21世纪本科院校土木建筑类创新型应用人才培养规划教材

建筑工程管理专业英语

主　编　杨云会
副主编　赵移山　龙　彬

内 容 简 介

本书对国际工程从招投标、实施至交工的项目全过程管理内容用英文进行了系统化的介绍；对国际工程项目参与各方的角色地位、责任和工作内容，FIDIC 合同条件、JCT 合同及 ICE 合同的简要对比，国际工程合同类型、国际工程招标程序、国际工程业主对承包商的选择和评估程序、承包商投标决策与风险分析、项目成本预算与控制、国际工程合同管理、项目进度控制、质量与安全管理、进度款申请与结算、项目风险管理等内容进行了阐述；对国际工程管理过程中的文件如世界银行标准招标文件、国际通用工程量清单、会议纪要、信函、月付款申请、项目结算和索赔等文件均通过实例予以清晰说明。本书还简要介绍了国际工程项目管理领域近年来的一些发展特征和最新知识，如 EPC、BOT、PPP、DB 总承包模式等高端项目管理模式和合同特点，建筑信息模型(BIM)的 3D/4D/5D 技术对国际工程项目管理的影响，国际工程咨询行业及其发展，国际大型项目的施工性评审等。此外，本书还增加了国际工程管理会议，合同和索赔谈判，谈判策略及跨文化交流技巧等内容，对国际工程管理中的难点内容(如变更管理和施工索赔)进行了重点介绍。

本书可作为高等学校工程管理专业及土木建筑类专业的教材，也可作为高职高专建筑工程技术、建筑工程管理、工程监理和工程造价等专业的教材，还可作为我国跨国承包商或外经公司的国际工程项目管理培训教材；同时，本书对国际工程承包公司、外经企业、招标代理机构、造价和监理等咨询机构的工程管理人员也具有参考价值。

图书在版编目(CIP)数据

建筑工程管理专业英语/杨云会主编．—北京：北京大学出版社，2013.8
(21 世纪本科院校土木建筑类创新型应用人才培养规划教材)
ISBN 978-7-301-22979-8

Ⅰ.①建… Ⅱ.①杨… Ⅲ.①建筑工程—施工管理—英语—高等学校—教材 Ⅳ.①H31

中国版本图书馆 CIP 数据核字(2013)第 182737 号

书　　　　名：	**建筑工程管理专业英语**
著作责任者：	杨云会　主编
策划编辑：	吴　迪　杨星璐
责任编辑：	伍大维
标准书号：	ISBN 978-7-301-22979-8/TU・0354
出版发行：	北京大学出版社
地　　　址：	北京市海淀区成府路 205 号　100871
网　　　址：	http://www.pup.cn　新浪官方微博：@北京大学出版社
电子邮箱：	编辑部 pup6@pup.cn　总编室 zpup@pup.cn
电　　　话：	邮购部 010-62752015　发行部 010-62750672　编辑部 010-62750667
印　刷　者：	北京虎彩文化传播有限公司
经　销　者：	新华书店
	787 毫米×1092 毫米　16 开本　19 印张　447 千字
	2013 年 8 月第 1 版　2024 年 6 月第 5 次印刷
定　　价：	46.00 元

未经许可，不得以任何方式复制或抄袭本书之部分或全部内容。
版权所有，侵权必究
举报电话：010-62752024　电子邮箱：fd@pup.cn

前　言

近年来，随着我国经济的快速发展和工业化水平的不断提高，我国承包商对外工程承包发展迅猛，我国已经进入世界承包商强国行列。然而，随着全球经济一体化的发展和国际工程项目大型化、复杂化的变化趋势，我国许多承包商在国际工程市场竞争中正面临对国际标准和项目管理惯例不熟悉的困难。本书以与国际接轨的视野，对国际工程项目管理的主要内容和特征，国际工程合同和国际惯例，以及国际工程从招投标、实施至交工的项目管理内容进行系统化的阐述，并根据工程管理专业学生从事国际工程项目管理的要求进行编写，以国际工程项目的全过程发展为主线，将国际工程项目管理的理论知识与实际工作内容相结合。本书的编写特点如下。

(1) 主线明确，结构清楚，内容完备，结合国际工程管理实践和工作实际需要，全面介绍了国际工程管理内容。本书介绍了国际工程项目参与各方的角色与作用，国际通用合同模式与国际工程合同类型，国际工程招标程序，世行标准招标文件，国际通用工程量清单，国际工程业主对承包商的选择和评估程序，承包商投标决策与风险分析，项目成本预算与控制，国际工程合同管理，工程信函写作，项目进度控制，质量与安全管理，进度款申请与结算，项目风险管理，国际工程管理会议及会议纪要，商业谈判策略，以及国际环境中的跨文化交流技巧等内容，尤其对国际工程管理中的难点内容如变更管理、施工索赔和争端解决等进行了重点介绍。

(2) 突出理论知识的系统性，注重实用性和可操作性。学生可通过对典型国际工程管理实例文件的学习，不断加深对国际工程管理理论知识的理解，提高工作实际问题的解决能力。例如，对国际工程项目管理涉及的过程文件和典型文件，如招投标文件、工程量清单、合同谈判、会议文件、信函、月付款申请、结算和索赔等文件均通过实例予以清晰说明；对熟悉国际工程惯例和管理经验，熟悉国际工程招投标文件、国际工程通用合同条件类型和管理模式，熟悉合同的谈判签订，熟悉国际工程项目施工合同的进度、质量与安全、造价控制，提高国际工程项目实际问题的分析能力和管理能力，具备工程谈判、案例分析和工程索赔的基本能力和项目风险管理能力都有很大的帮助。

(3) 介绍了全球国际工程管理的最新发展趋势。本书介绍了国际工程招投标和国际工程管理领域近年来的一些发展成果，如 EPC、BOT、PPP、DB 总承包模式等高端项目管理模式和合同特点，建筑信息模型(BIM)的 3D/4D/5D 技术对国际工程管理的影响，国际工程咨询行业及其发展，国际大型项目的施工性评审等，使学生能够接触国际工程管理的最新知识和操作实务，了解国际工程管理的现状和发展趋势，为将来参与国际工程管理打下良好的基础。

本书教学建议安排 60~80 学时，对于开设 40 学时左右的专业可以重点讲授第 1~16 单元的内容，阅读内容建议可作为选学与参考学习材料，作为对单元内容学习的巩固和提高。

本书由杨云会任主编，负责全书的总体策划及定稿，赵移山、龙彬任副主编，舒畅参与编写。本书具体编写分工如下：杨云会负责全书的编写，赵移山负责第1~16单元的翻译工作，龙彬编写第1~12单元的练习，舒畅编写第13~16单元的练习。

由于编者水平有限，本书不当之处在所难免，敬请读者、同行批评指正。

编　者

2013年4月

目 录

Unit 1 Development in Global Construction Market 1
Unit 2 Project Participants— Client/Consultant/Contractor 19
Unit 3 Contracts Used for Construction Projects 37
Unit 4 The Bidding/Tendering Process 56
Unit 5 The Contractor's Bid Decision 73
Unit 6 Project Cost Estimate and Cost Control 96
Unit 7 Project Contract Management 115
Unit 8 Payments and Final Accounts 134
Unit 9 Variations and Claims 149
Unit 10 Construction Planning and Scheduling 166
Unit 11 Construction Management Meeting 183
Unit 12 Construction Risk Management 201
Unit 13 Construction Negotiation Strategies and Skills 224
Unit 14 Construction Claims (1) 241
Unit 15 Construction Claims (2) 256
Unit 16 Contract Dispute Resolution 276
参考文献 296

Unit 1

Development in Global Construction Market

1. Fluctuating Construction Market Demand And Increasing Competition

The engineering and construction is one of the oldest industries which provides infrastructure for all other industries, and it is the largest industry in the world; it constitutes one of the largest services sectors in the economy – both in terms of its contribution to GDP and employment in most developed and many developing countries. The importance of the construction industry lies in the function of its products which provide the foundation for industrial production, and its impacts on the national economy cannot be measured by the value of its output or the number of persons employed in its activities alone.

International construction marketing in the 21st century is for better organization and the use of influence through new approaches, namely new business models including changed project delivery models and long-term supplier or service relationships to maintain competitiveness:

- Information knowledge (not just data) technologies;
- Increased "value" focuses (life cycle costs, flexibility, and resiliency);
- Performance-based standards and regulations;
- Human resources;
- Sustainability.

Those who accept these new fundamental shifts will be better off in the short and long term to compete well into the future. But market in the new millennium isn't easy, the international contracting community has been enduring difficult economic headwinds during the past five years. The world financial market collapse in recent years has affected and still affects the international construction market. Many international projects were delayed, put on hold, or cancelled at an unprecedented rate. However, even as the U.S. continues to fight off the prospect of a double-dip recession and European nations pull back from stimulus programs to stabilize the troubled Euro, opportunities are bubbling for international contractors in developing countries, particularly those rich in resources. The downturns in many major regions have caused an increase in competition as more firms enter unfamiliar markets; moreover, when global financial crisis persisted and world demand slumped, the global market competition has gotten downright vicious with technology improvement, therefore we have witnessed a fundamental shift of how construction operations are attracting business.

2. The Relationship with International Agencies and Its Importance

Before entering any of the global markets, a basic understanding of that market, namely, the likely sources of the projects and players including the employers, contractors, specialists and designers, understanding who will be making the decisions on procurement, including political influence, the role of the multilateral organizations such as the World Bank and a detailed knowledge of the various procurement and funding strategies is essential. The major multi-lateral organizations' projects are supported either by countries in the region or by international agencies such as the World Bank, International Finance Corporation that operate on a global basis, and agencies with more regional focus including the Asian Development Bank, the African Development Bank, the European Bank for Reconstruction and Development, the Commonwealth Development Corporation. In fact, the international agencies have, over the past few years, moved from mainly funding specific projects to supporting institutional strengthening.

Success in the construction industry requires effective inter-organizational management. That is, construction projects often require collaboration and management of diverse firms in order to achieve a common goal. With putting up the buildings, there are great numbers of projects activities around global market which are mainly supported by above agencies with some extent of promotional efforts.

3. Major Players of Global Construction Market

Mega-projects require cutting-edge technology; those included are hydroelectric projects, thermal and nuclear power projects, urban transport, roads, tunnels, bridges, tunnels, oil projects, and technology projects. Besides the technology the companies involved in mega-projects need the ability to deal with the extreme complexity of such projects which includes the ability to establish the necessary network around the project in any part of the world.

Many of the major corporations have had many years experience in the global market, particularly those in the oil and gas prospecting and processing industries such as BP and Shell, and the power sector. The oil and gas sector continues to expand in the Middle East, but Central Asia, Russia and Africa are the main growth areas, both to recover new sources and to lessen the dependence on the Middle East.

The international EPC (Engineering Procurement Construction) contractors who carry out major parts of the oil, gas and power construction works include Bechtel, Fluor and Parsons from the USA, Amec from the UK and a number of major contractors from Korea and Japan.

In the infrastructure field, major contractors with a global presence come primarily from Europe, the USA, Korea and Japan. Chinese contractors are becoming bigger competitors, since Chinese contractors have been pushing into the international market with some success, such as China Railway Group Ltd., China Railway Construction Corp. Ltd., China State Construction Engineering Corp., China Communications Construction Group and China Metallurgical Group Corp. etc.

4. Various Procurement and Funding Strategies

Many companies try to enter the global market without any knowledge of the various procurement and funding strategies used on specific projects. For those, the strategies of avoidance have become constructive. This knowledge is fundamental in understanding the entry point in the market as well as assessing the risks involved. These strategies can be summarized generally under five main headings:

- Traditional;
- Design and Build;
- Turnkey EPC;
- Financed;
- Cost Plus (Management/CM/Target Cost).

With the development and delivery of large, complex projects worldwide, one would expect the permanent combination of engineer and constructor in a permanent enterprise to promote innovation. The increasingly technical, procedural complexity of the projects requires the construction companies' active participation in all the phases of the projects. This is consistent with findings in industries that typically rely on an EPCM or EPC approach rather than those that rely on purpose assembled design and construction teams. Limited resources as well as other factors have caused the public sectors to consider the adoption of non-traditional procurement methods for the public projects. Similarly performance benefits from tighter integration of industry participants can be seen in the performance results for design-build projects, such as privatization and financed projects of PPP/BOT/PFI or DBO.

5. International Partnerships and Strategic Alliances

Construction services supplied internationally are typically related to large-scale projects, such as airports, harbours and petrochemical plants and are often undertaken by specialized contractors with local sub-contracting. In recent years, increasing competition among companies and the growing size and technical sophistication of projects have encouraged construction companies to enter into partnership agreements and strategic alliances in bidding for and implementing construction projects. Construction, architectural and engineering services are primarily traded through commercial presence, that is, the establishment of foreign affiliates and subsidiaries of foreign companies.

Allying with foreign partners would not only provide international companies the access to local markets, but also a better understanding of local environment. This strategy would also make international companies better use of their reputed technology and management skill in international markets, especially Africa and Asian markets, where these advanced services are highly demanded and cannot be fully provided by local companies.

Some of the major consultants operate on a global basis including the USA firms above, all now very strong in all markets, especially, Jacobs and AECOM are increasing their presence by purchasing UK and European companies. Consultancy firms from the UK, German, Denmark, the Netherlands and Japan dominantly ally with major contractors and operate worldwide.

6. Global Market Competition of Sustainable Tactics

The construction industry in global market is one of extreme competitive operations, with high risks and generally low profit margins when compared to other areas of the economy. Accordingly, major construction players have made several attempts to gain and sustain competitive advantage in the relevant industry all over the world. This often resulted in the adoption of new philosophies such as concurrent engineering, lean production and many others such as just-in-time (JIT), total quality management (TQM), benchmarking, business process reengineering (BPR) in service.

Construction industry has a significant impact on people and the environment; paying attention to the needs of building owners and occupiers, major construction players have aimed to market construction systems that are cleaner, healthier and more sustainable. This approach will gradually turn modern environmental requirements into real opportunities for sustainable construction.

Therefore, in order to sustain competitiveness and to survive in a national and international market, construction companies should properly understand how they are currently performing and how they need to perform in the future. Increasing competition is forcing companies to evaluate their status in the business environment and therefore make appropriate strategic decisions and plan strategic decisions in the long term.

7. Strategy and Competitiveness Change

With less construction work available and heavy competition for projects, many large global construction companies have been forced to reassess their strategies in order to remain viable. Some construction companies' confidence declined and organizations began to rethink their strategy and prepare for a dramatically changing landscape by analyzing their micro-environment: markets, customers and competitors. Many construction companies experienced problems adapting to the environmental changes, and, preparing for a change, they adopted a survival strategy rather than a growth strategy. These changes demand the construction company even larger capabilities, in terms of technology, human resources, capital, etc. While large global construction companies will probably weather the storm because they have a strong clientele base in the governmental sector and private sectors, as those companies have stable relations with client and strong competitive advantages in expertise, cutting-edge technology and management skills. Moreover, those companies have taken a number of options to continue working through tough periods:

➢ Integrate the construction industry value chain to enhance productivity and efficiency;

➢ Strengthen the international construction market image;

➢ Strive for the highest standard of quality, occupational safety, and health and environmental practices;

➢ Develop human resource capabilities and capacities in the international construction market;

➢ Innovate through research and development, and adopt new construction technologies;
➢ Leverage on information and communication technology in the international construction market;
➢ Upgrade the export of construction products and services.

Reading

Project Management for Construction

1. Definition of Project Management

1.1 Term of Project Management

The term project management is defined:
➢ by PMBOK(Project Management Body of Knowledge)as "The application of knowledge, skills, tools and techniques to project activities to meet project requirements."
➢ by PRINCE2 (Projects In Controlled Environments) as "The planning, monitoring and control of all aspects of the project and the motivation of all those involved in it to achieve the project objectives on time and to the specified cost, quality and performance."

1.2 Project Management Processes

Project management processes can be organized into five groups of one or more processes:
➢ Initiating processes: recognizing that a project or phase should begin and committing to do so.
➢ Planning processes: devising and maintaining a workable scheme to accomplish the business need that the project was undertaken to address.
➢ Executing processes: coordinating people and other resources to carry out the plan.
➢ Controlling processes: ensuring that project objectives are met by monitoring and measuring progress and taking corrective action when necessary.
➢ Closing processes: formalizing acceptance of the project or phase and bringing it to an orderly end.

2. Project Management for Construction

The construction industry is a conglomeration of diverse fields and participants that have been loosely lumped together as a sector of the economy. The construction industry plays a central role in national welfare, including the development of residential housing, office buildings and industrial plants, and the restoration of the nation's infrastructure and other public facilities.

The management of construction projects requires knowledge of modern management as well as an understanding of the design and construction process. Construction projects have a specific set of objectives and constraints such as a required time frame for completion. While the relevant technology, institutional arrangements or processes will differ, the management of such projects has much in common with the management of similar types of projects in other specialty or technology domains such as underground tunnel, chemical and energy developments.

Generally, project management is distinguished from the general management of corporations by the mission-oriented nature of a project. A project organization will generally be terminated when the mission is accomplished. Project management is the art of directing and coordinating human and material resources throughout the life of a project by using modern management techniques to achieve predetermined objectives of scope, cost, time, quality and participation satisfaction.

Specifically, project management in construction encompasses a set of objectives which may be accomplished by implementing a series of operations subject to resource constraints. There are potential conflicts between the stated objectives with regard to scope, cost, time and quality, and the constraints imposed on human, material and financial resources. These conflicts should be resolved at the onset of a project by making the necessary tradeoffs or creating new alternatives. Subsequently, the functions of project management for construction generally include the following:

➤ Specification of project objectives and plans including delineation of scope, budgeting, scheduling, setting performance requirements, and selecting project participants.

➤ Maximization of efficient resource utilization through procurement of labor, materials and equipment according to the prescribed schedule and plan.

➤ Implementation of various operations through proper coordination and control of planning, design, estimating, contracting and construction in the entire process.

➤ Development of effective communications and mechanisms for resolving conflicts among the various participants.

3. Construction Management Approach

Construction management is the coordinated effort of all parties involved in providing the employer with a successful project. The objectives of construction project management are to complete a project within the plans and specifications provided in accordance with the contract requirement. Moreover, the employer may, in time, continue the facility life cycle through the process of renovation or alteration to accommodate new requirements. With the complexity of the construction process increasing, employers demand accountability and accurate guidance during the entire planning and construction process. In recent years construction practices have changed dramatically, since technology, materials, financing, design, and engineering have all advanced fast.

3.1 Traditional Construction Management

The traditional construction management is usually for ordinary projects of moderate size and complexity, and employer often employs a designer (an architectural/engineering firm) which prepares the detailed plans and specifications for the constructor (a main/general contractor). The designer also acts on behalf of the employer to oversee the project implementation during construction. From the viewpoint of project management, the terms "employer" or "client" or "owner" are synonymous because they have the ultimate authority to make all important decisions. The contractor is responsible for the construction itself even though the work may actually be undertaken by a number of specialty subcontractors.

The employer may select a constructor either through competitive bidding or through negotiation. Public agencies are usually required to use the competitive bidding mode, while private organizations may choose either mode of operation. In using competitive bidding, the employer is forced to use the designer-constructor sequence since detailed plans and specifications must be ready before inviting bidders to submit their bids. If the employer chooses to use a negotiated contract, it is free to use phased construction if it so desires.

The general contractor may choose to perform all or part of the construction work, or act only as a manager by subcontracting all the construction to subcontractors. The general contractor may also select the subcontractors through competitive bidding or negotiated contracts. The general contractor may ask a number of subcontractors to quote prices for the subcontracts before submitting its bid to the employer.

Although the designer-constructor sequence is still widely used because of the public perception of fairness in competitive bidding, many private employer/owners recognize the disadvantages of using this approach when the project is large and complex and when market pressures require a shorter project duration than that which can be accomplished by using this traditional method.

3.2 Professional Construction Management

Professional construction management refers to a project management team consisting of a professional construction manager and other participants who will carry out the tasks of project planning, design and construction in an integrated manner. Contractual relationships among members of the team are intended to minimize adversarial relationships and contribute to greater response within the management group. A professional construction company is a firm specialized in the practice of professional construction management which includes(some issues will be deliberated in Unit 3):

➢ Work with employer/owner and the architectural/engineering firms from the beginning and make recommendations on design improvements, construction technology, schedules and construction economy;

➢ Propose design and construction alternatives if appropriate, and analyze the effects of the alternatives on the project cost and schedule;

➢ Monitor subsequent development of the project in order that these targets are not exceeded without the knowledge of the employer/owner;

➢ Coordinate procurement of material and equipment and the work of all construction contractors, and monthly payments to contractors, changes, claims and inspection for conforming

design requirements;
- Perform other project-related services as required by employer.

Professional construction management is usually used when a project is very large or complex.

4. Organization of Project Participants

There are two basic approaches to organize for project implementation, even though many variations may exist as a result of different contractual relationships adopted by the employer and builder. These basic approaches are divided along the following lines:

- Separation of organizations. Numerous organizations serve as consultants or contractors to the owner, with different organizations handling design and construction functions. Typical examples which involve different degrees of separation are:
  - Traditional sequence of design and construction;
  - Professional construction management.
- Integration of organizations. A single or joint venture consisting of a number of organizations with a single command undertakes both design and construction functions. Two extremes may be cited as examples:
  - Owner-builder operation in which all work will be handled internally by force account;
  - Turnkey operation in which all work is contracted to a vendor which is responsible for delivering the completed project.

Since construction projects may be managed by a spectrum of participants in a variety of combinations, the organization for the management of such projects may vary from case to case. There are many variations of management manners between these two extremes, depending on the objectives of the organization and the nature of the construction project. For example, a large chemical company with internal staff for planning, design and construction of facilities for new product lines will naturally adopt the matrix organization. On the other hand, a construction company whose existence depends entirely on the management of certain types of construction projects may find the project-oriented organization particularly attractive. While organizations may differ, the same basic principles of management structure are applicable to most situations.

New Words and Expressions

project management for construction 施工项目管理
PMBOK(Project Management Body of Knowledge) 项目管理知识体系
project management processes 项目管理流程
a workable scheme 切实可行的方案
taking corrective action 采取纠正措施
construction industry 建筑行业

Unit 1 Development in Global Construction Market

conglomerate 凝聚成团；聚合物
conglomeratation 兼并，重组
lumped together 聚集，合成
national welfare 国家福利
residential housing 住宅
office buildings 写字楼
industrial plants 工业厂房
nation's infrastructure 基础设施
public facilities 公共设施
knowledge of modern management 了解现代管理
design and construction process 设计与施工过程
a specific set of objectives and constraints 一系列具体的目标和约束
institutional arrangements 制度安排
underground tunnel 地下隧道
be distinguished from 有别于，不同
the general management of corporations 一般企业管理
predetermined objectives 预定目标
participation satisfaction 参与满意度
resource constraints 资源约束
tradeoff 折衷，权衡；交易
specification of project objectives 特定的项目目标
delineation 描述，画轮廓
procurement 采购，购买
implementation of various operations 实施各种操作
development of effective communications 开展有效的沟通
mechanisms for resolving conflicts 解决冲突的机制
general contractor 总承包
project implementation 项目实施
oversee 监督，审查；偷看到，无意中看到
synonymous 同义的，同义词的；同义突变的
ultimate authority 至高无上的权威
specialty subcontractors 专业分包商
competitive bidding 招标
competitive bidding mode 竞价模式
mode of operation 运作模式
bidders 投标人
negotiated contract 协商合同
quote prices 报价，询价
professional construction management 专业的施工管理

minimize 使减到最少；小看，极度轻视；最小化
adversarial 对抗的；对手的，敌手的
adversarial relationships 对抗性关系
design improvements 设计改进
construction technology 施工工艺
schedules 时间表
subsequent development of the project 项目的后续发展
payments 付款
changes 变更
claims 索赔
contractual relationships 契约关系
sequence of design and construction 设计与施工的顺序
a single command 单一的命令
vendor 供应商
variations of management style 各种各样的管理模式
in-house staff 内部员工
new product lines 新的产品生产线
matrix organization 矩阵组织
applicable to most situations 适用于大多数情况
construction practices 施工实践
financing 融资
facility life cycle 设备生命周期
accountability 有义务，有责任；可说明性

Exercises

I. Choose the best answer according to the text.

1. The construction industry plays a central role in national welfare, including _____.
   A. the development of residential housing, office buildings and industrial plants
   B. the restoration of the nation's infrastructure and other public facilities
   C. knowledge of modern management and an understanding of the design and construction process
   D. A and B

2. Subsequently, the functions of project management for construction generally include the following: _____.
   A. specification of project objectives and plans
   B. maximization of efficient resource utilization
   C. implementation of various operations and development of effective communications
   D. above all

3. According to the text, the employer may select a constructor _____.
   A. competitive bidding
   B. negotiation
   C. contract
   D. A and B
4. The general contractor may choose to perform _____.
   A. all or part of the construction work
   B. only as a manager by subcontracting all the construction to subcontractors
   C. the subcontractors through competitive bidding or negotiated contracts
   D. above all
5. We learn from the passage that Professional construction management refers to _____.
   A. minimize adversarial relationships and contributes to greater response within the management group
   B. a firm specialized in the practice of professional construction management which includes
   C. a project management team consisting of a professional construction manager and other participants who will carry out the tasks of project planning, design and construction in an integrated manner
   D. none of the above
6. The objectives of construction project management _____.
   A. are to complete a project within the plans and specifications provided in accordance with the contract requirement
   B. are the coordinated effort of all those involved in providing the employer with a successful project
   C. are depending on the objectives of the organization and the nature of the construction project
   D. are as the same with basic principles of management structure are applicable to most situations

II. Decide the following statements are true or false.

1. The management of construction projects requires knowledge of modern management or an understanding of the design and construction process.

2. The contractor is responsible for the construction itself even though the work may actually be undertaken by a number of specialty subcontractors.

3. Public agencies are required to use the competitive bidding mode, while private organizations may choose either mode of operation.

4. Monitor subsequent development of the project in order that these targets are not exceeded with the knowledge of the employer/owner.

III. Change the following words to another form and write down the Chinese meanings.

1. terms _____
2. application _____

3. performance ＿＿＿＿＿＿＿＿＿＿＿＿＿＿
4. undertaken ＿＿＿＿＿＿＿＿＿＿＿＿＿＿
5. conglomeration ＿＿＿＿＿＿＿＿＿＿＿＿＿＿
6. participants ＿＿＿＿＿＿＿＿＿＿＿＿＿＿
7. terminated ＿＿＿＿＿＿＿＿＿＿＿＿＿＿
8. oversee ＿＿＿＿＿＿＿＿＿＿＿＿＿＿
9. synonymous ＿＿＿＿＿＿＿＿＿＿＿＿＿＿
10. accountability ＿＿＿＿＿＿＿＿＿＿＿＿＿＿

IV. Give out the following words' synonym or other word in the closest meaning.

1. objectives   a. complete
2. project   b. involves
3. accomplish   c. beginning
4. executing   d. phase
5. encompasses   e. alteration
6. onset   f. evaluating
7. employer   g. targets
8. architectural   h. group
9. renovation   i. carry out
10. estimating   j. engineering
11. team   k. client

V. Put the following English into Chinese.

1. By PRINCE2 (Projects In Controlled Environments) as "The planning, monitoring and control of all aspects of the project and the motivation of all those involved in it to achieve the project objectives on time and to the specified cost, quality and performance".

2. Closing processes: formalizing acceptance of the project or phase and bringing it to an orderly end.

3. While the relevant technology, institutional arrangements or processes will differ, the management of such projects has much in common with the management of similar types of projects in other specialty or technology domains such as underground tunnel, chemical and energy developments.

4. Project management is the art of directing and coordinating human and material resources throughout the life of a project by using modern management techniques to achieve predetermined objectives of scope, cost, time, quality and participation satisfaction.

5. In using competitive bidding, the employer is forced to use the designer-constructor sequence since detailed plans and specifications must be ready before inviting bidders to submit their bids.

VI. Put the following Chinese into English.

1. 项目管理知识体系
2. 项目管理解决冲突的机制

3. 拥有至高无上的权利
4. 管理矩阵组织结构
5. 工程的后续维护

参 考 译 文

第1单元 全球建筑市场的发展

1. 建筑市场需求的波动和日益加剧的竞争

工程和建筑是最古老的行业之一,该行业为其他各行业提供基础设施,且它是世界上最大的行业;它构成了经济中最大的服务领域之一——就它对大部分发达国家和许多发展中国家GDP和就业两方面的贡献而言。建筑业的重要性在于它的产物的作用,这些产物为工业生产提供基础,且该行业在国家经济上的影响不能仅仅通过它的产值或者在其生产活动中所雇用的人数来衡量。

21世纪的建筑市场营销是为了更好地组织和运用其影响力,这一目的是通过新的途径,即新业务模式包括改变的项目交付模式和长期供应商或者服务联系从而保持竞争力来实现的:
- 信息知识(不仅是资料)技术;
- "价值"增加集中(生命周期成本、机动性和弹性);
- 基于工作情况的生产标准和规章制度;
- 人力资源;
- 可持续发展。

那些接受这些新的重要转变的人们将在短期和长期内更好地进入未来的竞争。但是新千年的市场并不轻松,在过去的五年中,国际承包市场一直忍受着艰难的经济逆流。世界金融市场近年来的崩溃影响到并且依旧影响着国际建筑市场。许多国际项目以史无前例的速度被误期、搁置或者取消。然而,正当美国继续竭力摆脱双下降的经济衰退,以及欧洲国家从为了稳定存在诸多问题的欧元而采取的刺激计划中撤出的时候,发展中国家的承包机会对于国际承包商来说却不断增加,尤其在那些资源丰富的发展中国家。随着更多企业进入不熟悉的市场,在许多主要地区的经济回落引起了竞争的加剧;此外,当全球金融危机持续不减和世界需求大幅下跌之时,随着技术的进步全球市场竞争彻底变得残酷,因此我们目睹了建筑运营怎样吸引业务的一个根本转变。

2. 与国际机构的关系及其重要性

在进入任何全球市场之前,一种对该市场的基本理解,即可能的项目来源和包括雇主、承包商、行家和设计师在内的参与者,以及谁将在采购上做决定,包括政治影响、像世界银行之类的多边组织的作用、各种不同采购的详细认识及资金策略等,是绝对必要的。主要的多边组织的项目要么由该地区的国家所支持,要么由国际机构诸如世界银行、以全球基础来运作的国际金融合作组织及带有更多区域重心的机构包括亚洲开发银行、非洲开发银行、欧洲复兴银行和英联邦开发公司来支持。事实上,在过去几年间,这些国际机构已经从主要对特定项目融资转移到对公共机构的支持。

在建筑行业的成功需要组织之间的有效管理。也就是说，为了实现一个共同的目标，建筑项目常常需要不同企业间的协作和管理。因为随着建筑物的拔地而起，围绕着全球市场正运作着大量的项目活动，这些项目活动主要由上述机构以某种程度的努力来支持。

3. 主要的全球建筑市场参与者

特大工程需要尖端技术；那些所包括的项目是水力发电工程、热能和核能工程、城市运输、公路、隧道、桥梁、石油工程和技术工程。除了技术之外，涉及特大工程的公司需要具有处理这种极端复杂性的工程的能力，这种能力包括在世界任何地方建立围绕工程的必要网络。

许多重要的公司在全球市场上已经有了多年的经验，特别是那些在石油和天然气勘探及加工行业的公司，诸如英国石油公司(BP)和壳牌石油公司(Shell)以及电力行业等。中东的石油和天然气行业继续扩展，但是中亚、俄罗斯和非洲却是主要的成长区域，它们既重新获得了新的源头又减少了对中东的依赖。

承揽石油、天然气和电力工程施工的 EPC(设计采购施工)承包商包括来自美国的柏克德工程公司(Bechtel)、福陆公司(Fluor)和派森斯公司(Parsons)，来自英国的艾铭集团公司(Amec)及来自韩国和日本的一些主要承包商。

在基础设施领域，这些跨国承包商主要来自欧洲、美国、韩国和日本。由于中国承包商以一些成功业绩向国际市场推进，像中国铁路集团有限公司、中国铁路建设集团有限公司、中国国家建筑工程公司、中国交通建设集团和中国冶金集团公司等一些中国承包商正在成为世界市场的主要竞争者。

4. 各种采购及融资策略

许多公司在不具备对特定项目的采购和融资策略的任何知识的情况下试图进入全球市场。对他们来说，回避策略已经变得有建设性。这种知识在理解市场切入点还有评估相关联的风险方面是最根本的。这些策略可以总体上概括成五个主要部分：
> 传统的；
> 设计和建造；
> EPC 交钥匙项目；
> 融资的；
> 成本加酬金项目(管理/施工管理/目标成本)。

随着世界性的大型、复杂项目的交付模式和发展，人们可以预期一个长久结合了工程师设计和建造者施工的长久性企业将推动建筑的革新。越来越技术化和程序化的复杂项目要求承包商积极参与到项目的所有阶段。这一点与行业研究发现的结果一致，即现代项目典型地依赖于一种 EPCM 或者 EPC 方式而非依赖于那些特定的设计和施工的独立的项目团队。有限的资源及其他因素使公共部门对公共项目考虑采用非传统的项目采购方法。类似的执行优势可以来自于项目行业参与者更紧密的设计和建造整合项目团队中，如私有化和融资项目的 PPP/BOT/PFI 或 DBO，可以看到项目执行的结果。

5. 国际伙伴关系和战略联盟

国际性建筑服务一般与大规模项目有关，诸如机场、港口和石油化工厂等，且常常由专业化的承包商承揽并分包给当地分包商。近年来，公司之间不断加剧的竞争、不断扩大的项目规模和技术复杂性，已经促使建筑公司在建筑项目的投标和实施中缔结合伙协议和战略联盟。施工、建筑和工程技术服务主要通过项目商业参与来进行交易，即建立外国子公司和外企附属公司。

与外国合伙人结盟不仅可以给国际公司提供当地市场的通道，而且可以对当地环境有更好的理解。这个策略也让国际公司更好地在国际市场上使用他们好的技术和管理技能，尤其在非洲和亚洲市场，这些先进的服务面临高度需求且不能完全由当地公司提供。

一些主要的包括上述美国公司在内的咨询公司在全球基础上进行运作，所有公司如今在所有市场上都非常强大，尤其是 Jacobs 和 AECOM 公司通过购买英国和欧洲的公司来增加他们的市场份额。来自英国、德国、丹麦、荷兰和日本的咨询公司主要与较大的承包商结盟并在全世界进行经营活动。

6. 可持续策略的全球市场竞争

全球市场的建筑业是极度竞争的行业之一，当与其他经济领域相比常常是风险高且利润低。相应地，在全世界范围内的相关行业中，主要的建筑参与者已经做了数种尝试去获得并维持竞争优势。这样做常常导致在服务中采用新经营哲学，比如并行工程、精益生产和其他像零库存、全面质量管理、标准程序和生产过程再设计等。

建筑行业对人们和环境有重大影响；当注意到业主和占有人的需要时，主要建筑参与者已经瞄准了更洁净、更健康和更持续的建筑体系的市场推广。这种途径将逐步使现代环境要求转变成针对可持续施工的真正机会。

因此，为了维持竞争力且在国际国内市场上求得生存，建筑公司应当正确地理解他们目前在怎样进行运作，以及在未来他们需要怎样去实施。日益加剧的竞争正迫使公司评估他们在商业环境中的地位，并且因此做出适当的战略决策并进行长期的战略规划。

7. 策略和竞争变化

由于可得到的建筑工程变得更少和激烈的项目竞争，为了保持持续的生存能力，许多大型全球建筑公司被迫重新评价它们的策略。一些建筑公司的信心有所衰退，并且一些组织开始重新考虑他们的战略并通过分析他们的微环境如市场、顾客和竞争对手而为戏剧性改变的前景做准备。许多建筑公司经历了适应环境改变的问题，并且在为改变做准备的同时，它们采纳了生存策略而非发展策略。这些改变甚至要求建筑公司在技术、人力资源、资金等方面具有更大的能力范围。而大型全球建筑公司将可能渡过难关，因为它们在政府部门和私营部门拥有强大的客户基础，且具有与委托人的稳定关系和在专门知识、尖端技术和管理技能方面的强大竞争优势。此外，那些公司采取了许多办法在整个艰难时期继续运营。

- ➤ 整合建筑业价值链以提高生产力和效能；
- ➤ 巩固国际建筑市场形象；
- ➤ 力争质量、职业安全及健康和环境业务的最高标准；
- ➤ 在国际建筑市场开发人力资源素质和能力；
- ➤ 通过研究和开发及采纳新建筑技术进行革新；

> 在国际建筑市场对信息和交流技术发挥杠杆作用；
> 升级建筑产品和服务出口。

阅读

建筑工程管理

1. 项目管理的定义

1.1 术语：项目管理

项目管理这个术语可以定义为：
> 由 PMBOK(《项目管理知识主体》)解释为"为达到项目要求而对针对项目活动的知识、技能、工具和工艺的应用"。
> 由 PRINCE2(《在被控环境中的项目》)解释为"为按时达成项目目标及针对确定的成本、质量和实施，项目所有方面的规划、监测和控制及涉及项目的所有方面的动机"。

1.2 项目管理过程

项目管理过程可以划分成五个阶段或更多阶段：
> 开始过程：确认项目或阶段应当开始且继续进行下去。
> 规划过程：设计并维持一个可行的项目业务目标方案。
> 执行过程：协调人脉和其他资源去完成计划。
> 控制过程：通过监控和测量进展情况并必要时采取校正行动确保项目目标的达成。
> 结束过程：使项目或阶段验收正式化且使项目有序终结。

2. 针对建筑的项目管理

建筑行业是一个由多种专业领域和参与者松散地组合在一起的经济聚合体。建筑行业在国家福利中扮演着中心角色，包括居民住宅、写字楼和工业产房的开发，以及国家基础设施和其他市政设施的重建。

建筑项目管理需要现代管理知识及对设计和施工流程的理解。建筑项目有一套特定的目标和约束，比如所需竣工期限。尽管相关技术、公共机构管理或进程将会不同，但是这样的项目管理却与相似的项目类型有着许多相同的方面，这些相似的项目处于其他专业或技术领域诸如地下隧道、化工和能源开发之中。

通常，项目管理不同于任务导向特征的一般公司业务管理。当一项任务完成的时候，一个项目组织通常会被终结。项目管理是一门指导和协调人力及物力资源的艺术，它通过使用现代管理技术在整个项目生命周期中实现预定的项目范围、成本、时间、质量及参与者的满意等目标。

明确地说，在施工中的项目管理包含一整套的目标，这些目标通过执行一系列的受制于资源约束的操作而得以实现。在关于项目范围、成本、时间和质量的既定目标和强加于人力物力及金融资源之上的约束之间，有着一些潜在的冲突。这些冲突应当通过进行必要的权衡或者创造新的供选方案，在项目一开始就解决掉。随后，针对施工的项目管理职能通常包括如下内容：

➢ 包括明确的范围描述、预算、进度、设定实施要求及选定项目参与者等内容的项目目标和计划。
➢ 根据规定的日程和计划,通过劳动力、原料和设备的采购,使有效资源利用最大化。
➢ 通过在整个进程中规划、设计、预算、发包及施工的恰当协调和控制,执行各项操作。
➢ 为化解各参与者之间的冲突,发展有效的沟通和机制。

3. 施工管理途径

施工管理是涉及提供给雇主一个成功的项目的所有当事方的协调性努力。施工项目管理的目标,是在根据合同要求而提供的计划和规范内去完成一个项目。此外,雇主可能及时通过革新或改变进程去顺应新要求而延续设施的生命周期。由于施工进程复杂性的增加,雇主在整个规划和施工过程中需要有人负责和精确指导。近年来,由于技术、材料、融资、设计和工艺全都有了快速的进步,所以施工惯例有了显著的改变。

3.1 传统施工管理

传统施工管理通常针对中等规模和复杂程度的普通项目,且雇主常常雇用一个设计师(一个建筑设计/工程公司),其为施工方(总承包商)准备详细的计划和规范。设计师也代表雇主在施工期间监督项目的实施。从项目管理的角度来看,"雇主"、"委托人"或者"业主"这几个术语是同义的,因为他们都有最终职权去做出所有重要的决定。承包商对施工本身负责,即使施工实际上可能由许多专业分包商来承担。

雇主通过竞争性招标或议标的方式选择施工方。公共项目代理商通常被要求使用竞争性招标模式,而私人组织可能会选择任何一种操作模式。在竞争性招标之中,由于在邀请投标人去投标之前,详细的计划和规范必须准备好,所以雇主必须使用设计师—施工方的顺序。如果雇主采用议标合同,且施工方也同意,即可自由使用分阶段施工。

总承包商可以选择完成施工工程的全部或一部分,也可以分包所有工程给分包商的方式而自己只扮演管理者的角色。总承包商可能通过竞争性招标或者议标合同来挑选分包商。总承包商可以在提交其标的给雇主之前要求一些分包商针对分包项目进行报价。

尽管设计师—施工方顺序因为在竞争性招标中的公共公平观念而仍然被广泛使用,但是,当项目很大很复杂或者市场压力要求一个比采用传统方式可以实现的更短的项目工期的时候,许多私人雇主/业主也承认使用这种方式的缺陷。

3.2 专业施工管理

专业施工管理涉及一个由专业施工经理和其他参与者组成的项目管理团队,施工经理和其他参与者将会执行整合方式中的项目规划、设计和施工等任务。团队成员之间的契约关系意在使对抗性关系最小化,并且促成管理团队内部更大的响应。一个专业施工公司是一个专门从事职业化施工管理业务的公司,职业化施工管理业务包括如下内容(有些问题将在第 3 单元深入探讨)。

➢ 从开始就与雇主/业主和建筑/工程公司一起开展工作,且在设计改善、施工技术、进度和建筑经济方面提出建议。
➢ 如果合适的话,提出设计和施工备选方案,且分析有关项目成本和进度的备选方案的结果。
> 对项目的后续发展进行控制,保证项目在雇主/业主不了解的情况下不能超过控制目标。
> 对原料和设备的采购、建筑承包商的工作,以及根据设计要求的按月对承包商的付款、变更、索赔和检查等进行协调。
> 落实雇主所要求的与项目有关的其他服务。

当项目巨大或非常复杂时,通常就会用到专业施工管理。

4. 项目参与者组织

即使许多变更可能作为由雇主和建造方所采纳的不同契约关系的结果而存在,仍然有两种针对项目的实施去组织的基本途径,这些基本途径沿着下面的方向被分类为:
> 管理组织的分离:一些组织以咨询师或者承包商的身份对雇主提供服务,不同的组织方式承担设计和施工职能。牵涉不同组织程度分离的典型例子是:
- 传统设计和施工程序;
- 专业施工管理。

> 组织的整合:一个或由一些组织所构成的独资或合资企业,既承担设计又承担施工职能的直线式组织管理。两种极端情况可能是:
- 业主—建设者方式运作,其中所有工作将通过自营的方式在内部运行;
- 交钥匙方式运作,将所有工程内容(设计和建造工作)承包给卖方,卖方负责交付竣工项目。

由于施工项目可以被以各种方式结合的许多参与者管理,所以针对这样的项目管理的组织可能会有这样或那样的不同。许多管理风格的变动,取决于组织的目标和施工项目的特性。例如,一家大型化工公司为了对新生产线的设施进行规划、设计和施工,将很自然地与内部员工一起接受矩阵组织模式。另一方面,如果施工公司的存活与否完全依赖于施工项目的管理的类型,它就可能会找到特别有吸引力的以项目为导向的组织。虽然组织可能不一样,但是相同的基本管理构架原则却适用于大部分情况。

Unit 2

Project Participants— Client/Consultant/Contractor

1. Roles of Project Participants

Pattern of Contractual Relationship

Construction management is the execution of the work as required by the contract documents. The construction stage includes the contractor's planning and scheduling activities, mobilization of equipment, material purchasing, fabrication of components, and construction. Construction management is a team effort that includes the contractors, subcontractors, testing agencies, architect/engineer, consultants, employer, product representatives, and others, all working toward the common goal of delivering the completed facility ready for its intended use.

The following diagram 2.1 illustrates the pattern of contractual relationship that exists between the various members of the design and execution team on conventional or traditional form of contract.

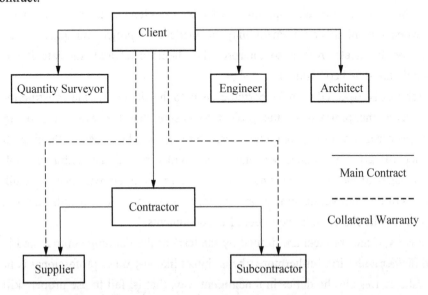

Figure 2.1　Participates Relations of Traditional Project Delivery Method

This may change depending on the type of contractual arrangement and the form of contract used.

It should be noted that the parties only entering into the main contract with client, there is no proxity between client's professional adviser and contractor. The contracts between the client / employer and his /her professional advisers are usually based on standard agreements produced by the respective professional institutions. Also the client's professional advisers could be liable to the contractor in default notwithstanding the absence of a contractual link. Thus, if the architect was to exceed his/her authority without the knowledge of the contractor, the contractor could recover any loss suffered in an action for breach of warranty of authority.

2. Client/Employer/Owner

The construction project manager requires a high level of expertise, in both theoretical knowledge and practical experience from all stages of planning, construction and management, and needs to have a holistic approach and the ability to manage the processes that are involved. The construction clients' role is to provide clear brief and make available necessary funds for the project. The construction client chooses the players that will be involved in the project and determines the conditions – from the planning stage to the point at which the final building of facility is put into commission. The client oversees the progress of a construction project from concept to implementation, and is responsible for the process to create the appropriate conditions for other participants in the construction process, including issues relating to technical systems and cooperation with specialists. Construction clients work in different ways, using their own resources or enlisting the help of consultants, thus, active and competent construction clients are essential for the sustainable development of the building.

3. Architect

The architect is traditionally appointed first by the client although now there are many occasions when the initial appointment may be made to a project manager or to any other consultant. The architects' role is to interpret the clients brief and translate it into a viable building within the stated constraints.

The architect is expected to make periodic visits to the site during the construction period to supervise/observe the progress of the project to ensure that the works are being executed generally in accordance with the contract. A written report will be issued containing observations and issues accordingly. The frequency of these visits will vary with the contractual obligations of the different stages of the project. During construction, the architect will also make all necessary interpretations of the contract documents and provide any supplemental details and/or instruction, which may be required to explain the intent of the documents.

The powers of the architect are limited by the term of the building contract and he/she does not exceed his/her authority, furthermore, the architect like any other professional is liable to the client if he/she carries out the duties in a negligent way, that is, fail to use proper skill and care. The root cause of disputes and complaints against architects is often an incomplete understanding of the architect's role and responsibilities in design, planning and construction processes.

During the construction period, meetings are scheduled generally weekly with architect, contractor and client. The architect, and their consultants when directly concerned, is expected to be present at these meetings. And the architect shall also be present, together with the client's representative, to conduct the final inspection of the building; the architect shall certify to the client's representative that the project has been completed in compliance with the contract.

In the past two decades, this traditional approach has become less popular for a number of reasons, particularly for large scale projects. The architect/engineer firms, which are engaged by the owner as the prime professionals for design and inspection, have become more isolated from the construction process. This has occurred because of pressures to reduce fees to architect/engineer firms, the threat of litigation regarding construction defects, and lack of knowledge of new construction techniques on the part of architect and engineering professionals.

4. Quantity Surveyor

The client will usually make the appointment of the quantity surveyor either direct or on the advice of the architect. If the architect or any other agent of the client makes the appointment, it is important to ensure that the principal is aware of his/her actions. The quantity surveyor, also known as a construction economist, or cost manager, is one of a team of professional advisers to the construction industry. The quantity surveyors works on projects ranging from office blocks, schools, hospitals, factories to bridges, railways, oil and mining development, shipbuilding and large process engineering works such as oil refineries to carry out calculate the quantities of works.

➤ At inception and feasibility stage, the quantity surveyor uses their knowledge of construction methods and costs to advise the clients on the most economical way of achieving their requirements, and to prepare initial budget estimate, feasibility proposals and cash flow projections.

➤ At pre-contract cost control stage, the quantity surveyor monitors cost implications during detailed design stage, review the construction cost of each package based upon the designs and specifications prepared by the architect, and ensure that the design remains on budget through cost management.

➤ At tender and contractual documentation stage, the quantity surveyor prepare tender and contract documentation in conjunction with the client and members of the specialists, take out quantities, prepare bills of quantities for rates and present detailed information on the costs of labour, plant and materials, etc.

After tendering, the quantity surveyor prepares report on tenders with appropriate recommendations and proposals, help the client to identify suitable tenderers based on considerations of cost, quality, service, financial status and experience, and determine the most suitable contractors.

➤ At project execution stage, the quantity surveyor interrogate contractor's statements, assess the amount of loss and expense of variation claims which are instructed by the architect or client, and prepare recommendations for interim payments to contractors, subcontractors and suppliers in accordance with contract requirements, and obtain sufficient substantiation to convince client or his representative and relevant architect of the legitimacy of the claim or variation order proposal, through working in and visiting sites. After construction they will be involved with settling the final account with contractors, if necessary or in dispute, mediation and arbitration.

The function of the quantity surveyor includes risk management system managing, and carrying out forecast final outturn values for cost, sales and margin. The quantity surveyor, like any other professional, owes a duty of care to the client to carry out his/her work and may be liable for professional negligence if fails to do so.

5. Other Consultants

The other consultants are structural engineers, mechanical and electrical engineers and any other specialist consultants depending on the complexity of the project. They may be hydraulic engineer, geo-technical engineer, and interior designer, building surveyor, land surveyor and landscape architect.

6. Main Contractor/ Contractor

Traditionally the function of the main contractor is to coordinate all tasks in a construction project, and the main contractor is appointed to be in charge of the construction of the whole project and coordinate the work of the various subcontractors. The main contractor is responsible for construction and delivery of the project according to the standards, workmanship and quality stipulated in the contract documents and according to the legal and statutory requirements. The main contractor is liable for defects in the subcontractors work. The relationship between the main contractor and the subcontractor depend on the terms of the sub-contract signed between the two parties and the responsibilities of each party depend on the contractual arrangement selected for the project.

7. Nominated Subcontractors & Specialty Contractors/Specialist Subcontractor

➢ Most standard forms of international construction contract enable the employer to select subcontractors, who are subsequently employed by the contractor or main contractor, via a "nomination" procedure. Those subcontractors that are nominated, selected or approved by the employer or the engineer are called "Nominated Subcontractors". Nominated subcontractors are usually specialists to carry out work for which a reference to prime cost item or provisional sum item, and contingency item used in the specification or other contract documents. For the purposes of the main contractor's final account, the main contractor is allowed to claim for a sum being a percentage rate of the actual price paid or due to be paid calculated attendances, overheads and profit for the nominated subcontractors' works.

➢ One method used by the clients to enable them to select subcontractors without the associated risks of nomination is to categorise all subcontractors as domestic subcontractor that will be selected by the main contractor directly. Whilst labelling all subcontractors as "domestic" may show what the parties intended at the time of entering into the building contract.

➢ Specialty contractors include mechanical, electrical, foundation, excavation, and demolition contractors among others. They usually serve as subcontractors to the main contractor of a project. In some countries, legal statutes may require a client to deal with various specialty contractors directly.

➢ The main contractor is also responsible for health and safety on the building site, and responsible for the acts, defaults and neglects of any subcontractor as fully as if they were the acts, defaults or neglects of the main contractor. The main contractor takes equivalent responsibilities or obligations consistent with those undertaken by any subcontractor.

8. Suppliers

The main contractor purchases most of the material required for the project from the suppliers. However the architect may nominate a particular source/firm for the supply of certain items. The roles of various parties connected with the building contract have been briefly outlined above. Major material suppliers include specialty subcontractors in structural steel fabrication and erection, sheet metal, ready mixed concrete delivery, reinforcing steel bar, roofing, glazing etc. Major equipment suppliers for industrial construction include manufacturers of generators, boilers and piping and other equipment. Many suppliers handle on-site installation to insure that the requirements and contractual specifications are met. As more and larger structural units are prefabricated off-site, the distribution between specialty contractors and material suppliers becomes even less obvious.

However, good team coordination and successful communication systems between each member of the team are necessary, if design and construction processes are to be effectively organized to achieve efficiency.

Reading

About the Project Life Cycle

1. Project Life Cycle

The project life cycle may be viewed as a process through which a project is implemented from cradle to grave. This process is often very complex; however, it can be decomposed into several stages. The acquisition of a constructed facility usually represents a major capital investment, whether its employer happens to be an individual, a private corporation or a public agency. Since the commitment of resources for such an investment is motivated by market demands or perceived needs, the facility is expected to satisfy certain objectives within the constraints specified by the employer and consultants.

From the perspective of an employer, the project life cycle for a constructed facility may be illustrated schematically in Figure 2.2. The cycle begins with the initial conception of the project and continues though planning, design, procurement, construction, start-up, operation and maintenance. It ends with the disposal of a facility when it is no longer productive or useful.

Various possibilities may be considered in the conceptual planning stage, and the technological and economic feasibility of each alternative will be assessed and compared in order to select the best possible project. The financing schemes for the proposed alternatives must also be examined, and the project will be programmed with respect to the timing for its completion and for available cash flows.

After the scope of the project is clearly defined, detailed engineering design will provide the blueprint for construction, and the definitive cost estimate will serve as the baseline for cost control. In the procurement and construction stage, the delivery of materials and the erection of the project on site must be carefully planned and controlled. After the construction is completed, there is usually a brief period of start-up or shake-down of the constructed facility when it is first occupied. Finally, the management of the facility is turned over to the employer for full occupancy until the facility lives out its useful life and is designated for demolition or conversion.

Since operation and maintenance of a facility will go on long after the completion and acceptance of a project, it is usually treated as a separate problem except in the consideration of the life cycle cost of a facility. All stages from conceptual planning and feasibility studies to the acceptance of a facility for occupancy may be broadly lumped together and referred to as the design/construct process, while the procurement and construction alone are traditionally regarded as the province of the construction industry.

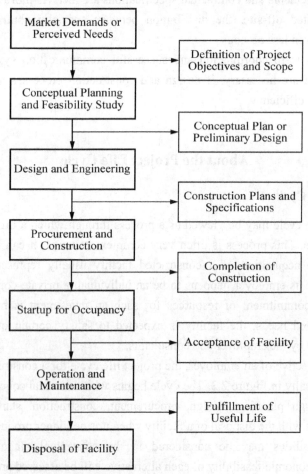

Figure 2.2 The Project Life Cycle of a Constructed Facility

The solutions at various stages are then integrated to obtain the final outcome. Although each stage requires different expertise, it usually includes both technical and managerial activities in the knowledge domain of the specialist. The employer may choose to decompose the entire process into more or less stages based on the size and nature of the project, and thus obtain the most efficient result in implementation. Very often, the employer retains direct control of work in the planning and programming stages, but increasingly outside planners and financial experts are used as consultants because of the complexities of projects.

Of course, the stages of development in Figure 2.2 may not be strictly sequential. Some of the stages require iteration, and others may be carried out in parallel or with overlapping time frames, depending on the nature, size and urgency of the project. Furthermore, an employer may have internal capacities to handle the work in every stage of the entire process, or he may seek professional advice and services for the work in all stages.

2. Project Contract Life Cycle

For construction contracts, from the contract formation to the contracts end, it usually takes a long period of time, sometimes even years, and it has many processes. Contract management must be carried out throughout the entire life period, and in different stages, contract management has different tasks and priorities. To common open tender projects, the construction contract usually goes through two main phases: the establishment of the contract and the implementation phase of the contract. The establishment of the contract phase has two processes which are bidding and contract negotiations. The implementation phase of the contract also has two phases, i.e., the construction and the maintenance. Some profound implications for the objectives and methods of project management result from this perspective:

➢ The project life cycle's costs and benefits from initial planning through operation and disposal of a facility are relevant to decision making. An employer is concerned with a project from the cradle to the grave. Construction costs represent only one portion of the overall life cycle costs.

➢ Optimizing performance at one stage of the process may not be beneficial overall if additional costs or delays occur elsewhere. For example, saving money on the design process will be a false economy if the result is excess construction costs.

➢ Fragmentation of project management among different specialists may be necessary, but good communication and coordination among the participants is essential to accomplish the overall goal of the project. New information technologies can be instrumental in this process, especially the Internet and specialized extranets.

➢ Productivity improvements are always of importance and value. As a result, introducing new materials and automated construction processes is always desirable as long as they are less expensive and are consistent with desired performance.

➢ Quality of work and performance are critically important to the success, so the owners will have to live with the results of the project.

New Words and Expressions

participate 分享，参与，参加；分享，分担
contractual relationship 契约关系
diagram 图解，图表用图解法表示
production team 制作团队
professional advisers 职业顾问
standard agreements 标准协议
respective professional institutions 各自的专业机构
default 违约
notwithstanding 尽管，依然；虽然，尽管
breach 违反，违背；打破，破坏
warranty of authority 诉讼权利
high level of expertise 高水平专业知识
theoretical knowledge 理论知识
practical experience 实践经验
holistic 整体的，全盘的
planning stage 规划阶段
building of facility 建筑设备
commission 佣金；授权，委托
enlisting 募征，支持；筹集
initial appointment 初始会议
stated constraints 国家限制条件
periodic visits 定期参观
in accordance with 与……一致，依照
written report 书面报告
contractual obligations 合同约定的义务，合同约定的责任
interpretations of the contract documents 对合同文件的阐释
supplemental details 补充细则
term of the building contract 建设合同条款
negligent 疏忽的，大意的
client's representative 业主代表
final inspection of the building 工程竣工验收
large scale projects 大型项目
prime professionals 首要专业
construction techniques 施工技术
threat of litigation 诉讼的威胁

engineering professionals 工程专业人员
quantity surveyor 造价师，工料测量师
construction economist 建设经济学家
office blocks 办公大楼
mining development 矿业发展
shipbuilding 造船
large process engineering works 大型加工工程
oil refineries 炼油厂
inception 起初；获得学位
feasibility 可行性，可能性
inception and feasibility stage 初步可行性研究阶段
the most economical way of achieving their requirements 以最经济的方法来满足他们的需求
initial budget estimate 初期预算估价
feasibility proposals 可行性建议
cash flow projections 现金流预测
pre-contract cost control stage 成本控制阶段
detailed design stage 详细设计阶段
tender and contractual documentation stage 投标与合同文件阶段
in conjunction with 联合，连接；有关系
bills of quantities 工程量清单
suitable tenderers 适合的投标者
the most suitable contractors 最适合的承包商
project execution stage 施工阶段
interrogate 询问，质问；审问，质问
contractor's statements 承包商的报表
expense of variation claims 各种各样的费用索赔
interim payments 临时付款，期中付款
substantiation 证实，实体化
sufficient substantiation 充分的证据
legitimacy of the claim 合法索赔
the final account 决算
mediation 调解，调节
arbitration 仲裁
structural engineers 结构工程师
mechanical and electrical engineers 机械和电气工程师
specialist consultants 专家顾问
hydraulic engineer 液压工程师
interior designer 室内设计师
building surveyor 建筑测量员

land surveyor 土地测量师
landscape architect 景观设计师
in charge of the construction of the whole project 负责整个工程项目
is appointed to 指定去
workmanship 工艺，手艺；技巧
stipulated 规定，约定
legal and statutory requirements 法律法规的要求
nominated subcontractors 指定分包商
specialty contractors/specialist subcontractor 专业承包商；专业分包商
international construction contract 国际建设施工合同
nomination procedure 候选人提名的程序
prime cost Item 最初的成本条款
provisional sum item 暂时的金额条款
contingency item 意外条款
categorise 分类，加以分类
mechanical 机械
electrical 电气
foundation 地基
excavation 挖掘
demolition 拆卸
legal statutes 法律法规
building site 建筑工地
defaults and neglects 违约与疏忽
suppliers 供应商
certain items 特定物品
structural steel fabrication and erection 钢结构制作与安装
sheet metal 钣金
mixed concrete delivery 混合混凝土配送
roofing 屋面材料
glazing 玻璃
industrial construction 工业建设
manufacturers of generators 发电机制造商
boilers and piping 锅炉与管道
on-site installation 现场安装
requirements and contractual specifications 合同要求与规格
structural units 结构单元
prefabricated off-site 现场预制
good team coordination 良好的团队协作
communication systems 通信系统
construction processes 施工组织过程

Unit 2 Project Participants — Client/Consultant/Contractor

Exercises

I. Choose the best answer according to the text.

1. The architects' role is to interpret _____.
    A. the clients brief and translate it into a viable building with in the stated constraints
    B. the client although now there are many occasions when the initial appointment may be made to a project manage
    C. make periodic visits to the site during the construction period to supervise/observe the progress of the project
    D. make all necessary interpretations of the contract documents and provide any supplemental details and/or instruction
2. According to this text, the root cause of disputes and complaints against architects _____.
    A. is scheduled generally weekly with architect, contractor and client
    B. is present, together with the client's representative, to conduct the final inspection of the building
    C. is often an incomplete understanding of the architect's role and responsibilities in design, planning and construction processes
    D. certifies to the client's representative that the project has been completed in compliance with the contract
3. The function of the quantity surveyor includes _____.
    A. risk management system managing, carrying out forecast final outturn values for cost, sales and margin
    B. a duty of care to the client to carry out his/her work
    C. being liable for professional negligence if fails to do so
    D. above all
4. Those subcontractors that are nominated or selected or approved by the Employer or the Engineer are called _____.
    A. specialty contractors
    B. specialist subcontractor
    C. nominated subcontractors
    D. none of the above
5. For the purposes of the main contractor's final account, the main contractor is _____.
    A. allowed to claim for a sum being a percentage rate of the actual price paid
    B. due to be paid calculated attendances, overheads and profit for the nominated subcontractors' works
    C. A or B
    D. A and B
6. We learn from the passage that major equipment suppliers for industrial construction

include _____.

    A. manufacturers of generators

    B. boilers and piping

    C. other equipment

    D. above all

II. Decide the following statements are true or false.

1. Also the client's professional advisers could be liable to the contractor in default notwithstanding the absence of a contractual link.

2. In the past two decades, this traditional approach has become popular for a number of reasons, particularly for large scale projects.

3. The main contractor takes equivalent responsibilities or obligations consistent with those undertaken by any subcontractor.

4. As more and larger structural units are prefabricated off-site, the distribution between specialty contractors and material suppliers becomes even more obvious.

III. Change the following words to another form and write down the Chinese meanings.

1. illustrates _____

2. notwithstanding _____

3. interpret _____

4. issued _____

5. negligent _____

6. quantity surveyor _____

7. inception _____

8. in conjunction with _____

9. geo-technical engineer _____

IV. Give out the following words' synonym or other word in the closest meaning.

1. conventional	a. instruction
2. owner	b. comply with
3. supervise	c. employer
4. issues	d. problems
5. supplemental details	e. obligations
6. in compliance with	f. observe
7. architect	g. be liable for
8. construction economist	h. traditional
9. is responsible for	i. quantity surveyor
10. responsibilities	j. engineer

V. Put the following English into Chinese.

1. The construction client chooses the players that will be involved in the project and determines the conditions – from the planning stage to the point at which the final building of facility is put into commission.

2. Construction clients work in different ways, using their own resources or enlisting the help of consultants, active and competent construction clients are essential for the sustainable development of the building.

3. The architect is traditionally appointed first by the client although now there are many occasions when the initial appointment may be made to a project manager or to any other consultant.

4. The client will usually make the appointment of the quantity surveyor either direct or on the advice of the architect. If the architect or any other agent of the client makes the appointment it is important to ensure that the principle is aware of his/her actions.

5. The quantity surveyor monitors cost implications during detailed design stage, review the construction cost of each package based upon the designs and specifications prepared by the architect; and ensure that the design remains on budget through cost management.

6. Whilst labeling all subcontractors as "domestic" may show what the parties intended at the time of entering into the building contract.

VI. Put the following Chinese into English.

1. 建筑施工组织过程
2. 钢结构制作与安装
3. 国际建筑施工合同
4. 机械工程师、电气工程师与岩土工程师
5. 初步可行性研究阶段
6. 工程竣工验收与竣工结算阶段

参 考 译 文

第 2 单元　项目参与方——业主/咨询师/承包商

1. 项目参与方的角色

合同关系的模式

施工管理即按合同文件的要求来施工。施工阶段包括承包商的规划和安排任务的进度、设备的动用、材料的采购、部件的组装和施工。施工管理需要团队的努力，这个团队包括承包商、分包商、测试机构、建筑师/工程师、咨询师、雇主、产品代表及其他人员，所有人员朝着交付竣工的供计划内使用的设施的共同目的努力。

图 2.1 说明了合同关系模式，这种模式存在于有关常规或者传统合同形式的各种设计和项目团队之间。

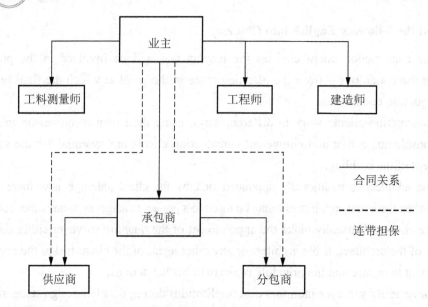

图 2.1 传统项目交付方式的项目参与者关系

合同关系的模式可能会根据合同约定的类型以及所使用的合同形式而改变。

应当指出的是，项目各方只与雇主签订主要合同，在业主的专业顾问和承包商之间没有合同关系。雇主和他/她的专业顾问之间的合同通常基于由各自的专业机构所制定的标准协议。同样，尽管缺乏合同联系，雇主的专业顾问仍可以使不履行合同职责的承包人受到处罚。这样，如果建筑师在没有对承包人了解的情况下超出了他/她的权限，那么承包人可以重新获得在因违反保证权的行动中所遭受的损失。

2. 雇主/业主

施工项目经理需要具有高水平的专业技能，既需理论知识又需来自规划、施工和管理的所有阶段的实践经验，并且必须具备管理所涉及的进程的整体处理能力。雇主的作用是提供清楚的项目纲要且筹集针对项目的可用必要资金。雇主选择将会涉及的参与方且决定工作条件——从规划阶段到设施的最后建造被交付使用那一刻。雇主监督施工项目从概念到实施的进展，且负责在施工过程中为其他参与方创造适宜的条件，包括有关技术系统及与行家合作中遇到的问题。施工雇主以不同的方式开展工作，利用他们自己的资源或者寻求咨询师的帮助，因此，积极、称职的施工雇主对于施工的可持续开发是必不可少的。

3. 建筑师

按照惯例，建筑师首先由雇主指派，但现在许多时候，最初都由项目经理或者咨询师指派。建筑师的作用是按照规定，解释雇主的项目纲要且把它转化成切实可行的建筑物。建筑师理应在施工期间对工地进行定期巡视，以监督项目的进展，从而确保施工总体上按照合同进行。相应地，他还应当对自己的巡视做书面报告。这些巡视的频率将随着项目的不同阶段的合同责任而变化。在施工期间，建筑师也应当对合同文件做出必要的诠释，且提供补充细节和/或指导，这些细节和/或指导可以是对文件含义的解释。

建筑师的权力由建筑合同条款来定,且其不能超越权限,而且,与其他任何专家一样,如果建筑师不认真履行职责,即未能使用恰当的技术和行动的话,他/她就要对雇主负责。由建筑师而引起的争端和投诉的根本原因常常是建筑师对设计、规划和施工进程中的角色和责任的不完全理解。

在施工期间,通常一周会有一次与建筑师、承包商和雇主的会议。当直接关系到他们的咨询师的时候,建筑师就也应出席这些会议。且建筑师将与雇主代表一起到场对建筑物实施最后检查,建筑师将向雇主代表证明该项目已经遵照合同完工了。

在过去二十年中,由于许多原因,特别是对于大规模项目,这种传统方式已经变得不受欢迎。作为雇主聘用从事设计和监理的首要专家的建筑师/工程师公司,已经在建筑工程构成中变得更加孤立了。这种情况的发生是由于为了降低建筑师/工程师公司的费用的压力、有关施工缺陷的诉讼威胁以及就建筑师和咨询行业来说的新施工技术知识的欠缺等。

4. 工料测量师

雇主通常会在建筑师的指导或者建议下委派工料测量师。如果建筑师或者任意其他的雇主代理商做了委派,那么应让雇主意识到其行动是很重要的。工料测量师,也以施工经济专家或者成本经理闻名,对于建筑业来说是专业顾问团成员之一。工料测量师在办公大楼、学校、医院、工厂、桥梁、铁路、石油和矿井开掘、造船以及炼油厂等大规模工程项目中开展工程量计算工作。

➤ 在项目开始和可行性研究阶段,工料测量师根据施工方法和成本知识按照雇主要求的最节约方式向雇主提出建议,编制初步概算、可行性研究建议和现金流动设想。

➤ 在签订合同前的成本控制阶段,工料测量师监测详细设计阶段的成本计划,评估基于由建筑师制定的设计和规范的每个一揽子交易的施工费用,并通过成本管理使设计与预算保持一致。

➤ 在标书与合同编制阶段,工料测量师与雇主和专家组成员协力编制标书与合同文件,计算工程量,准备针对费用的工程量表,并展示劳动成本、机械设备和材料等方面的详细情况。

➤ 投标之后,工料测量师以最恰当的建议和提案就投标撰写报告,帮助雇主去鉴别基于成本、质量、服务、财务状况和经验等方面都合适的投标人,并确定最恰当的承包商。

➤ 在项目实施阶段,工料测量师对承包商的报告书提出质疑,评估按建筑师或雇主要求的工程变更的损失和费用数额,根据合同要求,对承包商、分包商和供应商的中期付款提出建议,并且通过在工地工作或者巡视工地获得足够的实证,让雇主或其代表以及相关的建筑师对由于索赔的合法性和工程变更通知提议而信服。在完工之后,如果必要,或者在争论、调解和仲裁的情况下,他们还参与到与承包商就决算进行清算的问题。

工料测量师的职责包括对风险管理系统的管理以及成本、销售和盈余的产量终值进行预测。就像其他工程咨询专家一样,如果未能这样做,工料测量师就要对业主承担审慎职责,并且还要对疏忽工作承担责任。

5. 其他咨询师

其他咨询师包括结构工程师、机电工程师和任何其他专家顾问,这取决于项目的复杂程度。可能还包括液压工程师、地质技术工程师、室内设计师、建筑勘测师、土地勘测师和园林建筑师。

6. 总承包商/承包商

按惯例，总承包商的作用是协调建筑项目中的所有任务，掌管整个项目的施工，并协调各分包商的工作。总承包商根据合同规定的标准、工艺、质量以及法定要求负责项目的施工和交付。总承包商对分包商运作中的缺陷负责。总承包商和分包商之间的关系取决于双方之间签订的转包合同中的条款，且各方的职责由项目的合同约定。

7. 指定分包商和专业分包商

➢ 大部分国际建筑包工合同能够让雇主挑选分包商，分包商随后被承包商或者总承包商通过一个"指定"程序雇用。由雇主或工程师指定、挑选或批准的分包商被称作"指定分包商"。指定分包商通常是开展工作的专家，对于这些工作，"通用费用事项"、"暂定费用事项"和"应急费用事项"的参考和合同文件等将用于规范其工作。对于主承包商的决算意图，主承包商可以要求支付一笔费用，这笔费用是被支付的或者应当被支付的实际价格的一定比例，且该费用由对指定分包商的运作的服务费、管理费和利润计算出来。

➢ 在没有相关指定风险的情况下，由雇主用来挑选分包商的一种方法是把所有分包商归类为内部分包商，这些分包商将由总承包商直接挑选。同时，把所有分包商列为"内部的"，可以在签订建筑合同的时候表明各参与方身份。

➢ 专业承包商还包括机械、电气、地基、挖掘及拆除等承包商。他们对于项目总承包商来说通常起到分包商的作用。在一些国家，法定条例允许雇主与专业承包商直接打交道。

➢ 总包商要对建筑工地上的健康和安全负责，任何分包商的行动、违约和疏漏将被认为是总包商的行动、违约和疏漏，由总包商承担全部责任。总包商负责承担与任何分包商担负一样的责任和义务。

8. 供应商

总承包商从供应商购买项目所需要的大部分材料。然而，建筑师可能会针对某种名目的供应而指定一个特定的来源/公司。与建筑合同相关联的各参与方的角色已经简要地在上文中做了概述。主要材料供应商包括在钢结构、轻钢结构、混凝土运送、钢筋细部设计、屋顶和玻璃装配业等方面的专业分包商。针对工业建筑的主要设备供应商包括发电机、锅炉和管材及其他设备的制造商。许多供应商处理现场安装，以确保达到要求及合同规范。由于更多更大的结构单位是在工地外预制的，所以专业承包商和材料供应商之间的分配变得更不明显。

然而，如果为提高效率，将设计和施工流程有效地组织起来的话，在团队的每个成员之间，良好的团队协调和成功的沟通系统就必不可少。

阅读

有关生命周期

1. 项目生命周期

项目生命周期可以看作是项目从开始到结束的实施过程。这个过程通常十分复杂，该过程可以被分解成几个阶段。不管该项目的雇主是个人、私营公司还是公共机构，已完工设施的资产通常代表一项重大资本投入。由于针对这样一项投资的资源投入是被市场需求或者知觉需要所激发的，所以该项设施被期望在雇主和咨询师所确定的范围内去达到某种目的。

从雇主的角度来看，竣工的设施的生命周期可用图 2.2 概略地阐明。这个周期开始于该项目的最初设想，并通过规划、设计、采购、施工、运行启动、经营和维护而继续下去。当一个设施不再有益或有用被废弃时，其生命周期就结束了。

在设想规划阶段，各种可能性都会被考虑到，且为了挑选最合适的项目，每种供选方案的技术和经济可行性都会都评估和对照。对于被提议的供选方案的财务计划也必须被检验，且针对该项目的竣工和可用现金流的有关时间安排将做出规划。

在项目范围被清楚地界定以后，详细的工程设计将为施工提供蓝图，且明确的成本估算将作为控制成本的基础线。在采购和施工阶段，必须周密地计划和控制材料的运送和项目在现场的构架。竣工以后，当首次启用时，通常有一个已完工设施的运行启动或者试运行的简短时期。最后，设施的经营管理以完全占有的形式移交给雇主，直到该设施度过它的有效寿命并被拆除或改建。

由于对设施的经营和维护在项目竣工和验收很久以后仍将继续下去，除了考虑到项目的生命周期成本之外，经营和维护被看作是一个单独的问题。从设想规划和可行性研究到针对使用的设施验收的所有阶段，可以宽泛地合在一起考虑，且作为设计/建造过程来处理，而采购和施工单独地按惯例被看作是建筑业的范围。

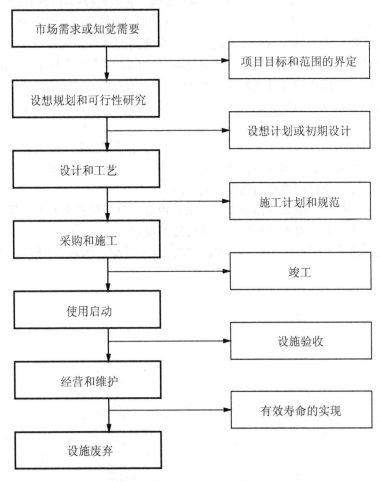

图2.2 竣工设施的项目生命周期

各个阶段的解决方案被整合起来以获得最终结局。虽然在每个阶段需要不同的专业知识或技能，但对于专业人士来说，它通常包括技术和管理两项活动。雇主可以把整个过程分解成或多或少的基于项目规模和特性的各个阶段，并因此在实施中获得最有效率的结果。在大多数情况下，雇主对规划和设计阶段进行直接控制，但是，由于项目比较复杂，局外的规划师和财务专家也常被用作咨询师。

当然，图 2.2 中的发展阶段不可能是严格有序的。有些阶段需要反复，而其他阶段可能并行或以重叠时段来实施，这取决于项目的特性、规模和紧迫程度。而且，一个雇主可能具有机构内部的能力以处理整个过程中每个阶段的运行，或者他可能为所有阶段的运作寻求专业意见和服务。

2. 项目合同生命周期

对于建筑合同，从合同的形成到合同的终止，它通常要花很长一段时间，有时甚至几年，并且它有许多步骤。合同管理必须在整个项目生命期间实施，且在不同阶段，合同管理具有不同的任务和重点。对于常见的公开投标项目来说，建筑合同通常经历两个主要阶段：合同的确立及合同的实施阶段。合同建立阶段有两个步骤，它们是投标和合同谈判。合同的实施阶段也有两个步骤，即施工和维护。以下是一些深刻的目标含义和项目管理方法。

➢ 设施从初始规划到经营到废弃的项目生命周期的成本和收益与决策有关。一个雇主关注一个项目从开始到结束的过程。建筑成本仅仅代表整个生命周期成本的一部分。

➢ 如果额外的成本或者延误发生在别的阶段，在项目进程的某一个阶段优化运作可能对整个项目并无益处。例如，假如结果是施工成本超支，在设计进程上节约资金将是一个错误的经济运作。

➢ 项目管理由不同专业人士进行分阶段管理可能很有必要，但是要实现项目的总体目标，在参与者中间的良好沟通和协调是必不可少的。新兴信息技术，尤其是因特网和专业化的外延网，在这个过程中将起到很大的作用。

➢ 生产率的提高一般来说都很重要且很有价值。只要这些东西不太昂贵且与所设计的运作情况相一致，就可引入新材料和自动化施工流程。

➢ 工程的质量和运行状况对一个项目的成功至关重要，因为业主将必须承担项目的最终质量结果。

Unit 3

Contracts Used for Construction Projects

1. Traditional Approach: Design—Bid—Build/DBB

The traditional approach is the appointment by the client of an architect or an engineer to design and administer the contract. Meanwhile the project is divided into small individual parts for construction, so it was called fragmented approach as well. The most outstanding character of DBB is that the procedure of the project construction has to follow the order of DBB. With a documented design contract, most of the design, including drawings and other design documentation, is prepared by consultants engaged by, or on behalf of the client. Tenders for the construction contract are not called until the whole of the work is designed. The DBB contract is typically based on the price of the bill of quantities. In a unit price contract, the risk of inaccurate estimation of uncertain quantities for some key tasks has been removed from the contractor. A documented design contract has the following risks:

➤ Delays during design will delay the project, since construction cannot commence until the design is completed;

➤ The volume and complexity of the tender documents increases the risk of errors and omissions that can give rise to variations and associated additional costs and delays;

➤ The procedure is linear and the lifetime is too long. Also the corresponding between the constructors, engineers, and contractors is difficult and the pre-investment finance can be very high.

Additional amounts are payable for changes to the client's requirements, errors and omissions in the client's tender documentation and, usually, circumstances such as unexpected adverse site conditions.

The FIDIC forms of contract have developed over the years as the contract of choice for many of the multi-lateral organizations. The Red Book is the FIDIC traditional form of contract. Those regular users of the ICE forms of contract, particularly the earlier editions, will recognize much of the wording in the FIDIC Red Book. This has now been developed into an additional versions (2006) referred to as the MDB harmonized edition for use on projects funded by the listed Multilateral Development Banks. Throughout the countries in the world where the United Kingdom has had a presence such as the common wealth nations, the influence of the JCT and ICE forms of building and civil engineering contracts can often be seen.

2. Design and Build Contract/D&B

For a design and build contract, the client provides a project brief or outline, which may include some concept design, and specifies performance and quality requirements. Commonly this team is a joint venture between an architect and a builder, while the contractor (builder) is the lead members of this team. The contractor takes overall responsibility for design, and engages consultants to prepare or complete the concept design, develop the design and prepare construction documentation. The contractor may also take responsibility for obtaining approvals from authorities.

Usually the design and build team will negotiate a fixed price/lump sum contract or tendered rates to complete the design and construction of the facility. In a lump sum contract, the owner has essentially assigned all the risk to the contractor, who in turn can be expected to ask for a higher markup in order to take care of unforeseen contingencies. Additional amounts are paid for variations to the client's requirements, but the client bears little of the risk of errors and omissions in tender documentation, since the contractor prepares the bulk of the design and documentation. The risk of latent conditions is generally allocated to the contractor.

A D&B contract has the following risks:

➢ If the tender documents are unclear or incomplete, the desired outcomes may not be achieved without disputes over interpretation, variations, additional expense and delays;

➢ Design activities are suspended during a relatively long tendering period, and progress may be delayed by complex tender reviews;

➢ Tender prices will include allowances for the additional design risks;

➢ Tender evaluation is complex and may increase costs and cause delays;

➢ Higher tendering costs and a lower number of competent tenderers may reduce competition and increase tender prices; and changes to the design requirements are likely to be costly, due to their potential to impact on the contractor's work and program.

The FIDIC form of contract for plant and design build is the Yellow Book, and in the UK the JCT design and build has developed as the contract of choice for design and build building projects.

3. EPC Turnkey Project

EPC is the abbreviation for Engineering Procurement Construction. EPC is one of the global construction contracting models, and it is also known as the turnkey project service. It is a typical type of contract for industrial plant construction sector, comprising the provision of engineering services, procurement of materials and construction. The term "turnkey" indicates that the system is delivered to the client ready for operations.

The feature of the EPC is that the ultimate price and time of the project have a great degree of certainty. The project is largely contractor managed, and the cost risk and control are weighted towards the contractor and away from the client. In this project delivery system, the EPC contractor holds all of the responsibility. It includes the provision of engineering services, procurement of materials and construction.

The FIDIC form of contract for EPC/Turnkey Projects is the Silver Book and is mainly used for projects in the power, process, oil and gas and industrial sectors, and usually an EPC/Turnkey Project is negotiated for a fixed price/lump sum contract as well.

An EPC contract, Engineering Procurement and Construction contract, is a direct agreement between the employer and EPC contractor, and the employer is not involved with the detailed design process, except in the event of variations and the quality control procedures.

The fundamental difference between design and build and EPC contracts, is that in the case of design and build, the client normally has an input into the outline design of the building. In the case of EPC industrial project the client normally only has a decision in the output e.g. megawatts of power or tons of cement and will not be involved in the detailed design process.

4. Financed Project

Entering the global market, many contactors can be confusing with referring to PFI, PPP, BOT, DBFO, etc. In those form models, the government defines and grants specific rights to an entity (usually a private company) to build and operate a facility for a fixed period of time. The government may retain the ultimate ownership of the facility and/or right to supply the services. In concessions, payments can take place both ways: concessionaire pays to government for the concession rights and the government may pay the concessionaire, which payment model provides under the agreement to meet certain specific conditions. Usually, the concessionaire makes investments and operates the facility for a fixed period of time after which the ownership reverts back to the public sector. Typical concession periods range between 5 to 50 years.

The UK has been in the forefront of these types of projects and the various formats are spreading rapidly worldwide. Financed projects normally entail the formation of Special Purpose Vehicles/SPV, to carry out not only the construction but also the operation and maintenance of the project. Many SPV are therefore a combination of contractors and facility managers.

A PFI project can be structured on minimum payment by the government over a fixed contract tenure, or minimum contract tenure for a fixed annual payment, or a combination of both payment and tenure. The Private Finance Initiative, PFI, used in the construction for hospitals, schools and in the work of national defence is a model where all of the finance is provided by the private sector. The client purchases its requirements based on an output requirement e.g. number of bed or school places.

Public Private Partnerships, PPP, are being used for example for light rail and tram projects, which were proposed for the stadium project in Ireland and most famously was being used on the London Underground initially. PPP uses a mixture of public and private money and as can be seen on the London underground complicated targets can lead to criticizing.

Build Operate and Transfer, BOT, often used for toll highways and bridges entails the private sector providing all of the finance and then receiving receipts, sometimes subsidized, over a period of say 25 years. At the end of the 25-year life of the project the ownership is transferred back to the central or local governmental authority. Design Build Finance Operate, DBFO, used on the channel tunnel but unlike BOT does not transfer back to the authority.

5. Management Contracts

5.1 Construction management

Construction management contracts have been the norm for many years in the USA, and have made a specialty of this type of contracting. The construction manager effectively acts as the overall manager and specialist contracts are entered into, often directly with the client. The CM (Construction Management) system in the USA is also influenced by the widespread use of 100% surety bonds whereby the bond holder steps in, in the event of the default of the construction manager.

5.2 Project Management Contract/ Managing Contractor

In project management consulting, the consultant is to be responsible for the successful completion of the project within a specific time frame and on a specific budget. There are different types of project management consulting, depending on the industry, the skill set required and the project to be completed.

Project management contract is related to the overall planning, coordination and control of a project from inception to completion aiming at meeting a client's requirements. Typically, this contract model includes the design, or procurement of the design on behalf of the client, the construction or procurement of the construction on behalf of the client. In particular instances, this contract model also covers other activities including, for example, site selection, site acquisition, permit approvals, advertising of the project, leasing or pre-leasing of the project, and/or other activities which might otherwise need to be performed by the client.

The project managing contractor will arrange the trade packages, tender and enter into the trade contracts on behalf of the client, perform the usual supervision, and report activities required on the project to keep the client informed of the progress of the works.

The attraction of this type of contract is its flexibility and the skills which the project management consulting may be able to bring to bear in the procuring the works, so as to assist the client.

6. Target Cost/Cost Reimbursable

Target cost and cost reimbursable contracts are widely used in the utilities sector. The client and contractor set a target cost and then share the profit or loss, often referred to as the Pain/Gain formula. Construction management seems to be less incentive for contractors to control the costs but the incentive of steady workloads appears to result in efficient working practices.

6.1 Guaranteed Maximum Price/GMP

Specifying a Guaranteed Maximum Price (GMP) can provide greater certainty of meeting the required project end cost and completion date. The GMP contract is designed to limit changes to the contract price or completion date and to reduce contract management effort by incorporating terms, and to reduce the contractor's entitlement to extensions of time, for example by disallowing claims on account of inclement weather or industrial disputes.

A GMP contract may include a provision requiring the contractor to provide offsets to maintain the original contract price by reducing the quality or scope of the work if the agency directs a variation. It may also allow a bonus for early completion. Unless the agency directs a change to the scope of the project, the contractor must complete the work for the tendered lump sum price.

6.2 Target Cost / Target Construction Sum

A project managing contractor contract is generally awarded early in the design phase, after a project brief or a concept design is developed. The tender document sets a target cost (or target construction sum) based on the estimated cost of the construction work, and a target date or dates for completion. The contract is awarded on the basis of non-price criteria and tendered management fees. For this development and management work, the contractor is paid the actual costs of consultants and service providers, often based on an "open book" approach, and the tendered management fee. To provide an incentive to manage the costs, the contractor is also entitled to share any cost savings upon completion, and is commonly paid 50% of the difference between the actual costs plus its fees (the actual construction sum).

The potential for incentive fees to be earned is the most important aspect of the project management contractor contract. It encourages the contractor to be efficient and make whatever savings are available. Other incentives linking aspects of performance to additional payments can also be incorporated into the contract.

Reading

Overview of FIDIC 1999

1. FIDIC 1999 introduction

In the contract for international engineering projects, the function of conditions of contract is of greatest importance providing the rights, obligation and responsibility for the parties concerned in the contract execution.

During the past half century, the International Federation of Consulting Engineers (FIDIC) has devoted itself to the compilation of management documents for all kinds of projects, among which the FIDIC conditions of contract are of the highest influence and are the most popular application. FIDIC, is also best known for its publications of high-quality standard contracts for the international construction contracting industry.

The first edition of FIDIC conditions of contract for works of civil engineering construction (use "Red Book" in the following) was compiled in 1957, and later its second, third, and fourth edition were issued in 1963, 1977, and 1987 respectively.

But these editions were mostly compiled in the reference of the related documents of the Institution of Civil Engineers (ICE). The FIDIC and European International Contractors (EIC) entrusted the University of Reading in 1966 to summarize the experience and to draw lessons from the application of the former documents.

With the investigation of the governments, employers, contractors and consulting engineers all over the world about their application of the "Red Book", 204 findings reports were returned. According to the findings, the FIDIC contract committee organized a group of experts to compile the new contract condition models to be applied in the 21st century.

The test edition of these models was published in 1998, and FIDIC solicited opinions throughout the world for additional time to publish the official texts in 1999.

Now FIDIC condition of contract has been applied worldwide, especially in the projects invested by World Bank, Asia Development Bank, Africa Development Bank etc.

The new models include :

FIDIC conditions of contract for construction, the (New Red Book);

FIDIC conditions of contract for plant and design/build, the (New Yellow Book) FIDIC conditions of contract for EPC turnkey projects, the (Silver Book);

FIDIC short form of contract, the (Green Book);

FIDIC conditions of contract (new edition) raised a higher requirement to the parties concerned in the area of contract management.

➤ The Red Book is the traditional form for civil engineering construction in which the contractor constructs to the employer's design. To give its full name, it is the conditions of contract for construction for building and engineering works designed by the employer.

➤ The Red Book is predicated on the employer designing and the contractor constructing, although there is provision for the contractor to carry out certain limited design where specified. The form maintains the traditional role of the engineer as certifier and first port of call for disputes and the payment mechanism is based on measure and value.

➤ The Yellow Book – conditions of contract for plant and design/build, it is used for design and build contracts and for plant contracts. Again, the engineer administers the contract, but the payment is based on periods or instalments of the lump sum.

➤ The Green Book is FIDIC's short form of contract, and it adopts the overall philosophy, broad structure of the Red and Yellow Books and provides for the contractor to undertake design where required. The payment provisions are very flexible: the basis of payment can range from lump sum, through lump sum with schedules of rates or bills of quantities, to cost reimbursable, although a multitude of traps lie in the space allowed for "details" to be inserted of that payment mechanism. It is intended for contracts of low capital value or simple contracts of short duration. There is no engineer. His place is taken by the employer.

➤ The Silver Book (conditions of contract) is different and used for EPC turnkey projects which has no engineer; instead the employer deals directly with the contractor. Risk is placed largely with the contractor. Payment is on periods or instalments of the lump sum.

➤ In 2006, FIDIC introduced the MDB (Multilateral Development Bank) harmonized edition, a variation of the Red Book. The rationale behind this contract was to reduce and standardize amendments routinely sought by multilateral lenders such as the World Bank. The revisions introduced consist largely of the introduction of lender friendly forms of performance security and provisions to ensure swift unimpeded access to this security.

➢ 2006 also saw the publication of the 4th edition of FIDIC's client/consultant model services agreement, the White Book, intended to be used in conjunction mainly with FIDIC's Red and Yellow forms.

➢ In 2008, FIDIC introduced us to the Gold Book, conditions of contract for design, build and operate projects. Essentially, this consisted of a Silver Book with a 20-years operating period added, reflecting an increasingly widespread practice of placing responsibility for operating and maintaining on the party which has built the plant, to lower the overall cost of ownership.

2. Characteristics of FIDIC

➢ The new edition was drafted as the "New Red Book", the "New Yellow Book" and the "Silver Book" by a workgroup under the leadership of the FIDIC contract committee. The contract form was not influenced by the former ICE framework, which was included in all 20 clauses. So if the clauses content could be unified, it would be under the same titles and expressions. In these three books, more than 80% of the content was consistent, and 85% of the definitions and expressions were the same. It is of great help for the users to understand them completely, saving study time.

➢ The new edition also shows more flexibility and adaptability. For example, in the old edition, the conditional performance guarantee was necessary, which the World Bank had different opinions of. While in the new edition, the guarantee forms were set by particular conditions which can be applied giving the employers better flexibility.

3. High-quality Provisions and Logical Clause Sequencing

Compared with the original "Red Book", the "New Red Book" has 163 clauses, nearly 40% being freshly compiled. An additional 40% were modified and given supplements. Only 20% were kept intact. The old edition adopted ICE's disorderly style bit in the clause sequence, while in the new edition, the related sub-clauses are put into one clause when possible, and convenient to the users.

4. More Specific Provisions Concerning the Rights And Obligations of The Contract Parties

Taking the clause of employer's default as an example, we can see that in contrast to the "Red Book", three points are added into the "New Red Book": two of them are concerned with payment. The above shows the strict requirements for the employer. However, the contractor shall institute a quality assurance system and submit to the engineer to audit any aspect of the system before execution. Monthly progress reports shall be prepared by the contractor to submit to the engineer every month, otherwise, the payment won't be given. Any kind of bribe can result in contractor's default. All of the above are high requirements for the contractor.

5. Changes in the Preparing Style

General conditions in the former edition were fairly concise; some recommendable clauses were given particular conditions. While in the new edition, there is a way around the regulations being that the general conditions are relatively comprehensive and detailed. An example would be advanced payment and adjustment formula. The new edition writers believe that it is more convenient for the users to delete the clauses they do not need than to write them in the "Particular Conditions" by themselves.

6. Application Prospect of FIDIC

The new edition has many advanced ideas and regulations such as standardizing of the contract words and expressions, clearer and stricter claim procedure, and emphasis on the protection of intellectual property rights. The traditional project management mode, which is universal in the world, has been applied in most of the engineering project management cases in the world.

FIDIC conditions of contracts have strict and clearly defined clauses and terms on the rights, obligations and responsibilities of client, engineer, and contractor in the contract, thus it will be possible for client and contractor to make a balanced risks distribution mechanism. A good contractor should seriously study and master the spirit of the contract documents, so as to improve construction project management and better safeguard his legitimate rights and interests.

New Words and Expressions

Design—Bid—Build/DBB 设计—投标—建设

appointment 委任，委托

administer the contract 管理合同

drawings 施工图纸

design documentation 设计文件

unit price of the bill of quantities 清单单价

unit price contract 单价合同

commence 开始，着手

tender documents 招标文件

additional costs 额外的成本费用

linear 线性的，直线的；长度的，线的

payable for changes to the client's requirements 符合客户的要求

unexpected adverse site condition 意想不到的不利现场条件

FIDIC forms of contract FIDIC 合同形式

multi-lateral organizations 多样化的多边组织

ICE forms of contract ICE 合同形式

additional versions 额外的版本

Multilateral Development Banks 多边开发银行

Unit 3 Contracts Used for Construction Projects

building and civil engineering contracts 民用建筑工程合同
design and build contract/D&B 设计与建造合同
concept design 概念设计
specifies performance 特定性能
joint venture 合资公司
overall responsibility for design 全面负责设计
construction documentation 工程文件
a fixed price/lump sum contract 固定价格合同，总价合同
tendered rates 投标率
unforeseen contingencies 不可预见的突发事件
the bulk of the design and documentation 大量的设计与施工图
latent conditions 潜在的条件
desired outcomes 理想的结果
additional expense 额外的费用
a lower number of competent tenderers 一群低能的投标人
EPC turnkey project EPC 工程总承包，EPC 交钥匙工程
abbreviation 缩写，缩写词
Engineering Procurement Construction/EPC 工程采购建设
global construction contracting models 全球工程承包模式
the turnkey project service 交钥匙工程服务
industrial plant construction sector 工业厂房的施工合同部门
project delivery system 项目交付系统
industrial sectors 工业领域
procurement and construction contract 采购和施工承包合同
detailed design process 详细设计过程
quality control procedures 质量控制程序
megawatts of power 几兆瓦的能量
tons of cement 几吨水泥
financed project 资助项目
ultimate ownership 最终的所有权
concession rights 特许权
concessionaire 特许经营者
the public sector 公共领域，公共部门
financed projects 融资项目
operation and maintenance of the project 项目的运营与维护
Special Purpose Vehicles/SPV 特殊目的机构
Private Finance Initiative/PFI 私人融资活动
Public Private Partnerships/PPP 公私合作伙伴关系
Build Operate and Transfer/BOT 建设—经营—转让

Design Build Finance Operate/DBFO 设计—建造—融资—经营
facility managers 设施经理
combination 联合，结合
a fixed contract tenure 一个固定合同期间
ministry of defense 防务部门
private sector 私人部门
light rail and tram projects 有轨电车与轻轨项目
stadium project 体育馆项目
London underground 伦敦地铁
toll highways and bridges 收费的公路和桥梁
receiving receipts 递交收据
central or local governmental 中央或地方政府
channel tunnel 海峡隧道
construction manager 现场施工经理
surety bonds 债券持有人
bond holder 债券保证人
project management contract 项目管理合同
managing contractor 管理承包商
project management consulting 项目管理咨询
overall planning, coordination and control 统筹规划、协调和控制
inception 构思，构想
meeting a client's requirements 满足业主的要求
in particular instances 在特定条件下
site selection 选址
site acquisition 现场采集
permit approvals 许可审批
leasing 租赁
supervision 监督，督促；监管
flexibility 灵活性，弹性；可变性
target cost contracts 目标成本合同
cost reimbursable contracts 费用补偿合同
utilities sector 公共事业部门
Guaranteed Maximum Price/GMP 保证最大价格
completion date 合同时间
incorporating terms 合同条款
contractor's entitlement to extensions of time 承包商延长时间的权利
inclement weather 恶劣的天气
industrial disputes 工业争端
original contract price 原有合同价格

offset 抵消，弥补

tendered lump sum price 一次性投标价格

project brief 项目概况

sets a target cost (or target construction sum) 确定目标成本

non-price criteria 非价格合同

tendered management fees 投标管理费用

cost savings 成本节省

actual construction sum 实际施工金额

potential for incentive fees 潜在的激励收费标准

project management contractor contract 项目承包管理合同

additional payments 额外支付

incorporated into 合并，并入

Exercises

I. Choose the best answer according to the text.

1. _____ have developed over the years as the contract of choice for many of the multi-lateral organizations and the Red Book is the FIDIC traditional form of contract.

 A. The FIDIC forms of contract

 B. The Design—Bid—Build contract

 C. The design and build contract

 D. The engineering procurement construction contract

2. EPC is one of the global construction contracting models, and it is also known as _____.

 A. the engineering procurement construction

 B. the turnkey projects

 C. the turnkey project service

 D. the quality control procedures

3. According to the text, the fundamental difference between design and build and EPC contracts is that _____.

 A. e.g. megawatts of power or tones of cement and will not be involved in the detailed design process

 B. in the case of design and build, the client normally has an input into the outline design of the building

 C. in the case of EPC the client normally only has a decision in the output

 D. B and C

4. In concessions, payments can take place both ways _____, which it provides under the agreement to meet certain specific conditions.

 A. concessionaire pays to government for the concession rights

 B. the government may pay the concessionaire

C. concessionaire pays to government for the concession rights and the government may pay the concessionaire

   D. none of the above

5. We learn from the passage that which statement is true? _____.

   A. The Red Book is the FIDIC traditional form of contract

   B. The FIDIC form of contract for plant and design build is the Yellow Book

   C. The FIDIC form of contract for EPC/turnkey projects is the Silver Book

   D. above all

II. Decide the following statements are true or false.

1. The most outstanding character of DBB is that the procedure of the project construction has to follow the order of DBB.

2. Tenders for the construction contract are called until the whole of the work is designed; the DBB contract is typically based on unit price of the bill of quantities.

3. The project is largely contractor managed and the cost risk and control are weighted towards the contractor and away from the client.

4. As with construction management there would seem to be incentive for contractors to control the costs but the incentive of steady workloads appears to result in efficient working practices.

5. To provide an incentive to manage the costs, the contractor is also entitled to share any cost savings upon completion, and is commonly paid 80% of the difference between the actual costs plus its fees (the actual construction sum).

III. Change the following words to another form and write down the Chinese meanings.

1. appointment _____
2. behalf _____
3. commence _____
4. omission _____
5. latent _____
6. comprising _____
7. entail _____
8. inception _____
9. provision _____
10. offset _____

IV. Give out the following words' synonym or other word in the closest meaning.

1. give rise to   a. important
2. brief   b. relate
3. contractor   c. outline

4. a fixed price contract   d. delegates
5. interpretation   e. lead to
6. entity   f. target cost
7. cost reimbursable   g. private company
8. critical   h. builder
9. associate   i. explanation
10. representatives   j. lump sum contract

V. Put the following English into Chinese.

1. In a unit price contract, the risk of inaccurate estimation of uncertain quantities for some key tasks has been removed from the contractor.

2. In a lump sum contract, the owner has essentially assigned all the risk to the contractor, who in turn can be expected to ask for a higher markup in order to take care of unforeseen contingencies.

3. The FIDIC form of contract for plant and design Build is the Yellow Book and in the UK the JCT design and build has developed as the contract of choice for design and build building projects.

4. A PFI project can be structured on minimum payment by the government over a fixed contract tenure, or minimum contract tenure for a fixed annual payment, or a combination of both payment and tenure.

5. The CM system in the USA is also influenced by the widespread use of 100% surety bonds whereby the bond holder steps in, in the event of the default of the construction manager.

6. The client and contractor set a target cost and then share the profit or loss, often referred to as the Pain/Gain formula.

7. The GMP contract is designed to limit changes to the contract price or completion date and to reduce contract management effort by incorporating terms, and to reduce the contractor's entitlement to extensions of time, for example by disallowing claims on account of inclement weather or industrial disputes.

8. It encourages the contractor to be efficient and make whatever savings are available. Other incentives linking aspects of performance to additional payments can also be incorporated into the contract.

VI. Put the following Chinese into English.

1. 建设项目承包管理合同
2. 建设项目管理咨询
3. 项目运营与维护，项目生命周期
4. 工程总承包，交钥匙工程
5. 民用建筑工程合同

参 考 译 文

第3单元 用于建筑项目的合同

1. 传统方式：设计—招标—建造/DBB

传统方式是由雇主任命建筑师或者工程师进行设计和管理的合同方式。同时，工程被分成小的单个部分进行施工，这种方式也被称为分阶段方式。DBB 最突出的特征是项目施工程序必须遵照 DBB 的规程。对于按文件程序进行设计的合同，包括制图和其他设计资料的大部分设计，由被雇主聘用的或者代表雇主利益的咨询师进行编制。对建筑合同的投标要到合同整体设计完成才会被邀标，且 DBB 合同一向以工程量清单的单价为基础。在单价合同中，对于一些关键任务的不确定数量的不精确评估的风险已经从承包商那里排除。按文件程序设计的合同具有如下风险：

- ➢ 由于施工要到设计完成才能开始，故设计期间的耽搁会延误项目进程；
- ➢ 投标文件的容量和复杂性会增加差错和遗漏风险，这种风险会导致变更、有关联的追加成本及误期；
- ➢ 程序是连续的且寿命周期太长。同样，施工方、工程师和承包商之间交流困难，且投资前的财务负担可能很高。

按雇主要求所做的变更和雇主在标书文件中出现的差错和遗漏，以及在通常情况下诸如不可预见的现场不利条件产生的额外费用要由雇主承担。

合同的菲迪克(FIDIC)形式作为许多多边组织的合同选择已经被采用了多年，且红皮书(Red Book)是菲迪克的传统合同形式。英国土木工程师学会(ICE)的合同形式，尤其是早期版本的固定用户，会认可菲迪克红皮书的许多措辞。如今这已经发展成为另外的版本(2006)，被称作在项目上使用的 MDB 协调版，由所列出的多边发展银行进行资助。世界上凡受到英国影响的国家如英联邦国家，受 JCT 和 ICE 合同形式影响的建筑和土木工程也屡见不鲜。

2. 设计和建造合同/D&B

在设计和建造合同中，雇主提供一个项目概要或提纲，它可能包括一些构思设计，且具体说明实施要求和质量要求。一般来讲，这个团队是建筑师或建造商作为组织者的合资企业，而承包商(建造商)是该团队的领导成员。承包商对设计全面负责，聘任咨询师去准备或者完成概念设计、改善设计并编制施工文件。承包商也可能需要对获得官方的批准负责。

通常，设计和创建团队将议定一个固定价格/总价合同或者投标费用去完成设施的设计和施工。在总价合同中，雇主从根本上把所有风险分派给承包商，承包商反过来理应可以要求更高的溢价，以便应对不可预见费用的出现。雇主对自己要求的变更可以额外付费，但是他几乎不承担投标文件中的差错和遗漏风险，因为承包商编制了大部分的设计和文件。潜在状况的风险一般都由给了承包商承担。

D&B 合同具有如下风险：

➢ 如果投标文件含糊不清或者不完整，那么在文件的解释、变更、额外开支和误期方面没有发生争端的情况下，期望的项目结果可能无法获得；
➢ 设计活动会在一个相对较长的投标期间被延期，且项目进展可能被复杂的投标评审程序延误；
➢ 投标价格将包括针对额外设计风险的补贴费用；
➢ 投标评估复杂且可能增加成本，引起延误；
➢ 更高的投标成本和更少的合格投标人将减少竞争且增加投标价格；由于对承包商项目运作和进度计划的潜在影响，设计要求变更的代价可能较高。

对于工厂和设计建造的菲迪克合同形式是黄皮书(Yellow Book)，在英国 JCT 设计和建造合同体系已经发展成为了针对设计和建造建筑项目的合同选择形式。

3. EPC 交钥匙项目

EPC 是设计采购施工(Engineering Procurement Construction)的缩写。EPC 是全球施工承包模式之一，且它也被认为是交钥匙项目服务。它是工业工厂建设领域典型的包工方式，包括提供工程设计服务、采购和施工。术语"交钥匙"表明，工程系统移交给了运营准备就绪的雇主。

EPC 模式的特征是，项目的最终价格和完成时间在很大程度是有确定性的。项目主要由承包商进行运作，且成本风险和控制问题偏向承包商而非雇主。在这种项目移交系统中，EPC 承包商负有全部责任。这种责任包括提供工程设计服务、材料采购和施工。

针对 EPC/总包项目的菲迪克合同形式是银皮书(Silver Book)，并主要用在电力、加工、石油和天然气及工业领域。通常情况下，EPC/总包项目也被议定为固定价格/总价合同。

EPC 合同，即设计、采购和施工合同，是雇主和 EPC 承包商之间的直接合同，且除了在有变更和质量控制程序的情况下，雇主不会牵涉到详细设计过程中。

设计和建造以及 EPC 合同之间的根本差异是，在设计和建造的情况下，雇主通常有一种对建筑的规划设计的投入。在 EPC 工业工程情况下，雇主通常只决定项目的产出诸如电力的兆瓦或者水泥的吨数，且将不会牵涉到详细设计过程。

4. 融资项目

进入全球市场，许多承包商在涉及 PFI、PPP、BOT、DBFO 时可能会感到莫名其妙。在该类模式中，政府规定并准许某一公司实体(通常是一家私人公司)在固定的一段时间内建造和运作一项设施。政府可能要保留该设施的最大所有权和/或提供服务的权利。在特许权下，付款可以采用两种方式：特许权获得者为特许经营权付款给政府，或者政府可以付款给特许经营权投资者，这将根据需要满足某些特定条款的合同。通常，特许权获得者进行投资且在一个固定的时期内经营该设施，在这个时期以后，所有权归还给公共部门。典型的特许权期限在 5～50 年之间变动。

英国已经处于这些项目类型的最前沿，且各种变化模式正在世界范围内快速蔓延。融资项目通常包括特别项目公司(SPV)，不仅要完成项目的建造，而且还要实施项目的经营和维护。许多特别项目公司(SPV)因此由承包商和设施管理者组合而成。

PFI 项目可以由政府在一个固定的合同保有期内以最少的付款，或者以针对一项固定的合同支付的最短合同保有期，或者以支付和保有期的结合，来进行构建。私人主动融资(PFI)，常常用于医院、学校和国防工程建设,是一种所有融资均由私人部门提供的项目模式。雇主购买这种基于产出需要的项目设施需求,例如对医院床位数量或学校场地等的需求。

公私合伙(PPP)模式,例如一直用于轻轨和有轨电车项目,最初用于爱尔兰体育场建设,最著名的是其被用于伦敦地铁项目。公私合伙(PPP)模式是利用公共和私人资金的混合体,且正如所能看到的那样,在伦敦地铁项目上,复杂的目标容易引起人们的批评。

建设—经营—转让(BOT)模式常常用于收费公路和桥梁,需要私营部门提供所有的融资,然后在一个时期比如说 25 年内收取进款,有时可能还要接受资金补贴。在项目 25 年的收费寿命结束时,所有权将转让给中央或当地行政当局。设计—建设—融资—经营(DBFO)模式,用于海峡隧道建设,但不像 BOT 模式那样,不需要转让回官方。

5. 管理合同

5.1 建造管理

建造管理合同多年来在美国已经成为标准,成为专业承包方式。建造经理以全面管理者的身份有效地采取行动,且行家合同常常直接与雇主签订。在美国,CM 系统管理也被 100%担保保函的广泛使用所影响,借此,一旦建造经理违约,保函持有人就会介入进来。

5.2 项目管理合同/管理承包商

在项目管理咨询合同方式中,咨询公司对在特定的期限和特定的预算内顺利完成项目负责。根据行业、所需专业技术和要完成的项目不同,目前有不同的项目管理咨询公司类型。

项目管理合同与项目从开工到竣工的全面规划、协调和控制有关,以满足雇主的要求为目标。典型地,该合同模式包括代表雇主利益的设计或者针对设计的采购以及施工或者针对施工的采购。在一些特定情况下,该合同模式还涵盖其他活动,比如工地选择、工地获得、许可证批准、项目广告、项目租赁或预租赁和/或其他除此之外的可能需要由雇主来实施的活动。

项目管理承包商会代表雇主安排一揽子交易、投标和签署交易合同,实施常规监理,且报告项目所需的活动,以让雇主对项目运作的进度有所了解。

这种合同类型的吸引力在于项目管理咨询公司可以在项目的采购上能够发挥灵活性和专业技术,以便对雇主有所帮助。

6. 目标成本/可偿还成本

目标成本/可偿还成本合同广泛用于项目设施领域。雇主和承包商设立目标成本,然后分享利润,分担损失,这种合同模式常常被认为是辛劳/获益准则。建造管理模式对承包商控制成本来说似乎只有更少的诱因,但稳定的工作量激励会获得有效率的工作实践。

6.1 保证最高价格/GMP

指定一个保证最高价(GMP)可以提供项目的最终成本和竣工日期。GMP 合同被设计来限制对于合同价格或竣工日期的改变,通过所包含的条款减少管理合同的精力,且削弱承包商的延期权利,例如驳回因恶劣天气或产业争端而要求的索赔。

如果代理人下达了变更指令,那么 GMP 合同可能包含一个要求承包商以降低质量或者减小项目范围的方式来维持原始合同价格的条款,以对冲变更价格。对于提早竣工,它也允许给承包商发红利。除非代理人下达了针对项目范围的变更,否则承包商必须按发包总价去完成项目。

6.2 目标成本/目标施工金额

项目管理承包商合同一般在项目概要或者概念设计成熟以后的设计初期授予。投标文件设定基于施工项目的预计成本的目标成本(或者目标施工金额),以及目标日期或者竣工日期。该合同以非价格标准和已投标管理费用来授予。对于这种开发和管理项目,承包商被支付给由咨询公司和服务者产生的实际成本,常常以"一目了然"的方式和已投标费用为基础。为了降低管理成本,承包商也可以分享在竣工上节省的任何费用,且一般会被付给在实际成本外加其费用(实际施工金额)之间50%的差额。

对于将被挣得的激励费用的可能性是项目管理承包商合同最重要的一个方面。它鼓励承包商做事要高效率且在各方面都节俭。其他与减少额外支付有联系的激励也可以被纳入合同之中。

阅读

FIDIC 1999 简单分析

1. 菲迪克(FIDIC)1999 介绍

在针对国际工程项目的合同中,合同条件的作用是最重要的,它为合同执行中的有关各参与方提供权利、义务和责任。

在过去半个世纪中,国际咨询工程师联合会,简称菲迪克(FIDIC),致力于汇编针对各种项目的管理文件。在这些文件中,菲迪克(FIDIC)合同条件具有最大的影响力,且发挥了最广泛的应用。菲迪克(FIDIC)也由于发行针对国际施工承包业的高质量标准合同而最为著名。

针对土木工程施工项目的菲迪克(FIDIC)合同条件的第一个版本(以下简称"红皮书")编制于 1957 年,之后它的第二、第三和第四版本分别发布于 1963、1977、1987 年。

但是这些版本大部分参照土木工程学会(ICE)的有关文件编制。菲迪克(FIDIC)和欧洲国际承包商(EIC)委托雷丁大学(University of Reading)在 1966 年从过去版本的应用中总结经验并进行借鉴。

世界范围内政府、雇主、承包商和咨询工程师对"红皮书"的应用进行了调查,204 项调查结果报告被返回来。根据这些调查结果,菲迪克(FIDIC)合同委员会组织一个专家小组,编制了应用于 21 世纪的全新合同条件模式。

这些模式的测试版于 1998 年发布,菲迪克(FIDIC)还征求了全世界范围内其他时间的意见,并于 1999 年出版了官方文本。

如今,菲迪克(FIDIC)合同条件已经被应用于全世界,尤其被应用于由世界银行、亚洲发展银行、非洲发展银行等银行所投资的项目中。

新模式包括:
菲迪克(FIDIC)施工合同条件(新红皮书)
菲迪克(FIDIC)工厂和设计/建造合同条件(新黄皮书)
菲迪克(FIDIC)EPC 总包项目合同条件(银皮书)
菲迪克(FIDIC)简易合同格式(绿皮书)

FIDIC 合同条件(新版)在合同管理方面对各方提出更高的要求。

➤ 红皮书是针对土木工程施工的传统形式,其中,承包商按雇主的设计进行施工。如果给出全称,它是"由雇主设计的建筑和工程项目施工合同条件"。

➤ 红皮书以雇主设计和承包商施工为基础,尽管有特定条款,针对承包商进行某种有限的设计。对于纠纷来说,这种形式保持了工程师作为证明者和第一停靠港的角色,而且付款机制以计量和计价为基础。

➤ 黄皮书——如给出全称是"工厂和设计/建造合同条件"被用于设计和创建合同以及工厂合同。还有,工程师管理合同,但此款项支付以时段或者分期付款为基础。

➤ 绿皮书是菲迪克(FIDIC)的合同简易格式,它采纳了综合原则、宽泛的结构以及红皮书和黄皮书,在需要时承包商承担设计。支付条款非常灵活——支付的方式可以在总价、有工程价格表或者工程量清单的总价合同之间变动,也可以是按费用支付,虽然这种合同允许设置一些陷阱在"明细(特殊)条款"里并插入付款条件中。这种合同是为资金小的项目合同或者短期简单合同而设计的。这种合同里不存在工程师,他的位置被雇主取代了。

➤ 银皮书则不同,且 EPC 总包项目没有工程师;取而代之的是,雇主直接应付承包商。风险主要转嫁给了承包商。支付则以总价分时段付款或者分期付款来进行。

➤ 2006 年,菲迪克(FIDIC)推出多边发展银行和谐版(MDB),即红皮书的变体。该合同背后的逻辑依据是减少修改,使修改标准化,这种修改通常由多边出借款人诸如世界银行来进行。这些被推介的修订主要靠采用出借方的履约保证的有利形势确保达成这种保证的快捷而无障碍的路径畅通。

➤ 2006 年,菲迪克(FIDIC)的雇主/咨询师示范服务协议第四版即白皮书出版,该版本主要针对菲迪克(FIDIC)的红皮书和黄皮书格式相结合使用而设计的。

➤ 2008 年,菲迪克(FIDIC)推出了其金皮书,即设计、建造和经营项目的合同条件。从根本上讲,金皮书总结了银皮书 20 年的运作经营,反映了一种日益广泛运作,且把经营和维护责任置于建造了工厂的参与方身上的做法,目的是降低所有权者的总体成本。

2. 菲迪克(FIDIC)的特征

新版本由菲迪克(FIDIC)合同委员会领导下的一个工作组以"新红皮书"、"新黄皮书"和"银皮书"来起草。合同格式不会受到先前包括所有 20 个条款的 ICE 构架的影响。因此,如果条款内容可以被统一的话,它将置于相同的标题和表述之下。在这三本书中,超过 80%的内容是一致的,且 85%的定义和表述是相同的。这对使用者完整地理解其内容一个极大的帮助,可以节约研读时间。

新版本也显示出更多的灵活性和适应性。例如,在老版本中,必须有条件履约保证,世界银行对此有着不同的看法。而在新版本中,保证形式由特殊条件来设定,这种特殊条件可以通过给予雇主更好的灵活性来得以应用。

3. 高质量条文和逻辑条款顺序

与最初的"红皮书"对照来看,"新红皮书"有 168 个条款,几乎 40%是新近编制的,额外的 40%做了修正和增补,只有 20%原封不动。老版本在条款顺序上采用 ICE 的凌乱条文顺序,而在新版本中,相关的次条款尽量被置于一个条款中,方便了用户阅读。

4. 更具体的有关合同各方的权利和义务

以雇主的违约条款为例,我们可以看到,在针对"红皮书"的合同里,有三点被加进了"新红皮书"里：其中两点与款项支付有关。上述内容表明了针对雇主的严格要求。然而，承包商会制定一个质量保证体系，且在执行之前呈交给工程师去审计该体系的各个方面。月份进度报告将由承包商准备好后每月向工程师提交，否则将不支付款项。任何形式的贿赂都可能导致承包商违约。上述所有内容都是对承包商的高标准要求。

5. 编制风格的变化

在以前版本中，一般条件非常简明；有些值得推荐条款被给予特殊条件。而在新版本中，有以规程为中心的方式，因为一般条款都相对综合、详细，比如预付款项和调整原则。新版本的编写者认为，对于用户来说，删除不需要的条款然后自己把这些条款写进"特殊条件"更加方便。

6. 菲迪克(FIDIC)的应用前景

新版本具有许多先进的理念和规章，比如合同措辞和表述的标准化、更清晰和更严格的索赔程序以及对知识产权保护的强调等。传统的在世界上普遍采用的项目管理模式已经被用在大多数工程项目管理的案例中。

菲迪克(FIDIC)施工合同有着严格和清晰的关于雇主、监理工程师和承包商合同权利、义务以及职责的定义，有可能让雇主和承包商平衡地分担风险。好的承包商应当认真研究和掌握被用于项目管理的合同文件精神，以便改善建筑工程管理，并更好地维护其合法权益。

Unit 4
The Bidding/Tendering Process

1. Introduction

A bid is the final price or "offer" which is submitted to the client by the contractor, is a sum of money for which he prepared to carry out the work, and will include not only the estimate but also the margin of overheads and profit. Bidding is the process by which an employer/client procures a building project.

The Biding process typically engages a number of parties, each of whom invests considerable time and money in the competition for a construction contract. Most of the rules of the competition are set out in the bid package. But the process also involves implied obligations and duties of fairness which do not appear in the documents and are not easily defined. For these reasons, the bidding process is one of the most contentious and highly-litigated aspects of the construction process.

Equally, it represents a high-risk area for the consultants who are retained to guide employers through this complicated process. The bidders compete not only with each other, but also with the employers to protect their profit. This is almost certainly as a result of the cost and uncertainty that is inherent in any competitive process. It is the very nature of a bidding process that all parties are in competition with each other and, each is fully entitled to act in their own interests.

2. Prequalification

Prequalification is a method of determining bidder responsibility before soliciting bids. Employers can use prequalification to restrict the bidding to a group of bidders who meet predetermined responsibility standards. Procedures are not rigid, and employers rate bidders according to their own special requirements. Responsibility standards may include the bidder's integrity, ability, experience, past performance, financial ability, safety record, bonding capacity, claims record, and available staff. Employers can use prequalification by projects or for a stated time.

The major international agencies such as the World Bank and the Asian Development Bank etc. typically will request all bidders to pass prequalification (some of the projects indicating post-qualification requirement). The successful execution of contracts for large buildings, civil engineering, supply and installation, turnkey, and design-and-build projects requires that contracts are awarded only to firms, or combinations of firms, that are suitably experienced in the type of work and construction technology involved, that are financially and managerially sound,

and that can provide all the equipment required in a timely manner. Prequalification usually consists of the following stages:
- ➢ Advertisement and notification;
- ➢ Preparing and issuing a prequalification document;
- ➢ Preparation and submission of applications;
- ➢ Opening and evaluation of applications;
- ➢ Updating and confirmation of bidder's qualification.

The Notification will be given in sufficient time to enable prospective bidders to obtain prequalification or bidding documents and prepare and submit their responses. Where large works or complex items of equipment are involved, this period will generally be not less than twelve weeks to enable prospective bidders to conduct investigations before submitting their bids. Various construction industry associations have excellent publications available for references on competitive bidding.

3. Bidding/Tendering Process

All qualified bidders will be rendered further instructions or information to bid. The International Competitive Bidding (ICB) process includes the following stages:

3.1 Preparing and Issuing a Bidding Document

For open bidding, employers publish an advertisement for bids newspapers and trade papers. This advertisement notifies all qualified bidders of the project in the international market.

When preparing and issuing of the bidding document, the employer will use the standard bidding documents issued by the World Bank, as it is mandatory requirement for contracts financed by the World Bank. The Section I Instructions to Bidders (ITB) and Section VII General Conditions of Contract (GCC) are subject to no modification or without suppressing or adding text to the document.

3.2 Bid Preparation and Submission

During this stage, the bidding documents may need modification. The employer will promptly respond to requests for clarifications from bidders and amend if needed, and addenda issued by the architect/engineer or employer transmits notice of modifications to all prospective bidders. The bidder is responsible for the preparation and submission of its bid. The conversion of the estimate into bid is undertaken by the bidder for all aspects of the project evaluation, other than pure costs are considered. Preparation during a bid process is not without risk, as the invitation to bid document is an invitation to treat (albeit creating a separate contract); the bid is hopefully an offer, capable of acceptance within a prescribed time; and the acceptance creates a binding contract.

3.3 Pre-bid Meeting/Conference

The employer will usually develop from submitted prequalification materials a selected list of qualified bidders, and conduct pre-bid meetings with prequalified bidders to familiarize bidders with the necessary documents and agreements relating to the project. Large or complicated projects usually require a pre-bid meeting, while small straightforward projects usually do not require a pre-bid meeting. The employer and architect/engineer conduct the pre-bid meeting to familiarize bidders with specifics of the project. Topics to address at the pre-bid meeting include the following:

- introduction of the architect/engineer and employer's construction representatives;
- project details and requirements;
- employer's bidding documents and construction procedures;
- unusual project requirements;
- question and answer period;
- site tour.

At the pre-bid meeting, the architect/engineer presents the project's details, conducts the question-and-answer session, and leads a tour of the project site. If necessary the architect/engineer will prepare records of the items discussed at the pre-bid meetings, issue an addendum to answer questions asked at the presentation or project site tour, including questions and answers, and distribute to all prospective bidders.

3.4 Bid Opening

Bid opening will be at a specified time, usually immediately after the receipt of bids. Attendance may be limited to the employer and architect/engineer, or the employer may also invite bidders. Bid opening is a critical event in the bidding process; the employer will appoint experienced staff to conduct the bid opening strictly following the procedures as specified in the instruction to bidders for all bids received not later than the date and time of the bid submission deadline. A bid for which a bid withdrawal or bid substitution notice was received on time shall not be opened, but returned unopened to the bidder. If encounter unexpected delay or unforeseeable circumstances, the employer may require cancellation of the bidding process and put off the procedures before bid opening.

The sequence in which bids are handled and opened is crucial. The employer will, however, verify at bid opening the validity of the documentation (power of attorney) or other acceptable equivalent document as specified in Instruction to bidders, confirming the validity of a bid modification, bid withdrawal, or bid substitution as the case may be, because a withdrawn or substituted bid shall not be opened and not read out consequently and, therefore, they shall not be further considered by the employer. Similarly, a bid modification shall be opened and read out to modify a bid that was received on time.

3.5 Bid Evaluation/Review

The employer is responsible for bid evaluation and contract award. The employer will appoint experienced architect/engineer to conduct the evaluation of the bids. The architect/engineer will review all bids received for responsiveness, participate in investigating the lowest and best responsible bidders and deliver a written recommendation to the employer about the award of, or rejection of, any bids for each construction contract. The architect/engineer and employer will have sole discretion to make the final decision on bid awards.

Usually, the architect/engineer and employer will conduct pre-award conferences with apparently successful bidders and will gather documentation for contract execution from such bidders. This is a matter of assessing the intention of the parties. Where the signing of a formal document is envisaged, the parties did not intend to be bound until the formal documentation has been prepared and signed. Making a counter-offer will have the effect of negating the original bid, if the bidder is asked to confirm that the bid remains open for acceptance on the revised basis.

3.6 Contract Award

After selecting the bidders, the employer prepares a notice of award (letter of intention) and sends it to the successful bidder. Attached to the notice are the construction agreement, the conditions of contracts, construction bonds, insurance requirements, and other documents. This notice sets forth the conditions regarding contract award and the time allowed to sign and return the agreement and other required documents. However, the notice does not authorize the start of construction. Construction starts after both parties execute the construction agreement and the employer issues a notice to proceed.

After the employer receives the signed agreement and other documents and finds everything satisfactory, the employer will execute the contract by signing the agreement. The employer then will send a copy of the executed contract to the successful bidder, now the contractor. If the successful bidder does not return the signed agreement and required documents within the time allowed, or if the required documents are not satisfactory, then the employer usually has the right to reject the bid and start proceedings with the next lowest bidder.

Reading

Contractor Selection

1. Competitive Bidding

Most construction projects in the international market are competitive bidding. Competitive bidding can be either open or closed. Open bidding allows all qualified bidders to submit a bid. Closed bidding allows only selected bidders to submit a bid. Most countries' public works employers predominantly use open bidding as required by their public law. An employer advertises the project, opens bids in public, and awards the contract to the lowest responsible bidder who submits a responsive bid.

The traditional competitive-bidding approach involves the employer contracting design services from an architect who develops the designs as per the employer's needs and directions. The architect prepares the contract documents (plans and specifications) for bidding and construction. He or she also assists the employer in competitively bidding the project and administering the construction contract (shop drawing review, review of application for payments, site observations and final project closeout services).

Since competitive bidding is still viewed by the architecture and design profession as the only way to control construction costs, lowest price tends to be over-emphasized at the expense of quality, value and service. It also assumes that all bidders will deliver the same quality product regardless of price. Therefore, it unfortunately often induces the bidder to choose the cheapest, rather than the best value approach in order to cut costs and win the bidding competition.

2. Negotiated Contracts

A negotiated contract is one in which an employer selects a contractor on the basis of factors other than cost, and subsequently awards the contract after negotiating the terms and cost. Most countries' public law normally prohibits direct selection and subsequent negotiated award on public works projects, thus negotiation procedures apply primarily to private works employers. Instead of inviting competitive bidding, private employers often choose to award construction contracts with one or more selected contractors. Employers can select a form of contracting that will meet the employer's and the project's design, construction, and management needs.

A major reason for using negotiated contracts is the flexibility of this type of pricing arrangement, particularly for projects of large size and great complexity or for projects which substantially duplicate previous facilities sponsored by the employer. An employer may value the expertise and integrity of a particular contractor who has a good reputation or has worked successfully for the employer in the past. If it becomes necessary to meet a deadline for completion of the project, the construction of a project may proceed without waiting for the completion of the detailed plans and specifications with a contractor that the employer can trust. However, the employer's staff must be highly knowledgeable and competent in evaluating contractor proposals

2.1 Negotiated Contracts Selection Process

Some employers prefer the direct selection process rather than conventional bidding because of the project type, the employer's capability or priorities, factors related to the construction process, cost or time, or other external influences.

Regardless of the reason for direct selection, the employer must use some method to make the selection. Following are some of those methods:

➤ Prequalification: the employer may ask a limited number of contractors to submit qualification statements. The employer selects a contractor after reviewing the information in the document.

➤ Advice from the architect/engineer: frequently the architect/engineer can recommend a contractor to the employer. For example, the employer wants to build faculty housing. The architect/engineer is familiar with a general contractor from similar housing projects, so the architect/engineer recommends that contractor. If the architect/engineer's recommendation satisfies the employer, then the employer selects the recommended contractor.

➢ Proposals: an employer may request proposals from a limited number of known contractors. Each contractor competitively bids the project on factors other than cost (e.g., time to complete the work). The employer selects a contractor after evaluating the proposals.

2.2 Factors to Consider Selection

When using direct selection, the employer considers the contractor's qualifications. The contractor is chosen from a list of contractors who have suitable experience and who are interested in doing the work. Factors to consider are the contractor's:

➢ reputation and performance;
➢ work specialty or expertise;
➢ schedule adherence;
➢ work quality;
➢ relationship with employers, architect/engineer, and subcontractors;
➢ financial stability;
➢ safety record.

2.3 Negotiation Process

After selecting the contractor, the employer must then negotiate the terms and cost of the contract. The terms may include the following:

➢ quality of materials;
➢ construction methods and sequence;
➢ subcontractors to use;
➢ time of construction;
➢ method of payment;
➢ contractor's staff.

Generally, negotiated contracts require the reimbursement of direct project cost plus the contractor's fee as determined by one of the following methods:

➢ cost plus fixed percentage;
➢ cost plus fixed fee;
➢ cost plus variable fee;
➢ target estimate;
➢ guaranteed maximum price or cost.

An employer realizes several advantages when using direct selection and negotiation. One advantage is that during the design phase, the contractor is a member of the project design team and can advise the architect/engineer on constructability, scheduling, and budgeting. Fast-track construction is another advantage of negotiated contracting, especially when using a cost-plus contract. Fast-track negotiated contracts may increase construction costs, but such contracts can produce high-quality projects in the shortest possible time.

The fixed percentage or fixed fee is determined at the outset of the project, while variable fee and target estimates are used as an incentive to reduce costs by sharing any cost savings. A guaranteed maximum cost arrangement imposes a penalty on a contractor for cost overruns and failure to complete the project on time. With a guaranteed maximum price contract, amounts below the maximum are typically shared between the employer and the contractor, while the contractor is responsible for costs above the maximum.

When deciding which form of contracting to use, the employer will base the decision on the employer's construction expertise and the staff available to administer the contract. Some forms of contracting require more employer's expertise and staff time during the construction process than others. For example, construction management and fast-track forms of contracting may require more staff expertise than the conventional lump-sum form. Multiple-prime contracts may also require more staff time. The employer can overcome lack of staff expertise and staff problems by hiring consultants to perform all project management duties or to supplement the employer's staff.

3. Characteristics of Bidding Competition

All other things being equal, the probability of winning a contract diminishes as more bidders participate in the competition. Consequently, a contractor tries to find out as much information as possible about the number and identities of potential bidders on a specific project. For certain segments, potential competitors may be identified through private contacts, and bidders often confront the same competitor's project after project since they have similar capabilities and interests in undertaking the same type of work, including size, complexity and geographical location of the projects. However, most contractors form an extensive network with a group of subcontractors with whom they have had previous business transactions. They usually rely on their own experience in soliciting subcontract bids before finalizing a bid price for the project.

The basic structure of the bidding process consists of the formulation of detailed plans and specifications of a facility based on the objectives and requirements of the employer, and the invitation of qualified contractors to bid for the right to execute the project. The definition of a qualified contractor usually calls for a minimal evidence of previous experience and financial stability. In the private sector, the employer has considerable latitude in selecting the bidders, ranging from open competition to the restriction of bidders to a few favored contractors. In the public sector, the rules are carefully delineated to place all qualified contractors on an equal footing for competition, and strictly enforced to prevent collusion among contractors and unethical or illegal actions by public officials.

Unit 4 The Bidding/Tendering Process

New Words and Expressions

the bidding/ tendering process 投标过程
overheads 一般费用；杂项开支；企业的日常管理费用
a margin of overheads and profit 一笔费用和利润
procure 导致；获得，取得
construction contract 建筑工程承包合同
invest considerable time and money 投入大量的时间与金钱
contentious 有争议的，有异议的；引起争议的；诉讼的
complicated process 复杂的程序
any competitive process 任何竞争过程
prequalification 资格预审
bidder responsibility 投标责任
meet predetermined responsibility standards 满足预定的责任标准
special requirements 特殊的要求
integrity 完整；廉正；诚实，正直
past performance 过去的表现
financial ability 财务能力
claims record 索赔记录
available staff 可利用的员工
the World Bank 世界银行
the Asian Development Bank 亚洲开发银行
large buildings 大型建筑物
civil engineering 土木工程
installation 安装
turnkey 工程总承包
construction technology 施工技术
a timely manner 及时的方式
issuing 公布，发布，出版
prequalification document 资格预审文件
submission of applications 提交申请
updating and confirmation of bidder's qualification 更新与确认投标人的资格
prospective bidders 潜在的投标人
large works or complex items 大型的工程或复杂的项目
construction industry associations 建筑行业协会
International Competitive Bidding (ICB) process 国际竞争投标过程
open bidding 公开招标

qualified bidders 合格的投标人
standard bidding documents 标准的招标文件
mandatory requirement 硬性要求，强制性的要求
clarification 澄清
addenda 附录，附加物
pure cost 纯粹的成本
prescribed time 规定的时间
a binding contract 一个有约束力的合同
prequalification materials 资格预审材料
familiarize 使熟悉
specifics of the project 具体项目
address 忙于，从事；地址；致辞，演讲，说话的技巧
construction procedures 施工程序
site tour 场地参观
addendum 附录
attendance 出席，到场；出席人数
bid opening 开标
appoint experienced staff 委托有经验的人员
withdrawal 撤退，收回；提款，取消
substitution 代替，代替物；置换
unexpected delay 意外的延迟
unforeseeable circumstances 不可预见的情况
cancellation of the bidding process 取消投标过程
put off 推迟，拖延
validity of the documentation 文件的有效性，文件的合法性
bid evaluation/review 评标
written recommendation 书面的建议
construction contract 建筑工程承包合同
discretion 谨慎，判断力；判定；考虑周到；自由裁决权
discretion to make the final decision 谨慎地做出最后的决定
signing of a formal document 签署一个正式文件
counter-offer 还价；还盘；反要约
contract award 合同授予
construction agreement 施工协议
the conditions of contracts 合同条款
construction bonds 施工契约
insurance requirements 保险要求
set forth 陈列；出发，宣布
signed agreement 签订的协议

execute the contract by signing the agreement 履行合同签署协议
successful bidder 中标人

Exercises

I. Choose the best answer according to the text.

1. The bidders compete not only with each other, but also with _____.
   A. the employers to protect their profit
   B. the cost and uncertainty
   C. the very nature of a bidding process
   D. the consultants who are retained to guide employers through this complicated process

2. Responsibility standards may include _____.
   A. the bidder's integrity, ability
   B. experience, past performance, financial ability
   C. safety record, bonding capacity, claims record, and available staff
   D. above all

3. According to text, prequalification usually consists of the following stages _____.
   A. advertisement, notification and preparing and issuing a prequalification document
   B. preparation and submission of applications and opening and evaluation of applications
   C. updating and confirmation of bidder's qualification
   D. above all

4. At the pre-bid meeting, the architect/engineer _____.
   A. presents the project's details, conducts the question-and-answer session, and leads a tour of the project site
   B. will prepare records of the items discussed at the pre-bid meetings, issues an addendum to answer questions asked at the presentation or project site tour
   C. A or B
   D. A and B

5. We learn from the passage that this notice sets forth the conditions _____.
   A. regarding contract award
   B. the time allowed signing and returning the agreement
   C. other required documents
   D. above all

II. Decide the following statements are true or false.

1. But the process also involves implied obligations and duties of fairness which do not appear in the documents and are easily defined.

2. Where large works or complex items of equipment are involved, this period will generally be not more than twelve weeks to enable prospective bidders to conduct investigations before submitting their bids.

3. Large or complicated projects usually require a pre-bid meeting; small, straightforward projects usually do not require a pre-bid meeting.

4. A bid for which a bid withdrawal or bid substitution notice was received on time shall not be opened, but returned unopened to the bidder.

5. Where the signing of a formal document is envisaged, the parties did intend to be bound until the formal documentation has been prepared and signed.

III. Change the following words to another form and write down the Chinese meanings.

1. overheads _____
2. procure _____
3. contentious _____
4. issuing _____
5. prospective _____
6. other than _____
7. put off _____
8. address _____

IV. Give out the following words' synonym or other word in the closest meaning.

1. bidding   a. review
2. employer   b. highly-litigated
3. obligations   c. modification
4. contentious   d. client
5. amend   e. engineer
6. meeting   f. duties
7. architect   g. conference
8. evaluation   h. tendering

V. Put the following English into Chinese.

1. Most of the rules of the competition are set out in the bid package.

2. Employers can use prequalification to restrict the bidding to a group of bidders who meet predetermined responsibility standards. Procedures are not rigid, and employers rate bidders according to their own special requirements.

3. The successful execution of contracts for large buildings, civil engineering, supply and installation, turnkey, and design-and-build projects requires that contracts are awarded only to firms, or combinations of firms, that are suitably experienced in the type of work and construction technology involved, that are financially and managerially sound, and that can provide all the equipment required in a timely manner.

4. The bidder is responsible for the preparation and submission of its bid, the conversion of the estimate into bid is undertaken by the bidder for all aspects of the project evaluation, other than pure cost are considered.

5. Bid opening, is a critical event in the bidding process, the employer will appoint experienced staff to conduct the bid opening, and conduct the bid opening strictly following the procedures as specified in the Instruction to bidders for all bids received not later than the date and time of the bid submission deadline.

6. Power of attorney or other acceptable equivalent document as specified in Instruction to bidders, confirming the validity of a bid modification, bid withdrawal, or bid substitution as the case may be, because a withdrawn or substituted bid shall not be opened and not read out consequence and, therefore, they shall not be further considered by the employer.

7. Making a counter-offer will have the effect of negating the original bid, if the bidder is asked to confirm that the bid remains open for acceptance on the revised basis.

VI. Put the following Chinese into English.

1. 履行合同签署协议
2. 投标人资格预审文件
3. 一个有约束力的合同
4. 标准的招投标文件
5. 企业日常管理费用

参 考 译 文

第 4 单元　招标过程

1. 导言

投标就是最终标价或"出价"，它由承包商提交给委托人，是承包商筹备好完成施工的款项。投标不仅包含费用估计，而且包含管理费和利润。投标就是一个过程，通过该过程承包商/雇主可以获得一个建筑项目。

通常，投标过程会有多个当事人参与，为了一个施工项目，他们会在竞争中投入大量的时间和金钱。大部分竞争规则被制订在一揽子投标文件里面。但是投标过程也涉及默示义务和公平责任，这些并不出现在文件中，且不太容易界定。由于这些原因，投标过程是建设过程中最易引起争论和高诉讼的方面之一。

同样，对于被请来在整个复杂的过程中指导雇主的咨询师来说，投标过程则代表着高风险。投标人不仅互相竞争，而且与维护各自利润的雇主竞争。这几乎无疑地是一种开支和不确定的结果，这种结果是任何竞争过程所固有的。这正是投标过程的特性，所有参与方都相互竞争，且每一方都被完全赋予了在他们自己的利益方面采取行动的权利。

2. 资格预审

资格预审指在招标之前决定投标人的责任。雇主可以使用资格预审将投标限制在一批达到预定的责任标准的投标人中。程序不是僵化的，雇主通过他们自己的特殊需要去评估投标人。责任标准可能包括投标人的诚信、能力、经验、以往表现、财务能力、安全记录、保函能力、索赔记录及可用全体员工。雇主可以通过项目或者一段既定时间来进行资格预审。

主要国际代理机构，诸如世界银行和亚洲开发银行等，会有代表性地要求所有投标人通过资格预审(有些项目还有资格后审要求)。针对大型建筑、土木工程、供应与安装、交钥匙工程及设计-建造项目，合同的成功执行要求合同仅被授予给公司或者公司联合体，这些公司或公司联合体必须在项目类型和涉及的施工技术上有相匹配的经验，必须是财务和管理健全的，而且能够以适时的方式提供所需设备。资格预审通常由下面步骤组成。

- ➤ 广告和通知
- ➤ 准备和发布资格预审文件
- ➤ 准备和提交申请
- ➤ 开启和评估申请
- ➤ 投标人资格的更新和确认

投标通知将在足够的时间内给出，使潜在投标人能够获得资格预审或者投标文件且提交回复。如果涉及大型工程或复杂的项目设备，这段时间将通常不少于十二个星期，使潜在投标人能够在提交他们的标书之前进行调查研究。投标人可查阅到各种建筑行业协会的优秀出版物的公开招标项目。

3. 投标/招标过程

所有合格的投标人将被给予更详细的投标指示和信息，国际竞标(ICB)过程包括如下步骤。

3.1 准备和发布投标文件

对于公开招标，雇主会在投标报纸和商业报纸上刊登广告，把国际市场上的项目通知给所有合格投标人。

当准备和发出投标文件的时候，雇主会使用世界银行发布的标准投标文件(SBD)，因为它是针对世界银行所提供资金的合同的强制要求。不得更改、压缩或者增加第一部分投标人须知(ITB)和第七部分通用合同条件(GCC)中的文件内容。

3.2 准备和提交标书

在该步骤中，可能需要修改投标文件。雇主会迅速针对来自投标人的阐释做出反应，且在需要时进行修订，并由建筑师/工程师或者雇主发布的附录将更改通知传送给所有潜在投标人。投标人负责准备和提交标书。投标人将项目估价转化为标书的报价是对项目所有费用进行估算，而不是仅考虑项目净成本。投标过程的准备是有风险的，且对投标文件的邀约就是一个交易的邀约(尽管会产生一个单独的合同)；投标通常就是一个报价，在法定期限内能够被认可；且认可会产生有约束力的合同。

3.3 标前会议

雇主通常会从所提交的资格预审材料中挑选列出合格投标人清单，且组织所有合格投标人参加标前会议，让投标人熟悉必要的文件和与项目有关的协议。大型或者复杂项目通常要求召开投标前会议，而小型或者简单项目一般不要求。雇主和建筑师/工程师组织投标前会议让投标人熟悉项目的具体情况。在标前会议上主要强调如下主题：

- ➤ 建筑师/工程师及雇主施工代表的介绍；

- 项目细节和要求；
- 雇主的投标文件和施工程序；
- 独特的项目要求；
- 问答时间；
- 现场参观。

在投标前会议上，建筑师/工程师展示项目细节，组织问答讨论，且带领项目现场参观。如有必要，建筑师/工程师会提前准备在投标前会议上讨论的条目记录，且发布在项目展示中或者项目现场参观中回答问题的补充材料，包括问题和答案，并分发给所有预期投标人。

3.4 开标

开标将在指定的时间进行，通常在收到标书以后立即进行。出席人一般是雇主和建筑师/工程师，雇主也可以邀请投标人。开标在投标过程中很重要，且雇主将委派老练的职员为所有在标书提交最后期限内所收到的标书组织开标，严格遵照如《投标人须知》(ITB)里所规定的程序。即时收到投标撤销或投标替换通知的标书将不被打开，而是原封不动地归还投标人。如果遭遇意外的延误或者不可预见的情况，雇主可以要求取消投标过程且在开标之前对投标程序进行延期。

处理和打开标书的顺序至关重要。雇主将在开标中核实文件资料的有效性(委任书)或者《投标人须知》(ITB)里所规定的其他可接受的相等文件，根据具体情况确认标书变更、标书撤销或标书替换的有效性，因为撤销或者更改的标书将不能被打开且因此不能当众宣读，因而，这些标书将不被雇主考虑。类似地，变更的标书将被打开和宣读。

3.5 评估/审查标书

雇主负责标书的评估和发包(合同授予)，他将指派有经验的建筑师/工程师组织标书的评估。建筑师/工程师将针对响应度评审所有收到的标书，共同考察出价最低和最尽责的投标人，针对每一个施工合同向雇主提供标书被接受或拒绝的书面材料。建筑师/工程师和雇主就授标做出最后的决定。

通常，建筑师/工程师和雇主会组织与最可能成功的投标人进行授标前会议，且会从投标人那里针对合同的履行收集文件资料，以评价参与方的意向。即使准备签署正式文件了，直到正式文件资料准备妥当且签署了，参与方与不想受约束。进行还标可以否认初始标价，如果该投标人被要求确认该标价对可接受的更改余地保持有效的话。

3.6 授标

选择好投标人之后，雇主将准备一个授标通知(意向书)并送交给中标人。随通知附有施工协议、合同条件、施工承诺以及其他文件。该通知包括有关合同授予及允许签署和返回协议和其他所需文件的时间。然而，该通知不能要求启动施工。施工将在施工协议生效和雇主发出开工通知以后启动。

在雇主收到并对已签协议和其他文件满意以后，雇主将通过签署协议来使合同生效。然后雇主会发送一份已生效合同的副本给中标人，即此时的承包商。如果中标人在允许的时间内不返回已签协议和所需文件，或者所需文件不符合要求，那么雇主可以驳回该标书，且与下一个出价最低的投标人开始商议投标进程。

阅读

选择承包商

1. 竞争性招标

国际市场上的大部分建筑项目竞争性招标。竞标可以是公开的，也可以是私下的。明标允许所有合格投标人递交标书，暗标只允许被选中的投标人提交标书。大部分国家的公共工程的雇主采用国际公法所要求的明标方式。雇主公布项目、公开开标，并把合同授予标价最低且最负责的投标人。

传统的竞标方式牵涉雇主合同设计服务，这种服务来自于按照雇主需要和指示去展开设计的建筑师。建筑师为投标和施工筹备合同文件(计划和规范)，协助雇主竞标项目，执行施工合同(施工图审查、付款申请审查、现场监测和最终完工服务)。

由于竞争性招标被建筑和设计行业看作是唯一的控制施工成本的方式，所以最低价格在质量、价值和服务上的开支被过分强调了。也可以做这样的假设，无论价格如何，所有投标人将交付相同质量的建筑产物。但很遗憾的是，为了降低成本和赢得投标竞争，投标人常常选择最便宜的而不是最有价值的投标途径。

2. 议标

议标是指雇主以某些要素而不是以成本来挑选承包商，接下来，在协商合同条款和成本之后进行授标。大部分国家的公法禁止在公共建设项目上直接挑选和紧随其后的议标，因此，议标程序主要适用于私人项目雇主。与邀请性竞标不同，私人雇主常常授予一个或更多的承包商施工合同。雇主可以选择承包形式，以满足雇主和项目的设计、施工和管理要求。

使用议标的主要原因是这种定价方式的灵活性，尤其是针对大规模和复杂的项目，或者针对实质上和以前设施相同的由雇主发起的项目。雇主可能很重视专家评价和特定承包商的诚信，这种承包商具有良好的声誉或者在过去已经成功地为雇主工作过。如果需要满足项目竣工的最后期限，那么在雇主可以信任的承包商的详细图纸和施工规范完成之前，项目就可以开始施工。然而，雇主的员工在评估承包商的提议时，必须有高度的见识和能力。

2.1 议标合同选择过程

由于项目类型、雇主的素质和考虑重点、有关项目施工过程的因素、成本或时间、或者其他外部影响，一些雇主更喜欢直接挑选而不是依照惯例来投标。

不管直接挑选的原因是什么，雇主必须做出选择。以下便是雇主选择的方式。

资格预审：雇主要求有限几个承包商提交资格陈述报告，然后审查文件信息，挑选承包商。

➢ 建筑师/工程师的推荐：建筑师/工程师经常向雇主推荐承包商。例如，雇主想要建造员工住房。由于建筑师/工程师熟悉来自类似住房项目的总承包商，所以建筑师/工程师就推荐那个承包商。如果建筑师/工程师的推荐使雇主满意，那么雇主就会选择被推荐的承包商。

➢ 建议：雇主会听取一些知名承包商的建议。每个承包商以竞争的方式对项目在要素上而不是成本上进行投标(如完成项目的时间)。雇主在评估这些建议之后选择承包商。

2.2 考虑挑选的因素

直接挑选承包商时，雇主一般只考虑承包商的资格。雇主从具有适宜的经验和对该项目感兴趣的承包商中选择。要考虑的因素是承包商的：
- 声誉和业务状况；
- 工程专长和专门知识；
- 进度遵守状况；
- 工程质量；
- 与雇主、建筑师/工程师和分包商的关系；
- 财务稳定性；
- 安全记录。

2.3 议标过程

选出承包商之后，雇主必须对合同的条款和成本进行商讨。条款可能包括如下内容。
- 材料的质量；
- 施工方法和顺序；
- 要使用的分包商；
- 施工时间；
- 付款方式；
- 承包商的员工。

一般来讲，议标合同要求直接项目成本外加付给承包商的报酬的补偿，如下所示。
- 成本外加固定比例；
- 成本外加固定费用；
- 成本外加可变费用；
- 目标估价；
- 保证最高价格或成本。

使用直接挑选和协商承包商有数项优势。优势之一是，在设计阶段，承包商是项目设计团队的一员，可以在施工性、进度和预算方面对建筑师/工程师提出建议。边设计边施工(Fast-track)是议标承包的另一个优势，特别是当使用成本加成合同的时候。边设计边施工(Fast-track)议标合同可以增加施工成本，但这种合同可以在最短的时间内产生高质量项目。

固定比例或固定费用是项目一开始就决定的，而可变费用和目标估价是通过分享任意成本节约的方式而作为激励来使用的。最高保证成本合同将针对超限成本和没能按时竣工强加给承包商处罚。对于最高保证价格合同，在最高价格以下的总额要在雇主和承包商之间分享，而承包商要对最高价格以上的成本负责。

雇主将根据自己的施工专门知识/技能和执行合同的可用员工，来决定使用哪种承包形式。一些承包形式更需要雇主具有专业技能和人力。例如，建造管理和边设计边施工(Fast-track)承包形式就比传统的一次付清形式要求有更多的员工专门知识/技能。多重主要合同(Multiple-prime contract)也需要更多的人力。通过聘用咨询师去履行所有项目管理职责或者增补员工，雇主能够克服员工专门知识/技能的不足和员工问题。

3. 竞争投标的特征

在所有其他方面都相同的情况下，参与到竞争的投标人越多，赢得合同的可能性越小。因此，承包商应设法发现尽可能多的潜在投标人。对于某些环节来说，潜在的竞争者可以通过私人接触来识别，且投标人常常在一个接一个的项目中遭遇相同竞争者，因为他们具有类似的能力和兴趣来承担相同类型的工程，如项目的规模、复杂性和地理位置。然而，大部分承包商与一群分包商形成广阔的网络，他们与这些分包商有过以往的业务交易。这些分包商通常依赖他们自己的经验，在针对一个项目定下投标标价之前要求分包报价。

投标过程由制订详细计划和设施的施工规范组成，这些计划和规范，以雇主的目标和要求及对为了实施项目的权利而去投标的合格承包商邀请为基础。承包商的界定通常要求出具以前的经验和财务稳定性等证明材料。在私营部门，雇主有相当大的挑选投标人的自由范围，这个范围在公开竞争到针对少数几个受青睐承包商的投标人的限制之间变动。在公共部门，这些规则被谨慎地界定为把所有合格的承包商放在一个平等的基础上竞争，且严格地防止承包商之间的串标和由公众官员做出的不道德或非法行径。

Unit 5
The Contractor's Bid Decision

1. Introduction

One of the most critical decisions that have to be made by contractors in the construction industry is whether or not to bid for a new project when an invitation has been received. Decision making at the earliest stages of construction projects involves a process of gathering information from various sources. In order to accomplish their projects perfectly, contractors often commit resources to a time-consuming and expensive process that requires them to adjust and adapt their business processes.

Smart contractors realise the importance of considering internal and external factors that affect the bid / no bid decision before committing themselves to a project. The decision making at this stage is accomplished by two related decisions:

➢ Bid / no bid decisions that consider factors would help to determine the benefit expected from a particular project and an appropriate bidding strategy;

➢ Mark-up decision, which is one of the consequences of the bidding strategy.

Not bidding for a project could result in losing a good opportunity to make substantial profit, improve the contractor's strength in the industry, gain relationship with the client, and more. However, bidding for inappropriate projects may result in large losses or the consumption of time and resources that could be invested in more profitable projects, ultimately even financial failure of the contractor.

2. Decision to Bid

Competitive bidding on construction projects involves decision making under uncertainty. One of the greatest sources of the uncertainty for each bidder is the unpredictable nature of his competitors. Each bid submitted for a particular project by a contractor will be determined by a large number of factors, including an estimate of the direct project cost, the general overhead, the confidence that the management has in this estimate, and the immediate and long-range objectives of management. As so many factors are involved, it is impossible for a particular bidder to attempt to predict exactly what the bids submitted by its competitors will be.

It will be necessary to plot income against expenditure using the programme of works and the bill of quantities, activity schedule, payments in arrears and retentions, over which both the employer and subcontractors must consider. Upon completion of the review, the contractor will grade the bid based on the interest to the company and decide whether or not to bid.

The technical process of predicting the net cost of the works is carried out by a team comprising the estimator, planning engineer, materials estimator, estimating technician, together with possible contributions from an experienced construction manager, if the work is of a specialist or complex nature. At the end of the process the team will produce the cost estimate. The estimate is the prediction of the cost to the contractor.

Thus, a bidding price may be dependent on the market or competitive environment in which it takes place. Bidding often involves two processes. First, the estimating process is the stage where the actual project costs are taken into account. This process may depend on the level of expertise in a contractor's estimating department. Second, the decision process is the stage where the directors of a firm will take a commercial view on the estimated cost, evaluating contractor's own particular circumstances, market conditions and risk. Thus, management will ultimately try to pitch the bidding price between cost and value in order to win the work.

3. Factors Affect Decision Making

From all indications, most contractors confront uncertain bidding conditions by exercising a high degree of subjective judgment, and each contractor may give different weights to various factors. The decision on the bid price, if a bid is indeed submitted, reflects the contractor's best judgment on how well the proposed project fits into the overall strategy for the survival and growth of the company, as well as the contractor's propensity to risk greater profit versus the chance of not getting a contract.

The intensity of a contractor's efforts in bidding a specific project is influenced by the contractor's desire to obtain additional work. The winning of a particular project may be potentially important to the overall mix of work in progress or the cash flow implications for the contractor. The bidding strategies of some contractors are influenced by a policy of minimum percentage markup for general overhead and profit. The contractor's decision is also influenced by the availability of key personnel in the contractor organization. The company sometimes wants to reserve its resources for future projects, or commits itself to the current opportunity for different reasons.

Making a decision to bid can depend on a number of factors including knowledge of the participants, complexity of the project, period between commencement and award, risk factors and language. However, the contractor has to apply a more precise form of decision making by considering a number of factors and then using a scoring system. The actual scoring systems will differ so greatly from contractor to contractor, but the following factors are generally included:

3.1 Client Relationship

The client relationship can be considered based on previous projects, knowledge of the client and any partnering or framework agreements. These considerations can be made because of previous business by contractor or associated and JV companies.

3.2 Third Party Relationships

The relationship with the prospective project involves the knowledge and previous experience of working with the various funders or parties on the project, whether they will be funders, contractors, consultants or specialist contractors. That means contractor get to know client through the third parties who have worked previously with either consultants or specialist contractors.

3.3 Sources of Funding

Determination of where the money is being sourced is a further consideration, which can include world aid agencies, international organization, soft loan, government, bank or financing corporation. Certain types of funding come with strings attached, restricting the nationality of the prospective bidders.

3.4 Countries of Origin

The countries of origin of the possible parties to the project is another factor to be considered, whether they will be the client, partners, funders, contractors, consultants or competitors. For example, dealing with participants from the USA brings all types of new laws relating to unions; participants from the Middle East bring the Sharia law; certain countries have a less than favourable record regarding corruption, etc.

3.5 Competitors

A review of the likely competitors is essential; bidding against companies from a country providing a soft loan to the project may be a high risk. Competing the companies with excellent expertise background or comparative advantages will be wasting money and energy.

3.6 Guarantees

One factor is whether the project is attracting export guarantees from, for example, the UK or USA which both have sophisticated export guarantees schemes. Most Middle East countries give price preferences to local bidders/contractors. In many of these countries it is mandatory for bidders to get the bid guarantee and other bank guarantees issued through local banks. Owing to this the bidder has to pay for the bank guarantee twice: once in the home country and once abroad. Many countries in the Middle East and North Africa (for example, Libya) have significant restrictions on imports (such as excessive import levies) which make it difficult to import machineries and other equipment in to those countries.

3.7 Legal Framework

This can be a source of confusion with the applicable law for the bidding project:
- form of contract;
- law of the contract, Common Law, Civil Code or Sharia;
- language of the contract; and

> location for dispute resolution (London, Paris, Hong Kong etc) all being in different countries or languages.

Other legal issues relate to bonds and guarantees, warranties and payment terms. A true problem relating to translation resulted, not in the subcontract, but the subcontractor being executed.

3.8 Payment Terms

An understanding of the payment terms including letters of credit, various forms of security and advance payment, together with an understanding of offset rules is paramount.

3.9 Local Business Requirements

Some countries only allow bidders with established companies and this can often be defined with minimum requirements, for example, a branch office or representative office. Other requirements may include a proportion of local input or a requirement to JV with a local company.

3.10 Local Customs

Other restrictions can include a limit on the use of international suppliers, use of local labour and working hours and holidays.

3.11 Risk

The bidding risk factor encompasses the initial inspection of the documents, inspection of the site, risk analysis, materials and subcontract enquiries, calculation of analytical unit rates, pricing of the bill of quantities. The factors of evaluating are related to the economic, contractual, political and physical environments in which construction projects take place and they tend to affect the way construction work is described, awarded, and documented. The technical factors include: necessity to price product before production, competitive tendering, low fixed-capital requirements, preliminary expenses, delays to cash-inflows, tendency to operate with too low working capital, seasonal effects, fluctuations and their effects, government intervention, activity related to development, uncertain ground conditions, unpredictable weather, and no performance liability or long-term guarantees. Whether the risks are acceptable or not, this could include the following:

> weather conditions, e.g. flooding, cyclone etc;
> suitability of materials – particularly filling material from quarries;
> reliability of subcontractors;
> non-recoverable costs, for example excesses on insurance claims;
> outputs allowed such as productivity;
> cost increases;
> terms and conditions in contract;
> ability to meet specification for price allowed/availability of labour/plant.

4. Contractor's Comparative Advantages

A final important consideration in forming bid prices on the part of contractors is the possible special advantages enjoyed by a particular firm. As a result of lower costs, a particular contractor may be able to impose a higher profit markup yet still have a lower total bid than competitors. These lower costs may result from superior technology, greater experience, better management, better personnel or lower unit costs. A comparative cost advantage is the most desirable of all circumstances in entering a bid competition.

Nowadays, international contractors are mitigating risk by declining work perceived as too risky, subcontracting large portions of their work to others, and apportioning risk in wage structures. In essence, they are passing risk on to others in the supply chain. So, they seem adept at managing risk.

Careful project selection is the first step to the success of the construction company and it should not be carried out in a careless manner. However, the causes of contractors' failure in bidding decision call for more reviews on evaluating project profitability and linking the strategy with individual projects.

Reading

Standard Bidding/Tendering Documents

The aim of studying standard bidding documents for procurement of works is to assist practitioners to thoroughly understand biding processes and its documents. It provides an at-a-glance description of bidding documents and biding activities, which occur from the decision to request bidders through to the award of a contract or engagement. The other types of bidding documents may vary from little to great extent; however, understanding of standard bidding documents is the necessity to the contractors competing in the international market.

The standard bidding documents for procurement of works have been prepared by the World Bank to be used for the procurement of admeasurement (unit price or rate) type of works through international competitive bidding in projects that are financed in whole or in part by the World Bank. These bidding documents are not suitable for lump sum contracts without substantial changes to the method of payment and price adjustment, and to the bill of quantities, schedules of activities, and so forth.

The process of prequalification shall follow the procedure indicated in standard prequalification documents: procurement of works, issued by the World Bank. Prequalification is usually used for all major works or complex works. After obtaining approval of the World Bank (post-qualification might be appropriate), an alternative Section III, evaluation and qualification criteria could possibly be applied as an exception.

PART 1——BIDDING PROCEDURES

Section I. Instructions to Bidders (ITB)

This section provides relevant information to help bidders prepare their bids. Information is also provided on the submission, opening, and evaluation of bids and on the award of contracts. All Section I contains provisions are to be used without modification, if the project is wholly or partially funded by the World Bank.

Contents of Clauses of Section I

A. General

1. Scope of Bid
2. Source of Funds
3. Fraud and Corruption
4. Eligible Bidders
5. Eligible Materials, Equipment, and Services

B. Contents of Bidding Document

6. Sections of Bidding Documents
7. Clarification of Bidding Documents, Site Visit, Pre-Bid Meeting
8. Amendment of Bidding Documents

C. Preparation of Bids

9. Cost of Bidding
10. Language of Bid
11. Documents Comprising the Bid
12. Letter of Bid and Schedules
13. Alternative Bids
14. Bid Prices and Discounts
15. Currencies of Bid and Payment
16. Documents Comprising the Technical Proposal
17. Documents Establishing the Qualifications of the Bidder
18. Period of Validity of Bids
19. Bid Security
20. Format and Signing of Bid

D. Submission and Opening of Bids

21. Sealing and Marking of Bids
22. Deadline for Submission of Bids
23. Late Bids
24. Withdrawal, Substitution, and Modification of Bids
25. Bid Opening

E. Evaluation and Comparison of Bids

26. Confidentiality
27. Clarification of Bids

28. Deviations, Reservations, and Omissions
29. Determination of Responsiveness
30. Nonmaterial Nonconformities
31. Correction of Arithmetical Errors
32. Conversion to Single Currency
33. Margin of Preference
34. Evaluation of Bids
35. Comparison of Bids
36. Qualification of the Bidder
37. Employer's Right to Accept Any Bid, and to Reject Any or All Bids

F. Award of Contract
38. Award Criteria
39. Notification of Award
40. Signing of Contract
41. Performance Security

Section II. Bid Data Sheet (BDS)

This section consists of provisions that are specific to every procurement, and that supplement the information or requirements included in instructions to bidders are also specific to each procurement. The employer must specify in the bid data sheet only the information that the instructions to bidders requests are specified in the bid data sheet. To facilitate the preparation of the bid data sheet, its clauses are numbered with the same numbers as the corresponding instructions to bidders clause.

Section III. Evaluation and Qualification Criteria

This section contains all the criteria that the employer will use to evaluate bids and qualify bidders. In accordance with instruction to bidders, no other methods, criteria and factors will be used. The bidder shall provide all the information requested in the forms included in Section IV (bidding forms).

The World Bank requires bidders to be qualified by meeting predefined, precise and minimum requirements. The method entails setting pass-fail criteria, which, if not met by the bidder, results in disqualification. Therefore, it will be necessary to ensure that a bidder's risk of having its bid rejected on grounds of qualification is remote, if due diligence is exercised by the bidder during bid preparation. For this purpose, clear-cut, fail-pass qualification criteria need to be specified in order to enable bidders to make an informed decision whether to pursue a specific contract and, if so, either as a single entity or in joint venture. The criteria adopted must relate to characteristics that are essential to ensure satisfactory execution of the contract, and must be stated in unambiguous terms.

Contents of Criteria of Section III

1. Evaluation

1.1 Adequacy of Technical Proposal

1.2 Multiple Contracts

1.3 Completion Time

1.4 Technical Alternatives

1.5 Domestic Preference

2. Qualification

2.1 Update of Information

2.2 Financial Resources

2.3 Personnel

2.4 Equipment

1.1 Adequacy of Technical Proposal

Evaluation of the bidder's technical proposal will include an assessment of the bidder's technical capacity to mobilize key equipment and personnel for the contract consistent with its proposal, regarding work methods, scheduling, and material sourcing in sufficient detail and fully in accordance with the requirements stipulated in Section VI (employer's requirements).

1.2 Multiple Contracts

Works are grouped in multiple contracts and pursuant to the Instructions to bidders, the employer will evaluate and compare bids on the basis of a contract, or a combination of contracts, or as a total of contracts in order to arrive at the least cost combination for the employer by taking into account discounts offered by bidders in case of award of multiple contracts.

2.1 Update of Information

The bidder shall continue to meet the criteria used at the time of prequalification. Updating and reassessment of the following information which was previously considered during prequalification will be required:

(a) Eligibility

(b) Pending Litigation

(c) Financial Situation

2.2 Financial Resources

Using the relevant forms in Section IV (bidding forms) the bidder must demonstrate access to, or availability of, financial resources such as liquid assets, unencumbered real assets, lines of credit, and other financial means.

2.3 Personnel

The bidder shall provide details of the proposed personnel and their experience records in the relevant information forms included in Section IV (bidding forms).

Because the managerial and technical competence of a contractor is largely related to the key personnel on site, the bidder should demonstrate having staff with extensive experience, and should be limited to those requiring critical operational or technical skills. The prequalification criteria will refer to a limited number of such key personnel, for instance, the project or contract manager and those superintendents working under the project manager who will be responsible for major components (e.g., superintendents specialized in dredging, piling, or earthworks, as required for each particular project).

2.4 Equipment

The bidder must demonstrate that it has the key equipment listed. In most cases bidders can readily purchase, lease, or hire equipment; thus, it is usually unnecessary to assess a contractor's qualification which depends on the contractor's owning readily available items of equipment. The pass–fail criteria adopted will be limited only to those bulky or specialized items that are critical for the type of project to be implemented, and that may be difficult for the contractor to obtain quickly, such as heavy lift cranes and piling barges, dredgers, asphalt mixing plants, etc. Even in such cases, contractors may not own the specialized items of equipment, and may rely on specialist subcontractors or equipment–hire firms, or the availability of such subcontractors.

Section IV. Bidding Forms

This section contains the forms which are to be completed by the bidder and submitted as part of his bid.

The employer will include in the bidding documents all bidding forms that the bidder shall fill out and include in his bid. As specified in Section IV of the bidding documents, these forms are the bid submission sheet and relevant schedules, the bid security, the bill of quantities, the technical proposal form, and the bidder's qualification information form for which two options are attached.

Section V. Eligible Countries

This section contains information regarding eligible countries, ineligible counties' contractor will be excluded. Consistent with international law, the proceeds of the World Bank's loans, equity investment or guarantees shall not be used for payment to persons or entities or for any import of goods, if such payment or import is prohibited by a decision of the United Nations Security Council taken under Chapter VII of the charter of the United Nations. Persons or entities, or suppliers offering goods and services, covered by such prohibition shall therefore not be eligible for the award of World Bank-financed contracts.

PART 2——WORKS REQUIREMENTS

Section VI. Works Requirements

This section contains the specification, the drawings, and supplementary information that describe the works to be procured.

PART 3——CONDITIONS OF CONTRACT AND CONTRACT FORMS

Section VII. General Conditions (GC)

This section contains the general clauses to be applied in all contracts. The text of the clauses in this section shall not be modified.

Section VIII. Particular Conditions (PC)

As the standard text of the general conditions chosen must be retained intact, any amendments and additions to the general conditions will be introduced in the particular conditions.

The contents of this section supplement the general conditions and will be prepared by the employer. Whenever there is a conflict, the provisions herein shall prevail over those in the general conditions.

The use of standard conditions of contract for all civil works will ensure comprehensiveness of coverage, better balance of rights or obligations between employer and contractor, general acceptability of its provisions, and savings in time and cost for bid preparation and review, leading to more economical prices.

The particular conditions take precedence over the general conditions. It is good practice to have a list of tax and custom regulations applicable in the country, to be provided as non-binding general information, attached to the bidding documents.

Section IX. Annex to the Particular Conditions – Contract Forms

This section contains forms, which shall be completed by bidders, will form part of the Contract. Section IX of the bidding documents also contains forms for the contract agreement, the performance security, and the advance payment security. After notification of award, the employer will prepare the contract agreement using the contract agreement form and send it to the successful bidder. The successful bidder shall sign the contract agreement and return it to the employer together with the performance security and the advance payment security, using the respective forms provided in Section IX.

The notification of award will be the basis for formation of the contract as described in Instructions to bidders. This standard form will be filled in and sent to the successful bidder, after evaluation of bids has been completed.

New Words and Expressions

the contractor's bid decision 承包人的投标决策
construction industry 建筑行业
construction projects 建设项目
business processes 业务流程
internal and external factors 内部与外部的影响因素

Unit 5 The Contractor's Bid Decision

a particular project 一个特定的项目
an appropriate bidding strategy 一个合适的投标决策
losing a good opportunity 失去一个好的机会
make substantial profit 赚取可观的收入
improve the contractor's strength 提升承包商的实力
profitable projects 有利可图的项目
under uncertainty 在不确定性下
competitive bidding on construction projects 工程项目竞争性投标
a large number of factors 大量的因素
estimate of the direct project cost 工程造价的直接估计
immediate and long-range objectives of management 直接而长期的管理目标
expenditure 支出，花费
bill of quantities 工程量清单
activity schedule 工程进度
the net cost of the works 工程净成本
estimator 评估师
planning engineer 规划师
materials estimator 材料测量师
estimating technician 估计技术员
an experienced construction manager 一个有经验的施工经理
factors affect decision making 影响决策的因素
indications 显示，标志；适应症
uncertain bidding conditions 不确定的投标条件
a high degree of subjective judgment 高度的主观判断
different weights 不同的权重
overall strategy 整体战略
propensity to 倾向，习性；癖好，偏好
additional work 额外的项目
cash flow implications 现金流的影响
contractor organization 承包组织
current opportunity 当前的机会
scoring system 得分系统
partnering and framework agreements 合作框架协议
third party relationships 第三方关系
consultants 顾问
specialist contractors 专业承包商
aid agencies 援助机构
soft loan 软贷款
corporation 企业，公司

strings attached 附带的条件
prospective bidders 潜在投标人
nationality 国籍；国家，民族；部落
partners 合伙人
funders 资助人
corruption 贪污，腐败；堕落
guarantee 保证，担保
sophisticated 复杂的，精致的；使变得世故，使迷惑；篡改
sophisticated export guarantees schemes 完善的出口保证方案
local bidders/contractors 当地的投标人(承包商)
price preferences 价格优惠
mandatory 强制的，强加的
bank guarantee 银行保函
home country 本国
significant restrictions on imports 明显限制进口产品
excessive import levies 过度进口关税
import machineries and other equipment 进口机械设备与其他设备
legal framework 法律框架
Common Law 普通法律
Civil Code 民法典
dispute resolution 解决争议
legal issues 法律问题
warranties and payment terms 担保与付款方式
payment terms 支付条款
letters of credit 信用证
advance payment 预付款
paramount 至高无上的；最重要的，主要的；最高统治者
local business requirements 当地商业需求
a branch office or representative office 一个分支机构或代表处
local customs 当地风俗习惯
international suppliers 国际供应商
initial inspection of the documents 初始检查文件
inspection of the site 场地巡查
calculation of analytical unit rates 计算分析单位价格
pricing of the bill of quantities 工程量清单定价
tender adjudication meeting 投标人裁决会议
weather conditions 气候条件
cyclone 飓风
suitability of materials 材料的可获取性

quarries 矿山
reliability 可靠度，可靠性；忠诚度
insurance claims 过度的保险索赔
non-recoverable costs 不可回收的成本
specification 规范，规格；说明书
contractor's comparative advantages 承包商的比较优势
forming bid prices 形成竞标价
superior technology 先进的技术
greater experience 丰富的经验
lower unit costs 降低单位成本
comparative cost advantage 比较优势成本
most desirable of all circumstances 最理想的情况
call for more investigation 呼吁更多的调查
evaluating project profitability 评估项目利润率
competitive environment 竞争环境
estimating process 估算过程
level of expertise 专业水平
contractor's estimating department 承包商评估部门
take a commercial view on the estimated cost 以商业的观点估计成本费用
evaluating contractor's own particular circumstances 评估承包商的特定环境
market conditions and risk 市场状况与风险
competitive tendering 竞争性投标
low fixed-capital requirements 低的固定资本需求
preliminary expenses 初步费用
delays to cash-inflows 现金流的短缺
seasonal effects 季节性影响
fluctuation 波动，振动，震荡
government intervention 政府干预
uncertain ground conditions 不确定的地基状况
performance liability 绩效责任
long-term guarantees 长期的保证
wage structures 薪金结构，工资结构
supply chain 供应链

Exercises

I. Choose the best answer according to the text.

1. One of the most critical decisions that have to be made by contractors in the construction industry is _____.

A. whether or not to bid for a new project when an invitation has been received

B. involves a process of gathering information from various sources

C. commit resources to a time-consuming and expensive process that requires them to adjust and adapt their business processes

D. the importance of considering internal and external factors that affect the bid / no bid decision before committing themselves to a project

2. The decision making at this stage is accomplished by two related decision _____.

A. bid/no bid decisions that consider factors would help to determine the benefit expected from a particular project and an appropriate bidding strategy

B. mark-up decision, which is one of the consequences of the bidding strategy

C. A or B

D. A and B

3. According to text, the winning of a particular project may be potentially important to _____.

A. the bidding strategies of some contractors are influenced by a policy of minimum percentage markup for general overhead and profit

B. the overall mix of work in progress or the cash flow implications for the contractor

C. the contractor's decision is also influenced by the availability of key personnel in the contractor organization

D. none of the above

4. Making a decision to bid can depend on a number of factors including _____.

A. knowledge of the participants

B. complexity of the project

C. period between commencement and award, risk factors and language

D. above all

5. We learn from the passage that the decision process which is the stage where the directors of a firm _____.

A. will ultimately try to pitch the bidding price between cost and value in order to win the work

B. are related to the economic, contractual, political and physical environments in which construction projects may take place

C. will take a commercial view on the estimated cost, evaluating contractor's own particular circumstances, market conditions and risk

D. may depend on the level of expertise in a contractor's estimating department

II. Decide the following statements are true or false.

1. One of the greatest sources of the uncertainty for each bidder is the unpredictable nature of his competitors.

2. As so many factors are involved, it is possible for a particular bidder to attempt to predict

exactly what the bids submitted by its competitors will be.

3. Owing to this the bidder has to pay for the bank guarantee twice in the home country and once abroad.

4. Careful project selection is the first step to the success of the construction company and it should not be carried out in a careless manner.

III. Change the following words to another form and write down the Chinese meanings.

1. accomplish _____
2. consequences _____
3. substantial _____
4. overhead _____
5. comprising _____
6. commencement _____
7. considerations _____
8. L/C _____
9. paramount _____
10. in essence _____

IV. Give out the following words' synonym or other word in the closest meaning.

1. adjust   a. bidders
2. propensity to   b. contractors
3. corporation   c. equipments
4. factors   d. adapt
5. participants   e. company
6. bidders   f. stakeholders
7. machineries   g. tend to
8. encompass   h. include
9. tenders   i. considerations

V. Put the following English into Chinese.

1. It will be necessary to plot income against expenditure using the programme of works and the bill of quantities–activity schedule–payments in arrears and retentions, both from the employer and to subcontractors must be considered. Upon completion of the review, the contractor will grade the bid based on the interest to the company and recommend whether or not to bid.

2. The bidding strategies of some contractors are influenced by a policy of minimum percentage markup for general overhead and profit.

3. A true story relating to translation resulted, not in the subcontract, but the subcontractor being executed.

4. Nowadays, international contractors are mitigating risk by declining work perceived as too risky, subcontracting large portions of their work to others, and apportioning risk in wage

structures. In essence, contractors are passing risk on to others in the supply chain; therefore, they seem adept at managing risk.

VI. Put the following Chinese into English.

1. 评估承包商的特定环境
2. 以商业的观点来估计工程成本
3. 工程量清单计价，定额计价
4. 建筑工程项目竞争性投标
5. 比较优势成本理论

参 考 译 文

第 5 单元　承包商的投标决策

1. 导言

建筑业中必须由承包商做出的最关键决策之一是，当收到一个投标邀请函时是否去参加新项目的投标。建筑项目的最早阶段的决策涉及从各种源头收集信息的过程。为了理想地完成项目，承包商常常把资源尽量用于需要他们调整和适应他们的业务程序的耗时耗资的建筑施工过程中。

明智的承包商了解内部和外部因素的重要性，这些因素会在他们承揽一个项目之前决定投标/不投标。在此阶段的决定由两个相关的决策来实现：

➢ 考虑因素的投标/不投标决定将有助于确定来自于一个特定项目的预计益处和恰当的投标策略。

➢ 加价决策，这是投标策略的重要性之一。

不参与项目的投标可能会失去可观利润、降低承包商在业内的实力、破坏与委托人的良好关系，以及更多方面好机会的丢失。然而，参与一个不适合的项目的投标可能造成巨大损失或者消耗掉可以投入到更加有利润的项目中的时间和资源，最终甚至是承包商财务的失败。

2. 投标决策

建筑项目的竞争性投标牵涉到不确定情况下的决策。对于每个投标人最大的不确定性之一是他的竞争者的不可预见性。由承包商针对一个特定项目而提交的每份标书将由许多因素决定，包括直接项目成本估算、综合管理费用、管理部门对该估算的信心以及目前和长期的管理目标。由于牵涉到这么多的因素，投标人试图精确地预测他的竞争者提交的标书有什么内容是不可能的。

应该利用项目的工程计划和工程量清单、工作进度、拖欠和保留款项来周密对待项目的收支平衡，雇主和分包商都必须考虑到这些因素。一旦完成项目评审，承包商将以公司的利益为基础对标书评级，并决定是否参与投标。

如果工程较专业或较复杂，工程净成本预算的技术过程将由预算师、项目计划工程师、材料预算师、估算技术人员，连同可能做出贡献的有经验的施工经理组成的团队来完成。

在预算过程结束时，该团队将做出成本预算。该预算对于承包商来说是对项目成本的预测。

这样一来，投标价格就受其所发生的市场或竞争环境影响。投标常常涉及两个过程。第一，评估过程是实际项目成本被考虑的阶段。该过程可能取决于承包商评估部门的专门知识水平。第二，决策过程是公司负责人对预计成本进行商业评审的过程，同时对承包商自己的特殊情况、市场条件和风险进行估价。于是，为了赢得工程，管理部门将最终设法对成本和价值之间的投标价格做出定位。

3. 影响决策的因素

从所有迹象来看，大部分承包商通过发挥高度的主观判断来正视不确定的招标条件，且每个承包商可能给予各种因素不同的权重。如果承包商明确地提交了一份投标书，在投标价格上的决策反映了承包商在所提议的项目怎样很好地与企业的生存和发展整体战略相符方面的最好判断，以及承包商冒险获得更大的利润与不能获得一份合同的机会相比的倾向性。

承包商对某个特定项目的投标努力程度受承包商想获得额外工程的愿望的影响。对于承包商来说，特定项目的中标对在建工程的全面整合或者现金流可能有潜在的重要影响。一些承包商的投标策略往往受公司针对综合管理费和利润的最低比例的加价政策的影响。承包商的投标决策也受承包商组织里可调配的关键项目管理人员的影响。公司有时候想要为未来项目保留其关键资源，或者由于不同的原因而致力于对当前机会的努力。

做出决策去投标受许多因素影响，包括对参与者的了解、项目复杂程度、项目的开工和授标之间的期限、风险因素和合同语言。然而，承包商不得不通过考虑许多因素，然后使用一个计分系统去应用更加周密的决策形式。承包商之间的计分系统有极大的不同，但是下面这些因素一般要包括在内：

3.1 与业主关系

与业主的关系可以基于以前项目、对业主的了解及任何的合作和框架协议来考虑。做这些考虑是由于承包商或有关联的公司和合资公司以前的业务。

3.2 第三方关系

无论是投资者、承包商、咨询公司还是专业承包商，跟预期项目的关系都涉及与各种有关项目的投资者或项目参与方一起工作的认识和先前经验。这就意味着承包商可以通过咨询公司或者专业承包商对业主非常了解。

3.3 资金来源

确定资金来源是要深入的考虑又一个问题，资金可以源于国际援助机构、国际组织、优惠贷款、政府、银行或金融公司。特定的资金类型会伴随附加条件并对潜在投标人的国籍有限制。

3.4 国籍因素

对于项目可能的参与方国籍是另外需要考虑的因素，无论他们是业主、伙伴、投资人、承包商、咨询公司还是竞争者。例如，处理来自美国的参与方会带来与工会有关的所有类型法律问题；来自中东的参与方会带来伊斯兰教教法；某些国家具有关于腐败记录的不良因素，等等。

3.5 竞争者

对可能的竞争者的评审是必不可少的；以那些来自提供优惠贷款给项目的国家的公司为竞争对手的投标可能是高风险的。与具有卓越专业技术背景和相对竞争优势的公司竞争将是浪费金钱和精力。

3.6 担保

一个因素是，项目是否吸引出口担保，例如来自英国和美国这两个都具有完善的出口担保方案的国家。大部分中东国家给予当地投标人/承包商价格优惠。在许多这些国家中，获得投标担保及其他由当地银行提供的银行担保的要求是强制性的。基于这一点，投标人必须支付给银行两次银行费用：一次是在本国，另外一次是在国外(项目所在国)。许多中东和北非国家(例如利比亚)在进口方面有极大的限制(例如，收取过高的进口关税)，这种限制使这些国家进口机械和其他设备很困难。

3.7 法律体制

以下方面对投标项目可能会引起关于适用法律的混乱：
- 合同形式；
- 合同法、普通法、民法或者伊斯兰教教法；
- 合同语言；
- 争端解决场所(伦敦、巴黎、香港等等)。以上这些在不同国家或者不同语言里都有。

其他合法问题与债券和担保、保函和付款条件有关。与法律相关的真正问题不在分包合同中，而在分包商的施工过程中。

3.8 付款条件

对付款条件的理解，包括对信用证、各种保函、预付款以及抵消规则的理解，是最重要的。

3.9 当地业务要求

有些国家对投标规定了最低门槛要求，仅允许在当地成立了公司的投标人投标，例如在当地有分公司或者办事处。其他要求可能包括当地公司一定比例的入股或者与当地公司合资。

3.10 当地风俗

其他管制可能包括对国际供应的限制，使用当地劳工以及上班时间和节假日要求。

3.11 风险

投标风险因素包括投标文件的初始检查、现场视察、风险分析、材料和分包合同查询、单价的计算分析、工程量清单定价。估价因素与经济的、合同的、政治的和物理的环境有关，在这些环境中，施工项目产生了且倾向于影响施工工程被描述、授予和提供文件的方式。技术因素包括：在生产之前对产品进行定价的必要性、竞争性招标(公开招标)、低固定资本需要量、初期费用、现金流的误期、操作太低运营资本的倾向、季节影响、波动及其影响、政府干预、有关开发的活动、不确定地面状况、不可预测天气及无责任或长期担保的执行。无论这些风险可以接受与否，都可能包括如下内容：

> 天气条件，如河流泛滥和气旋等；
> 材料的合适性——尤其是来自采石场的填充材料；
> 分包商的可靠性；
> 不可恢复成本，如保险索赔的超额；
> 允许的产量例如生产量；
> 成本增加；
> 合同中的条款；
> 针对允许价格/劳工/工厂可用性的满足规范的能力。

4. 承包商的比较优势

就承包商而言，在形成投标价格上的最后一项考虑是由特定公司具有的特殊优势。由于具有较低成本，某个承包商也许能够加上更高利润的溢价，却仍然具有比竞争者更低的总出价。这些更低成本可能是由于具有较高的技术、更多的经验、更好的管理、更好的员工或者更低的单位成本。比较成本优势是进入一项投标竞争的所有条件中最重要的。

如今，国际承包商通过谢绝已察觉到太冒险的工程、把工程的很大一部分转包给其他人，以及把风险分摊到工资结构中来缓解风险。本质上，他们是在供应链上把风险传递给其他人。因此，他们似乎精于对风险的驾驭。

谨慎选择项目是建筑公司成功的第一步，而不应以粗心的态度来实施。然而，对承包商在投标决策中失败的原因，要求更多地对项目盈利性的预算评估以投标策略与特定项目的结合来考虑。

阅读

标准投标/招标文件

对项目采购的标准投标文件进行研究，是为了帮助实习者彻底理解投标过程和投标文件。它提供一份看一眼就描述的投标文件和一个投标活动，这一点产生于要求投标人直到授标或者签约的决策。其他类型的投标文件变化很大；然而，对标准投标文件的理解对于承包商角逐国际市场来说是一种迫切需要。

项目采购的标准招标文件(SBDPW)由世界银行编制，由世界银行完全或部分提供资金的项目需通过国际竞争性招标，这些标准文件用于单价(单位价格或费率)类型的采购。在没有对付款方式和价格调整以及对于工程量清单和工作进度等的实质性的改变的情况下，这些投标文件不适合于总价合同。

资格预审过程将遵照标准资格预审文件(SPD)规定：由世界银行发布的项目采购的程序进行。资格预审通常被用于重大项目或复杂项目。在获得世界银行的批准(可能还需要资格后审)之后，可供选择的第三节，评价和资格标准可能有例外。

第一部分——招标程序

第一节 《投标人须知》

该节提供帮助投标人准备他们的标书，提供在标书投递、开标和评标及授标等方面的信息。如果项目完全地或部分地由世界银行提供资金的话，整个第一节内容包含的规定条件不得更改。

第一节的条款目录：

1. 总则
1.1 投标范围
1.2 资金来源
1.3 欺诈和腐败
1.4 有资格投标人
1.5 合格材料、设备以及服务
2. 投标文件内容
2.1 投标文件章节
2.2 投标文件阐述、现场参观、投标前会议
2.3 投标文件修正
3. 标书编制
3.1 投标成本
3.2 标书语言
3.3 组成标书的文件
3.4 投标函和表格
3.5 可选标书
3.6 标价和折扣
3.7 投标货币和付款
3.8 组成技术提案的文件
3.9 确定投标人资格的文件
3.10 标书(投标)有效期
3.11 投标担保
3.12 标书格式和签署
4. 提交和开启标书
4.1 标书的加封和标记
4.2 标书提交最后期限
4.3 迟到标书
4.4 标书的撤销、替换和修改
4.5 开标
5. 标书评价和比较
5.1 保密条款
5.2 标书阐述
5.3 偏差、保留(附加条件)和遗漏

5.4 响应性确定
5.5 实质性不符
5.6 计算错误纠正
5.7 单一货币转化
5.8 优惠差额
5.9 评标
5.10 比标
5.11 投标人资格
5.12 雇主接受任何标书，以及拒绝任何或所有标书的权利
6. 授标
6.1 授标准则
6.2 中标通知
6.3 合同签署
6.4 履约保函

第二节　标书数据总表(BDS)

该节对每项采购都有很具体的规定，且在投标人须知里对每项采购都是有很具体的补充信息或者要求。雇主必须在投标数据总表里仅仅详述《投标人须知》所要求的、在投标数据单表里被详述的信息。为了使投标数据单表的准备更便捷，它的条款标有与相应的投标人须知条款相同的序号。

第三节　评价和资格标准

该节包含雇主将用来评价标书和选择投标人资格的所有标准。根据《投标人须知》，再没有其他方法、标准和因素。投标人将提供第四节(投标表格)表格所要求的所有信息。

世界银行要求投标人须满足预先确定的、明确的和最低门槛要求而通过资格审查。该方法使得设定通过-失败标准非常必要，如果被投标人不满足该标准，则资格审查不合格。因此，应确保投标人持有以资格为理由而被拒绝的标书的风险很小，如果在标书编制期间投标人采取了适当行动的话。因此，清晰的失败-通过的资格标准应当是明确的，以便使投标人决定是否去竞争某个特定合同(参加投标)，如果去竞争，是作为单一实体，还是组成联合体投标。所采纳标准必须关系到能确保合同满意履行的某种特征，这点很关键，且必须以明确的条款来进行陈述。

第三节的标准内容：
1. 评价
1.1 技术提案的充分性
1.2 打包合同
1.3 竣工时间
1.4 技术可选方案
1.5 当地公司优惠
2. 资格
2.1 信息更新
2.2 财务资源

2.3 员工
2.4 设备

1.1 技术提案的充分性

对投标人的技术提案的评价包括投标人针对合同去调动关键设备和人员且与其提案相一致的技术能力，关系到施工方案、进度计划和材料来源，以足够的细节和完全根据第六节(雇主的要求)里所规定的要求来进行。

1.2 打包合同

在项目由多个合同组成的情况下，依照《投标人须知》的规定，雇主将项目在单个合同、合同组合、作为一个总合同的基础上去评审和比较标书。雇主在考虑投标人所提供的标价折扣以达成最低的项目成本组合的情况下，授予投标人打包合同。

2.1 信息更新

投标人将继续去达到资格预审要求的标准。下面几条是在资格预审期间考虑过的需要更新和评估的信息：
(a) 资质
(b) 未决诉讼
(c) 财务状况

2.2 财务资源

使用在第四节(投标表格)里的相关表格，投标人必须证实诸如流动资产、无债务真实资产、信用额度及其他财务手段等财务资源的使用通道或者可用性。

2.3 员工

投标人将在第四节(投标表格)里所包含的相关信息表格里提供所提议的员工及他们的阅历记录的详细资料。

因为承包商的管理和技术能力主要与现场的关键工作人员有关，所以投标人应当证实他们拥有经验丰富的员工，且只限于在招标书里要求的关键性管理或者技术人员。资格预审标准将参考数量不多的这样一些关键人员，例如，项目或者承包经理及那些在项目经理下面工作的主管人员，这些主管人将负责项目的主要部分(如：每个特定项目所要求的专攻挖掘、打桩或者土方工程的主管人)。

2.4 设备

投标人必须证明其具有所要求的关键设备。在大多数情况下，投标人可以容易地购买、租借或租赁设备；这样一来，通常就不必要通过设备评估承包商了。通过-失败准则将仅仅限制在那些重型、大型和专业设备，类似的设备对于要去实施的项目是决定性的，并且承包商很难快速获得此类设备，比如重型吊车和打桩机、挖掘机、沥青混合搅拌机等。在这样的情况下，承包商不一定拥有这些专门的设备，则可以依赖于专业分包商或者设备租赁公司，或者分包商的可用设备。

第四节 投标表格

该节包含要由投标人去完成并且作为其标书的一部分进行提交的表格。

雇主将把所有投标人必须填写且包含在其标书中的投标表格列入投标文件中。正如投标文件第四节所规定的那样,这些表格是标书提交总表及相关的表格、投标担保、工程量清单、技术方案表及投标人资格信息表,这些表格中包括两种选择。

第五节 有资格的国家

这一节是关于国家有资格的情况,无资格国家的承包商将被排除在外。与国际法一致,世界银行贷款的盈利、产权投资或者担保将不被用于对自然人或者实体或者针对任何商品进口的付款,前提是,这样的付款或者进口被联合国宪章第七章的规定做出的决定所禁止的话。提供商品或者服务的涉及这种禁止的自然人、实体或者供应商,将没有资格获得世界银行提供资金的授标。

第二部分——项目要求

第六节 项目要求

该节包含描述所获得项目规格、制图和其附加信息。

第三部分——合同条件和合同格式

第七节 通用条件(GC)

该节包含用在所有合同中的一般条款。该节中的条款正文不能被修改。

第八节 特别条件(PC)

所选择的一般(通用)条件的标准文本必须保持完整无缺,任何对一般条件(通用)的修改和添加将被列入特别条件里去。

该节的内容对一般条件做了补充且将由雇主进行编制。如果存在冲突,此处的条款将优先于通用条件里的条款。

针对土木工程的合同标准条件的使用将确保合同覆盖范围宽广、雇主和承包商之间权利和义务的更好平衡、其条款的广泛接受性及针对标书编制和审查的时间和成本的节约,从而实现更经济的价格。

特别条件比通用条件具有优先权。最好列出该国适用的税收和关税的法规条例清单,并将这个清单作为非约束一般信息附在投标文件中。

第九节 特别条件附件-合同格式

该节介绍合同格式,这些合同格式将由投标人完成且作为合同的一部分。投标文件的第九节也介绍针对合同协议、履约担保及预付款担保的合同格式。在接到中标通知书以后,雇主将用合同格式来编制合同协议且把它发送给中标人。中标人将使用第九节中介绍的合同表格签署合同协议并连同履约担保、预付款担保一起返还给雇主。

正如《投标人须知》中所描述的那样,中标通知书是合同形成的基础。需要认真填写该标准表格,并在标书的评审完成之后发送给中标人。

Unit 6

Project Cost Estimate and Cost Control

1. Project Cost Management

Cost management is very much more than simply maintaining records of expenditure and issuing cost reports. Cost management means understanding how and why costs occur and promptly taking the necessary response in light of all the relevant information. Keeping a project within budget depends on the application of an efficient and effective system of cost control. From the information generated in the progress of the project, cost management should be not only to identify past trends but also forecast the likely consequence of future decisions including final out-turn cost, that is, the final account. Cost management helps the project team to better establish the appropriate project contract strategy, and cost management should be placed in which contract and possibly the form of contract be adopted. Cost management can also help identify possible programme restraints both in contract preparation and execution. Without an effective company-wide cost-control system this would result in substantial risk to any contractor's slender margins.

2. Project Cost Estimate

Cost estimate is one of the most important steps in project management. Cost estimate establishes the baseline of the project cost at different stages of development of the project; moreover, estimates of the cost and time are prepared and revised at many stages throughout the project cycle. These are all predictions and should not be considered 100% accurate, but the degree of realism and confidence achieved will depend on the level of definition of the work and the extent of the risk and uncertainty. The principles and techniques of cost estimate are utilized in the application of scientific methods to the problem of cost estimation, cost control and profitability. Virtually all cost estimation is performed according to one or some combination of the following basic approaches:

2.1 Production Function

The relationship between the output of a process and the necessary resources is referred to as the production function. In construction, a production function relates the amount or volume of output to the various inputs of labor, material and equipment. The relationship between the size of a building project (expressed in square meter) and the input labor (expressed in labor hours per square meter) is an example of a production function for construction.

2.2 Empirical Cost Inference

Empirical estimation of cost functions requires statistical techniques which relate the cost of constructing or operating a facility to a few important characteristics or attributes of the system. The preparation of the first estimate would be based on a variety of techniques, for example, historic data or approximate quantities. Major projects often have substantial elements that are unique and for which there is no relevant historic data. The role of statistical inference is to estimate the best parameter values or constants in an assumed cost function. Usually, this is accomplished by means of regression analysis techniques.

2.3 Unit Costs for Bill of Quantities

A unit cost is assigned to each of the facility components or tasks as represented by the bill of quantities. The total cost is the summation of the quantities of the products multiplied by the corresponding unit costs. The unit cost method is straightforward in principle but quite laborious in application. The initial step is to break down or disaggregate a process into a number of tasks. Create Work Breakdown Structure(WBS) is the process of subdividing project deliverables and project work into smaller, more manageable components. Collectively, these tasks must be completed for the construction of a facility. Once these tasks are defined and quantities representing these tasks are assessed, a unit cost is assigned to each task and then the total cost is determined by summing the costs incurred in each task. The level of detail in decomposing into tasks will vary considerably from one estimate to another.

2.4 Allocation of Joint Costs

Allocations of cost from existing accounts may be used to develop a cost function of an operation. The basic idea in this method is that each expenditure item can be assigned to particular characteristics of the operation. In many instances, however, a causal relationship between the allocation factor and the cost item cannot be identified or may not exist. For example, in construction projects, the accounts for basic costs may be classified and allocated proportionally to various tasks which are subdivisions of a project. It usually according to:
- labor;
- material;
- construction equipment;
- construction supervision;
- general office overhead.

2.5 Detailed Estimating Method

Activity-based detailed or unit cost estimates are typically the most definitive estimating techniques, and use information down to the lowest level of detail available. They are also the most commonly understood and utilized estimating techniques. The accuracy of activity-based detailed or unit cost techniques depends on the accuracy of available information, resources spent to develop the cost estimate and the validity of the bases of the estimate. A work statement and set of drawings or specifications may be used to identify activities that make up the project. Each activity is further decomposed into detailed items (WBS) so that labor hours, material costs, equipment costs, and subcontract costs are itemized and quantified.

Cost estimates must consider the overall costs of the works, including labor, materials, equipment, services, facilities, inflation allowance or contingency costs. Moreover, cost estimates must also consider the causes of variation of the final estimate and various costing alternatives for purposes of better project management. It is necessary to analyse the project in as many individual work sections as can be identified, if possible, to prepare indicative quantities and consider the resources necessary to carry out the work, including location of project and access thereto, especially with regard to heavy and large loads, availability of labour and the possible need of accommodation for workmen, off-site construction, temporary works. Cost estimates may increase or decrease as the project progresses and additional detail become known. The accuracy of a cost estimate of a project will improve as the project progresses through its life cycle.

3. Cost Control

Cost control is the manipulation and analysis of all costs pertaining to the project. Cost control is also a method or system used to record, compare, track and effect the cost of the project for profitability. For control and monitoring purposes, the original detailed cost estimate is typically converted to a project budget, and the project budget is used subsequently as a guide for management. The final or detailed cost estimate provides a baseline for the assessment of financial performance during the project. To the extent, that costs are within the detailed cost estimate, then the project is thought to be under financial control. Overruns in particular cost categories signal the possibility of problems and give an indication of exactly what problems are being encountered. Expense oriented construction planning and control focuses upon the categories included in the final cost estimation.

In general, construction cost control consists basically of monitoring actual performance against cost estimates and identifying variances. The cost control methods based on the detection of variances appears to assume that the causes of deviation will be apparent and the appropriate corrective action obvious. Cost control includes:

3.1 Project Performance Reviews

Project performance review is to compare cost performance over time, schedule activities or work packages, planned value, and milestones. The construction plan and the associated cash flow estimates can provide the baseline reference for subsequent project monitoring and control. For schedules, progress on individual activities and the achievement of milestone completions can be compared with the project schedule to monitor the progress of activities. Compares actual project performance to planned or expected value, and examines project performance over time to determine if performance is improving. Expenses incurred during the course of a project are recorded in specific work elements cost accounts, and then comparing it with the original cost estimates in each category to ascertain if the budget is under control. Two related outcomes are expected from the periodic monitoring of costs:

➢ Identification of any work items whose actual costs are exceeding their budgeted costs, with subsequent actions to try to bring those costs into conformance with the budget;

➢ Estimating the total cost of the project at completion, based on the cost record so far and expectations of the cost to complete unfinished items.

3.2 Variance Analysis

The purpose of variance analysis is to describe how cost variances are managed, such as monitoring cost performance to detect and understand variances from plan, ensuring changes are acted on time, preventing unauthorized changes from being included, managing the actual changes when and as they occur, then ensure the acceptable range of variance decreases as the project progresses.

3.3 Project Management Estimating Software

Project management estimating software is computerized cost accounting and integrated cost control system which is used to track planned cost versus actual cost and to forecast the effects of cost changes. Project management software spreadsheets and simulation/statistical tools are widely used to assist with cost estimating; it can simplify the use of the techniques and facilitate more rapid consideration of costing alternatives, provide a means of comparing actual with budgeted expenses in a timely manner, develop a database of productivity and cost-performance data for use in estimating the costs of operations that are deviating from the project budget, and generate data for valuing variations and changes to the contract and potential claims for additional payments.

4. Summary

In conclusion, an effective cost-control management should contain the following characteristics:

➢ A detailed budget for the project set with a contingency sum to be used at the discretion of the project manager;

➢ Costs should be forecast before decisions are made to allow for the consideration of all possible courses of action;

➢ The cost-recording system should be cost-effective to operate, the actual costs should be compared with forecasted costs at appropriate periods to ensure conformity with the budget and to allow for corrective action if necessary and if possible;

➢ Actual costs should be subject to variance analysis to determine reasons for any deviation from the budget;

➢ The cost implications of time and quality should be incorporated into the decision-making process.

Reading

Bill of Quantities

1. Objectives of Bill of Quantities

The objectives of the bill of quantities are
- ➢ to provide sufficient information on the quantities of works to be performed to enable bids to be prepared efficiently and accurately; and
- ➢ when a contract has been entered into, to provide a priced bill of quantities for use in the periodic valuation of works executed.

In order to attain these objectives, works should be itemized in the bill of quantities in sufficient detail to distinguish between the different classes of works, or between works of the same nature carried out in different locations or in other circumstances which may give rise to different considerations of cost. Consistent with these requirements, the layout and content of the bill of quantities should be as simple and brief as possible.

2. Consist of Bill of Quantities

The bill of quantities is divided generally into the following sections:
- ➢ Preamble;
- ➢ Work items (grouped into parts);
- ➢ Daywork schedule; and
- ➢ Summary.

2.1 Preamble

The preamble should indicate the inclusiveness of the unit prices, and should state the methods of measurement that have been adopted in the preparation of the bill of quantities and that are to be used for the measurement of any part of the works.
- ➢ The bill of quantities shall be read in conjunction with the instructions to bidders, general and special(particular) conditions of contract, technical specifications, and drawings.
- ➢ The quantities given in the bill of quantities are estimated and provisional, and are given to provide a common basis for bidding. The basis of payment will be the actual quantities of work ordered and carried out, as measured by the contractor and verified by the engineer and valued at the rates and prices bid in the priced bill of quantities, where applicable, and otherwise at such rates and prices as the engineer may fix within the terms of the contract.
- ➢ The rates and prices bid in the priced bill of quantities shall, except insofar as it is otherwise provided under the contract, include all constructional plant, labor, supervision, materials, erection, maintenance, insurance, profit, taxes, and duties, together with all general risks, liabilities, and obligations set out or implied in the contract.
- ➢ A rate or price shall be entered against each item in the priced bill of quantities, whether quantities are stated or not. The cost of items against which the contractor has failed to enter a rate

or price shall be deemed to be covered by other rates and prices entered in the bill of quantities.

➢ The whole cost of complying with the provisions of the Contract shall be included in the Items provided in the priced bill of quantities, and where no items are provided, the cost shall be deemed to be distributed among the rates and prices entered for the related items of work.

➢ General directions and descriptions of work and materials are not necessarily repeated nor summarized in the bill of quantities. References to the relevant sections of the contract documentation shall be made before entering prices against each item in the priced bill of quantities.

➢ Provisional sums included and so designated in the bill of quantities shall be expended in whole or in part at the direction and discretion of the engineer in accordance with the conditions of contract.

➢ The method of measurement of completed work for payment shall be in accordance with [SMM7 the Principles of Measurement (International) for Works of Construction (June 1979, reprinted 1988, 1991, 1994, 2001, 2002 and 2004), as published by the Royal Institution of Chartered Surveyors with amendments made to suit local practice and conditions. Method of measurement: SMM7; CESMM; measurement and coverage rules].

➢ Errors will be corrected by the employer for any arithmetic errors in computation or summation as follows:

● where there is a discrepancy between amounts in figures and in words, the amount in words will govern; and

● where there is a discrepancy between the unit rate and the total amount derived from the multiplication of the unit price and the quantity, the unit rate as quoted will govern, unless in the opinion of the employer, there is an obviously gross misplacement of the decimal point in the unit price, in which event the total amount as quoted will govern and the unit rate will be corrected.

➢ Rock is defined as all materials that, in the opinion of the engineer, require blasting, or the use of metal wedges and sledgehammers, or the use of compressed air drilling for their removal, and that cannot be extracted by ripping with a tractor of at least 150 brake hp with a single, rear-mounted, heavy-duty ripper.

2.2 Work Items

The items in the bill of quantities should be grouped into sections to distinguish between those parts of the works that by nature, location, access, timing, or any other special characteristics may give rise to different methods of construction, phasing of the works, or considerations of cost. General items common to all parts of the works may be grouped as a separate section in the bill of quantities. When a family of price adjustment formulae are used, they should relate to appropriate sections in the bill of quantities. The bill of quantities usually contains the following part bills, which have been grouped according to the nature or timing of the work(for example):

Bill No.1——General Items(Preliminaries & General Items);

Bill No.2——Substructure (It INCLUDES basement and foundation excavations; piers, piles, pedestals, beams and strip footings; foundation walls; drop aprons; hardcore filling; work slabs and damp-proofing or other membranes; floor structures; subsoil drainage; ducts, pits, bases and service tunnels; entrance steps, ramps and their finishes; steps and ramps in the one floor level; structural screeds and toppings; covered swimming pools; all other work up to but excluding the lowest floor finish.);

Bill No.3——Superstructure;

Bill No.4——Waller;

Bill No.5——Roof Covering;

Bill No.6——Finishing;

Bill No.7——Sundries(It may includes pipe runs from the external face of buildings; inspection pits; sumps; road gullies; culverts; box drains; grated trenches; runs from pools and fountains; outfalls and head walls; agricultural and sub-soil drains; connections to existing runs and pits.);

Bill No.8——Site Works(It includes demolitions; site clearance; general levelling and filling; hoardings; retaining walls; removal of any paving, fences, trees and services; temporary diversions of services; underpinning to adjacent buildings.);

Bill No. 9——Mechanical & Electrical services;

Bill No.10——Provisional Quantities and Sums.

2.3 Quantities

Quantities should be computed net from the drawings, unless directed otherwise in the contract, and no allowance should be made for bulking, shrinkage, or waste. Quantities should be rounded up or down where appropriate, and spurious accuracy should be avoided(the revised 7th Edition of the Standard Method of Measurement).

The following units of measurement and abbreviations are recommended for use (unless other national units are mandatory in the country of the employer).

Unit	Abbreviation	Unit	Abbreviation
cubic meter	m^3 or cu m	millimeter	mm
hectare	ha	month	mon
hour	h	number	nr
kilogram	kg	square meter	m^2 or sq m
lump sum	sum	Square	mm^2 or sq mm
meter	m	millimeter	
metric ton (1,000 kg)	t	week	wk

2.4 Daywork Schedule

A daywork Schedule should be included if the probability of unforeseen work, outside the items included in the bill of quantities, is relatively high. To facilitate checking by the employer of the realism of rates quoted by the bidders, the daywork schedule should normally comprise:

> a list of the various classes of labor, materials, and contractor's equipment for which basic daywork rates or prices are to be inserted by the bidder, together with a statement of the conditions under which the contractor will be paid for work executed on a daywork basis; and

> a percentage to be entered by the bidder against each basic daywork Subtotal amount for labor, materials, and plant representing the contractor's profit, overheads, supervision, and other charges.

2.5 Provisional Quantities and Sums

Provision for quantity contingencies in any particular item or class of work with a high expectation of quantity overrun should be made by entering specific "provisional quantities" or "provisional items" in the bill of quantities, and not by increasing the quantities for that item or class of work beyond those of the work normally expected to be required. To the extent not covered above, a general provision for physical contingencies (quantity overruns) should be made by including a "provisional sum" in the summary of the bill of quantities. Similarly, a contingency allowance for possible price increases should be provided as a "provisional sum" in the summary of the bill of quantities. The inclusion of such provisional sums often facilitates budgetary approval by avoiding the need to request periodic supplementary approvals as the future need arises.

The estimated cost of specialized work or of special goods (to be carried out or supplied by a nominated subcontractor) should be indicated in the relevant part of the bill of quantities as a particular provisional sum with an appropriate brief description. A separate bidding procedure is normally carried out by the employer to select the specialists, who are then nominated as subcontractors to the main or prime contractor. To provide an element of competition among the main bidders (or prime contractors) in respect of any facilities, amenities, attendance, etc., to be provided by the successful bidder as prime contractor for the use and convenience of the specialist or nominated subcontractor, each related provisional sum should be following by an item in the bill of quantities inviting a percentage (to be quoted by the main bidder) payable on the actual expenditure from the provisional sum.

2.6 Summary

The summary should contain a tabulation of the separate parts of the bill of quantities carried forward, with provisional sums for daywork, for physical (quantity) contingencies, and for price contingencies (upward price adjustment) where applicable.

New Words and Expressions

expenditure 支出，花费
issue 发行，出版
application 进度款申请，应用，实践

identify 确定；辨认，辩护；识别
account 账户，账目；总数，合计
adopt 采纳，通过；收养，领养
execution 实施，执行
contractor 承包商
company-wide 全公司的，公司性的；企业水平的
slender 微薄的；苗条的；细长的
margins 利润；边缘
project cost estimate 项目成本估算
profitability 利润
virtually 几乎地，完全地
production function 生产函数
in construction 在施工中
amount 数量，总量
volume 体积，容积
square meter 平方米
empirical cost inference 实证成本推理
facility 设施，公共设施
attribute 特质，属性；归属，归于
approximate 近似的，相似的
parameter values 参数值
constant 常数，恒量；经常的，恒定的
regression analysis 回归分析
unit costs 单位成本
assign 分配，分派，安排，指定
facility components 设备部件
summation 总和，合计
multiply 乘法，乘以；累积
laborious 艰苦的，费劲的；勤劳的
break down 终止；制服，毁掉，失败
disaggregate 解聚，分解；分解，崩溃
collectively 而且，然而
assess 评估，估价
decomposed into 分解，腐烂
allocation 分配，配置；安置
existing accounts 现有客户，现存账户
proportionally 按比例地
subdivision 细分，分部；供出卖而分成的小块土地
construction equipment 施工设备

Unit 6 Project Cost Estimate and Cost Control

construction supervision 建设监理
general office overhead 一般办公室开销
definitive 确切的，准确的
validity 有效性，有法律效力
work statement 工作报表
specification 规格，规范
subcontract 分包合同
itemize 分条列述，详细列表
quantified 定量化的
inflation allowance 通货膨胀津贴
contingency costs 意外事故成本
off-site construction 现场施工
temporary works 临时工程
manipulation 操纵，操控
assessment of financial performance 财务业绩评价
overruns 超出限度，泛滥成灾
encounter 遭遇，遇到，碰到
expense oriented construction planning 以费用为导向的规划建设
category 种类，类别；范畴
assume 假设；认为，认定
project performance reviews 项目绩效考核
work packages 工作包
milestones 里程碑
associated 相关的，有关联的
cash flow 现金流量
completion 完成，结束；实现
planned value 计划值
expected value 期望值
ascertain 确定，确认
conformance 符合；顺应，一致性
variance analysis 方差分析
unauthorized 未经授权的
computerized 使电脑化，使计算化；用电脑处理
cost accounting 成本会计
simulation 仿真；模拟，模仿
cost-performance data 性价比数据
deviate 偏离，偏向
potential claims 潜在的要求
additional payments 额外的支付

contingency sum 应急金额，应急资金
discretion 自由裁决权；考虑周到；谨慎，判断力
conformity with 符合；顺应，一致性
be subject to 服从，顺从
implication 影响；暗示；牵连，卷入；含义
be incorporated into 纳入

Exercises

I. Choose the best answer according to the text.

1. From the information generated in the progress of the project, cost management _____.
   A. should be not only to identify past trends
   B. but also forecast the likely consequence of future decisions including final out-turn cost
   C. helps the project team to better establish the appropriate project contract strategy
   D. should be placed in which contract and possibly the form of contract be adopted

2. The relationship between the output of a process and the necessary resources is referred to as _____.
   A. the amount
   B. the volume
   C. the production function
   D. the input labor

3. The total cost is the summation of the products of _____.
   A. the quantities division by the corresponding unit costs
   B. the quantities multiplied by the corresponding unit costs
   C. the corresponding unit costs multiplied by the quantities
   D. B or C

4. Construction cost control consists basically of _____.
   A. monitoring actual performance against cost estimates
   B. identifying variances
   C. pertaining to the project
   D. A or B

5. Cost control includes: _____.
   A. project performance review
   B. variance analysis
   C. project management software
   D. above all

II. Decide the following statements are true or false.

1. With an effective company-wide cost-control system this would result in substantial risk to any contractor's slender margins.

Unit 6 Project Cost Estimate and Cost Control

2. These are all predictions and should not be considered 100% accurate, but the degree of realism and confidence achieved will depend on the level of definition of the work and the extent of the risk and uncertainty.

3. The unit cost method is straightforward in application but quite laborious in principle.

4. The accuracy of a cost estimate of a project will improve as the project progresses through its life cycle.

5. The cost implications of time and quality should be corporate into the decision-making process.

III. Change the following words to another form and write down the Chinese meanings.

1. application _____
2. efficient _____
3. out-turn cost _____
4. execution _____
5. attributes _____
6. parameter _____
7. constants _____
8. laborious _____
9. break down _____
10. classified _____

IV. Give out the following words' synonym or other word in the closest meaning.

1. issuing   a. out-run cost
2. account   b. may not exist
3. disaggregate   c. classified
4. cannot be identified   d. monitor
5. allocated   e. break down
6. control   f. changes
7. in general   g. finish
8. variances   h. conformity with
9. completion   i. publishing
10. conformance with   j. all in all

V. Put the following English into Chinese.

1. Keeping a project within budget depends on the application of an efficient and effective system of cost control. From the information generated in the progress of the project, cost management should be not only to identify past trends but also forecast the likely consequence of future decisions including final out-turn cost, that is, the final account.

2. Major projects often have substantial elements that are unique and for which there is no relevant historic data. The role of statistical inference is to estimate the best parameter values or constants in an assumed cost function.

3. Activity-based, detailed or unit cost estimates are typically the most definitive of the estimating techniques and use information down to the lowest level of detail available.

4. It is necessary to analyze the project in as many individual work sections as can be identified, if possible, to prepare indicative quantities and consider the resources necessary to carry out the work, include location of project and access thereto, especially with regard to heavy and large loads, availability of labor and the possible need of accommodation for workmen, off-site construction, temporary works.

5. Compares actual project performance to planned or expected value, examines project performance over time to determine if performance is improving, expenses incurred during the course of a project are recorded in specific work elements cost accounts to be compared with the original cost estimates in each category to ascertain if the budget is under control.

VI. Put the following Chinese into English.

1. 实证成本推理
2. 建设施工监理
3. 企业财务业绩评价
4. 项目绩效考核
5. 费用为导向的规划建设

参 考 译 文

第6单元 项目成本估算和成本控制

1. 项目成本管理

成本管理远远不只是简单地记录支出情况，以及发布成本报告。成本管理是指了解成本如何和为什么发生并且迅速地根据所有相关信息采取必要的回应。只有应用高效率和有效果的成本控制系统，才能使项目保持在预算之内。从产生于项目进展中的信息，成本管理不应当仅仅去识别过去的动向，而且还要预测未来决策的可能后果，包括最后的收入成本，即决算。成本管理有助于项目小组更好地制订恰当的项目合同策略，同时成本管理应当被置于合同及合同被采纳的情形之中。成本管理也有助于在合同的准备和履行两方面鉴别可能的方案限制。如果没有一个有效的公司范围内的成本控制系统，任何承包商都可能只能获得微薄的利润。

2. 项目成本预算

成本估算是项目管理中最重要的步骤之一。在项目发展的不同阶段，成本预算组成都是项目成本的基础；此外，成本和时间的预算在项目周期的许多阶段都会进行准备和修正。这些预测不应当被认为是100%精确，但是成本预算的可靠性和所获得的信任将取决于对项目范围、风险范围和不确定性的确定程度。成本估算的原则和技巧被用于针对成本估价、成本控制和盈利性问题的科学手段应用上。实际上，所有成本预算都根据下列基本途径的一种或其组合来实施。

2.1 生产量函数

在工序的产出和必要的资源之间的关系被定义为生产量函数。在施工当中,生产函数把产出的总额或者数量与劳动、材料和设备的各种投入联系起来。建设项目的规模(以平方米表示)与劳动投入(以每平方米劳动小时数表示)之间的关系就是一个针对施工的生产量函数的例子。

2.2 经验成本方法

成本函数的经验估算需要统计技术,该技术把建造或者运营一个设施的成本与少数几个重要的估算系统特征或者属性联系起来。首次估算将以多种技巧为基础,例如历史数据或近似工程量。重大项目常常具有基本的独特要素,且对于这种要素来说,没有相关的历史数据。统计推断的作用是在一个假定成本函数中去估计最好的参数值或者常数。通常,这一点是通过回归分析技巧的方式来完成的。

2.3 对于工程量清单的单位成本

单位成本被分配给工程量清单所显示的每一个设施组件或者每一项任务。总成本是产品数量与相应的单位成本相乘的总和。单位成本法的原理简单易懂,但在应用上却十分费时费力。最初就是把一个过程分类或者分解成许多任务。建立任务分解结构(WBS)即将项目可交付产品和项目工程细分为更小和更易控制的任务成分。以协同的方式,这些任务必须针对一个设施的施工来完成。一旦这些任务被规定且表示这些任务的数量被核定,一个单位成本就被分配给每个任务,然后总成本就由每个任务所引起的成本的求和来决定。在分解成任务的过程中,细节层次将在一个估算到另一个估算之间有相当大的变化。

2.4 联合成本的分配

来自现存账户的成本分配可以被用于生成某项任务的价值函数。这种方式的基本理念是,每项支出可以归因于运营任务的特性。然而,在许多情况下,分配因素和成本项目之间的因果关系不能被鉴别或者可能不存在。例如,在建筑项目中,对于基本成本的账户可以分类并按比例分配到各种任务中,这些工作是对项目的细分。它通常按照以下内容细分:

- ➢ 人工;
- ➢ 材料;
- ➢ 施工机械;
- ➢ 施工监督;
- ➢ 总管理费。

2.5 详细估算法

基于活动性的详细的或单位成本预算是典型的最具决定性的估算技术,且使用最低层面的详细信息。它们也是最被理解和使用的估算技术。基于活动性的详细的或单位成本技术的精确性取决于可用信息的精确性、消耗在开展成本估算上的资源和估价基础的有效性。工作报告、工程图纸或者规范可用来鉴别那些弥补项目的活动。每项活动被进一步分解成详细条目(WBS),这样劳动小时数、材料成本、设备成本及分包成本就可以被条目化和量化。

成本预算必须考虑工程的全部成本,包括劳动、材料、设备、服务、设施、通胀补贴或者不可预见费用。此外，为了达到更好的项目管理目的，成本预算也必须考虑引起决算变化的原因及不同成本计算的替代方案。应尽可能地将项目进行分析并详细划分分项工程，如果可能的话，还要对工程量与完成项目的必要资源进行考虑，包括项目的位置和进入的通道，尤其是有关重大装载(设备、机械)，劳动力可用性和工人可能的住宿需要，工地外施工及临时工程。随着项目进展和工程情况明朗化，成本预算可能增加或者减少。项目的成本预算的精确性将随项目周期进度的发展而提高。

3. 成本控制

成本控制涉及对项目所有成本的操纵和分析。成本控制也是针对可盈利而用于记录、比较、跟踪和引起项目成本的一种方法或系统。对于控制和监测的目的而言，原始的详细成本预算代表性地转变成了一种项目预算，且项目预算随后作为(成本)管理指导。最终或详细的成本估算为评估项目期间的财务状况提供了一个基准。某种程度上，如果项目造价包括在详细成本预算之内，则项目被认为已处于财务控制之中。某些项目类别的成本超支情况会表露出可能的问题并且确切显现遇到的问题的迹象。以开支为导向的施工计划和控制以被包含在最终成本预算里的各项目类别为焦点。

总的来说，施工成本控制基本上由对成本预算与实际项目执行的(成本)监测和对(成本)偏差的识别所组成。基于偏差的观察成本控制方法似乎可以这样假设，(成本)偏差的原因将会很明显，且适宜的改正措施也将显而易见。成本控制包括：

3.1 项目执行情况审查

项目执行情况评审就是将施工成本与时间、进度工作或者所有工程项目、计划成本及计划日期进行对比。施工计划和相关的现金流估算可以为后续的项目监控提供基准参考点。对于进度计划，把单独的工作进度和完成的计划日期与项目进度计划进行对比可以监控工作进度。把实际项目执行情况与计划成本或拟完成成本进行对比，在一段时间内检验项目执行状况以确定项目执行状况是否在改善。在项目进程期间已发生费用是否在明确的工作类别成本账户中记录，该费用将与在每个类别中的原成本预算进行对比，从而清楚项目预算是否处于控制之中。两个相关结果的预测分析从定期的成本监控中获得：

➢ 如果确认任一项工程其实际成本将超出预算成本，然后采取行动设法使其工程成本与预算成本相一致；

➢ 项目在竣工时的总成本预算，以目前的成本记录和拟完成成本去完成未完工程的成本为基础。

3.2 成本偏差分析

成本偏差分析的目的是描述怎样处置成本偏差，比如监控实际成本去查明和理解计划成本的偏差，确保变更按时执行，防止非授权的变更的执行，管理实际应对变更，然后确保成本偏差在可接受范围随着项目进展而减小。

3.3 项目管理软件

项目管理预算软件是计算机化的成本会计和综合成本控制系统，该系统用于跟踪计划成本与实际成本的比值，且预测成本变化的结果。项目管理软件电子数据表和模拟/统计工具广泛用于辅助成本预算，且它可以简化技术和设施的使用，以更快捷的计算替代方案成本的考虑，提供一种以及时的方式将预算费用与实际费用进行对比的方法，开发一个以生产量和成本状况来评估执行成本偏离项目预算的数据库，生成可以计量对合同工程的变更和能增加付款的潜在索赔的数据。

4. 总结

综上所述，有效的成本控制管理应当包括如下特征：
- ➢ 对于项目的详细预算，设置一笔项目经理可以支配的不可预见的费用；
- ➢ 在做出决定前进行成本预测，以便考虑所有的可能行动过程；
- ➢ 成本记录系统操作起来应当很划算，且实际成本应当与在任何恰当时期所预测的成本进行对比，以确保与预算一致，如果必要的话，可以采取纠正措施；
- ➢ 对项目实际成本应进行偏差分析，以查明与项目预算的任何偏离；
- ➢ 对时间和质量的隐含成本应当纳入决策过程。

阅读

工程量清单

1. 工程量清单的目的

列置工程量清单有如下目的。
- ➢ 对实施的工程量提供足够的信息，以便能高效和精确地准备标书；
- ➢ 签署合同时，提供标价的工程量清单，以便对完成工程量进行定期计量。

为了达到这些目的，工程应当以足够的细节在工程量清单中条目化，以区别不同类别的工作，或者区别相同性质的工作在不同位置或其他情形下可能导致的不同成本考虑。为了与这些要求一致，工程量清单的布置和内容应当尽可能简单并简短。

2. 工程量清单的组成

工程量清单通常由以下几部分组成：
- ➢ 序言；
- ➢ 工程事项(归纳成几个部分)；
- ➢ 计日工价格表；
- ➢ 总结。

2.1 序言

序言应当指出单价包含的内容，且陈述在准备工程量清单过程中所采用的测量方法，以及被用于测量工程任何部分的测量方法。
- ➢ 工程量清单应当与《投标人须知》、通用和特殊合同条件、技术规范和工程图纸结合起来阅读。
- ➢ 在工程量清单中给出的工程量是估算的、暂定的，为投标提供一个平等的基础。付款要根据要求和完成的实际工程量，由承包商计量而且由工程师核实，如果价格适用，以标书中标价工程量清单中的费用或单价来进行费用计量，否则，单价可能由工程师按照合同条款确定。

> 在标书中标价的工程量清单中的费用或价格，除了按合同条款另外表明，还应当包括施工机械设备、人工、监督、材料、装配、维护、保险、利润、税费和关税，以及所有普遍风险、责任和义务，这些都是在合同中表明或隐含的。

> 在标价工程量清单中，无论工程量是否有，应当逐项填写费用或价格。承包商未能填报费用或价格的项目，将被认为包括在工程量清单中填报的其他项目的费用和价格中。

> 按照合同条款的完全费用将包含在标价工程量清单所提供的项目里，且在没有提供项目的情况下，这项费用被认为是分配给了填报的其他相关工作项目的费用和价格。

> 对工作和材料的一般说明和描述没有必要在工程量清单中重复，也没有必要总结。填报标价工程量清单里的每个项目的价格，必须参考合同文件的相关部分。

> 指定包括在工程量清单中的暂定金额将根据合同条件在工程师的指导和支配下全部或部分开支。

> 针对付款的完成工程的测量方法将依据[SMM7 建筑工程(国际)测量原则(1979 年 6 月出版，1988 年、1991 年、1994 年、2001 年、2002 年、2004 年再版)，由英国皇家特许测量师学会出版，有适合各地实际和条件的修订版。测量方法：SMM7；CESMM；测量和范围原则]。

> 在计算与总和中的任何运算错误将由雇主进行纠正。列举如下：

● 如果小写金额和大写金额有不符，则执行大写金额；

● 如果单价和单价与数量相乘的总额不符，将执行所报出的单价，除非在雇主看来，在单价中有明显的小数点错放的情况，在该情形中，所报出的总额将起支配作用，且单价将被纠正。

> 在工程师看来，岩石被定义为所有这样的材料，它们需要爆破，或者需要使用金属楔和大锤，或者需要风钻使其移走，并且，通过带有后挂式的和重型的凿裂齿且用至少 150 制动马力的牵引机进行冲破，它们也不能被取出。

2.2 工作项目

工程量清单中的项目应当被归类成许多部分，以通过性质、位置、通道、时间安排或者其他任何特殊特征，在那些工程的组成部分之间进行辨别，这些组成部分可能导致不同的施工方法、工程分段安排或者费用考虑。工程所有部分共同的通用项目可能被归类成工程量清单中的单独部分。当使用一组价格调整公式时，它们将涉及工程量清单中的合适部分。工程量清单通常包含下列的部分清单，这些清单根据工程的性质和时间安排(例如)归类如下：

清单 1——一般事项(通用费项目)。

清单 2——下部结构(它包括地下室和地基开凿；墙墩；桩；基座；横梁和条形基础；基墙；反梁；碎石填充；板及防潮或其他隔膜；地面结构；地下排水；管道井；坑；底部和地下管道；入口台阶；斜坡及其面层；地板平面上的台阶和斜坡；结构找平层和保护层；有顶游泳池；所有其他工程但不包括在最低地板处的面层)。

清单 3——上部结构。

清单 4——墙体。
清单 5——屋面结构。
清单 6——建筑装饰。
清单 7——杂项(它可能包括来自建筑物外部表明的管道；检修井；集水坑；道路沟渠；涵洞；方沟；带格栅深沟；来自水池和喷泉的出水口；出水口和拱面墙；农用和地下排水沟；与现有出口和井点的连接)。
清单 8——现场工程(它包括拆毁；场地清理；一般整平和填充；临时围篱；挡土墙；路面石、树木和公共设施的移除；公共临时设施管道的改向；临近建筑支护)。

2.3 工程量

工程量应当从图纸进行净计算，除非以另外方式在合同中做了规定，且针对增量、缩水或者浪费没有进行补贴。在适当的地方，工程量应当以四舍五入法来计算，且应当规避伪造的精确性。(《标准测量方法》修订第七版：SMM7)

推荐使用下列测量单位和缩写形式(除非雇主所在国家强制使用其他单位)。

单位	缩写形式	单位	缩写形式
立方米	m^3 or cu m	毫米	mm
公顷	ha	月份	mon
小时	h	数目	nr
千克	kg	平方米	m^2 or sq m
一次所付款项	sum	平方	mm^2 or sq mm
米	m	毫米	wk
公吨 (1,000 kg)	t	星期	

2.4 计日工价格表

除了包含在工程量清单中的事项之外，如果不可预见工作相对较多，则计日工价格表应当包括在内。为方便雇主对投标人所报价格的真实性进行核查，计日工价格表通常包含：

➢ 由投标人(承包商)填入的人工、材料和机械设备费用和价格的计日工价格表清单，承包商将在各类工作情况下按照计日工价格表对实施的工作而获得付款；

➢ 投标人可以按照人工、材料和机械设备的计日工价格表对每个项目小计计入一定百分比例的代表承包商利润、管理费、监督和其他费用。

2.5 暂定工程量和金额

对任何预计工程量很有可能超量的特定项目或工作类别的意外工程量，应在工程量清单中计入特定的"暂定工程量"或"暂定项目"，而不是对那些超过预期要求项目或工作类别增加工程量。就以上没有涵盖的范围来说，通用的不可预见费用(工程量超量)应当把"暂定款项"包含到工程量清单的合计中。类似地，对于可能的价格上涨的不可预见费用补贴，应当把"暂定款项"列在工程量清单的合计中。将来需要时，包含这样的"暂定款项"常常可以免于做定期的补充，而便于获得预算批准。

附有简要说明的专业工程或者专业设施(由指定分包商完成)的预算费用应当在工程量清单的相关部分里作为特别的"暂列款项"。单独的挑选专业分包商的投标程序通常由雇主操作，这些专业分包商将被指定为总包商分包商。为了保证在主投标人(总包商)中所有的设备、设施和服务等的竞争，由成功的投标人作为总包商向专业分包商或者指定分包商提供便利和服务，总包商按照工程量清单中的项目对每项有关的"暂列款项"，填报一定比例(由主投标人报价)的服务费，并依照"暂列款项"实际费用进行(由雇主)支付。

2.6 总计

总计应当包含前面所提的工程量清单单独部分的表格，如适用，还需附有暂定计日工合计，意外(工程量)费用，以及意外价格费用的"暂列款项"(向上调整价格)。

Unit 7

Project Contract Management

1. Introduction

Contract management plays a significant role in construction project management system, since construction project management involves groups of people representing different disciplines, from project managers, contract managers, and division managers to subcontractors, architects, engineers, suppliers, and clients—all trying to collaborate on a multitude of issues and changes while juggling multiple documents and contracts. From the signing of the contract, the implementation of the contract, and finally the termination of the contract, main contractor must guarantee the project running smoothly and they receive the final expected result.

Construction contract management involves the activities necessary to effect and determine the fulfillment of the contract requirements by the parties to the construction contract. Construction contract management begins when the agreement between the employer and contractor is executed and ends when final payment is accepted by the contractor.

Contract managers must monitor cost, scope, quality, and time frame and must ensure that all contract conditions are met. This important work affects both the financial and the actual success of the project or company. Contract management must ensure that:

- the employer's interests are protected and its obligations are met;
- the contractual obligations of the service provider are met;
- contract milestones are duly discharged;
- key deliverables are received;
- contract related processes are completed;
- any variations, claims, issues, disputes, and any additional funding requirements are managed.

2. The Targets of Contract Management

The important targets of a contract are to manage the contract within the following constraints:

- time
- cost
- quality

Cost is the responsibility of quantity surveyor whether you are contractor's quantity surveyor or the consultant's quantity surveyor. There is a close relationship between planning and management. The quantity surveyor uses the bill of quantity as the management tool in managing the project.

In managing the time of a construction project, a construction program prepared by the contractor and accepted by the engineer is used to manage the time, since the all activities required to complete the project is identified, and relationships between different activities and durations are identified and can be easily monitored. If deviations occur, the remedial action could be taken to mitigate the delay. There is a close relationship between cost and time. Delay in the completion of the project inevitably means increases in cost. The costs on a project depend on the quantity of the work, duration of the work and site establishment costs. Moreover, it is apparent that nonconformance of quality will cause many secondary problems such as schedule delay, cost overruns, sub-contractor insolvency etc.

3. The Contract Documents

Incomplete or inaccurate contract documents require additional time and effort on the part of project participants, and progress may be delayed while interpretations or revisions are being prepared. Contract modifications are typically required to resolve issues resulting from incomplete or inaccurate contract documents. The time and effort required to prepare and respond to the contract modifications may distract contractor from concentrating on the project. Negotiating price and time revisions often result in disagreement or conflict.

3.1 Contract Documents

The contract documents are listed and enumerated in the agreement and referred to in the conditions of the contract for the work to be performed. They are the legal documents which describe the work requirement. The contract documents describe the proposed construction works that result from performing services, furnishing labor, and supplying and incorporating materials and equipment into the construction works.

3.2 Contracts and Agreements

Contract documents consist of both written and graphic elements and typically include the following:

These include contracting forms (agreement) and conditions of the contract (general and supplementary conditions, or employer furnished general or particular special conditions) as well as various named attachments and forms. Revisions, clarifications, and modifications are changes applicable to the contract documents such as addenda issued during the procurement process or change orders issued during the course of the work.

3.3 Specifications

These include specific written requirements for the work. Specifications define the quality requirements for products, materials, and workmanship upon which the contract is based and establish requirements for administration and performance of the project.

3.4 Contract Drawings

Contract drawings are those named in the agreement and can be supplemented by various forms of interpretations and modifications including small-size sketches. These include large graphic illustrations of the physical form of the work to be performed. They show the quantitative extent and relationships of elements to one another. They help to establish the extent of the work and are complementary with the specifications. Contract drawings are generally bound separately because of their larger size.

3.5 Record Drawings

The contract documents may require record drawings. Often the architect may issue new versions of drawings to indicate changes and field conditions. Concealed conditions and utility locations are the most common information required. The contract documents indicate the type of information required to be included on the record drawings. These record drawings are as a permanent record of the actual conditions of the completed work.

There are several types of drawings, reports, and specifications that may be utilized during construction but may not be included with the contract documents. These may include surveys, hazardous material reports, assessments, and geotechnical data. The contract documents are interrelated and they provide different types of information required to carry out the work.

The contract documents consist of in order of precedence the following:
- Letter of acceptance
- Contract agreement
- MOU if any
- Particular conditions of contract
- Contract data
- General conditions of contract
- Copies of guarantees and bonds
- Insurance
- Drawings
- Specifications
- Bills of quantities
- Any other pertaining documents

4. The Main Objects of Contract Management

4.1 Finance Management

The main tasks of financial management include resource planning, cost estimation, cost planning, and cost control. Before signing a contract, everything possible has to be taken into account, to assure that every party has their own responsibilities lined up more specifically than their financial obligations. According to the cost planning, measures would be taken to correct any deviations that are bound to occur, maximize the financial benefit for the project.

4.2 Subcontract Management

It will probably take a huge amount of the main contractor's time and energy to manage subcontractors, including designated sub-contractor, nominated subcontractor and domestic subcontractors. The main contractor takes equivalent responsibilities or obligations consistent with those undertaken by any subcontractor. The main contractor may be held liable for defective work carried out by a subcontractor and responsible for the acts, defaults and neglects of any subcontractor as fully as if they were deemed as the defaults or neglects of the main contractor. The main contractor is also responsible for health and safety on the building site.

4.3 Progress Management

A construction contract will generally set a period for completion of the works. That period may be specified in the tender documents or otherwise agreed with the contractor before a contract is awarded. The contract may impose liquidated damages, in the form of a charge per day or per week on the contractor, for failing to meet the specified completion time. In order to finish the project on time, the importance of progress management is to makes sure certain tasks are finished on schedule.

Tasks in progress management include schedule making, project follow-ups, schedule updates, and reports. These tasks usually take place in the control department, and are assorted into the engineering department, the procurement department, the construction department, and the quality department. If a delay occurs that is not within the contractor's control, the main contractor is entitled to request for the time for completion to be extended.

4.4 Quality Management

Maintaining good quality is one of the main objectives of construction management in addition to meeting designated schedule and cost. In addition, quality is one of the important factors considered when determining the success of a project. Quality in construction projects can be classified in various ways. There are various objects and methods of quality control according to phases of the project life cycle. Quality management includes the processes required to ensure that the project will satisfy the needs for which it was undertaken. It includes all activities of the overall management function that determine the quality policy, objectives, and responsibilities and implements them by means such as quality planning, quality control, quality assurance, and quality improvement, within the quality system. Documentation quality management contributes to the smoothness or otherwise of the construction process, and may influence cost and time to a degree.

4.5 Health, Safety, and Environment Management

The target of health, safety, and environment management is to guarantee people's health and safety, protect nature, reduce pollution, and stimulate sustainable development. When a project management organization is established, the parties' obligations are largely set out in the contract documents, however, there are also regulatory requirements created by government law that will not be specified in the contract documents. The regulatory requirements of the health, safety, and environment protection are different in different countries. The contractor is liable for compliance with all statutory requirements, if the contractor just follow the domestic requirements without paying attention to the local requirements; this may cause the project to fail when examined. The contractor is responsible for the giving of all notices necessary to comply with regulatory requirements and the payment of all necessary fees, charges and other imposts, other than those notices and imposts to be given or paid by the client under the contract.

4.6 Managing Variations and Claims

If the client's representative or engineer instructs (directs) a variation, the contractor is obliged to carry out the instruction. A variation becomes part of the contract and all the contract conditions apply to the changed work, including provisions for extensions of time and site conditions (if applicable). There is a risk that actions of the client may delay the completion of a construction contract, thus it is therefore important to manage variations effectively in order to reduce the risk of exceeding the budget and completing the project late. Variations are one of the main reasons for cost and time overruns in construction contracts (please refer to last unit for more information).

The contractor will be entitled to claims for additional payment and for an extension to the period for completion following a variation instruction. The additional payment may include additional costs for delay, acceleration and/or disruption associated with the variation. Construction contracts involve various matters for which the contractor may make a claim against the client. Most frequently, these claims are for payment and/or additional time. Claims for additional payment can arise for a multitude of reasons including disputes over variations, changes in circumstances, prolongation claims and disruption claims.

5. Summary

In brief, contract management should contain the following characteristics:
- Control construction project's contracts, budgets, forecast costs, and deliverables;
- Collaborate between project managers, contract managers, administrators, subcontractors, architects, engineers, suppliers, and clients;
- Ensure project changes are resolved, payment is made, and claims are avoided;
- Be prepared for the unexpected and have the information necessary to negotiate cost and schedule details to final resolution;
- Track daily reports, meeting minutes, and materials delivered against purchase orders;
- Instantly reflect cost or schedule impact of any change, and identify which contractors are impacted;
- Analyze comparative trends and cause/effect among projects to maximize efficiency while minimizing project costs, risks and safety issues;

➢ Manage, implement, administer, conduct, and guide effective contracts administration function for the organization from proposal through contract close.

Reading

Business Message Writing

1. Prewriting

The exchange of information is basic to business. Without it business could not function. Every transaction needs communication. The message is a common business communication medium. If business writers want to send successful business message, they should always keep in mind that they are going to have a talk with their audience. The prewriting stage is to work out a message they want to send. Before business writers put thoughts and ideas down on paper, they should conduct research, gather data, or collect any information they need to write the message. The writers of business message should consider these questions before they begin to write.

➢ Purpose: What is my purpose of writing? What is my objective?
➢ Audience: Who is my audience, and what response do I expect?
➢ Length: How long should this message be? Or how long does it need to be?
➢ Medium: What form is best for this message—letter/fax, memo, email message?

It is important to outline the ideas and organize their thoughts before writing; the prewriting stage is also the time to determine the objective and main idea of the message, so as to make sure the writing is focused and effective.

2. Planning Business Message

In addition to considering audience, length and medium for a business message, business writers must also determine the main idea, choose supporting information and adjust the message for the audience or receiver.

2.1 Identify the Objective

The objective is what they want to achieve through a message. The objective may be to
➢ promote good will which is a principle of vital significance;
➢ inform what is the urgent matter for advancing of the project;
➢ request what should be instructed by Engineer or Client;
➢ record a memo what has been decided by Engineer or Client verbally;
➢ persuade Client to hold a meeting to discuss about the recent change of the works.

2.2 Determine the Main Idea

After determine the objective of a message, the next step is to identify the main idea. The main idea is the central theme or the most important thought which the message is to convey to the audience, or receiver.

2.3 Choose Supporting Information

Supporting information includes essential facts that explain, reinforce, or justify the main idea in terms receivers can understand and from which they can benefit. As writers gather information during the prewriting stage, they should keep receivers needs in mind, and think over what receivers need to know to be able to respond to the message.

2.4 Adjust the Message for the Receiver

When adjusting the content of a message, the writers should put themselves in the place the receivers. Through empathy, the writers can see the situation from the receivers' perspective and compose the message accordingly. Considerate messages address the receivers' level of interest, involvement, or opinions regarding the subject. Considerate messages use supporting information that receivers will benefit from understanding and appreciation.

3. Nonverbal Symbols in Written Messages

The appearance and correctness of a written document as well as the timeliness of the response send critical nonverbal messages and deserve careful attention. Letterhead stationery, plain sheets, and envelopes should be made of high-quality bond paper and have the same color. The typefaces and design of the letterhead and logo should convey a professional image. Drawings, photographs, charts, and graphs should be appropriate to the content and enhance the message. The print should be crisp and easy to read.

Documents should not include any errors in capitalization, grammar, number expression, punctuation, spelling, or word usage. Accurate content, especially amounts, addresses, and other facts, is essential. Error-free documents send a nonverbal message that the sender is reliable and considers quality important. Documents that contain errors send a negative message about the sender.

Example of Claim letter to Client

21 November 2001

The Project Director
Jade Real Estate Development Company
5th Floor, 18 Kent Street
Pretoria
South Africa
Attention: Mr. Andrew Smith

Dear Sir,
Re.: St. James Court Project-Delayed Payment and Variations Claim

Please refer to our monthly statement No.11, which was submitted on 10th August 2001 to your quantity surveyor Mr. Michael Robert, who is on behalf of Jackson & Michael Quantity Surveyor Associates to certify our payment statement. We noticed, with regret, that there was a big difference between our application and quantity surveyor's corresponding certification and the certified amount was far less than we applied. We must forward to you, the client, herewith our complaints on following aspects:

1. Variations Claim

The variations claim has been the most serious issue in our statement, because some of the variations orders were instructed by architect or the client verbally without writing instructions, although we sent out our letters promptly to the architect to confirm concerned works with necessary evidences while we were carrying out those works. Still we are waiting for the formal confirmations to obtain certification from Jackson & Michael Quantity Surveyor Associates. Your quantity surveyor: Mr. Michael Robert insists that all variations claim should be presented together with necessary supporting documents and evidences stipulated in the contract, thus most of the variations claims were consequently neglected. On the telephone conversation with the architect and the quantity surveyor, we are aware that an acceptable settlement will be reached for implementation of arrangements in the coming project meeting among the client, the architect and the quantity surveyor; we hope the outcome will acceptable to us as well.

2. Delayed Interim Payments

We must remind you that the interim payments are not advancing with the progress step of the project in accordance with the contract too. Our monthly statement is usually certified two or three months later than the agreed tempo in terms of the principle in the contract, therefore, the interim payments are delayed accordingly. We believe there is a growing trend for the deteriorated situation as the variations claim accumulated. We thence reiterate our statement of payments and claims for the project to be reviewed and expedited without further delay.

3. Nonperformance of Nominated Subcontractors

The another serious issue we must address is the poor performance of nominated subcontractors, namely, IBL Lift Co. Ltd., Super Window & Door Co. Ltd. and Smart Intercom Co. Ltd., they are holding up the overall progress of the building and interrupting the programme of the project for several weeks, although we have raised this issue on various occasions to you, we perceived no improvement of their performance so far. As you know these nominated subcontractors remain fully paid, controlled and directed by the client. We must point out that we will take no responsibility for the delay caused by those nominated subcontractors as they are beyond our power and command, furthermore, we will reserve the right to claim for the time extension and consequence damages.

In conclusion, we wish the client will arrange a meeting with the presence of the architect, quantity surveyor and us to work out the difference among all the parties and solve the problems of the project being suffering. We have already demonstrated our preparedness to cooperate with all the parties; we are maintaining the performance and delivery of the services to the general satisfactory level though we are in difficult financial situation due to delayed interim payments.

Our clear intention is to take a positive approach of suggestion to the negotiations and, given an appropriate timetable for negotiations and other processes. We believe the claims we have made will be justified, as all the variations claims have been substantiated with detailed documents, and all the works were measured by the Jackson & Michael Quantity Surveyor Associates.

We are awaiting your comment on above.

Yours sincerely

Ralph Groves
General Construction Co. Ltd.
Quantity Surveyor
C.C.: Mr. Francis Lim—ARC Architect & Consultancy
　　　Mr. Michael Robert—Jackson & Michael Quantity Surveyor Associates
Ralph Groves

New Words and Expressions

objective 目标，目的；目标的，客观的
discipline 学科，纪律，惩罚；训练，训导
project managers 项目管理
contract managers 合同管理
subcontractors 分包商
clients 合作者，顾客
multitude 多数，群众
juggling 欺骗的，变戏法的；欺骗，杂耍
multiple 多重的，许多的；关联，倍数
document 文件，证件，文档；用文件证明
signing of the contract 签订合同
implementation 履行，实现；安装启用
termination 结束，终止
scope 规模，范围，跨度
conditions 条件，状况；困境
obligations 义务，责任，职责
contractual 合同的，契约的
discharged 免除，放出；排除，流出
deliverable 可交付使用的，可以传达的
claim 索赔，声称；主张，要求
quantity surveyor 预算师或造价师

bill of quantity 工料清单，工程量清单
contractor 承包商
identified 识别的，辨别的，辨认的
deviation 偏差；偏离，偏向
remedial 补救的，治疗的；矫正的
mitigate 减轻，缓和下来；使缓和，使减轻
delay 耽搁，延误
duration 持续
contract documents 合同文件
precedence 优先，居先
letter of acceptance 接收函
mou 谅解备忘录
bond 约定，债券；结合，团结在一起
specifications 规格，详细说明
pertaining 有关的，附属的；关于
finance management 财务管理
taken into account 考虑，思考，认为
financial obligations 财务责任
maximize 使最大化，使最大限度
financial benefit for the project 项目的财务效益
subcontract management 分包管理
designated subcontractor 指定分包商
nominated subcontractor 指定分包商
domestic subcontractors 国内分包商
undertaken 承担；着手，开始
consistent with 符合，一致性；遵守
defaults 违约；拖欠，不到场；缺席，缺乏
defective 有缺陷的，不完美的
building site 建筑场地
progress management 进度管理
tender documents 招标文件
liquidated 已偿付的
specified completion time 指定的完成时间
project follow-ups 工程随访
schedule updates 时间表的更新
control department 控制部门
engineering department 工程部门
procurement department 采购部门
construction department 建设部门

the time for completion 竣工时间
satisfy 满足，满意
quality assurance 质量保证
comply with 满足，符合；遵守，遵照
unsatisfactory performance 不理想的业绩
sustainable development 可持续发展
regulatory requirements 监管要求
be liable for 承担，负有责任和义务
compliance with 满足，符合；遵守，遵照
statutory requirements 法规要求，法令要求
be responsible for 承担，负有责任和义务
impost 关税，税款
other than 而不是
claims 要求，声称；索赔，主张
be obliged to 有义务的，有责任的
site conditions 场地条件，场地状况
provision 规定，准备；供给食物及必需品
client 委托人
overruns 超出限度；泛滥成灾
acceleration 加速，促进；加速度
disruption 分裂，瓦解；破坏，毁坏
make a claim against the client 索赔客户
prolongation 延长，延长部分；延期
purchase orders 订单
comparative trends 比较趋势

Exercises

I. Choose the best answer according to the text.

1. According to the text, contract managers must monitor _____.

    A. cost, scope, quality

    B. time frame

    C. ensures that all contract conditions are met

    D. above all

2. The important targets of a contract are to manage the contract with in the following constraints _____.

    A. time and cost

    B. cost and quality

    C. time, cost and quality

    D. time, cost, quality and progress

3. The main aspects of Contract Management are _____.

    A. finance management and subcontract management

    B. quality management and health, safety, and environment management

    C. managing variations and claims

    D. A, B and C

4. We learn from the passage that contract management should contain the following characteristics _____.

    A. control construction project's contracts, budgets, forecast costs, and deliverables

    B. instantly reflect cost or schedule impact of any change, and identify which contractors are impacted

    C. analyze comparative trends and cause/effect among projects to maximize efficiency while minimizing project costs, risks and safety issues

    D. above all

II. Decide the following statements are true or false.

1. From the signing of the contract, the implementation of the contract, and finally the termination of the contract, main contractor must guarantee the project runs smoothly and they receive the final expected result.

2. Delay in the completion of the project evitable means increases in cost.

3. If a delay occurs that is within the contractor's control, the main contractor is entitled to request for the time for completion to be extended.

4. The contractor will be entitled to claims for additional payment and for an extension to the period for completion following a variation instruction.

III. Change the following words to another form and write down the Chinese meanings.

1. multitude _____
2. implementation _____
3. termination _____
4. obligations _____
5. deliverables _____
6. project _____
7. eliminate _____
8. stimulate _____
9. statutory _____
10. applicable _____

IV. Give out the following words' synonym or other word in the closest meaning.

1. significant   a. obligations

2. objectives   b. complete

3. depend on   c. directs

4. responsibilities
5. taken into account
6. completion
7. instructs
8. consistent with
9. is liable for
10. clients

d. crucial
e. comply with
f. targets
g. is responsible for
h. customers
i. consideration
j. rely on

V. Put the following English into Chinese.

1. In managing the time of a construction project, a construction program prepared by the contractor and accepted by the engineer is used to manage the time, since the all activities required to complete the project is identified, and relationships between different activities and durations are identifies and can be easily monitored.

2. The main contractor may be held liable for defective work carried out by a subcontractor and responsible for the acts, defaults and neglects of any subcontractor as fully as if they were deemed as the defaults or neglects of the main contractor.

3. The contractor is responsible for the giving of all notices necessary to comply with regulatory requirements and the payment of all necessary fees, charges and other imposts, other than those notices and imposts to be given or paid by the client under the contract.

VI. Put the following Chinese into English.

1. 合同履行与签订
2. 工程量清单计价规则
3. 竣工结算时间
4. 对客户进行索赔
5. 工程跟踪调查与随访

参 考 译 文

第 7 单元　项目合同管理

1. 引言

在施工项目管理系统中，合同管理扮演着一个重要角色，由于施工项目管理涉及代表不同专业学科的人群，这些人群的范围为从项目经理、合同经理以及部门经理到分包商、建筑师、工程师、供应商和雇主——所有这些人都在设法尽力应对多种文件和合同的同时，在大量争端和变更上面进行协作。从合同的签署、合同的履行到最终合同的终止，主要承包商必须保证项目顺利运转且他们得到最终所期望的结果。

施工合同管理涉及影响和决定经由施工合同各方的合同要求的履行的必要活动。施工合同管理在雇主和承包商之间的协议生效时开始，且在承包商收到最终付款时结束。

合同经理必须监控成本、范围、质量和期限并且确保所有合同条件得到满足。该重要工作影响到项目或公司财务和实际两方面的成功。合同管理必须确保：

- ➢ 雇主的利益受保护且其义务要尽到；
- ➢ 服务提供商的合同义务要尽到；
- ➢ 合同里程碑事件准时执行；
- ➢ 关键交付之物被收到；
- ➢ 合同的相关程序被完成；
- ➢ 任何变更、索赔、问题、争执和任何额外资金要求被管理。

2. 合同管理的目标

合同的重要目标是在下列约束之内管理合同：
- ➢ 时间
- ➢ 成本
- ➢ 质量

无论是承包商的工料测量师还是咨询公司的工料测量师，成本都是工料测量师的责任。在规划和管理之间有着密切的关系。在管理项目过程中，工料测量师使用数量清单作为管理工具。

在建筑项目的时间管理中，由承包商编制且由工程师所接受的施工计划被用来管理时间，由于完成项目所需的所有活动是公认的，不同活动和期限之间的关系也是被认同的，且能够很容易就被监控。如果发生了偏差，可以采取补救措施去缓和延误。成本和时间之间有着密切的关系。项目竣工的延误必然意味着成本的增加。项目的成本取决于施工的数量、施工期限以及建立现场的成本。此外，质量不合格将会引起许多附加问题，比如日程误期、成本超支、分包商无力偿还债务等。

3. 合同文件

就项目参与方而言，不完整或不准确的合同文件需要额外的时间和精力，且在解释和修改的准备期间，进度可能会被延误。不完整或不准确的合同文件常导致需要修改文件。需要准备和对合同更改做出反应的时间和精力会使承包商从对项目的专注中分心。对价格和时间修订进行谈判常常会导致分歧和冲突。

3.1 合同文件

合同文件会在协议中列出和列举出来，且在承包商的合同条件中针对要实施的工程而被提及。它们是描述工程要求的法定单证。合同文件描述被提议的施工工程，这些工程产生于服务的实施、装修工作以及材料和设备的供应并纳入施工工程的实施。

3.2 合同及协议

合同文件由书面和图形元素组成，并一向包括下列事项：
签约形式（协议）及合同条件（总体和辅助条件，或者雇主提供的总体或特殊条件）还有若干指定的附件和表格。修订、澄清和更改是适用于合同文件的变化，比如在采购过程中所发布的附录或者在工程实施期间发布的变更指令。

3.3 规范

这些规范包括针对工程的具体书面要求。规范界定出产品、材料和技艺的质量要求，合同就是以此为基础并对工程的管理和实施确定相关要求。

3.4 发包图样

发包图样是在协议中指定的且能够由若干(包括小尺寸草图在内)解释和更改形式来进行补充的文件。这些资料包括要实施的工程物理形式的大型图示说明。它们表明工程的数量范围和要素的相互关系。它们有助于确立工程的范围并由规范来进行补充。由于尺寸较大，发包图样一般必定是分开的。

3.5 竣工图纸

合同文件可能需要竣工图纸。建筑师通常会发布图纸的新版本，指出变化和野外条件。隐藏条件和效用定位是最普遍的所需信息。合同文件指出将要包括在竣工图纸里的所需信息的类型。这些竣工图纸将作为已竣工工程的实际状况的永久记录。

竣工图纸有图纸、报告和规范等数种类型，它们可能在施工期间被使用但不一定包括在合同文件中。它们可能包括测绘、危险材料报告、评估和地质技术数据。合同文件是相互关联的，且提供对完成工程所需的不同类型的信息。

合同文件由内容组成，这些内容按优先顺序排列。
- 接收函
- 承包合同
- 谅解备忘录(如需要)
- 合同特殊条件
- 合同数据
- 合同通用条件
- 履约担保副本
- 保险
- 图纸
- 规范
- 工程量清单
- 任何其他有关文件

4. 合同管理的主要方面

4.1 财务管理

财务管理的主要任务包括资源规划、成本估算、成本计划以及成本控制。在签署合同之前，必须尽可能考虑到一切，以确保各方更明确地准备承担他们自己的责任，而不仅仅是尽到财务义务。根据成本计划，应当采取措施去纠正必定要发生的偏差，使项目的财政收益最大化。

4.2 分包合同管理

管理分包商，包括指定分包商、提名分包商和国内分包商，可能将会花费主要承包商的庞大时间和精力。主要承包商承担与任何分包商所承担的相等的责任和义务。主要承包商要对有缺陷的由分包商所完成的作业负责，并对任何分包商的行动、违约和疏忽尽可能充分地负责，如果缺陷被认为是主要承包商的违约或疏忽的话。主要承包商也要对建筑现场的健康和安全负责。

4.3 进展管理

建筑合同通常会设定一个项目竣工的期限。该期限可能在投标文件中规定，或者相反，在合同裁决之前采纳承包商的意见。由于未能满足规定的竣工时间要求，合同要求支付清偿损失额，对承包商方面以每天或者每星期的收费形式进行。为了按时完成项目，进度管理的重要性体现在确保某些任务按时间表完成。

进度管理的任务包括计划制定、项目跟进、进度更新和进度报告。这些任务通常由控制部门完成，且被分为工程部任务、采购部任务、施工部任务和质量部任务。如果是承包商力所不能及的延误，总包商应要求延长竣工的时间。

4.4 质量管理

除满足指定的日程和成本之外，保持良好质量是施工管理的主要目标之一。质量还是考察工程成功与否的关键因素之一。建筑工程中的质量可以按多种方式分类。根据项目生命周期阶段的不同，存在质量控制的各种对象和方法。质量管理包括所需的确保项目将满足其要求的过程管理。它包括所有全面管理职能的活动，这些活动将决定质量方针、目标和责任，并且通过质量体系以内的诸如质量规划、质量控制、质量保证以及质量改善的方式来执行它们。质量管理的文件资料对施工进程的顺畅与否影响很大，且在某种程度上影响到施工成本和时间。

4.5 健康、安全以及环境管理

健康、安全和环境管理的目标是保证人们的健康和安全，保护自然、减少污染以及促进可持续发展。当项目管理组织建立起来的时候，各方的义务很大程度上在合同文件中就规定了，然而，也有一些由政府法律建立的没有在合同文件中确定的规定性要求。有关健康、安全和环保的法定要求在不同的国家是不同的。承包商应对服从所有法定要求负责，如果承包商只是遵守境内要求而没有注意当地要求，这可能导致在审查时项目的失败。承包商要对给出所有必要的通知负责，遵从法定要求和支付相关费用，根据合同条款由雇主给出或支付的通知和费用除外。

4.6 管理变更和索赔

如果雇主代表或工程师指示（指导）了一个变更，承包商就要执行该指示。变更成为合同的一部分且所有合同条件适用于改变了的工程，包括时间延伸和现场状况的条款（如果合适的话）。有这样一个风险，即雇主的活动可能延误建筑合同的完成，于是，为了减少超过预算和推迟竣工的风险，有效地管理变更因此就十分重要。变更是建筑合同中成本和时间超过限度的主要原因之一。（更多信息请参考最后一个单元）

承包商有权索赔在遵守变更指令后发生的额外付款和竣工延期。额外付款可能包括针对与变更有关的延误、加速和/或中断的额外成本。施工合同涉及承包商可以为其对雇主提出索赔的若干问题。最常见的是，这些索赔是针对付款和/或额外延期的。针对额外付款的索赔可能因为许多原因引起，包括就变更、情况改变、延期索赔和中断索赔等方面的争执。

5. 总结

简而言之，合同管理应当具有如下特征：
- 控制建筑项目的合同、预算、预测成本以及项目的可交付；
- 在项目经理、合同经理、经理、分包商、建筑师、工程师、供应商和雇主之间进行协作；
- 确保项目改变的解决、支付的实现和索赔的避免；
- 为意外事件做好准备，并具有商谈成本的必要信息和对于最终解决问题的时间表详细资料；
- 跟踪日报单、会议记录以及针对购买订单而送交的材料；
- 立即对任何改变的成本或时间表冲突做出考虑，且辨别哪个承包商受到了影响；
- 分析项目之中的比较趋势和原因/结果，在使项目成本、风险和安全问题最小化的同时使效率最大化；
- 在组织上从项目开始至合同终止，在管理、完成、监督、管理、执行中对合同管理职能进行有效管理。

阅读

商务消息写作

1. 写前构思

对于商务来说，信息交流是最基本的。没有信息交流，商务就不能运行了。每一笔交易都需要沟通。消息是普遍的商务沟通媒介。如果商务写作者想要成功发送商务消息，他们应当记住他们其实打算与他们的读者进行一次谈话。写前构思阶段是设计出他们想要发送的消息。在商务写作者把思考和想法写到纸上之前，他们应当进行研究、集合数据或者收集他们写消息所需的任何信息。在开始写作之前，商务消息的写作者应当考虑以下问题。
- 意图：我的写作意图是什么？我的目标是什么？
- 读者：谁是我的读者，且我期望得到什么反应？
- 长度：该消息应当有多长？或者它需要多长？
- 媒介：对于该消息的最好形式是什么——信函/传真、备忘录、电子邮件消息？

在写作之前应对想法列提纲并组织好他们的想法，写前构思阶段还是决定该消息的目标和主旨的时间，应确保该写作是集中的和有效的。

2. 构思商务消息

除了考虑商务消息的读者、长度和媒介之外，商务写作者还必须决定主旨，选择支持信息并针对读者或者接受者进行调整。

2.1 辨识目标

目标是他们通过消息想要获得的东西。目标可能是：
- 促进重大意义的原则的良好意愿；
- 告知针对项目推进的紧迫问题；

> 要求应当由工程师或雇主指示什么；
> 记录有工程师或雇主口头决定的事情的备忘录；
> 说服雇主举行会议讨论最近工程的改变。

2.2 决定主旨

在定好消息的目标之后，下一步就是确定主旨。主旨是中心主题或者消息要传达给读者或接受者的最关键的问题。

2.3 选择支持信息

支持信息包括解释、加强或者证明主旨的根本实事，接受者可以在商谈中理解这个主旨，且从主旨获益。像作者在写前构思阶段收集信息那样，他们应当把接受者的需要记在心里，且仔细考虑接受者需要知道什么，以便能够对消息做出反应。

2.4 针对接受者调整消息

调整消息的内容时，作者应当把自己放到接受者的位置。通过移情作用（同感），作者能够看到从接受者的视角并相应地对消息进行创作。周到的消息会考虑到关于主题接受者的兴趣、参与或者认识水平。周到的消息使用证明信息，以致接受者将从理解和欣赏中获益。

3. 书面消息中的非言辞符号

书面文件的外观和正确性还有反响的适宜性发出一个关键的非言辞信息且值得仔细关注。带信头的信笺、纸张和信封应当由高质量的证券纸制成，且具有相同的颜色。信头的字体和设计以及专用标志应当传达出一种专业形象。图纸、照片、图表和曲线图应当适合于内容且增强信息。印刷应当整洁且易于阅读。在字母大写、语法、数字表达、标点符号、拼写或用词方面，文件不应出任何错误。精确的内容，尤其是数额、地址和其他事实是绝对必要的。无差错文件发出一种非言辞信息，即发送者是可靠的且认为质量很重要。有错误的文件反映出有关发送者的负面信息。

向雇主索赔的例子

2001 年 11 月 21 日

南非
比勒陀利亚
肯特大街 18 号 5 楼
玉石房地产开发公司
项目负责人
致：安德鲁·史密斯先生

尊敬的先生：
关于：St. James 法院项目延误付款和变更索赔

请查阅我们每月 11 号的报表，该报表已于 2001 年 8 月 10 日提交给了贵公司工料测量师 Michael Robert 先生，他代表 Jackson & Michael 工料测量师协会证实我们的付款结算。我们很遗憾地得知，在我们的申请和工料测量师相应的证明之间有一个很大差异，且所证实的总额远远低于我们所申请的数额。我们必须转发给贵方，即雇主，随同此信附上我们就以下方面的投诉。

1. 变更索赔

在我们的声明中，变更索赔已经是最严重的问题，因为一些变更指令由建筑师或雇主口头做出而没有任何书面指示，尽管在我们实施项目的时候，我们迅速发出敝函给建筑师以必要的证据证实相关的工作。我们仍然在等待正式的确认，以获得来自 Jackson & Michael 工料测量师协会的认证。贵方的工料测量师 Michael Robert 先生坚持认为所有的索赔应当与必要的证明文件及合同中约定的证据一起呈现，这样变更索赔的大部分会因此而被忽略。在与建筑师和工料测量师的电话交谈中，我们知道，一个可接受的解决办法将针对解决的执行在即将到来的项目会议上达成，参会方为雇主、建筑师及工料测量师；我们也希望结果大家都能接受。

2. 延期临时付款

我们必须提醒贵方，临时付款也没有按照合同随着项目的进展而推进。就合同中的原则而言，我方月报表通常迟于所约定的进度之后两到三个月才得到证实，因此，临时付款也相应地延迟了。我方认为，对于因为变更索赔的堆积而恶化的情况，存在一个增长的趋势。我方因此重申我方的付款报告和没有更多延迟的、将被评审和加速进展的项目索赔。

3. 指定分包商的不履行

我方必须提出的另一个严重问题是，指定分包商，即 IBL 电梯有限公司、超级门窗有限公司以及 Smart 内部通话系统有限公司的糟糕表现，他们阻碍了建筑的总体进展且中断项目计划几个星期，虽然我方在各种场合向贵方提出该问题，但我方感觉迄今为止他们的表现没有任何改善。如贵方所知，这些指定分包商仍然由雇主完全付款、控制和指导。我方必须指出，由于他们超越我方的权限和指挥，我方将对由指定分包商所引起的延误不负任何责任，而且，我方将保留对时间延长和后续损失的索赔权。

最后，我方希望雇主安排一个由建筑师、工料测量师和我方共同出席的会议来解决各方之间的分歧和项目正面临的问题。我方已经表露出与各方合作的准备；尽管我方因延期进度付款而处于艰难财务状况之中，我方对于项目仍然保证了总体满意水平。

我方的明朗意向是找到协商的积极途径，并给出一个恰当的谈判时间表和程序。我方相信，我方所进行的索赔是合理的，由于所有变更索赔都有详细的证明文件，且所有工程都由 Jackson & Michael 工料测量师协会进行了测量。

我方等待贵方就上述内容发表看法。

谨启

General 建筑有限公司

工料测量师

抄送：Francis Lim 先生——ARC 建筑师&顾问

　　　Michael Robert 先生——Jackson & Michael 工料测量师协会

Unit 8

Payments and Final Accounts

1. Construction Payments Introduction

Payments are of major concern to contractors and employers. As the duration of the construction projects are usually long, contract sums involved are large and payments are only progressively paid rather than on delivery, thus the payments are lifeblood of the construction Industry. They constitute the primary mechanism by which the contractor gets paid for the work carried out. This becomes the cash flow between the employer and the contractor. In construction contracts payments may be classified into three categories:

> ➢ Advance payments
> ➢ Interim payments
> ➢ Final payments Account

2. Advance Payments

An advance payment, or simply an advance, is the part of a contractually due sum that is paid in advance, while the balance will only follow after completion of the works. Advance payment is needed by the contractor for their cash flows purpose and for complete performance under one or more contracts as well. They are expected to be liquidated from payments due to the contractor incident to performance of the contracts. Since they are not measured by performance, they differ from partial, progress, or other payments based on the performance or partial performance of a contract. Advance payments may be made to contractors for the purpose of making advances to subcontractors. Under the FIDIC 1999 "Red Book" an advance payment is required but discretional; it is not an automatic right.

Advance payments are typically between 15% and 20% of the contract amount, but this depends on the nature of the works. The prerequisites of Employer to make an advance payment are the contractor has furnished the performance guarantee/bond and advance guarantee/bond to the employer.

3. Interim Payments

Interim payment occurs throughout the contract construction period. Generally the interim payment will occur at pre-determined intervals in the contract. These payments are determined by the value of the work carried out by the contractor during this period. In general they may be called monthly valuations. However this is determined in the tender document and the contract. Sometimes the interim valuations can be called stage payments or milestone payments paid at specific times when the contractor achieves the various stages of completion (e.g. Completion of substructure etc).

➢ In order to arrive at stage payments it is advisable for the quantity surveyor to carry out a contract sum analysis so that unrealistic stage payments are not given in the contract. A contract sum analysis will become the basis for valuing variations. Where a project is subject to stage payments and where there is no detailed pricing document, in such cases variations can be valued at the contract rates, day works or by obtaining quotations from the contractor and approving them prior to executing the variation.

➢ Under FIDIC contracts the commonly used document to value interim payments are the bill of quantities, and the schedule of rates. It is important to define the time period of submitting an interim application and the time period for evaluation by the engineer and the time period for honouring the payment by the employer.

4. Interim Payment Certificates

"Interim payment certificates" means a payment certificate issued under the clause "contract price and payment", other than the final payment certificate (FIDIC Conditions of Contract Definition). Interim payment certificate shall be issued when completed amounts are ascertained by the engineer as payable to the contractor by the employer. In 14.3 of FIDIC contracts, the contractor shall submit a statement to the engineer after the end of each month, FIDIC Sub-Clause 14.6 stipulates that the engineer shall have the discretion to make the interim valuation whenever he considers necessary for issuing the interim certificate, which is to be issued within 28 days after receiving a statement/application and supporting documents.

The following table generally gives frequency of the issue of interim certificates under various forms of contract.

contractor's application to issue of certificate	JCT 80	ICE 6	FIDIC
frequency	monthly	monthly	within 28 days from date of application by the Engineer
period of honouring	14 days	28 days	within 28 days from date of certificate delivery to the employer
valuation date	7 days before Certificate	none noted	none noted

➢ Most standard forms of contract state an entitlement on the part of the contractor to interim payment, the interim payments are therefore sums paid on-account of whatever the contractor might eventually be entitled to recover from the employer. In the international construction market, FIDIC construction contracts have claims or payment application and certification provisions, which are usually applied and implemented on monthly or stage payment basis. Interim or progress payment claims are usually prepared by the contractor and submitted to the engineer or quantity surveyor for valuation, and then for certification.

➤ It is a matter of fact whether payment for work carried out is a statement of acceptance or approval. Most contract provisions for interim certification and payment are based on cumulative valuation of work done, and are only for payments on account. They are neither binding nor conclusive of acceptance of the work.

➤ The certification process in the construction industry has been in place for many a long year and is an integral part of both building and civil engineering. It involves employer, consultant, main contractor and subcontractor alike. On many standard forms of main contract the contractor is entitled to be paid the sum which is certified by the architect, engineer or contract administrator. The widely used standard forms of contract published by the FIDIC, JCT and ICE provide provisions for the architect, contract administrator or engineer to issue a payment certificate at regular intervals normally monthly, which under the terms of the contract is the sum which the employer is required to pay.

➤ The employer is required to pay within a specified period after having received the said interim payment certificate from the engineer or quantity surveyor, who usually acts as the contract administrator of the project. FIDIC standard forms of construction contract provide for payment application and certification clauses. The relevant payment clauses in respect of the conditions of contract require the contractor to submit sufficient details/particulars to the engineer for him to value and ascertain the works (including materials and goods on site), and issue interim certificate for contractor's entitlement to payment. The materials and plant on site shall be reasonably, properly and not prematurely delivered with adequate protection against weather or other casualties.

➤ Where any form of advanced payment or payment on account is involved there is always a fear on the employer that there may be an overpayment followed closely by the insolvency of the contractor who has received payment. Certainly, architects and the quantity surveyors are well aware of the dangers of over certifying, therefore, they usually certify much less amount of the contractor's application provide the financial advice to the employer to defer payment.

5. Final Account/Payment

In basic terms of construction contracts, a final account is the agreed statement of the amount of money to be paid at the end of a building contract by the employer to the contractor. In construction contracts, it is generally common practice for both the employer (or the employer's representative) and the contractor to sign the final account statement to signify that the final account figure represents the full and final settlement of all claims etc. The settlement of the final account negotiations between the contractor, and the architect or quantity surveyor will in due course trigger the issue of the final account statement and ultimately, enable the architect to issue the final certificate.

The final account stage of a contract is the process during which the quantity surveyor determines the final cost of a project, based on the following documents:

- The form of contract
- Original priced bill of quantities
- Variations
- Drawings
- Agreed contractor's claims

After the architect has issued the certificate of practical completion, the contractor must supply the quantity surveyor with all the necessary documentation in order that the final account (adjustment) can be prepared. The quantity surveyor then has an additional three months to prepare the final account (adjustment); there is no stipulated penalty stated in the contract if these deadlines are not met. The final account which is prepared by the quantity surveyor is composed of the following:

- Statement of final account
- Final account summary
- Adjustment of prime cost sums if used
- Adjustment of provisional sums
- Adjustment of provisional items
- Adjustment of variation account
- Adjustment for fluctuations
- Adjustment for contractor's claims

A final account brings about a sense of finality to the negotiations leading up to the agreement of the final account between the parties to the contract. The final accounts also finalize (subject to formal proceedings) disputes under the contract – normally those arising from valuations, quality of work, decisions on extensions of time and loss and/or expense. That is why clauses dealing with final accounts often reach the conclusion unless objection is made within a prescribed period. Disputing elements of the final account means in effect either adjudication or arbitration.

6. Retention Money

Retention money is amount retained by the employer for any defective works that may occur during the construction period and the defects liability period. The contractor should complete all contracting works, and then entitled payment for only 90%~95% of that amount. The money held back is the retention, typically 5%~10% of the total contract price. There are often two levels of retention on a project. The employer will withhold retention from the general contractor. The general contractor, in turn, withholds retention from each of his subcontractors.

Outstanding retention has never been more prevalent than today in the international construction market. The most common alternative for retention money is the retention guarantee/bond. For a number of years retention bonds have been offered by surety companies as an alternative to retention. However, such a bond does not remove the difficulties of operating a retention system, and it simply shifts the mechanism by which the security is provided. It is kept by the employer on behalf of the contractor and his responsibility to release the bond as stated in the contract, once the defects are rectified to the satisfaction of the engineer. Normally fluctuations (variations to the price) are paid net and subject to retention, and similarly any formulae fluctuation provisions are also subject to retention.

Reading

Sample of Interim Certificate and Final Account

1. Example of Interim Payment Certificate

Sun Trust Office Building PROJECT-PORT LOUIS

Payment Certificate No. 22 For Works Executed by George Contractor as at Feburary 2001

Sun Trust GEORGE CONTRACTOR

Title	Rs.	Rs.
Bill No. 1——Preliminaries		5,000,000.00
Bill No. 2——Basement	3,181,503.18	—
Bill No. 3——Superstructure	21,053,564.20	—
Bill No. 4——Waller	1,907,698.55	—
Bill No. 5——Roof Covering	31,209.00	—
Bill No. 6——Windows & Doors	—	—
Bill No. 7——Finishings	3,867,568.80	—
Bill No. 8——Sundries	411,890.00	—
Bill No. 9——P.C. & Provisional Sum	1,088,644.58	31,542,078.31
SUM		36,542,078.31
add: variations fluctuation		2,999,802.83
		604,382.71
		40,146,263.85
less: retention (5%)		2,007,313.19
		38,138,950.66
add: advance payment		2,094,406.10
		40,233,552.76
less: reimbursement on advance payment		38,138,950.66
less: as per subcontract		3,468,883.20
		34,670,067.46
less: previous certified		34,245,815.32
amount certified under this valuation		Rs. 424,252.00

(Signed of)   (Signed of)
QUNTITY SURVEYOR   FINANCIAL DIRECTOR

2. Example of Final Account

Sun Trust Office Building FINAL ACCOUNT

Sun Trust

Revised contract sum as per enclosed final account	81,918,232.41
Add Additional preliminaries	2,464,096.00
Fluctuation	1,035,904.00
Final contract sum	85,418,232.41

Note: Authorised deductions as follows will be computed in the final certificate.

CEB bill CEB	9,278.65
direct payments made to subcontractor by client	238,092.00
direct payment made to supplier	610,436.00

We hereby certify that in respect of this contract, we have no further claim beyond the amount stated above and agree to accept the final contract sum of rupees eighty five million four hundred and eighteen thousand two hundred and thirty two and cents forty one (Rs. 85,418,232.41) in full and final settlement of this contract and all matters arising therefrom.

Dated this ………………………………………day of ……………… 20 …....

Signature……………………………………………………

In the capacity of………(Manager)………………

For…………………………….(Company)….

<u>Sun Trust Office Building</u>

FINAL ACCOUNT

MAIN SUMMARY

<u>Sun Trust</u>

original contract sum	Rs. 96,794,170.40
adjustment for remeasurement (Annexure I)	OMIT (16,259,212.72) 80,534,957.68
adjustment for variation (Annexure II)	ADD 1,383,274.73
revised contract sum	Rs. 81,918,232.41

ADJUSTMENT FOR RE-MEASUREMENT

<u>SUMMARY</u>

Title	OMISSION	ADDITION
Bill No. 1——Preliminaries	—	—
Bill No. 2——Basement	1,190,700.00	995,616.10
Bill No. 3——Superstructure	6,838,740.00	6,729,190.00
Bill No. 4——Waller	138,438.30	81,992.80
Bill No. 5——Roof Covering	—	—
Bill No. 6——Windows & Doors	9,650,000.00	—
Bill No. 7——Finishings	—	—
Bill No. 8——Sundries	—	—
Bill No. 9——P.C. & Provisional Sum	37,692,150.00	31,444,016.68
sum	55,510,028.30	39,250,815.58
less	39,250,815.58	
net omission carried to main summary	Rs. 16,259,212.72	

New Words and Expressions

final accounts 决算
contractors 承包商
employers 雇主
duration 持续时间
lifeblood 生命线；生命的根源；生命必需的血液
the construction industry 建筑行业
constitute 组成，构成；任命，建立
primary mechanism 主要机制
cash flow 现金流
advance payments 预付款
interim payments 临时付款
final payments account 最后付款账户
liquidated 以偿付的；清偿，清理
discretional 自由裁量权的；考虑周到的；谨慎的，有判断力的
prerequisites 先决条件，前提
performance guarantee /bond 履约保函(债券)
advance guarantee /bond 预先保函(债券)
contract construction period 合同工期
pre-determined intervals 预先决定阶段
monthly valuations 每月的估算
tender document 招标文件
stage payments 阶段支付款项
quantity surveyor 预算师或造价师
detailed pricing document 详细的定价文件
quotations 报价单；引用语，引证
schedule of rates 进度率
Interim Payment Certificates 期中支付证书
clause 条款，子句
Final Payment Certificate 最终支付证书
payable 应付的
stipulate 规定，认为；指出
discretion 自由裁决权
statement/application 声明与应用
contractor's application to issue of certificate 承包商的申请证书
construction market 建筑市场
payment application 付款申请

Unit 8   Payments and Final Accounts

progress payment 按进度付款
certification 认证，确认
contract provisions 合同条款
binding 装订；捆绑；有约束力的
conclusive 决定性的
civil engineering 建筑工程
integral 完整的，整体的；积分的
contract administrator 合同管理员
payment application and certification clauses 付款申请与认证条款
materials and goods on site 现场材料与产品
prematurely delivered 过早交付
casualties 人员伤亡
insolvency 破产，无力偿还；倒闭
final account/payment 决算账户与付款
common practice 通常做法
sign the Final Account Statement 签订决算报表
trigger 引起，激发
original priced bill of quantities 原始清单定价
finality 定局，终结，结尾；最后的事物或言行
conclusively 决定性地，结局地；推论地，定局地
objection 异议，反对；妨碍；缺陷，缺点；拒绝的理由
prescribed period 规定的时期
adjudication 判决，裁定；破产之宣言
arbitration 仲裁，公断
stipulated 保证，规定
deadline 截止日期，截止期限
adjustment of provisional sums 临时费用的调整
adjustment of provisional items 临时项目的调整
retention 扣留，滞留；保留；记忆力
retention money 滞留金
liability period 责任期内
retention bonds 债券保留
surety companies 担保公司
fluctuations 起伏，波动

Exercises

I. Choose the best answer according to the text.

1. In construction contracts payments may be classified into _____ three categories.
    A. advance payments
    B. interim payments

C. final payments account

D. above all

2. According to the text, which statement is true? An advance payments the part of _____.

   A. a contractually due sum that is paid in advance, while the balance will only follow after completion of the works

   B. the contractor for their cash flows purpose and for completes performance under one or more contracts as well

   C. 15% and 20% of the contract amount, but this depends on the nature of the works

   D. the purpose of making advances to subcontractors

3. We learn from the passage that under FIDIC contracts the commonly used document to value interim payments _____.

   A. will occur at pre-determined intervals in the contract

   B. can be called stage payments or mile stone payments paid at specific times

   C. is the bill of quantities, and the schedule of rates

   D. will become the basis for valuing variations

4. The settlement of the final account negotiations between the contractor, and the architect or quantity surveyor will in due course trigger _____.

   A. the parties' conclusively unless objection is made within a prescribed period

   B. a sense of finality to the negotiations leading up to the agreement of the final account between the parties to the contract

   C. the agreed statement of the amount of money to be paid at the end of a building contract by the employer to the contractor

   D. the issue of the final account statement and ultimately, enable the architect to issue the final certificate

5. We learn from the passage that the money held back is the retention, typically _____ of the total contract price.

   A. 90%~95%

   B. 5%~10%

   C. 10%~15%

   D. 75%~85%

II. Decide the following statements are true or false.

1. An advance payment, or simply an advance, is the part of a contractually due sum that is paid in advance, while the balance will only follow after completion of the works.

2. In order to arrive at stage payments it is advisable for the quantity surveyor to carry out a contract sum analysis so that unrealistic stage payments are given in the contract.

3. In the international construction market, FIDIC construction contracts have claims or payment application and certification provisions, which are usually applied and implemented on four weeks or stage payment basis.

Unit 8   Payments and Final Accounts

4. The quantity surveyor then has an additional one months to prepare the final account (adjustment); there is no stipulated penalty stated in the contract if these deadlines are met.

5. However, such a bond does not remove the difficulties of operating a retention system it simply shifts the mechanism by which the security is provided.

III. Change the following words to another form and write down the Chinese meanings.

1. constitute _____
2. classified _____
3. categories _____
4. interim _____
5. liquidated _____
6. performance _____
7. FIDIC _____
8. intervals _____
9. valuations _____
10. stage payments _____

IV. Give out the following words' synonym or other word in the closest meaning.

1. mile stone payments	a. adapt to
2. details	b. variations to the price
3. final account	c. advance guarantee/bond
4. adjustment	d. delegates
5. quantity surveyor	e. particulars
6. finalize	f. structures
7. mechanics	g. stage payments
8. performance guarantee/bond	h. engineer
9. representatives	i. subject to
10. fluctuations	j. final payment

V. Put the following English into Chinese.

1. Since they are not measured by performance, they differ from partial, progress, or other payments based on the performance or partial performance of a contract.

2. Sometimes the interim valuations can be called stage payments or mile stone payments paid at specific times when the contractor achieves the various stages of completion.

3. Where a project is subjected to stage payments and where there is no detailed pricing document, in such cases variations can be valued at the contract rates, day works or by obtaining quotations from the contractor and approving them prior to executing the variation.

4. Where any form of advanced payment or payment on account is involved there is always a fear on the part of the paying party that there may be an overpayment followed closely by the insolvency of the party who has received payment.

5. It is kept by the employer on behalf of the contractor and it his responsibility to release it as stated in the contract once the defects are rectified to the satisfaction of the engineer. Normally fluctuations (variations to the price) are paid net and subject to retention similarly any formulae fluctuation provisions are also subject to retention.

6. That is why clauses dealing with final accounts often impose on the parties' conclusively unless objection is made within a prescribed period.

VI. Put the following Chinese into English.

1. 履约保函
2. 项目合同工期
3. 付款申请与认证条款
4. 按工程进度支付价款
5. 决算报表的签订

参 考 译 文

第 8 单元 支付与结算

1. 建筑支付介绍

支付对于承包商和雇主来说都是大事情。由于建筑项目的期限往往较长，涉及的合同金额巨大且支付只能是日渐增加的而非交货付款，因此，支付是建筑业的命脉。它们构成了首要的机制，通过该机制承包商获得针对所完成工程的付款。这成为了雇主和承包商之间的现金流转。在建筑合同中，支付可以分成三类：

➢ 预先付款
➢ 临时付款
➢ 结算付款

2. 预付款

预付款或称首付款，是预先支付的到期合同金额的一部分，而余额只能在工程完成之后得到。预付款是由于承包商的现金流转需要，也是为了承包商能够完全履行某一个或更多合同而得到的预付款项。预付款将由承包商在后续的（项目）合同履行中返还。预付款不是以履约情况来估算的，所以它不同于基于合同履行或部分履约的进度款，或者其他支付款。预付款付给承包商可能是为了让承包商能给分包商预付款项。根据菲迪克(FIDIC)1999"红皮书"的条款，要求预付款但是由业主自主决定；它不是一种自动的权利。

预先付款一般是合同总额的 15%～20%，这由工程的性质决定。雇主预付款的先决条件是承包商已经对雇主提供履约担保/保证书和预先担保/保证书。

3. 中期付款

整个合同施工期间都可能有临时付款。一般来讲，临时付款将发生在合同的预先裁定间隔期间。这些付款由在此期间承包商所完成的工程价值来决定。总的来说，它们可以被称为月份估价。然而，这要在投标文件和合同中来决定。有时，当承包商实现了各种阶段的完工(如：地下结构的完工等)，临时估价可称为阶段付款或特定时间支付的里程碑付款。

> 为了获得阶段付款，工料测量师最好做出合同金额分析，以便给出实际的阶段付款。合同点价分析将成为对变更做出估价的基础。在项目以阶段付款方式或没有详细定价文件的情况下，变更可以由合同进度和计日工作量来估价，或者在执行变更之前由承包商报价并获得批准。

> 在菲迪克(FIDIC)合同条件下，经常用来估价临时付款的文件是工程量清单，以及价格表。界定提交临时申请时间期限和由工程师评估的时间期限以及由雇主进行的承兑付款的时间期限很重要。

4. 期中付款证书

"期中付款证书"意味着以"合同价格和支付"条款为依据所发放的付款证书，除了最终付款证书(FIDIC 合同定义条件)之外。菲迪克(FIDIC)合同条件的 14.3 款规定，承包商应当在每个月末向工程师提交月进度款申请。期中付款证书将在完工总量由工程师查明雇主可以对承包商支付的时候再发放。FIDIC 分条款 14.6 规定，无论何时如果工程师觉得有必要发放期中付款证书，将具有进行期中付款估价的裁决，期中付款证书应当在收到声明/申请和证明文件后 28 日内发放。

以下表格在总体上给出了在各种合同形式下期中付款证书的发放频率。

承包商对于付款证书发放的申请	JCT 80	ICE 6	FIDIC
频率	每月	每月	由工程师提出申请之日起 28 天以内
承兑期限	14 天	28 天	从付款证书送交雇主之日起 28 天内
评估日期	付款证书前 7 天	未注明	未注明

> 大部分标准合同形式规定了对期中付款的承包商一方的资格，期中付款因此是承包商最终有资格从雇主那里取回的分期支付的金额。在国际建筑市场上，FIDIC 建筑合同具有索赔或支付申请以及认证规定，这些规定通常以按月份或阶段付款的方式来应用和执行。期中或进度付款索赔通常由承包商准备并提交给工程师或工料测量师进行评估，然后进行认证。

> 事实是，对于完成工程的付款是接受或批准了的申报。大部分针对期中认证和支付的合同条款以所完成工程的累积估价为基础，并且仅仅针对账目付款。期中付款既没有约束性，也不是对项目工程量的最终接受。

> 在建筑业中，付款证书过程已运行了多年，并且是建筑和土木工程两方面的主要部分。它同样涉及雇主、咨询师、主承包商和分包商。在许多标准主合同形式中，承包商有资格支付由建筑师、工程师或合同经理批准的金额。广泛使用的由 FIDIC、JCT 和 ICE 所公布的标准合同形式的条款中，建筑师、合同经理或者工程师通常应当按月依据合同条款定期发放付款证书，该付款证书代表着要求雇主支付的金额。

> 雇主被要求在收到上述的来自工程师或者工料测量师(常常是项目合同经理)的期中付款证书的特定期限内付款。FIDIC 建筑合同的标准合同形式提供了支付申请和认证条款。

合同支付条款要求承包商提交足够的详细资料/细目给工程师,以为其估价和查明工程(包括现场的材料和物品),并按照对承包商应付款项发放期中付款证书。现场的材料和机械应当合理、恰当而非过早地抵达现场,同时须采取足够抵抗天气或其他严重事故的防护措施。

➢ 在预付款或分期付款的任何形式所涉及的任何地方,就雇主而言,总是存在一个担心,即承包商收到付款后紧接着无力偿付超额付款。建筑师和工料测量师当然能意识到超额批准付款的危险,通常他们批准的付款额都大大低于承包商的申请额,同时会向雇主建议推迟付款。

5. 结算/支付

在施工合同基本条款中,结算是施工合同结束时经双方同意由雇主支付给承包商的金额总数。在施工合同中,对于雇主(或雇主的代表)和承包商两者来说,这已经是惯例,即签署结算报表和结算数额意味着索赔等问题的完全和最终解决。承包商、建筑师或者工料测量师之间的结算谈判的清算将在一定的时候引起结算书的发放,并且最后促使建筑师发放最终竣工证书。

在合同的结算阶段,工料测量师以下列文件为基础,结算项目的最终成本。

➢ 合同协议
➢ 原始标价工程量清单
➢ 变更
➢ 图纸
➢ 接受的承包商索赔

在建筑师发放实际竣工证书之后,承包商必须提供所有必要的文件资料给工料测量师,以便准备好结算(调整金额)。如果这些最后期限没有被满足,在合同中没有阐明规定的惩罚;工料测量师则有额外的三个月准备结算(调整金额)。由工料测量师准备的结算包括下列内容:

➢ 结算申请
➢ 结算总述
➢ 通用费(开办费)调整(如果有)
➢ 暂定金额调整
➢ 暂定事项金额调整
➢ 变更金额调整
➢ 汇率波动金额调整
➢ 承包商索赔金额调整

合同双方对结算谈判达成协议的结算书将是终局性的结果。结算也按照合同终结条款受限于正式工作程序所有的争端;正常情况下争端起因于工程量计算、工程质量、工期延长以及损失和/或费用的决定。这就是为什么处理结算的条款常常表示达成最终协议,除非争议能在规定期限内提出。结算的争端实际上意味着争端评判或者仲裁。

6. 保留金

保留金是由雇主针对施工期间和保修期间可能发生的任何缺陷工程保留的数额。承包商应当完成合同工程，然后仅仅有资格获得该总额的 90%～95%的付款。被扣留的这笔款项就是保留金，通常保留金是合同总价的 5%～10%。在一个项目上常常有两种保留金。雇主扣留总承包商的保留金。反过来，总包商扣留他的每个分包商的保留金。

在国际工程市场上，未清偿的保留金从来没有像如今如此盛行。最普遍的替代保留金的方案是保留金担保/保函。多年来保留金保函作为替代方案由担保公司提供。然而，这样一种保留金保函并不能排除运作保留金系统的困难，且通过保函提供以转变机制。一旦承包商完成所有缺陷工程的修复并得到工程师的认可，由雇主代表承包商保存的保留金保函将按照合同解除保函责任。正常情况下，价格波动(对于价格的变化)被净支付且受限于保留金中，类似地，任何公式的价格波动条款也受限于保留金中。

阅读

期中付款证书和结算实例

1. 期中付款证书例子

<u>Sun Trust 办公大楼项目——路易港</u>
<u>针对由 George Contractor 于 2001 年 2 月所完成工程的第 22 号付款证书</u>

标题	卢比	卢比
工程量表 1——通用费/开办费		5,000,000.00
工程量表 2——地下室	3,181,503.18	—
工程量表 3——地上结构	21,053,564.20	—
工程量表 4——墙体	1,907,698.55	—
工程量表 5——屋面结构层	31,209.00	—
工程量表 6——窗和门	—	—
工程量表 7——建筑装饰	3,867,568.80	—
工程量表 8——杂项	411,890.00	—
工程量表 9——暂定费用和暂定金额	1,088,644.58	31,542,078.31
合计		36,542,078.31
增加：变更 　　　价格波动		2,999,802.83 604,382.71 40,146,263.85
减少：保留金(5%)		2,007,313.19 38,138,950.66
增加：预付款项		2,094,406.10 40,233,552.76
减少：预付款偿还		38,138,950.66
减少：按照分包合同		3,468,883.20 34,670,067.46
减少：先前批准		34,245,815.32
本次核算批准总额		Rs.　424,252.00

签名　　　　　　　　　　　　　签名
工料测量师(签名)　　　　　　　财务主管(签名)

2. 结算例子

Sun Trust 办公大楼结算

修证合同金额(根据所附结算书)	81,918,232.41
增加　通用费/开办费	2,464,096.00
价格波动	1,035,904.00
最终合同金额	85,418,232.41

注：如下的授权扣除将在最终付款证书里进行计算。

票据	9,278.65
由雇主直接付给分包商的付款	238,092.00
付给供应商的直接付款	610,436.00

我们特此证明，关于本合同，我们没有更多超出上述总额的索赔，且同意接受捌仟伍佰肆拾壹万捌仟贰佰叁拾贰卢比肆拾壹分整的结算金额，以及该合同的最终结算和由此产生的所有法律问题。

　　签名＿＿＿＿＿＿＿＿＿＿＿＿＿＿＿＿＿＿＿＿＿＿＿＿＿＿
　　以＿＿＿＿＿的身份＿＿＿＿＿＿＿＿(经理)＿＿＿＿＿
　　致＿＿＿＿＿＿＿＿＿＿＿＿＿(公司)＿＿＿＿＿＿

Sun Trust 办公大楼
结算
主要总计

原合同金额	卢比　96,794,170.40
工程量测量的调整(附录Ⅰ)	减项 (16,259,212.72) 80,534,957.68
变更调整(附录Ⅱ)	增加　1,383,274.73
修正合同金额	卢比　81,918,232.41

工程量测量的调整
总计

标题	减项	增加
工程量表 1——通用费	—	—
工程量表 2——地下室	1,190,700.00	995,616.10
工程量表 3——地上结构	6,838,740.00	6,729,190.00
工程量表 4——墙体	138,438.30	81,992.80
工程量表 5——屋面覆盖层	—	—
工程量表 6——窗和门	9,650,000.00	—
工程量表 7——建筑装饰	—	—
工程量表 8——杂物	—	—
工程量表 9——暂定费用和暂定金额	37,692,150.00	31,444,016.68
合计	55,510,028.30	39,250,815.58
减少	39,250,815.58	
计入总计净减少额	Rs. 16,259,212.72	

Unit 9

Variations and Claims

1. Variations in Construction Projects

Variations are inevitable on building and civil engineering projects and may range from small changes having little consequential effects to major revisions, which result in considerable delay and/or disruption to the project. Variations in construction contracts can mean changes to the terms of the contract or can mean changes to the scope or character of the works. In construction projects, a variation usually refers to an alteration or a modification to pre-existing conditions, assumptions or requirements. It can be caused by either internal or external factors. Different variations may have different effects or consequences. Variations to the scope of construction works are necessary because no project is impeccable and variations are required to meet unforeseen circumstances or changed requirements. Thus, variation can be in the form of additions, omissions or substitutions.

2. Causes of Variation

The causes of project variations may originate from either external or internal pressures that are being applied to the project. External causes may be due to technological changes, changes in the customer expectations and tastes, changes in competitor's activities, changes in government and policies, changes in the economy and finally demographic changes in the society. At a more detailed level, the causes of construction project variation are usually generated from either design or construction activities, including: inadequate briefing from the employer, inconsistent and late instructions from the employer, incomplete design, lack of meticulous planning at the design stage, lack of coordination of specialist design work and late clarification of complex details. The design generated causes include design changes, design errors, omissions and operational improvements. Construction driven causes are often linked to the unsatisfactory site conditions that hinder good workmanship, material handling and plant operation. Furthermore, changes may occur due to the employer's desire to include the latest technology. One example of variation is that the contractor is required to change the timing, order or sequence of the work.

3. Type of Variations

3.1 Extra and Changes in the Work

Construction contracts generally include a clause that gives the employer the right to order extras and changes. Standard contracts like FIDIC do include time provisions for payments to the contractor for basic contract work but not for extra work. Some forms of variation require the contractor to perform the work in a different way. This may result in a need for more or different equipment and labour skills. In such circumstances variations required by the employer do not usually need the contractor's consent. It should be apparent that some changes could bring extra work and incur over cost into contactor. The impact from the change should be compensated for in addition to the direct costs of the changed work and in contract completion time. The employer should provide a time extension and payment for performing the change.

3.2 Variation in Quantity

Many fixed-price contracts incorporate unit pricing. This entails the employer's setting forth estimated quantities of materials needed to accomplish the work into units. For example, the employer might estimate quantities of cubic meters of concrete poured, the quantities being a combination of materials and work. The entire contract could be unit priced, if the design is complete, the key is the degree to which quantities can be reasonably estimated. In complex projects, unit price contract becomes more difficult, the contractor generally takes more of a risk if unit price is used in such cases. Wrong estimates can result in substantial losses or in windfall profits for either party. If the actual quantity is significantly lower than estimated, the contractor may not be able to recover his fixed cost for the work. In other instances, he may be overly compensated.

4. Valuating of Variation

4.1 Method of Valuing Variations

➢ The traditional method of valuing variations, both on building and civil engineering works, is to base the valuation of the variations on the rates or prices contained within the bill of quantities or rate of schedules. The standard form creates what is known as an admeasurement contract by which the employer undertakes to pay for the actual quantities of work executed reflecting the engineer's design of the permanent works calculated based on the latest drawings and schedules. The Red Book of FIDIC form is designed for use on civil engineering projects based on a bill of quantities. The quantities set out in the bill of quantities are the estimated quantities of the work.

➢ This approach of valuing variations often led to disagreement between the parties with the employer's quantity surveyor wishing to rigidly adhere to the rates in the bill and the contractor wanting the rates to reflect the true cost as incurred or likely to be incurred. The valuation of variations has been a popular topic of litigation in the international construction market. If the varied works are complex, the parties need to be skilled negotiators and be prepared to adopt a give-and-take attitude in order to bring about a satisfactory settlement. Under the traditional approach, compromise was often required for there was seldom one correct solution.

➢ Indeed the parties might consider alternative approaches before selecting the appropriate strategy. Many standard conditions of contracts introduce the requirement for the contractor to submit a lump-sum quotation for the variation, prior to receipt of the official variation order and before carrying out the work. Additional supervision, additional field office expenses, added temporary utility costs, added sanitary control costs, cleaning costs, and in some cases additional project management costs should be included. The advantage to the employer in this approach is that the final commitment, including disruption and extended time, is known prior to the instruction and the majority of the risk is transferred to the contractor. The advantage to the contractor is the certainty of obtaining adequate recompense for the variation.

4.2 Procedures of Valuing Variations

It is common enough to have provisions in the contract that no extra work shall be paid for unless it is ordered in writing by the engineer, and if such conditions are properly made, and there is nothing fraudulent or iniquitous in the way they are carried out, these conditions would be quite sufficient and effectual.

A variation will be valued in accordance with schedule rates so far as applicable or, in the absence of agreement, by determining a reasonable rate or a price. Each variation will be priced using the following order of precedence as this is a matter of interpretation of the contract:

- ➢ prior agreement;
- ➢ applicable rates or prices in the contract;
- ➢ rates or prices in a priced bill of quantities, schedule of rates or schedule of prices, even though not contract documents, to the extent that it is reasonable to use them; and
- ➢ reasonable rates or prices, which shall include a reasonable amount for profit but not overheads.

A variation is usually effected through an instruction from the employer's representative, engineer or architect. Such instructions are usually required to be in writing, namely a letter signed by the engineer or architect. Whether this is a pre-requisite to the contractor's right to recover payment will depend on whether the requirement is a condition precedent. The contractor's option is to send a letter to the engineer to confirm the variation in case of verbal instruction within three days.

5. Application of Variations and Claims

5.1 Application of Variations

The contractor will ultimately be required to give notice of their intention to claim a variation and provide the employer with supporting documentation within a specified period. Failure to provide such information will result in the application being rejected. Moreover, some contracts provide for a time limit to provide this information and failure to do so within the specified time may result in rejection of the application. In construction contracts, the basis of payment to the contractor in respect of any variation will usually be established in the contract, e.g. bill of quantities. The engineer may have authority to agree variations, including the assessment of compensation and time extensions. The variations amount shall be added to or deducted from the contract sum. Depending on the contract terms, the engineer's authority is subject to the employer's approval. Such as FIDIC, the engineer may need to give a formal decision independently of the parties.

5.2 Application of Claims

➢ Variations must not be confused with claims. It is often said that a contractor is claiming a variation, but this actually means that they are making an application for variation. Any claim in respect of the variation only occurs if the employer or engineer rejects the application, and the contractor disagrees with the decision and wishes to pursue a claim.

➢ Variation generally occurs as a result of a change made to the scope of works, consequently, changes can just as easily decrease the scope of works as increase it. Some contracts contain a provision that triggers a variation in the event of certain quantities being increased or decreased in excess of a fixed percentage, thus, it is the threshold that the contractor will decide if to file a claim or not. For example in FIDIC Red Book 1999, the value of changed work should be not to exceed 10% of the contract price.

➢ Claims by the contractor however usually arise from failure on the part of the employer. It is also possible that the claim may arise because of some outside event that has affected the contractor's work, while the employer is usually supposed to be liable.

Variation is almost an inevitable part of any construction claim. Given the competitive environment that the international construction market is usually in, many contractors probably rely on the employer's variations to make a reasonable return for their contracts. In addition, variation works commonly affect the completion date and, therefore, impact on delay claims by the employer(counter-claim). This explains, to some extent, why the resolution of issues concerning variations is never easy, especially if the dispute is hard way after the building is completed and records are scarce, making physical measurement of the works completed is difficult.

Reading

Conversations

1. Discuss the Difference

(Mr. Ralph Groves, quantity surveyor of the contractor of General Construction Co. Ltd. is calling Mr. Michael Robert of Jackson & Michael Quantity Surveyor Associates to make an appointment to discuss the variations claims of an office building: State Bank Project).

Operator: Good morning, Jackson & Michael Quantity Surveyor Associates. Can I help you?

Mr. Ralph Grove: Good morning. I'd like to speak to Mr. Michael Robert, please.

Operator: Who's calling please?

Mr. Ralph Groves: Mr. Ralph Groves, I'm from General Construction.

Operator: Will you hold the line a moment, Mr. Ralph Groves? I'll see if Mr. Michael Robert is free.

Unit 9   Variations and Claims

Mr. Ralph Groves: Yes, thank you.

Mr. Michael Robert: Hello, Michael speaking.

Operator: Oh, hello, Mr. Robert. Mr. Ralph Groves from General Construction is on the line. Can you speak to him now?

Mr. Michael Robert: Oh, yes. Put him through, please.

Operator: You're through now, Mr. Ralph Groves.

Mr. Michael Robert: Hello, Mr. Ralph Groves, What can I help you?

Mr. Ralph Groves: Good morning, Mr. Michael Robert. I'm calling for the State Bank Project No. 11 payment certificate I have just received yesterday, I'm not happy with the figure you certified after I checked my application.

Mr. Michael Robert: Well, It's a tricky question. What are your opinions about it?

Mr. Ralph Groves: You know, Mr. Michael Robert. You have omitted lots of variations claims in our monthly application consecutively for three months and you haven't given us the good reasons for that.

Mr. Michael Robert: Well, Mr. Ralph Groves. I'm very sorry about that. But I can do nothing about it, because I've not found sound backup for your variations claims according to the Contract. You see, I can not violent the rules of quantity surveying to give you the extra works amount without the architect's authorizations.

Mr. Ralph Groves: Mr. Michael Robert, It's not fair. It seems as if you were kicking ball game with me, I would not be able to reach the ball as it were passed to another constantly. When I talked with the client, Mr. Andrew Smith last month, he said he would ask you to evaluate the extra works we claimed and do some helps to us, but you're saying now you're waiting for the architect's decision. I think we can not hold on any longer, as we have been draining our own finance to run on this big project's expenses on plants, materials and labour, and all the subcontractors under the circumstances of delayed payments for several months.

Mr. Michael Robert: I understand your situation; I would try to help you if I could. You know, I must be loyal to my duty. Let's see what we can do.

Mr. Ralph Groves: Good, thank you for your consideration. I suggest that we fix a date when you are free, then I will bring all the variations claims that you have not approved with relevant supporting documents to your office, we will check together and see what variations are without the justified backup you think, and sort out the unacceptable variations with you.

Mr. Michael Robert: It sounds good. I have gone through all your files, some of them lack the contractual procedures proof. I think you had better ask the architect Mr. Francis Lim to give you the authorization.

Mr. Ralph Groves: Well, I will talk to the Architect. But I don't think we need all the variations authorizations from the architect, because some of the variations we had sent letters timely to confirm them to the client or to the architect for those oral instructions, and we also made copy to you, some of them we could trace the confirmation from the minutes of site meeting.

Mr. Michael Robert: Yes, I know that. I have talked with the client about this, and we probably will work on this issue in the next project meeting held by the client. Anyway, let's have a meeting to see what we can do. Mr. Ralph Groves, what's your suggestion?

Mr. Ralph Groves: We sit down to see what we can reach for the variations and what the differences are. If we can't solve these problems, I will write to the architect and the client to tell them the remaining issues, and I will try to ask the client to arrange a meeting with all concerned parties to work out the differences. You see, the project is coming to the completion and the payments can't be dragged on any more.

Mr. Michael Robert: Alright, I agree with you. We meet and discuss first.

Mr. Ralph Groves: Will you be available for us to meet on next Thursday?

Mr. Michael Robert: Let me check with my secretary, I will ask her to give you a call to confirm our appointment. If so, we can fix on two o'clock in the afternoon, as I'm always busy in the morning.

Mr. Ralph Groves: That's good, so see you next Thursday two P.M. Thank you, have a nice day!

Mr. Michael Robert: OK, Thank you, Bye.

2. Negotiating a Contract

(Mr. Weston Hunt, quantity surveyor from Capital Construction Company. He is negotiating the terms of contract with Mr. Marsh Murray, the Project Director of the client, who gave him a letter of intention).

Mr. Marsh Murray: Good afternoon, Mr. Weston Hunt, thank you for coming.

Mr. Weston Hunt: Good afternoon, Mr. Marsh Murray.

Mr. Marsh Murray: Well, Mr. Weston Hunt, let's continue from where we left off yesterday. At yesterday's meeting, we talked about the clauses to be covered by the contract, including formation of the contract documents, specifications, questions of payment, provision of guarantee as well as the arbitration clause. We also discussed some of the items in detail. We've covered quite a lot of ground, haven't we?

Mr. Weston Hunt: Yes, Mr. Marsh Murray, it seems to me we've come quite a long way, but there's still a fair few points left over to clear up.

Mr. Marsh Murray: OK, let's go back to the original plan and see where we have got to. The preliminary target of project commencement is due to start in September this year, is that right?

Mr. Weston Hunt: Yes, that's right. We set up a time schedule in September. We'll take over the site in next month until the middle of August if you're ready…

Mr. Marsh Murray: Very encouraging. Your action is to reach our target and generally mobilization activity was good. So what was the next step?

Mr. Weston Hunt: Well, as you know, the plan is to move the plants of excavators, lorries to site quickly so as to begin the earth works as our tender was accepted.

Mr. Marsh Murray: Good, let's go over terms of payment. Would you be agreeable to payment by bi-monthly transfer from Commercial Bank?

Mr. Weston Hunt: I'd suggest in a month, we can open an account in Commercial Bank.

Mr. Marsh Murray: OK, we accept it. Now what about deliveries of goods in view of those required from importation? Can you guarantee the completion date if the those goods are not available or short of supply?

Mr. Weston Hunt: I've been looking into the question of having the goods sent by sea. The goods will be less liable to damage and quick, as the materials will be packed and delivered in container. We will arrange them ahead of programme to get rid of risk of hold up due to strikes etc.

Mr. Marsh Murray: There's only one thing there. If we run the project in terms as we've already previously agreed, this might mean we need warehouse to store them or an extra substantial expense and increase in cost.

Mr. Weston Hunt: Really, I believe it would be worthwhile. I noticed that you have an empty building for the next phase developing just beside the site, and we would pay you with the extra costs incurred if we could use it as a temporal warehouse.

Mr. Marsh Murray: I'm certainly with you in principle, but I've to take the matter up when I get back to Camp town. Perhaps I should make a special note of that.

Mr. Weston Hunt: We will appreciate your help.

Mr. Marsh Murray: The next point is the guarantee. We should like to have a performance guarantee of 15% contract sum for at least twenty months in accordance with the standard contract form.

Mr. Weston Hunt: No trouble about that. We offer a standard guarantee of performance in all the projects in accordance with contract terms, and I think this project should be no exception.

Mr. Marsh Murray: So a guarantee would be written into our contract also?

Mr. Weston Hunt: Certainly. Then, one of the things we haven't decided properly yet is who's going to be responsible for insurance.

Mr. Marsh Murray: You'll be prepared to look after that side entirely. This is the contractor's responsibility as well. The only thing I would propose is that you should provide a furnished site office for the architect and a signboard placed beside the entrance when you are at work.

Mr. Weston Hunt: That's fine, but perhaps we should consult the architect about the site office later, and we would like to be suggested for the adaptation over there.

Mr. Marsh Murray: Of course we'd be only too pleased to get your ideas and cooperation from your side.

Mr. Weston Hunt: Right, we probably conclude all the issues. When will be the contract signing due to take place?

Mr. Marsh Murray: Next week actually, on 15th and 16th July.

Mr. Weston Hunt: Well, I'm very happy with the frank exchange of views and our discussion outcome.

Mr. Marsh Murray: Yes, I think we will turn over a new leaf from this project. We hope that we shall do more business in the future.

Mr. Weston Hunt: I certainly will.

New Words and Expressions

variation 变化；变异，变种
civil engineering 土木工程
revision 修改；修正，修订本；复习
having little consequential effects 几乎没有间接影响
consequential 随之发生的；结果的；间接的；重要的
disruption 中断，终止；分裂，破坏，毁坏
alteration 变更；修改，改变
modification 改变；修改，改正
assumption 假定，设想；担任，采取
impeccable 无可挑剔的，无瑕疵的；没有缺点的
addition 增加物；添加，加法
omission 省略，疏忽；遗漏；冗长
substitution 代替，置换；代替物
technological changes 技术变革
demographic changes 人口结构的变化
design or construction activities 设计或施工活动
specialist 专家的，专业的；专家，专门医师
coordination 协调，调和；对等，等同
coordination of specialist design work 协调的专业设计工作
clarification 澄清，说明；净化
site conditions 场地条件，场地状况
workmanship 手艺，工艺；技巧
plant operation 工厂运作，工厂运行
provision 规定，准备
consent 赞成，答应；同意，赞成；一致
contract completion time 合同完成时间
compensate 弥补，补偿
incorporate 体现；合并，混合
entail 必需，承担；限定继承权，限定继承的财产
setting forth 陈列，出发；宣布
cubic meters of concrete poured 大批立方米混凝土
quantities 工程量
substantial losses 重大损失
windfall 意外的收获，意外的钱财；被风吹落的果子
windfall profits 暴利
overly compensated 过度补偿

the bill of quantities 工程量清单
admeasurement 计量，大小；分配
drawings and schedules 图纸和时间表
disagreement 分歧，不一致，不协调
popular topic 热门话题；焦点
litigation 诉讼，起诉
give-and-take attitude 互相让步的态度
satisfactory settlement 令人满意的解决方案
compromise 妥协，折衷；让步
submit a lump-sum quotation 提交一个一次性的报价单
supervision 监管，监督
additional field office expenses 额外的现场办公费用
sanitary 卫生的，清洁的；公共厕所
commitment 承诺，保证；承担义务；委托，献身
fraudulent 欺骗性的，不正确的
iniquitous 不公正的，邪恶的
in accordance with 按照，根据
order 规则，顺序；整理，订购
precedence 优先
interpretation 解释；翻译；演出
applicable 可使用的，适用的；合适的
overheads 一般费用；杂项开支；企业的日常管理费用
namely 即，那就是
pre-requisite 先决条件
precedent 首列，先列；在前的，在先的
intention 意图，打算；想法
assessment of compensation and time extensions 评估时间延长
deducted from the contract sum 从合同金额中扣除
depending on the contract terms 根据合同的约定
making an application for variation 做一项申请变更
threshold 门槛，极限；入口；开始，临界值
dispute 争议，争论；辩论

Exercises

I. Choose the best answer according to the text.

1. Variations in construction contracts can mean _____.
   A. changes to the terms of the contract
   B. changes to the scope or character of the works
   C. an alteration or a modification to pre-existing conditions, assumptions or requirements
   D. A and B

2. In construction projects, a variation usually refers to _____.
   A. an alteration or a modification to pre-existing conditions, assumptions or requirements
   B. can mean changes to the terms of the contract or it can mean changes to the scope or character of the works
   C. may range from small changes having little consequential effects to major revisions
   D. may have different effects or consequences

3. According to the text, which statement is true? _____.
   A. The causes of project variations may originate from neither external nor internal pressures that are being applied to the project
   B. At a more detailed level, the causes of construction project variation are usually generated from either design or construction activities
   C. In such circumstances variations required by the employer usually need the contractor's consent
   D. The contractor's option is to send a letter to the engineer to confirm the variation in case of verbal instruction within two days

4. The traditional method of valuing variations, both on building and civil engineering works, is to _____.
   A. set out in the bill of quantities are the estimated quantities of the work
   B. led to disagreement between the parties with the employer's quantity surveyor wishing to rigidly adhere to the rates in the bill
   C. reflect the true cost as incurred or likely to be incurred
   D. base the valuation of the variations on the rates or prices contained within the bill of quantities or rate of schedules

5. We learn from the passage that it is common enough to have provisions in the contract that no extra work shall be paid for _____.
   A. unless it is ordered in writing by the engineer
   B. if such conditions are properly made
   C. there is nothing fraudulent or iniquitous in the way they are carried out
   D. above all

6. A variation is usually effected through an instruction from the employer's engineer or architect. Such instructions are usually required to be in writing, that is, _____.
   A. a pre-requisite to the contractor's right
   B. a letter to the engineer to confirm the variation in case of verbal instruction within three days
   C. a letter signed by the engineer or architect
   D. none of the above

II. Decide the following statements are true or false.

1. Standard contracts like FIDIC do include time provisions for payments to the contractor

Unit 9　Variations and Claims

for base contract work but not for extra work.

2. If the actual quantity is significantly more than estimated, the contractor may not be able to recover his fixed cost for the work.

3. For example in FIDIC red book 1999, the value of changed work should be to exceed 10% of the contract price.

4. Variation is almost an inevitable part of any construction claim.

5. Variation generally occurs as a result of a change made to the scope of works, consequently, changes can just as easily increase the scope of works as decrease it.

6. In such circumstances variations required by the employer do usually need the contractor's consent.

III. Change the following words to another form and write down the Chinese meanings.

1. substitutions _____
2. variations _____
3. inconsistent _____
4. completion time _____
5. incorporate _____
6. entails _____
7. agreements _____
8. employer _____
9. in accordance with _____
10. overheads _____

IV. Give out the following words' synonym or other word in the closest meaning.

1. disruption   a. driven
2. alteration   b. lead
3. foreseen   c. requires
4. omission   d. destroy
5. generated   e. according to
6. cause   f. forecast
7. entails   g. explain
8. in accordance with   h. negative
9. interpretation   i. valuation
10. assessment   j. modification

V. Put the following English into Chinese.

1. Thus, variation can be in the form of additions, omissions or substitutions.

2. The standard form creates what is known as an admeasurement contract by which the employer undertakes to pay for the actual quantities of work executed reflecting the engineer's design of the permanent works calculated based on the latest drawings and schedules.

159

3. This approach of valuing variations often led to disagreement between the parties with the employer's quantity surveyor wishing to rigidly adhere to the rates in the bill and the contractor wanting the rates to reflect the true cost as incurred or likely to be incurred.

4. Many standard conditions of contracts introducing the requirement for the contractor to submit a lump-sum quotation for the variation prior to receipt of the official variation order and before carrying out the work.

5. Claims by the contractor however usually arise from failure on the part of the employer. It is also possible that the claim may arise because of some outside event that has affected the contractor's work.

6. This explains, to some extent, why the resolution of issues concerning variations is never easy, especially if the dispute is hard way after the building is completed and records are scarce, making physical measurement of the works completed difficult.

VI. Put the following Chinese into English.

1. 项目合同完成工期
2. 提交一个一次性的报价单
3. 额外的现场办公费用
4. 工程索赔条款
5. 工程项目管理变更

参 考 译 文

第9单元 变更和索赔

1. 建筑项目中的变更

在建筑和土木工程项目里变更点是不可避免的，变更可以是那种产生的后果影响不大的小修改，也可以是会导致项目产生严重延误和/或中断的重大修改。在建筑合同中，变更可能意味着对合同条款的改变或对工程范围或特性的改变。在建筑项目中，变更通常指对先前存在的条件、设想或要求的改动或变更。它既可以由内部因素引起，也可由外部因素引起。不同的变更具有不同的影响或结果。对建筑工程的变更是必要的，因为没有一个项目是无瑕疵的，且人们也需要用变更去满足未预见的情况或者变化了的要求。因此，变更的形式可以是附加、删减或者替代。

2. 变更的起因

项目变更的起因可能源于外部或者内部施加于项目的压力。外部原因可能是技术的改变、客户期望和品位的变化、竞争者活动的变化、政府和政策的变化、经济的变化，以及最后的社会上人口结构的变化。在更详细的层面上，建筑项目的变更通常产生于设计或者施工活动，包括雇主的不充分的情况简介、雇主不一致和迟到的指令、不完整的设计、设计阶段缺乏一丝不苟的规划、专业设计工作协调不足以及迟到的详细资料。设计产生的原因包括设计更改、设计差错、遗漏和操作改良。施工所促使的原因常常与不符合要求的现场状况相关联，这些状况妨碍了良好的工艺、物料处理和设备操作。此外，改变可能由于雇主渴望加入最新的技术而发生。举一个变更的例子，如承包商被要求改变工程的时间安排、顺序或程序。

3. 变更的类型

3.1 工程的附加和变更

建筑合同通常包括一个给予雇主去指令附加和变更的权利的条款。像 FIDIC 标准合同一定包括针对基本合同工程而非额外工程的付款给承包商的时间条款。一些变更形式要求承包商以不同的方式来完成工程。这可能导致对于更多或不同设备和劳工技能的需要。在这种情况下，由雇主所要求的变更通常不需要承包商的同意。一些变更可能带给承包商附加工程，招致额外成本。来自变更的影响应当除对已变更工程的直接成本做补偿之外，还要对合同竣工时间进行抵偿。雇主应当针对改变的变更而提供时间延长和付款。

3.2 数量的变更

许多固定价格合同纳入了单位定价，这使得雇主阐明完成工程所需材料的估计数量变得很必要。例如，雇主可能会估计所浇灌的混凝土的立方(米)数量、组合材料的数量以及工作量。标了单价的整个合同，设计完成后，关键就是工程量估算的合理程度。在复杂项目中，单价合同变得更加困难，且如果单价在这种情形下被使用了，承包商通常要冒更多的风险。错误估计可能导致重大损失或两者中任一方的意外利润。如果实际数量显著低于估计数量，承包商也许不能收回他的工程固定成本。在其他情况下，他可能得到过度补偿。

4. 变更计量

4.1 变更计量的方法

➢ 传统的变更计量方法，在建筑和土木工程两方面的变更都是以包含在工程量清单或价格表里的有关费率和价格为计量基础。标准合同创建了被认为是测量合同的形式，通过这种形式，雇主承担对实际完成工程数量的付款，实际工程量反映了以最新工程师的设计图纸和计划为基础来计算的永久性工程。FIDIC 形式的红皮书设计用于基于工程量清单的土木工程项目。工程量清单中设置的工程数量是估计数量。

➢ 这种计量变更的方式常常导致各方之间的分歧，由于雇主的预算师希望严格地遵循清单中的费用，承包商则要求费用反映的是所发生的或可能发生的真实成本。在国际市场上，变更计量已经成为诉讼的一个普遍话题。如果已经变更的工程很复杂，为了达成满意的解决方案，各方需要成为熟练的谈判者且准备采取折中的态度。在传统方式之下，妥协常常是很好的正确解决办法。

➢ 的确，在挑选恰当的策略之前，各方可能会考虑可选择的方式。在收到正式变更通知和完成工程之前，许多标准合同条件针对变更对承包商提出提交总价报价的要求。额外监督费用、额外现场办公费用、附加临时设施费用、附加卫生费用、清洁费用以及有些情况下的额外项目管理费用应当包括在内。这种方式对雇主的好处是，包括中断和时间延长在内的最终承诺在指令之前被知晓，且大部分风险转嫁给了承包商。对承包商的好处是获得足够的变更补偿的确定性。

4.2 计量变更的程序

按惯例在合同中规定任何额外工程将不被支付，除非它由工程师以书面形式来指令。如果适当地规定这种条件，且在实施过程中没有欺骗或不公正，则应规定这些条件。

变更将根据适用的价格表来计量，或者，在缺乏协议的情况下，通过确定合理的费用或价格来进行。由于这是合同解释的关键所在，因此每项变更将使用以下优先顺序来定价。

- ➢ 先前的协议；
- ➢ 合同中适用的费用和价格；
- ➢ 标价工程量清单中适用的费用求价格、价格表(即使没有合同文件，对于合理使用它们的范围来说)；
- ➢ 合理的费用或价格，其应当包括合理的利润而不包括管理费。

变更通常受雇主代表、工程师或者建筑师的指令的影响。这些指令常常要求以书面形式，也就是由工程师或建筑师签字的信函来传达。变更对承包商得到付款来说是否是一件首要事情将取决于该要求是否是一个先决条件。如果是口述指令，承包商则可在三天内寄送函件给工程师以确认变更。

5. 变更和索赔的申请

5.1 变更申请

承包商最终将被要求给出其对变更提出索赔的想法的解释，并在指定的期限内提供证明文件给雇主。不能提供这些资料将导致申请被驳回。此外，一些合同规定一个时间限制去提供这些资料，且在指定时间内不能提供会导致申请被拒绝。在施工合同中，关于任何变更的对承包商的付款基础将通常立足于合同中，如工程量清单。工程师有权同意变更，包括补偿金额和时间延长的核定。变更的数量将添加到合同中或从合同金额中扣除。根据合同条款，工程师的职权需要由雇主批准。例如 FIDIC，工程师需要给出一个正式的独立于各方的决定。

5.2 索赔申请

- ➢ 变更不能混同于索赔。通常所说的承包商在对变更提出索赔，这实际上意味着他们在进行变更申请。如果雇主或工程师拒绝了变更申请，且承包商不同意变更决定并希望进行索赔，任何与更变有关的索赔才会发生。
- ➢ 变更一般是对工程范围进行改变的结果，因此，变更可能是减少工程范围，就像增加工程范围一样容易发生。有些合同包含一个条款，该条款在工程量增加或减少超出某一固定百分比的情况下引发合同索赔，于是，这就成为承包商决定提交合同索赔申请与否的门槛。例如，在 FIDIC 红皮书 1999 中，变动的工程量应当不超过合同价格的 10%。
- ➢ 然而，由承包商提出的索赔通常起因于雇主一方的疏忽。也有一种可能，即索赔由于影响承包商运作的一些外部事件而产生，这些事件通常被认为是雇主的责任。

变更几乎是任何施工索赔的一个不可避免的部分。考虑到国际工程市场通常处于其中的竞争环境，许多承包商或许依赖于雇主的变更去为他们的合同产生一个合理的回报。另外，变更工程一般会影响竣工日期，因此会造成由雇主提出的工程延误索赔(反索赔)。这在一定程度上解释了为什么与变更有关的问题解决从来都不容易，尤其是在建筑竣工之后和记录缺乏的情况下，在进行已经完成的隐蔽工程的物理测量的时候，争端是个艰难的过程。

阅读

对　话

1. 讨论分歧

(Ralph Groves 先生，General 建筑有限公司承包商的预算师，正在打电话给 Jackson & Michael 预算师协会的 Michael Robert 先生就讨论 State Bank 项目办公大楼的变更索赔进行预约。)

电话接线员：早上好，Jackson & Michael 预算师协会。需要帮忙吗？

Ralph Groves 先生：早上好，我找 Michael Robert 先生。

电话接线员：您是哪位？

Ralph Groves 先生：我是 General 建筑公司的 Ralph Groves 先生。

电话接线员：请稍等。Ralph Groves 先生？我看看 Michael Robert 先生是否有空。

Ralph Groves 先生：好的，谢谢。

Michael Robert 先生：你好，我是 Michael。

电话接线员：噢，你好，Robert 先生，General 建筑公司的 Ralph Groves 先生在等你电话。您现在可以跟他讲话吗？

Michael Robert 先生：噢，可以。请接通他的电话。

电话接线员：Ralph Groves 先生，你的电话接通了。

Michael Robert 先生：你好，Ralph Groves 先生，我能帮您什么忙吗？

Ralph Groves 先生：早上好，Michael Robert 先生。我打电话来是为了我昨天刚收到的 St. James 法院项目的 11 号付款证书的事。在核对了我的申请之后，我对您所证明的数字不太满意。

Michael Robert 先生：喔，这是个棘手的问题。关于这个问题你的看法是什么？

Ralph Groves 先生：您知道，Michael Robert 先生。您连续三个月遗漏了我们每月申请中的许多变更索赔，且您没有为这一点对我们给出令人满意的理由。

Michael Robert 先生：噢，Ralph Groves 先生，对此我非常抱歉。但是我不能对此做任何事情，因为根据合同，我没有发现对你们变更索赔的可靠证据。您是知道的，没有建筑师的授权，我不能违背预算规则给您额外的工程量。

Ralph Groves 先生：Michael Robert 先生，这不公平。看样子似乎是您在跟我玩踢球游戏，在球不变地传给另一个人的时候，我是不能抓着球的。当我上个月跟委托人 Andrew Smith 先生谈论的时候，他说他将请您评估我们索赔的额外工程并给予我们一些帮助，但是您现在却说您要等待建筑师的决定。我认为我们再也不能拖延了，因为在几个月的延迟付款的情况下，我们正在耗尽我们自己的资金来维持有关设备、材料和人工费用以及所有分包商方面的这笔巨大项目开支。

Michael Robert 先生：我理解你的处境；如果可以我也想尽力帮您。您知道，我必须忠于我的职责。让我们看看我们能做点什么。

Ralph Groves 先生：很好，谢谢您的体谅。我建议我们定一个您有空的日期，到时我带上所有您没有批准的变更，并且带有相关证明文件的索赔资料到您办公室，我们将一起检查并发现什么变更没有您认为的合理证据，且与您一起解决不可接受的变更。

Michael Robert 先生：可以。我已经审查过您的所有卷宗，有些缺乏合同程序证明。我认为您最好请建筑师 Francis Lim 先生给您批准。

Ralph Groves 先生：噢，我将与建筑师商谈。但是我认为我们不需要来自建筑师的所有变更核准，因为对有些变更来说，我们适时的寄了确认信函给委托人或者建筑师对那些做了口头指令，且我们也做了副本给您，而对于有些变更我们可以追踪来自现场会议记录的确认。

Michael Robert 先生：是的，我知道。我已跟委托人谈过这一点，并且我们或许会在下一次由委托人举行的项目会议上继续这个议题。不管怎么说，让我们碰个面看看我们能做点什么。Ralph Groves 先生，您觉得呢？

Ralph Groves 先生：我们坐下来看看我们就变更能达成什么结果以及我们的分歧是什么。如果我们不能解决这些问题，我将写信给建筑师和委托人告知他们这个遗留的争端，并且我将设法请委托人安排一次所有相关各方参加的会议来解决分歧。你知道，项目正接近竣工，付款再也不能拖延了。

Michael Robert 先生：行，我同意你的意见。我们首先碰面讨论。

Ralph Groves 先生：我们下星期四碰面，您方便吗？

Michael Robert 先生：让我与秘书核对一下，我将让她给你打电话来确认我们的预约。如果可以，我们可以在下午两点整碰面，因为我早上总是很忙。

Ralph Groves 先生：那很好，那么下星期四下午两点见。谢谢！祝您度过愉快的一天！

Michael Robert 先生：好的，谢谢，再见。

2. 商谈合同

(Weston Hunt 先生，Capital 建筑公司的预算师。他正与发给他意向书的 Marsh Murray 先生，委托人的项目主任，协商合同条款。)

Marsh Murray 先生：下午好，Weston Hunt 先生，谢谢您的光临。

Weston Hunt 先生：下午好，Marsh Murray 先生。

Marsh Murray 先生：噢，Weston Hunt 先生，让我们从昨天停止的地方继续吧。在昨天的会议上，我们谈论了合同所涉及的条款，包括合同文件的构成、规范、付款问题、担保规定以及仲裁条款。我们也详细讨论了一些事项。我们已经涉及了很大范围，对吧？

Weston Hunt 先生：是的，Marsh Murray 先生，对我来说似乎我们已经走过很长一段路，但是仍然存在相当数量的遗留事项需要处理。

Marsh Murray 先生：好吧，让我们回到原始计划看看我们已经讨论的地方。初步的项目开工目标是今年九月份应当启动，对吗？

Weston Hunt 先生：是，对的。我们在九月份设定了一个时间表。如果你们准备好了的话，我们将在下个月接管施工现场直到八月中旬。

Marsh Murray 先生：太好了！你们的行动定将达到我们的目标且动员活动总体看也非常充分。那么下一步是什么？

Weston Hunt 先生：喔，正如你所知，为了像我们的投标所认可的那样开始土方工程，计划尽快把挖掘机、卡车运到现场。

Marsh Murray 先生：很好。让我们转到支付条款。您同意两月一次从商业银行转账付款吗？

Weston Hunt 先生：我建议每月付款一次，我们可以在商业银行开一个账户。

Marsh Murray 先生：好的，我们接受建议。要求进口的那些货物交货情况如何？如果这些货物缺货或者短缺，你们能保证完工时间吗？

Weston Hunt 先生：我一直在调查通过海路运送货物的问题。由于材料将被包装且放入集装箱运送，所以货物将更少受到损坏且快捷。我们将在计划之前对货物做出安排以避免由于罢工等造成的耽搁风险。

Marsh Murray 先生：还有一件事情。如果像先前已经同意的协议条件来运作项目的话，这可能意味着我们需要存储货物的仓库或者大量额外开支和成本的增加。

Weston Hunt 先生：确实，我认为这很值得。因为我注意到你们有一幢针对下一个发展阶段的空置大楼刚好在现场旁边，而且，如果我们能够用它作为暂时的仓库的话，我们将把额外产生的成本付费给你们。

Marsh Murray 先生：我原则上当然与你站在一起，但是当我回到 Camp 镇时，我不得不着手处理此事。或许我应当对此事做点特殊标注。

Weston Hunt 先生：我们将对您的帮助表示感谢。

Marsh Murray 先生：下一事项是担保。按照标准合同我们想要至少 20 个月的合同金额 15%的履约保函。

Weston Hunt 先生：没问题。我们将根据合同条款提供项目总额的标准履约保函，且我认为该项目应该没有异议。

Marsh Murray 先生：那么担保也将写进我们的合同吗？

Weston Hunt 先生：当然。还有，我们还没有恰当处理的事务之一是谁将对保险负责。

Marsh Murray 先生：贵方应当完全对这事负责，且这也是承包商的责任。我唯一提议的事情是，当你们进入现场的时候，贵方应当为建筑师提供一间装修过的现场办公室和一块置于入口处的布告板。

Weston Hunt 先生：这不错，随后我们咨询建筑师有关现场办公室的事，且我们愿意对其改造接受建议。

Marsh Murray 先生：当然，我们非常乐意获知贵方的想法和合作态度。

Weston Hunt 先生：正好，我们也可以解决所有问题了。什么时候应该进行合同的签署？

Marsh Murray 先生：实际上在下星期，7 月 15 和 16 号。

Weston Hunt 先生：噢，我对我们坦诚交换意见和商讨的结果非常满意。

Marsh Murray 先生：是的。我认为从这个项目我们将翻开新的一页，且我希望我们将在未来有更多的合作。

Weston Hunt 先生：我当然愿意。

Unit 10
Construction Planning and Scheduling

1. Introduction

Construction planning and scheduling are the important aspects for the successful completion of a project. Construction planning is a fundamental and challenging activity in the management and execution of construction projects. It involves the choice of technology, the definition of work tasks, the estimation of the required resources and durations for individual tasks, and the identification of any interactions among the different work tasks. The proper planning and utilization of resources play important role in cost and time optimization. A good construction plan is the basis for developing the budget and the schedule for work. Project scheduling is intended to match the resources of equipment, materials and labour with project work tasks over time.

2. Construction Plan

2.1 Factors of Construction Plan

Developing the construction plan is a critical task in the management of construction, even if the plan is not written or otherwise formally recorded. Essential aspects of construction planning include the generation of required activities, analysis of the implications of these activities, and choice among the various alternative means of performing activities. In addition to these technical aspects of construction planning, it may also be necessary to make organizational decisions about the relationships between project participants and organizations to be included in a project. For example, the extent to which sub-contractors will be used on a project is often determined during construction planning. There are numerous possible plans available for a given project. Although past experience is a good guide to construction planning, each project is likely to have special problems or opportunities that may require considerable ingenuity and creativity to overcome or exploit. Construction planners face the various problem of choosing the best among numerous alternative plan; a planner also must imagine the final facility as described in the plans and specifications.

2.2 Categories of Construction Plan

In developing a construction plan, it is common to adopt a primary emphasis on either cost control or on schedule control. Some projects are primarily divided into expense categories with associated costs. In these cases, construction planning is cost or expense oriented. Within the categories of expenditure, a distinction is made between costs incurred directly in the performance of an activity and indirectly for the accomplishment of the project. Traditional scheduling procedures emphasize the maintenance of tasks precedence or efficient use of resources over time. Finally, most complex projects require consideration of both cost and scheduling over time, so that planning, monitoring and record keeping must consider both dimensions. In these cases, the integration of schedule and budget information is a major concern.

2.3 Construction Plan Techniques

Currently, construction planners mainly use the principles and techniques of the project management approach in preparing their plans, include:

➤ Work Breakdown Structure (WBS): The work content of the project is decomposed into a set of main activities, and each of those in turn is decomposed into a set of sub activities.

➤ Dependency analysis: The project activities established by WBS are ordered according to the dependency relationships between them.

➤ Duration estimates: The time required to achieve each activity is calculated.

➤ Network development: Using one of the networking techniques (mainly CPM or PERT), activities are graphically presented. Details regarding activity durations and precedency relationships are illustrated on the network.

➤ Resource allocation: The appropriate type and size of resources are committed to each activity, taking into consideration the time span along which the resources are needed.

➤ Cost estimations: The cost of each activity is calculated, depending on its work content, duration and resource needs.

3. Construction Scheduling

➤ Usually the planning of project schedule is subject to factors of weather, local construction practices, construction methods, and resource availability. Two important procedures in the development of project schedule are identifying the activities and estimating the activity durations. Identification of project activities requires reviews of the project plan, drawings, specifications, and other considerations, such as general requirements and special conditions. The estimation of activity duration is then based on the resource availability to reflect the resource productivity on expected project site conditions.

➤ In addition to assigning dates to project activities, project scheduling is intended to match the resources of equipment, materials and labor with project work tasks over time. Good scheduling can eliminate problems due to production bottlenecks, facilitate the timely procurement of necessary materials, and otherwise insure the completion of a project as soon as possible. In contrast, poor scheduling can result in considerable waste as laborers and equipment wait for the availability of needed resources or the completion of preceding tasks. Delays in the completion of an entire project due to poor scheduling can also create havoc for employers who are eager to start using the constructed facilities.

➢ The most widely used scheduling technique is the Critical Path Method (CPM) for scheduling, often referred to as critical path scheduling. This method calculates the minimum completion time for a project along with the possible start and finish times for the project activities. Indeed, many texts and managers regard critical path scheduling as the only usable and practical scheduling procedure. Computer programs and algorithms for critical path scheduling are widely available and can efficiently handle projects with thousands of activities.

➢ Program (Project) Evaluation and Review Technique (PERT) is a project management tool used to schedule, organize, and coordinate tasks within a project. It is basically a method to analyze the tasks involved in completing a given project, especially the time needed to complete each task, and to identify the minimum time needed to complete the total project. PERT planning involves the following steps:
- Identify the specific activities and milestones;
- Determine the proper sequence of the activities;
- Construct a network diagram;
- Estimate the time required for each activity;
- Determine the critical path;
- Update the PERT chart as the project progresses.

4. Presenting Project Schedules

Project planning is often conducted by producing network representations of greater refinement until the plan is satisfactory. The use of graphical project representations is an important and extremely useful aid to planners and managers. Graphs and diagrams provide an invaluable means of rapidly communicating or understanding a project schedule. With computer-based storage of basic project data, graphical output is readily obtainable and should be used whenever possible. An extremely useful project network diagram is to draw a time-scaled network. In time-scaled network diagrams, activities on the network are plotted on a horizontal axis measuring the time since project commencement. Another useful graphical representation tool is a bar or Gantt chart illustrating the scheduled time for each activity. The bar chart lists activities and shows their scheduled start, finish and duration, but bar chart presentation carries much less information than other ways.

5. Schedule Control

➢ While the network model of project activities is an extremely useful device to represent a project, many aspects of project plans and activity inter-relationships cannot be represented or have not been represented in other models. When the construction phase starts, the attention is focused then on monitoring the implementation of the original plan, measuring the progress of work in terms of time, cost and quality, and comparing planned versus actual performance by means of network. If any departure from the original plan is realized, corrective actions must be adopted to bring back the work progress to the desired performance.

➢ After the project schedule is developed, this scheduled plan in execution is constantly reviewed by the project team with comparisons to the real project progress to make necessary changes. In the monitoring and control stage of the construction process, the construction manager has to keep constant track of both activities' durations and ongoing costs. These monitoring efforts along with the implementation are the keys to the successful management of project schedule. Cost overrun is an unfavorable situation just like a project delay. In fact, the budget plan is closely related to the schedule plan.

➢ Thus, a schedule plan can reveal the potential cost information in the project life cycle. The "S" curve method is frequently used to depict the relation of project schedule and cost. In the "S" curve, one can see whether the project is ahead of the schedule or behind the schedule, and the anticipated expenditure for the project. The cost control and schedule control need constant monitoring of project cash flow against work plan. Whether they are short-term plan, long-term plan, day-to-day, or monthly basis, the basic cost control methodology is analogous to that of schedule control. Constant evaluation is necessary until the construction of the facility is complete. Many employers require detailed construction schedules to be submitted by contractors as a means of monitoring the work progress. The actual work performed is commonly compared to the schedule to determine if construction is proceeding satisfactorily.

6. Scheduling Problems

➢ Unreasonable schedule requirements often result in conflict between project participants. If contractor is not allowed a reasonable period of time to complete his work, contractor may incur costs and inefficiency because of increased crew size or overtime work, may cut corners to appear to maintain the schedule, and may utilize means and methods that produce the quickest result rather than the desired result. Proper work sequencing may be set aside to increase productivity in order to make up time. These occurrences may negatively impact the completed facility.

➢ Unplanned, extensive, or an excessive number of changes to the project scope requested by the employer may result in incomplete or inaccurate contract documents and, when combined with unreasonable schedule requirements, may have a negative effect on contractor. Under these circumstances, change orders for modifications to the contract price, contract duration, or both need to be processed. These changes also impact purchase orders and scheduling, and usually result in a higher cost to the contractor.

Reading

Development of Scheduling Techniques

1. Introduction

➢ Projects will often be confronted by time, resources and organizational constraints. The construction management requires a highly accurate planning, scheduling and management of the process of the project which will enable the overall optimization of the cost, time and resources. It can be recognized that construction planning affects most of the project life cycle, and thus, project success is related, to a great extent, to the efficiency of construction planning. The construction planning is the process of determining appropriate strategies for the achievement of predefined project objectives. In construction projects, the objective of planning is the completion of a prescribed amount of work within a fixed time, at a previously estimated cost, and to specified standards of quality.

➤ Construction project scheduling is to assign staff to project tasks, display resource requirements profiles, and adjust the schedule of slack tasks so resource requirements more closely fit those available in the organization. Construction project scheduling is a topic that has received extensive research over a number of decades. A variety of special techniques have been developed to address specific circumstances or problems. With the availability of more powerful computers and software, the use of advanced scheduling techniques is becoming easier and of greater relevance to practice. These techniques address some important practical problems, such as:

- scheduling in the face of uncertain estimates on activity durations;
- integrated planning of scheduling and resource allocation;
- scheduling in unstructured or poorly formulated circumstances.

➤ The traditional approach for scheduling and progress monitoring techniques like bar charts, Critical Path Method (CPM), Programme Evaluation Review Techniques (PERT) etc. is widely used by the project managers for planning. There is a gradual increase in the pressure on the project managers to shorten the delivery time and decrease the costs involved in the process, without a decrease in the quality of the building. Therefore, new practices and increasing complexity of today's construction projects have resulted in an increase in the number of commercially available computerized planning and scheduling tools.

2. Scheduling with Uncertain Durations

It has been noted that uncertainty is not an exceptional state in the process of construction work. Activity durations are estimates of the actual time required, and there is liable to be a significant amount of uncertainty associated with the actual durations. During the preliminary planning stages for a project, the uncertainty in activity durations is particularly large since the scope and obstacles to the project are still undefined. Activities that are outside of the control of the employer are likely to be more uncertain. For example, adverse weather, trench collapses, or labor strikes make duration estimates particularly uncertain.

First, the uncertainty in activity durations may simply be ignored and scheduling done using the expected or most likely time duration for each activity. Formal methods of introducing uncertainty into the scheduling process require more work and assumptions. The use of predicted activity durations typically results in overly optimistic schedules for completion;

Second, the use of single activity durations often produces a rigid, inflexible mindset on the part of schedulers. Clearly, the use of fixed activity durations in setting up a schedule makes a continual process of monitoring and updating the schedule in light of actual experience essential. Otherwise, the project schedule is rapidly outdated.

Thus, the number of possible plans and schedules is enormous, so considerable insight to the problem must be used in generating reasonable alternatives. With improved graphic representations and information availability, man-machine interaction has been developed as scheduling procedures and provided various alternatives. Many commercial software programs are available to perform these tasks, such as Primavera P6 Professional Project Management.

GERT (Graphical Evaluation Review Technique) is a stochastic network analysis technique used in project management that allows for conditional and the probabilistic treatment of the logical relationships between the project's activities following randomly determined sequence of observations. The logical relationships between the project's activities are primarily based on the dependency between the two project activities or the dependency between a project activity and milestone. The key objective of the GERT is to evaluate on the basis of the network logic and estimated duration of the activity and derive inference about some activities that may not be performed.

Venture Evaluation Review Technique(VERT) is another scheduling of network analysis technique used in project management. The basic purpose of VERT is to support management in the assessment and quantification of the risk involved in new ventures and projects, to provide estimates of capital requirements, and to evaluate ongoing projects, programs, and systems. VERT is totally computerized. It permits analyses of risk in three parameters – time, cost, and performance. More importantly, it permits the user to scope his problem in any level detail desired.

3. Information Technology Development and Detailed Simulation

3.1 Simulating Construction Process

Formal scheduling procedures have become much more common with the advent of personal computers on construction sites and easy-to-use software programs. Sharing schedule information via the Internet has also provided a greater incentive to use formal scheduling methods. In forming a construction plan, a useful approach is to simulate the construction process either in the imagination of the planner or with a formal computer-based simulation technique. Three dimensional geometric models in a Computer-Aided Design (CAD) system can be helpful in simulating space requirements for operations and for identifying any interference. Similarly, problems in resource availability identified during the simulation of the construction process can be effectively forestalled by providing additional resources as part of the construction plan.

3.2 Detailed Activities Planning

The actual computer representation of the project schedule generally consists of a list of activities along with their associated durations, required resources and predecessor activities. Graphical network representations rather than a list are helpful for visualization of the plan and to insure that mathematical requirements are met. The actual input of the data to a computer program may be accomplished by filling in blanks on a screen menu, reading an existing data file, or typing data directly to the program with identifiers for the type of information being provided. Neither the project schedule, nor its cost can be controlled accurately. It is important for the construction plan and schedule to have detailed activities. A master program does not show all the detailed activities that occur in a project. The planning activities should be elaborated as more details are required. In the construction plan and schedule, it is very difficult for the project planners to consider the detailed activities, resource allocation and space requirement. Project planners pay a lot attention to the master program but tend to neglect detailed activities. They understand that resource allocation is a key factor in the construction plan and schedule but they lack mathematical method to analyze resource allocation.

3.3 Detailed Activities 4D Planning

➢ The space required by construction activities is the most difficult element for planners to analyze as space is static stage and dynamic. Since spaces required by activities change in all three dimensions through time, the time-space may conflict between activities. A detailed 4D planning and scheduling is required to compute the duration of each activity and associated space required. Such as the activity of concreting wall, it includes many types of activity related to time-space. Fixing reinforcement, erecting formwork and falsework, casting concrete and dismantling formwork and falsework will require process time, space for crews to work and to temporarily store and manage the materials and equipment items needed. There are many factors to be considered in this simple activity, and all of them are directly related to the construction planning and scheduling.

➢ The project manager can use the visualization aspects at any stage of the project to monitor the activities and cost flow, and use 4D methods and simulation for effective resource allocation, which makes the project sequence easier to understand. Different stages of the construction process and activities are generated in different layers using simulation software. At a specific time interval, one can utilize the actual building model and the scheduled building model to compare the work flow. By observing the result, comparisons among difference from plans or problems with the existing plan can be identified. 4D simulation can be further used to assist the project managers in control and analysis, monitoring of work by creation of a front-end application, by synchronizing the construction work in three dimensions and its schedule. This would help all parties involved in a project to visualize the progress in a natural way, hence minimizing the delays and cost overruns. In addition to monitoring of work flow, 4D simulation can be further used to monitor the quantities, costs and resources.

4. Information Technology Challenges in Construction Management

Due to the nature of construction practices, the integration of project information will be a difficult process and take a long way. Currently, most of new building information resides in isolated databases contained in hundreds of incompatible software applications from different vendors. With the consideration of complex situations in conducting a construction project, most construction firms take more conservative attitudes toward technological innovation than firms in other industries because of tight budgets restricting, some of the new technologies may lack the engineering experience, technical background, and common sense to decide the most appropriate use of a particular programme package. Conversely, engineers with years of experience in the construction industry may not have comprehensive computer-related knowledge to support them to choose the right information technology system and configuration to perform their tasks. Besides, unlike other business software, there is limited choice of construction specific software available in the market. These limitations negate the efforts of the firms in developing a universal configuration of information technology systems. That is one important factor responsible for this slow rate of technology assimilation in construction management.

New Words and Expressions

construction planning and scheduling 建设规划与调度
interactions 相互作用，相互交流；交互
optimization 最佳化，最优化；最佳，最优
production bottlenecks 生产瓶颈
facilitate 促进，帮助；使便利，使容易
procurement 采购；获得，取得；电子采购
construction plan 施工方案
formally recorded 正式记录
alternative means 替代手段；可选择的方法
project participants 项目参与者
a given project 一个指定的项目
considerable 相当大的，相当多的；重要的，值得考虑的
ingenuity 心灵手巧，独创性；精巧；精巧的装置；独创性，独出心裁
overcome 克服，战胜
exploit 利用；勋绩，功绩；开发，开拓；剥削；开采，开发
specifications 规格；说明书；性能规范，技术规范
oriented 以……为导向，以……为方向
expenditure 支出，花费；经费，消费额，开支
scheduling procedures 调度程序
precedence 优先，居先；优先次序
over time 随着时间的过去；超时，加班
dimension 维度，尺寸；容积；规格的
integration 集成；综合，整合；积分
project management approach 项目管理方法

Work Breakdown Structure (WBS) 工作分解结构
in turn 一次，按顺序
be decomposed into 被分解成
dependency analysis 关联分析
networking techniques 网络技术
activity durations 活动持续时间，工程持续时间
taking into consideration 考虑，思考
be committed to 致力于，奉献于
the time span along… 随着……时间的跨度
planning of project schedule 项目进度规划
construction practices 施工实践
construction methods 施工方法
resource availability 资源的可利用性
review 评审，检查；回顾，复习，评论；检讨，检阅
drawings 工程图纸
other considerations 其他因素
in addition to 除了
match 使比赛；使相配；敌得过，比得上；相配；与……竞争
havoc 大破坏；浩劫；蹂躏；严重破坏，损毁
Critical Path Method (CPM) 关键路径法
critical path scheduling 关键路径调度
computer programs 计算机程序
algorithms for critical path scheduling 关键路径调度算法
Program (Project) Evaluation and Review Technique (PERT) 计划(项目)评估和审查技术(网络)，计划评审技术
construct a network diagram 构建网络图
update the PERT chart as the project progresses 随着项目进程更新网络图
representations 代表；表现；表示法；陈述
refinement 精制；文雅；[化工][油气][冶] 提纯；精致，精炼
graphical project representations 图形项目陈述
graphs and diagrams 图形与图表
invaluable 无价的；非常贵重的；无可估量的，价值连城的
graphical output 图形输出
project network diagrams 工程网络图
time-scaled network diagrams 时间刻度网络图
horizontal axis 水平坐标轴
commencement 开始，发端；毕业典礼；开始
plot 密谋；策划；绘制，绘图
bar or Gantt chart 柱状图或甘特图

schedule control 进度控制
construction phase 施工阶段
departure 离开；违背；出发，启程
construction manager 现场施工经理
keep constant track of 保持持续追踪
project life cycle 项目生命周期
"S" curve method S 形曲线法
cash flow 现金流
proceeding satisfactorily 顺利进行，顺利施工

Exercises

I. Choose the best answer according to the text.

1. Although past experience is a good guide to construction planning, but each project which is likely to have special problems or opportunities _____.
   A. may also be necessary to make organizational decisions about the relationships between project participants
   B. may require considerable ingenuity and creativity to overcome or exploit
   C. will be used on a project is often determined during construction planning
   D. face the various problem of choosing the best among numerous alternative plans

2. Two important procedures in the development of project schedule are _____.
   A. identifying the activities
   B. estimating the activity durations
   C. A or B
   D. A and B

3. According to the text, which statement is true? _____.
   A. In developing a construction plan, it is common to adopt a primary emphasis on neither cost control nor on schedule control
   B. Dependency analysis: the project activities established by CPM are ordered according to the dependency relationships between them
   C. Good scheduling can eliminate problems due to production bottlenecks, and otherwise insure the completion of a project as soon as possible
   D. Poor scheduling cannot result in considerable waste as laborers and equipment wait for the availability of needed resources

4. According to the text, many aspects of project plans and activity inter-relationships _____.
   A. is focused then on monitoring the implementation of the original plan
   B. must be adopted to bring back the work progress to the desired performance
   C. cannot or have not been represented in network models
   D. is constantly reviewed by the project team with comparisons to the real project progress to make necessary changes

5. We learn from the passage that one can see _____ in the "S" curve.
   A. whether the project is ahead of the schedule or behind the schedule
   B. the anticipated expenditure for the project
   C. the basic cost control methodology is analogous to that of schedule control
   D. whether the project is ahead of the schedule or behind the schedule, and the anticipated expenditure for the project

II. Decide the following statements are true or false.

1. The bar chart lists activities and shows their scheduled start, finish and duration, but bar chart presentation carries much more information than other ways.

2. The most widely used scheduling technique is the Critical Path Method (CPM) for scheduling, often referred to as critical path scheduling.

3. Indeed, many texts and managers regard critical path scheduling as the only usable and practical scheduling procedure.

4. Many aspects of project plans and activity inter-relationships can or have been represented in network models.

5. Cost overrun is an unfavorable situation just like a project delay. In fact, the budget plan is closely related to the schedule plan.

III. Change the following words to another form and write down the Chinese meanings.

1. fundamental _____
2. identification _____
3. utilization _____
4. eliminate _____
5. procurement _____
6. ingenuity _____
7. creativity _____
8. overcome _____
9. in addition to _____
10. match _____

IV. Give out the following words' synonym or other word in the closest meaning.

1. critical   a. related
2. considerable   b. exceed
3. associated   c. focus on
4. emphasize   d. important
5. breakdown   e. draw
6. presented   f. numerous
7. CPM   g. completion
8. depict   h. critical path method

9. complete
10. overrun

i. illustrated
j. decomposed into

V. Put the following English into Chinese.

1. Although past experience is a good guide to construction planning, each project is likely to have special problems or opportunities that may require considerable ingenuity and creativity to overcome or exploit.

2. In contrast, poor scheduling can result in considerable waste as laborers and equipment waiting for the availability of needed resources or the completion of preceding tasks.

3. It is basically a method to analyze the tasks involved in completing a given project, especially the time needed to complete each task, and to identify the minimum time needed to complete the total project.

4. While the network model of project activities is an extremely useful device to represent a project, many aspects of project plans and activity inter-relationships cannot be represented or have not been represented in network models.

VI. Put the following Chinese into English.

1. 建设项目规划与调度
2. 工程项目进度计划
3. 计划(项目)评估和审查技术(网络)或者计划评审技术
4. 时间刻度网络图
5. 关键路径调度算法

参 考 译 文

第 10 单元 施工组织设计与进度计划

1. 引言

施工组织设计和进度计划对于项目的顺利竣工来说非常重要。施工组织设计在建筑工程管理和实施中是一项基本的和有挑战性的活动。它涉及技术的选择、工程任务的确定、所需资源和各项任务工期的预算以及相关工程任务之中的交叉作业的辨别。合理的进度计划和资源利用对项目成本和时间最优化非常重要。一个好的施工组织是进行预算和计划的基础。项目进度计划趋向于将机械设备、材料和人工与随进度推移的项目工程任务相匹配。

2. 施工组织设计

2.1 施工组织设计的因素

制订施工组织设计是施工管理中的关键任务,即便这个组织设计不是书面或正式的记录。施工组织设计包括所需工作任务的安排,分析这些工作任务的工作内容,以及对实施各种工作任务的可选方案的选择。除这些施工计划的技术方面之外,对项目参与方和将参与在项目中的组织之间关系的组织决策也很必要。例如,用在项目上的对于哪一个分包商的参与程度常常是在施工组织设计期间做出的决定。对于特定的项目，存在许多可能的可用组织设计。虽然过去的经验对施工组织设计来说是良好的指导，但是每个项目可能有着特殊的问题或机会，这些问题或机会可能需要相当多的智谋和创造力去战胜和开发。施工组织设计者面临着在许多可选择的组织设计中做出最好选择的问题，且施工组织设计者也必须设想按照施工组织设计和规范中所描述的最终设施。

2.2 施工组织设计的类别

在制订施工组织设计中，通常的控制重点要么是成本控制要么是进度控制。一些项目主要被分成与成本关联的费用类别。在这些情形中，项目施工组织设计是成本导向型或费用导向型的。在费用型类别中，在工作任务的实施中直接引起的成本和为了项目的完成间接引起的成本之间形成了区别。传统的进度计划程序强调任务优先关系的维持或者随进度推移对资源的有效使用。最后，大部分复杂项目要求随着进度推移对成本和进度计划两者进行考虑，以致施工组织设计、监控和记录保存必须考虑到两个维度。在这些情形中，进度计划和预算信息的整合是主要的关注点。

2.3 施工组织设计技术

目前，在计划准备之中，施工组织设计者主要使用项目管理方法的原则和技术，这些原则包括：

➢ 工作分解结构(WBS)：项目的工程内容被分解成一系列主要的工作任务，且每套工作任务依次被分解成一系列次工作任务。

➢ 关联性分析：通过 WBS 建立起来的项目工作任务根据它们之间的依赖关系来安排。

➢ 期限评估：实现每项工作任务所需时间是被计算的。

➢ 网络开发：通过使用网络技术(主要是 CPM 或 PERT)，工作任务以图表的形式呈现。有关工作任务期限的详细情况和优先关系在网络上进行阐明。

➢ 资源分配：资源的恰当类型和规模被固定在每项工作任务上，同时顾及到时间跨度和所需的资源。

➢ 成本估价：根据工作任务的工程内容、工期和资源需求，计算出每项工作任务的成本。

3. 施工进度计划

➢ 通常，项目进度计划受天气、当地施工实际、施工方法以及资源可用性等因素的影响。在项目进度计划中两个重要的步骤是识别工作任务和估计工作任务期限。项目工作任务的识别需要对项目施工组织设计、图纸、规范和其他要考虑事项(比如一般需要和特殊条件等方面)进行审查。工作任务期限的估计以资源可用性为基础，这种可用性反映出所期望的项目施工现场状况的资源生产率。

➢ 除把日期分配给项目工作任务之外，项目进度计划的目的是把在施工期间的设备资源、材料和对于项目工程任务的人工进行匹配。合理的进度计划能够消除因生产瓶颈引起的问题，减轻必须材料及时采购的困难，而且确保项目尽快竣工。相比而言，不良的进度计划将导致人工和设备的窝工等待，可用所需资源或者等待紧前任务的完成造成的极大浪费。由于不合理的进度计划导致的整个项目竣工的延误也可能引起急于使用建设项目的雇主的大混乱。

Unit 10　Construction Planning and Scheduling

➢ 用得最广泛的进度计划技术是关键路径法(CPM)，常常被称作关键路径进度计划。该方法计算出项目最少完成时间及项目工作任务的可能开始和结束时间。的确，许多教科书和项目经理把关键路径进度计划看做是唯一可用和实际的进度计划程序。关键路径进度计划的计算机程序和运算法则的可用范围很广，且能够高效率地处理包括成千上万种工作任务的项目。

➢ 计划(项目)评审技术(PERT)是用来在一个项目之内对任务进行日程安排、组织和协调的项目管理工具。从根本上说，它是分析在完成一个指定项目过程中所涉及的任务，尤其是分析完成每项任务所需要的时间，以及鉴定完成全部项目所需要的最少时间的方法。PERT 规划的步骤如下：
- 识别具体工作任务和里程碑事项；
- 确定工作任务的恰当顺序；
- 建立网络图表；
- 估计每项工作任务所需的时间；
- 决定关键路径；
- 随着项目进展更新 PERT 图表。

4. 展现项目进度计划

项目施工组织设计常常通过建立更精细的网络而展现，直到计划设计令人满意。对于策划人和项目经理来说，使用图表项目展现是一个重要的且极其有用的手段。网络计划图表和曲线图提供了快速传达或者理解项目进度计划的非常有价值的方法。由于基于计算机的基本项目数据的贮存，曲线图的输出很容易获得，且无论什么时候都可以使用。一个非常管用的项目网络曲线图就是用来时标网络计划图。在时标网络图中，网络上的工作任务在水平轴上标出，以便测量项目开始以来的时间。另一个有用的曲线图展现工具是针对每项工作任务阐明计划时间的横道图或甘特图。横道图列出工作任务并且表明它们的已安排日程的开始、结束和期限，但是横道图展现的信息比其他方式少得多。

5. 进度控制

➢ 项目工作任务的网络模式是一种极其有用的描绘项目的工具，项目计划和工作任务的许多方面和相互关系在其他模式中不能或者没有被描绘。施工阶段开始的时候，注意力于是集中在对原计划执行的监控上，同时从时间、成本和质量几方面测量工程的进展，且通过网络计划图对计划与实际完成情况进行对照。如果任何违背原计划的工作被发现，就必须采取纠正措施把工程进展调整到所需要的状况。

➢ 编制项目进度计划以后，该项执行中的进度计划会不断地受到项目小组的检查，以对实际项目的进展做必要的更改。在施工过程的监测和控制阶段，施工项目经理必须经常对业务工作任务工期和进展中的成本进行跟踪。这些监测方面的努力连同执行是项目进度管理成功的关键。成本超支是一种不利情况，就像是项目的延误。事实上，预算计划与进度计划有紧密的关系。

➢ 如此一来，在项目的生命周期中，进度计划可以透露潜在的成本信息。"S"曲线法经常被用来描述项目进度和成本之间的关系。在"S"曲线中，人们可以看到项目是处于进度之前还是进度之后，以及对于项目的预期支出。成本控制与进度控制需要不断监控与工程计划与项目现金流的对比。无论它们是短期计划、长期计划、每天计划还是以月份为基础的计划，基本的成本控制成套方法与进度控制方法是类似的。在设施建设完成前，不断的评估是必要的。许多雇主需要详细的施工进度计划作为监测承包商工作进展的一种手段。通常以实际完成的工程进度与施工进度计划对比，以确定施工进度是否令人满意。

6. 进度计划问题

➤ 完成工程不合理的进度要求常常导致项目参与方之间的冲突。如果不给承包商完成工程的合理期限，那么承包商可能因为增加的职工数量或加班工作而招致成本增加和无效率，也可能会走捷径以维持进度，并且可能利用一些产生最快的结果而非所想要的结果的手段和方法。为了赶时间，恰当的工程顺序安排可能会被搁置一边从而增加生产率。这些事件可能会消极地影响到竣工的设施。

➤ 由雇主所要求的、对于项目范围无计划的、大规模的或者过度的变更数量，可能引起不完整或者不准确的合同文件，并且，当与不合理的进度要求相结合时，可能对承包商产生负面影响。这种情况下，需要对合同价格、合同期限或者两者的变更指令做出处理。这些变更会影响购买订单和进度计划，并且通常会导致承包商更高的成本。

阅读

进度计划技术的发展

1. 引言

➤ 项目通常受到时间、资源和组织的制约。施工管理需要高度精确的规划、进度计划和项目过程的管理，这样才能使成本、时间和资源的全面优化成为可能。的确，施工规划影响到项目生命周期的大部分，因此，在很大的程度上，项目的成功与施工规划的功效有关系。施工规划是为了预先确定的项目目标的完成而决定适当的策略的过程。在建筑工程项目中，规划的目标是在一个固定的时间内，以预算的成本以及明确的质量标准，完成规定工程总量的项目。

➤ 几十年中，项目施工进度计划编制受到广泛的研究，已经被开发出了各种各样的专业技术来用以解决特定的情况或问题。借助更强大的计算机和软件技术，应用先进的进度计划编制技术使计划变得更加容易且更切合实际。这些技术可以应对一些重要的实际问题，比如：

- 在工作任务工期面对不确定的估算进行进度计划编制；
- 整合的进度计划编制规划和资源分配；
- 在松散的或者规划拙劣的情况下进行进度计划编制。

➤ 项目经理广泛使用横道图、关键路径法(CPM)、计划评估审查技术(PERT)等进度计划编制和进展监控技术的传统方式被做规划。在项目经理身上存在一个不断增加的压力，需要缩短交付时间，减少在(施工)过程中涉及的成本但不能降低建筑物的质量。因此，如今建筑工程项目的新实践和不断增加的复杂性导致了商业上可用的、计算机化的规划和进度计划编制工具数量的增加。

2. 编制不确定工期的进度计划

已经特别提到，不确定性是施工过程中的通常状态。工作任务的工期是实际工作所需时间的估计，且常常存在着与实际完成时间的很大的不确定性。在项目的初期规划阶段，因为对项目的范围和障碍仍然不明确，所以工作任务工期的不确定性特别巨大。雇主的控制之外的工作任务更加不确定。例如，不利的天气、深沟的倒塌或者劳工的罢工会使工期估计特别不确定。

首先，工作持续时间的不确定性可能被简单地忽略，且进度计划编制通过对于每项工作任务所期望的或者最有可能的持续时间来进行。将不确定性引入进度计划编制过程的正式方法需要做更多的工作和设想。使用预测工作持续时间的方法常导致得到对完工过分乐观的进度计划。

其次，单一持续时间工作任务的使用常常使进度计划者产生固定、无弹性的思维倾向。显然，基于必不可少的实际经验，在进度计划的编制中使用固定持续工作时间可以在过程中持续对进度计划进行监控和更新。否则，项目进度计划会很快不适用。

于是，可能的施工组织设计和进度计划的数量巨大，因此，对于施工问题的重要领悟必须用来设计合理的可选方案。凭借改进的网络图表描绘和可用信息技术，人机互动作为进度计划编制程序得到发展并提供了多种可选方案。许多商业软件程序可以用来执行这些任务，例如 Primavera 公司的 P6 专业项目管理软件。

GERT(图表评审技术)是用于项目管理中的一项随机网络分析技术，它给予项目任务之间逻辑关系的有条件和概率处理办法，这些任务紧跟随机决定的观察顺序。项目任务之间的逻辑关系主要以两种项目任务之间的依赖性或者一个项目任务和转折点之间的依赖性为基础。GERT 的关键目标是评价网络逻辑基础和估计的任务工期，得出可能不被实施的一些任务的推论。

风险评审技术(VERT)是另一种用于项目管理的进度计划网络分析技术。VERT 的基本目的是支持牵涉到新风险企业和项目中的风险评定和量化中的管理、提供资金需要量的估计，以及评价进行中的项目、计划和系统。VERT 被完全计算机化。它允许对三个参数——时间、成本和执行中的风险进行分析。更重要的是，它允许用户以需要的任何水平的细节查清其问题。

3. 信息技术发展和详细模拟

3.1 模拟施工过程

随着个人电脑和易于使用的软件程序在施工现场的出现，正式的进度计划编制程序变得更加普遍了。通过因特网共享进度计划信息也提供了使用正式进度计划编制方法的更大诱因。在形成施工组织设计的过程中，一个很有用的方法就是模拟施工过程，要么以规划者的想象，要么以基于计算机的模拟技术。在计算机辅助设计(CAD)系统中的三维几何模型，在对工作任务操作空间(作业面)要求进行模拟并识别任何相关的作业面干涉方面是很有帮助的。类似地，对施工过程的资源可用性的辨识问题进行模拟，通过提供额外资源作为施工组织设计的一部分，可以有效地对问题进行预先阻止。

3.2 详细工作任务规划

项目进度计划的实际计算机描述一般由一列工作任务及其相关工期、所需资源和紧前工作任务构成。网络图示而非一个清单对于计划的可视化和确保精确要求得到满足来说很有帮助。对计算机程序的实际数据输入可以通过填满屏幕菜单上的空格、阅读一个现存的文档,或者用针对被提供信息的类型的标识符直接对程序输入数据来完成。项目日程和它的成本两者都不能被精确地控制。对于施工规划和进度计划来说,具有详细的工作任务很重要。总进度计划并没有出现在项目中的所有详细工作任务。正如需要更多详情那样,应对规划工作任务应当进行详尽说明。在施工规划和进度计划中,考虑详细工作任务、资源配置和作业面需要对于项目规划者来说非常困难。项目规划者对总进度计划关注较多而对详细工作任务有忽视的倾向。他们懂得,资源配置在施工规划和进度计划中是关键因素,但是他们缺乏分析资源配置的数学方法。

3.3 四维规划的详细工作任务

➤ 施工工作任务所需的操作空间(作业面)对于规划者来说是最难满足的要素,因为场地是静态的场所且处于不断变化中。由于工作任务所需的操作空间(作业面)在一段时间内在所有的三个维度变化,时间-空间可能在工作任务之间发生冲突,因此需要详细的四维规划和进度计划去计算每项工作任务的工期和相关联的所需的操作空间(作业面)。例如混凝土墙体施工工作任务,它包括许多类型的与时间-空间有关的工作任务。(绑扎钢筋、安装模板以及脚手架、浇筑混凝土、拆卸模板和脚手架将需要处理的时间、为工作人员进行作业并临时贮存的场所和操作所需的各种材料和设备。在这个简单的工作任务中有许多因素要考虑,且所有这些因素直接关系到施工规划和进度计划。

➤ 项目经理可以在项目的任何阶段使用可视化手段去监控施工工作任务和成本流程,且使用四维方式和模拟进行有效的资源配置,并可以使项目的工作流程更容易理解。通过使用模拟软件生成不同阶段在不同的(空间和操作)层面的施工流程和工作任务。在一个具体的时间段内,人们可以利用实际的建筑和计划的建筑模型对作业流程进行对比。通过观察结果,对照现行计划可以识别与计划的不同或问题。四位模拟可以进一步用于协助项目经理进行作业控制、分析和监控,通过创建前锋线的应用对在三维空间的建筑施工进度与进度计划同步进行。这种做法可能会帮助所有项目参与方以一种自然的方式对项目进度形成形象化的认识,因此最大限度地减少工程延误并使成本超支最小化。除监控作业流程之外,四位模拟可以用来进一步监控工程量、成本和资源。

4. 施工管理中信息技术的挑战

由于施工行业的实际情况,项目信息的整合将非常困难且非常漫长。目前大部分新建项目信息存在于孤立的数据库中,这些数据库存在于来自不同卖方的成百上千个互不兼容的软件应用程序中。由于建筑施工项目中情况复杂,大部分建筑公司由于紧缩的预算限制对技术革新比其他产业中的公司持更保守的态度,因此,一些新技术在决定一个特殊程序包的最恰当使用时,可能会缺乏工程经历、技术背景和基本常识。相反地,具有多年建筑行业经验的工程师在执行他们的任务时,可能没有综合的与计算机有关的知识来支持他们选择正确的信息技术系统和配置。此外,与其他商务软件不一样,在市场上只有有限的特定施工软件可供选择。这些局限使建筑公司在开发信息技术系统的通用配置的努力徒劳无功。那是造成这种信息技术在施工管理中同化进度缓慢的重要因素。

Unit 11

Construction Management Meeting

1. Introduction

During the course of a contract, various meetings are held on a regular basis to provide platforms for those parties involved in the delivery of the project to come together to discuss those items, issues, processes, procedures etc. that are required to complete the project, as required by contract, and to ensure a common understanding of any issues and to facilitate the actions required. These platforms will also provide a vehicle to identify and track the responsibility of those parties involved with specific issues, and the status and progress of various items and issues. Some of the typical project meetings include pre-construction meeting, weekly site meeting, coordination meetings monthly schedule update, and construction management meetings.

These meetings are crucial for the identification of project concerns and priorities, and the development of the associated action plans and corrective actions essential for the success of the contract and project. The meetings also provide the means for refocusing the parties and bringing in new stakeholders, especially during long and complex projects. In addition, meetings such as coordination meetings, change order negotiation meetings, notice of non-compliance and project memorandum resolution meetings are commonly used for problem prevention and resolution.

2. Responsibilities of the Project Manager

The Project Manager (PM) of employer, or architect/engineer, is primarily responsible for meeting coordination, meeting notification, agenda preparation, meeting minutes preparation and distribution, and follows up on issues that require action by the various participants of the meetings. The project manager is also responsible for conducting these meetings.

The PM of employer is ultimately responsible for project delivery and is the focal point of all issues related to the assigned project. In some programs, the PM assumes primary responsibility for assembling the construction management team, defining and communicating the roles and responsibilities of the individual team members, and promoting effective team interaction. The PM is also responsible for overseeing the management approach taken with the contractor. The PM must stay in touch with the project while it is in construction. The PM must monitor the project so that changes and/or unanticipated conditions do not unnecessarily impact cost, schedule, or quality of the project.

The contractor's project manager and/or superintendent is responsible for attending all required meetings, ensuring that the appropriate subcontractor, supplier, vendor, etc. is notified of required attendance (as necessary), and preparation and distribution of contractor-required documentation such as the contractor's monthly/weekly progress schedule.

3. Pre-Construction Meeting(Kick off Meeting)

The pre-construction meeting is arranged as soon as possible after the contract has been awarded. Its purpose is to establish a relationship and to discuss the mechanics under which the contract is to be administered. The pre-construction meeting provides the project participants with a basic project orientation of the roles, responsibilities, processes and procedures, and frontend priorities for the project. The lines of communication, the project-required processes and procedures for items such as subcontractor approval and/or substitution, payment process, requirements, submittals, request for information, and change orders will be addressed in this meeting. The pre-construction meeting is usually held within one or two weeks after issuance of the notice to commencement. The pre-construction meeting is held as there are several benefits to site communication which may arise from such a meeting, including the following:

➤ It allows people to get to know each other; this is likely to lead to better communication and less confrontational attitudes as the work progresses;

➤ It provides the opportunity to decide on how communication will operate;

➤ It provides the opportunity to define points of contact at each organisation;

➤ It can be used to ensure that all people have the contact details for others working on the project.

4. Weekly Site Meetings

The weekly site meetings are held to discuss general project status, specific problems related to construction, and outstanding items to be resolved. The site meeting is utilized to monitor progress and identify issues hindering construction of a specific project. During the site meetings, the PM reviews and discusses the progress of the project, including schedule variances and problem areas; responsibilities are assigned and timeframes established for resolution of identified issues. There are likely to be communication and building quality improvements from an appropriate number of well structured meeting participants. The responsible parties report back in subsequent meetings on progress being made toward resolution of previously identified issues, and reports any additional issues identified. The contractor should establish a timeline for resolving all outstanding items. The PM will establish the responsible party and a time limit for processing each outstanding variation instruction.

5. Monthly Schedule Update Meeting

The monthly schedule update meetings are held to review and discuss required monthly submittals, such as progress payments, schedules and trade staffing levels. In addition, some of the issues and topics discussed in the weekly site meetings may also be addressed in these meetings, if necessary. PM's staff and the contractor may elect not to have a monthly meeting, if the issues to be addressed in the monthly meeting are covered and addressed in the weekly meetings. The attendees and procedures are the same as the above weekly site meeting. Depending on the size of the project, it may be possible to combine this meeting with the weekly site meetings.

6. Project Management Co-ordination Meeting

The co-ordination meeting is utilized to ensure uniformity in managing all of the construction works within a program. The PM and the engineer are supposed to meet regularly to evaluate and monitor the contractor's performance under the contract. These meetings are different from site meetings held to discuss matters related to the work being carried out, and are intended to promote co-operation and efficiency. The benefits from such meetings will make the time spent notable. Trade co-ordination meetings have also often proven to be particularly worthwhile, especially at helping site work to progress smoothly and informal agreements between trades to be established. The meetings will handle current issues affecting the contracting community and understand how they may impact current and future construction projects. All concerned parties will present lessons learned during construction and find ways to prevent similar problems from reoccurring in the future.

7. Attendees of Meetings

The attendees of above meetings may include the following individuals or organization representatives:

- employer/owner/client representative;
- Project Manager (PM);
- engineer;
- architect/designer representative;
- quantity surveyor;
- contractor's project manager, superintendent, major subcontractors and Suppliers.

However, the attendees of project management co-ordination meeting are usually the parties' high profile delegates or senior members.

8. Meeting Minutes

The PM or engineer's personnel usually prepares the meeting agenda. After preparation of the agenda, written notification of the meeting is distributed to required and requested attendees. The status of the attendee, either required or requested, should be indicated on the notification. The notice also includes a copy of the agenda, and the time, place and date of the meeting. Preparation for the meeting should include a sign-in sheet, and any required handouts and notes for the meeting.

Meeting minutes are prepared to provide a record of items discussed and decisions made, and can be utilized to track and follow-up on the task and responsibilities issues at the meetings. Every effort shall be made to report the acts of the meeting without bias. The PM or engineer's personnel is responsible for taking notes at the meeting, preparing meeting minutes, and expeditiously distributing to all parties. Comments and corrections to the meeting minutes shall be forwarded in writing to the author prior to the next meeting or brought up for discussion at the next meeting if any party forwards to comment or correction. The minutes of the previous meeting may be amended, as required, and approved at the following meeting. The author reviews the comments and corrections submitted, and applies any necessary changes to the meeting minutes.

Reading

Site Meeting Minutes

DATE: 20th December 2004
PROJECT: William Shopping Center
CLIENT: Lexicon Investment Co. Ltd.
CONTRACTOR: Sigma Construction Co. Ltd.
START DATE: 6th January 2004
COMPLETION DATE: 1st November 2005
MEETING VENUE: Site Office
PRESENT:

ATTENDEE:	COMPANY NAME:
Kyle Davis	Lexicon Investment Co. Ltd.
Roy Martin	Lexicon Investment Co. Ltd.
Paul Henry	ATI Architects
Keith Thompson	ATI Architects
Lewis Anderson	Blanch Mechanical Engineering Associates
Lance Foeman	Lance Quantity Surveyor Associates
James Bond	Sigma Construction Co. Ltd.
Lewis Anderson	Sigma Construction Co. Ltd.
Jesse Rivera	Joinery Works Company—Subcontractor
Ed Rushing	Bay Mechanical and Electrical Corp.—Subcontractor
John Smith	John & Son Metal Works Company—Subcontractor

A. OBSERVATIONS AND DISCUSSIONS

A site meeting was held at 3:00 p.m on Tuesday, 20th December 2009. There was a review of the site meeting minutes dated 13th December 2009.

The following items were discussed and observations made.

B. GENERAL ACTION

1. Questioned by the architect, the main contractor stated that they remain on schedule for the contract completion date. Main contractor distributed Revision 5 to their internal schedule.

2. With respect to submittals –John & Son is awaiting the following.

Skylight shop drawings: John & Son is questioning architect on the details of the skylight for his interpretation. Revised shop drawings should be received by John & Son 13/1/10.

3. Main contractor is comfortable with the response from architect regarding the lift shaft decoration change. They are working on revising the shop drawings and they will be resubmitted as soon as possible.

4. Relative to item No. 5 of the previous meeting minutes concerning the parking ramp, architect has forwarded to Sigma the revised partition wall and general information regarding the shopping center parking passage. Paul requested that James contact Keith if he has any specific questions.

The signage package will be the directional signage to be addressed by client. There will be no need for a building directory.

5. Relative to item No. 6 of the previous meeting minutes, Bay Mechanical reported that the sprinkler shop drawings have been supplemented with revised calculations of the water curtain. They are waiting architect's review and acceptance.

6. Relative to item No. 7 of the previous site meeting minutes, when the main contractor has disassembled the ceiling and completed the sprinkler work, architect will be here on the 4th of Jan. to look at the ceiling before it is re-installed.

7. Relative to item No. 8 of the previous site meeting minutes concerning coordination drawings, the final item to be addressed within the coordination drawings are the ceiling height adjustments relative to the electrical duct. Bay Mechanical took field measurements of the ductwork size.

8. Concerning item No. 9 of the previous meeting minutes with respect to Manhole 57 as reflected in Proposal Request No. 17.1 which is included in Change Order No. 2, there has been a slight revision which has been reflected as a revised Proposal Request No. 17.1a. Main contractor is authorized to proceed with this work and if there are any minor amount money revisions, he is to send it to the architect immediately. James suggested installing a mud flap at the bottom of the manhole once the exact invert of the piping has been established.

Main contractor will be accomplishing some revision work in the bottom of the manhole for drainage, which was reviewed at this meeting. This includes a water dam at the corner penetration, as well as adding a small sump pit. This is scheduled to be submitted tomorrow.

9. Relative to item No. 10 of the previous site meeting minutes with respect to the 8" slab placement over electrical vault, this area will be full load tested at the expense of the main contractor. Main contractor stated the remainder of the concrete for stairs etc. needs to be placed and cured for at least 30 days before the full load test. This can now be load tested at any time. It will be load tested as soon as Bay Mechanical is done working in the area.

10. Concerning item No. 11 of the previous site meeting minutes, Kyle expressed his concern with respect to the louver detailing. The issue is moisture in the wall cavity. The detailing needs to be closely watched during installation to make sure that not only the sill but the

jambs and heads are addressed as well.

11. Concerning item No. 12 of the previous site meeting minutes with respect to the existing tunnel cap, main contractor reported that they have removed the existing waterproofing over the concrete cap. There are some minor areas of tar left on the concrete. Main contractor will have the supplier review the condition and approve prior to scheduling placement of concrete. John & Son is recommending installing expanded metal mesh for concrete preparation. Client authorized this to proceed but response to proposal request needs to be reacted to by the main contractor as soon as possible.

12. Relative to item No. 15 of the previous meeting minutes, the main contractor indicated that they still expect 12mm of the glass shipment in February.

13. Concerning item No. 16 of the previous meeting minutes, main contractor reported that the failed interior plastering sample has been replaced. They are waiting for architect's instruction to proceed.

14. Relative to item No. 17 of the previous meeting minutes, there will need to be cosmetic correction addressed for the curved columns that abut the main entrance. It is not a flush installation at the present time.

Also, there are a number of areas of cast in place concrete walls that most likely to need skim coat on plaster overcoat to address cosmetic issues.

Paul reviewed with client and main contractor various cast in place concrete conditions. The main contractor will be asked to provide a proposal for a sand float finish after the concrete has been rubbed down per the original contract document. This would be for all public areas. An area has been identified as acceptable sample from the main contractors that he had prepared for the architect.

15. Relative to item No. 18 of the previous meeting minutes, main contractor had a suggestion for consideration of applying a trowel finish on the exterior face of the concrete block backup for the atrium. The idea does have merit and the architect asked the main contractor to formally provide a price through Lance for consideration.

16. Relative to item No. 19 of the previous meeting minutes, main contractor had a question concerning the colour of the glaze base. Paul reviewed this area with the main contractor and client. A proposal request will be issued through ATI from main contractor to John & Son. Also, Paul reviewed the existing south wall brick condition. The infills for the existing brick openings shall be flush per direction from architect. Also, the cast in place concrete below this area should be addressed by pre-cast. Paul will be issuing a proposal request for this.

17. Relative to item No. 20 of the previous meeting minutes, main contractor will be issuing a utility shut-down request for water tentatively scheduled for 10th January 2010.

18. Relative to item No. 21 of the previous meeting minutes, the client request for removal and replacement of the existing vestibule door sets for Vestibule 50C. Client is requesting doors, frames, and hardware be replaced. Architect will issue a proposal request to Joinery Works.

19. Relative to item No. 22 of the previous meeting minutes, the client will be purchasing,

receiving and installing all of the home equipment outside of this contract. Relative to the furniture package, the built-in furniture and the required blocking for the built-in furniture will be issued to Joinery Works as a proposal request. The remainder of the furniture package is still being developed between Joinery Works and client.

20. Concerning item No. 24 of the previous meeting minutes, Sigma indicated that it seems likely that blocking off a portion of the parking stalls in the parking lot north of the project will not be needed. Delivery of parking lot is tentatively scheduled for 22 February 2010.

21. Concerning item No. 26 of the previous meeting minutes, client indicated that at the present time Lewis will only accept Bay Mechanical listed pre-manufactured sprinkler head guards. Facilities management of Lexicon will discuss this with Lewis.

22. With respect to item No. 27 of the previous meeting minutes, architect requested main contractor forward the information on the concrete screed for the atrium floor.

23. The condition of the existing aluminum door frame and thresholds in the main entrance was discussed. Client is requesting that these be removed and replaced with new designs. Architect will issue a proposal request to John & Son.

24. Main contractor indicated that there was a fair amount of water usage that appears on Bay Mechanical's bill for responsibility. Ed Rushing asked for a breakdown.

25. Electrical shut down is tentatively scheduled for 11th March through 20th March 2010. Main contractor is aware of the requirements for this type of work and is encouraged to get it started as soon as possible.

C. PROGRESS STATUS REVIEW

1. Overall project is approximately 55% complete.
2. Excavation 99% complete.
3. Drainage/Sewer 99% complete.
4. Structural concrete 99% complete.
5. Bricklaying 65% complete.
6. Landscaping 55% complete.
7. Site improvements 50% complete.
8. Structural steel 90% complete including fabrication.
9. Carpentry-structural 95% complete.
10. Pre-plaster 50% complete.
11. Electrical rough in 70% complete.
12. Roofing 75% complete.
13. Plumbing 45% complete.
14. Windows installation 70% complete.
15. Fire services 99% complete.
16. Gas services 99% complete.
17. Mechanical 50% complete.

18. Plasterer 35% complete.

19. Carpenter fixing 25% complete.

20. Production on site over past two weeks has only been 50% due to inclement weather.

D. PROJECT PAYMENT

1. Client stated that project budget was reviewed. And it was noted that project payment was tracking similar to previous months, all the interim payment effected in accordance with quantity surveyor's certification.

2. Sigma confirmed that they had received payment for their last payment application.

3. Bay Mechanical and Joinery Works complained their last payments were deferred, Lance would issue payment certificate within next week, Bay Mechanical and Joinery Works were supposed to back up their outstanding items in next application.

E. EXTENSION OF TIME

1. Inclement Weather

Total claims for loss of 26 days has been received and approved to date. Only leaves 15 days in delay clause. Another 11 days is under reviewing during July.

2. Other Claim

Claim (16 days) received for time lost due to preparing steel shop drawings. Following original rejection, Sigma has submitted additional information to substitute claim. Main reason for claim is lack of details on architectural drawings and some changes to steel structure as a result. This is being considered.

F. MEETING INFORMATION

The next site meeting will be held in two weeks Tuesday, January 3rd, 2010 at 3:00 p.m at the site office.

G. DISTRIBUTION

All the parties attended this meeting.

The preceding is assumed to be a complete and correct account of the items discussed, directions given, and conclusions drawn, unless this office is notified to the contrary immediately.

New Words and Expressions

construction management 施工管理
platform 平台
items 条款，项目
issues 问题

Unit 11　Construction Management Meeting

processes　流程，过程
procedures　程序，规程
facilitate　促进，帮助
vehicle　工具，传播媒介
track　追踪，跟踪
pre-construction　施工前
stakeholders　利益相关者，利害关系人
change order　工程变更通知单
non-compliance　不符合，不遵守
memorandum　备忘录，便签
project manager　项目经理
coordination　沟通，协调
notification　通知，通告，告示
construction management team　施工管理团队
contractor　承包人
unanticipated conditions　不可预料的状况
superintendent　负责人，主管，监督人
subcontractor　分包商，转包商
vendor　卖主，卖方
documentation　文件材料
progress schedule　进度计划，进度安排
awarded　授予，判定
mechanics　技术，结构
substitution　代替，置换
submittals　提交，建议
commencement　开始，发端
confrontational　对抗的，对抗性的
schedule variances　进度变更
quality improvements　质量改进
variation instruction　变更指令
progress payments　付款程序
staffing levels　人员编制，人员职级
attendees　出席者，在场者
co-ordination　协调，配合
uniformity　一致，均匀性，同样
worthwhile　值得做的，值得花时间的
representatives　代表
quantity surveyor　预算师或造价师
delegates　代表

handouts 讲义，宣传册子
bias 偏见
client 委托人，顾客，客户
venue 集合地点，发生地点
observations 评论，观察
completion 完成，结束，实现
signage 引导标示，标记指示
drainage 排水，排水系统
louver 天窗，百叶窗
excavation 挖掘，发掘
bricklaying 砖墙
landscaping 景观美化
carpentry 木工手艺

Exercises

I. Choose the best answer according to the text.

1. These meetings are crucial for the identification of project concerns and priorities, it also provide the means for _____.

    A. refocusing the parties

    B. bringing in new stakeholders

    C. during long and complex projects

    D. A and B

2. The Project Manager (PM) of employer is primarily responsible for _____.

    A. meeting coordination and meeting notification

    B. agenda preparation, meeting minute's preparation and distribution

    C. issues that require action by the various participants of the meetings

    D. above all

3. According to the text, which statement is true? The pre-construction meeting has several benefits including the following: _____.

    A. it allows people to get to know each other; this is likely to lead to better communication and less confrontational attitudes as the work progresses

    B. it provides the opportunity to decide on how communication will operate and to define points of contact at each organization

    C. it can be used to ensure that all people have the contact details for others working on the project

    D. above all

4. We learn from the passage that some of the subcontractors will not be able to attend

Unit 11 Construction Management Meeting

pre-construction meeting_____.

 A. the parties' high profile delegates

 B. senior members

 C. as they may have not been designated yet at that time

 D. none of the above

5. One of the main purposes for which QS is employed by the client is_____.

 A. to avoid budget overrunning and benefiting to the client

 B. to draw the attention of contractor to tendering issues

 C. to make the financial difficulties of the contractor and known to the clients

 D. to discuss project management with consultant

II. Decide the following statements are true or false.

1. Some of the typical project meetings include pre-construction meeting, weekly site meeting, coordination meetings monthly schedule update, notice of non-compliance and project memorandum resolution meetings

2. The architect/engineer, is primarily responsible for meeting coordination and notification, agenda preparation, meeting minute's preparation and distribution.

3. The pre-construction meeting provides the project participants with a basic project orientation of the roles, responsibilities, processes and procedures, and frontend priorities for the project.

4. The monthly schedule update meetings are held to review and discuss required monthly submittals, such as schedule payments, processes and trade staffing levels.

5. Some of the subcontractors will be able to attend pre-construction meeting as they may have not been designated yet at that time.

III. Change the following words to another form and write down the Chinese meanings.

 1. items _____
 2. vehicle _____
 3. stakeholders _____
 4. superintendent _____
 5. kick off meeting _____
 6. substitution _____
 7. agreements _____
 8. employer _____
 9. profile delegates _____
 10. completion _____

IV. Give out the following words' synonym or other word in the closest meaning.

 1. issues   a. key
 2. prominent   b. profession

3. monitor
4. academics
5. institution
6. crucial
7. liaise
8. mechanics
9. submittals
10. representatives
11. comment

c. associate
d. initial
e. tender
f. suggestions
g. delegates
h. sector
i. conservation
j. structures
k. problems

V. Put the following English into Chinese.

1. These meetings are crucial for the identification of project concerns and priorities, and the development of the associated action plans and corrective actions essential for the success of the contract and project.

2. The PM is ultimately responsible for project delivery and is the focal point of all issues related to the assigned project.

3. The pre-construction meeting provides the project participants with a basic project orientation of the roles, responsibilities, processes and procedures, and frontend priorities for the project.

4. Current issues affecting the contracting community and understand how they may impact current and future construction projects. Lessons learned during construction and find ways to prevent similar problems from reoccurring in the future.

5. Comments and corrections to the meeting minutes shall be forwarded in writing to the author prior to the next meeting or brought up for discussion at the next meeting if any party forward to comment or correction.

VI. Put the following Chinese into English.

1. 进度变更
2. 预算师或造价师
3. 项目总进度计划
4. 项目管理团队建设
5. 混凝土结构工程

参 考 译 文

第 11 单元　施工管理会议

1. 引言

在合同期间，各种会议定期举行，为那些涉及项目交付的各方聚在一起讨论项目竣工所需的、正如合同所要求的那些事项、争端、进程、步骤等提供一个平台，确保对任何争端的共同理解且推进必需的行动。这些平台也将提供一种手段去鉴别和跟踪那些与具体争端以及各种事项和争端的状况和进展有密切关系的当事人的责任。比较典型的项目会议有施工前会议、每周现场会议、每月日程更新协调会议以及施工管理会议。

　　这些会议对于项目重要和优先事项的确定、相关行动计划的展开以及针对合同和项目成功的必要矫正行动来说，是至关重要的。这些会议也会重新集中各方并带来新的利益相关者，尤其对于长期和复杂项目。另外，像协调会、变更谈判会、不服从通知和项目备忘录决议会这类会议，一般都是用来预防和解决问题的。

2. 项目经理的职责

　　雇主的项目经理(PM)或者建筑师/工程师主要负责会议协调、会议通知、议程准备、会议记录准备和分发，以及对争端进行跟踪，这些争端要求由会议的各参与方做出行动。项目经理也负责主持这些会议。

　　雇主项目经理(PM)最终要对项目的交付负责，而且是与所分配的项目有关的所有争端的焦点。在有些计划中，项目经理主要负责组合施工管理团队、定义和传达每个团队成员的角色和责任，以及推动有效的团队配合。项目经理也负责监督承包商所实施的管理方式。在施工过程中，项目经理必须保持与项目的联系。项目经理必须对项目进行监控，以使变更和/或未预料到的情况不会不必要地影响到项目的成本、日程或质量。

　　承包商的项目经理和/或主管负责出席所有必需的会议，确保恰当的分包商、供应商、销售商等被通知到必需的会议出席(作为必需事项)，以及确保诸如每月/每周进度计划之类的承包商所需文件资料的准备和分发。

3. 施工前会议(启动会议)

　　施工前会议会在合同授予之后尽快安排。它的目的是建立一种关系，并讨论合同将根据其而被执行的技术性细节。施工前会议对项目参与方提供基本的项目角色目标、责任、进程和步骤及项目的紧前工作优先事项。针对诸如分包商同意和/或替换、付款程序、必要条件、文件提交、信息要求以及变更指令等事项的沟通路线、项目所需的进程和步骤将在会议上进行议定。施工前会议通常在施工通知发布之后一到两星期之内举行。施工前会议的举行对于现场沟通有许多好处，具体内容如下：

- ➢ 让人们变得互相认识，随着工程的进展，人们之间会有更好的沟通和更少的对抗；
- ➢ 决定如何沟通；
- ➢ 它提供机会去确定每个组织中的联系人；
- ➢ 使所有人员拥有与项目有关的其他人的详细的联系方式。

4. 每周现场会议

　　举行每周现场会，目的是讨论总体项目状况、与施工有关的具体问题及要解决的突出事项。现场会议用来监控进展和发现阻碍特定施工工作的问题。在现场会议期间，项目经理检查和讨论项目的进展，包括进度偏离和问题区域；被分配的责任和针对已鉴定问题的解决方案的时间框架。可能有来自组织得很好的恰当数量的会议参与者的交流和建筑质量的改善。责任方在下次会议中汇报对于先前发现的问题的解决所取得的进展，并且报告所发现的其他问题。承包商应当建立一个解决所有遗留问题的时间表。项目经理将确定责任方和处理每项遗留变更指令的期限。

5. 每月日程更新会议

举行每月日程更新会议是为了检查和讨论每月必需提交的文件，例如施工进度付款、进度计划和项目各方人员编制。另外，如果必要的话，在每周现场会议上讨论的一些议题和话题也可能在这些会议中议定。如果在每月会议上要进行商议的问题在每周会议上被涉及和议定，项目经理的成员和承包商可以决定不举行每月会议。出席者和程序与每周现场会议相同。根据项目大小不同，可以决定是否把这种会议与每周现场会议合并召开。

6. 项目管理协调会议

项目管理协调会议用来确保管理所有的施工工作与工程进度计划的统一性。项目经理和工程师应该定期碰面，并根据合同评估和监控承包商的工作情况。这些会议不同于所举行的去讨论与正在实施的工程有关事务的现场会议，而是希望在项目上促进合作和效率。召开这种会议的好处是使时间花得可知可觉。项目分包工作协调会也常常被证明特别有价值，尤其在促使现场工作平稳进展和各分包之间将要建立的协作之间的非正式协议的签署方面。项目协调会议将处理影响缔约各方的现行问题，以及理解它们可能对当前和未来的建筑工程的影响。所有相关参与方将得出施工期间得到的教训，并找到方法去防止未来类似问题的再发生。

7. 会议出席人员

上述会议的出席人员可能包括下列个人或组织代表：
- 雇主/业主/雇主代表；
- 项目经理(PM)；
- 工程师；
- 建筑师/设计师代表；
- 工料测量师；
- 承包商的项目经理、监管人、主要分包商和供应商。

然而，项目管理协调会的出席者通常是各方高级别的代表或资深人员。

8. 会议记录

项目经理或工程师的员工通常要准备会议议程。在议程准备好之后，会议的书面通知将分发到必需的和被要求参会的出席者手中。出席者的身份，无论是必需的还是被要求的，应当在通知上标明。通知也包括议程的复印件，以及会议的时间、地点和日期。对会议的筹备应当包括签到单，以及会议的任何必需的印刷品和笔记簿。

会议记录用来提供所讨论事项的记录和所做出的决定，并且可以用来跟踪会上发布的任务和责任。每项工作努力应当没有偏袒地报告会议的决议。项目经理或工程师的员工负责在会上做笔记，准备会议记录，并迅捷地分发给所有当事人。对会议记录的评论和修改应当在下次会议之前以书面形式提交给评论人，或者在下次会议上提出讨论，如果有任何当事人提出评论和更正的话。上次会议的会议记录按要求可以在接下来的会议上被修正以及被认可。评论人审查所提交的评论和更正，并申请对会议记录的任何必要更改。

Unit 11　Construction Management Meeting

阅读

现场会议记录

日期：2009 年 12 月 20 日
项目：William 购物中心
雇主：Lexicon 投资有限公司
承包商：Sigma 建筑有限公司
开工日期：2009 年 1 月 6 日
竣工日期：2010 年 11 月 1 日
会议地点：现场办公室
出席情况：

出席人员	公司名称
Kyle Davis	Lexicon 投资有限公司
Roy Martin	Lexicon 投资有限公司
Paul Henry	ATI 建筑师
Keith Thompson	ATI 建筑师
Lewis Anderson	Blanch 机械工程事务所
Lance Foeman	Lance 工料测量师事务所
James Bond	Sigma 建筑有限公司——总包商
Lewis Anderson	Sigma 建筑有限公司——总包商
Jesse Rivera	Joinery 工程公司——分包商
Ed Rushing	Bay 机械电力公司——分包商
John Smith	John & Son 金属工程公司——分包商

A. 简评和讨论

现场会议于 2009 年 12 月 20 日星期二下午 3:00 举行。有一个对标有 2009 年 12 月 13 日的现场会议记录的回顾。

该会议对以下事项进行了讨论，且做了简评。

B. 总体行动

1. 建筑师提出质疑，总承包商申明他们仍然按照合同竣工日期的时间计划。总承包商分发了他们内部进度计划的第 5 号次修订方案。

2. 关于提交文件——John & Son 公司等待着如下事项。

天窗施工图：John & Son 公司询问建筑师有关天窗施工大样的说明。John & Son 公司应在 2010 年 1 月 13 日收到修订的施工图。

3. 总包商对建筑师有关电梯装饰的变更的答复很满意。他们正在对施工图做修订，且这些施工图会尽快重新提交。

4. 上次会议记录的第 5 事项是关于停车场斜坡的问题，建筑师已将有关购物中心的停车通道的修改隔断墙和全部信息送给总包商(Sigma)了。建筑师 Paul 要求 James(总包商)与

Keith(建筑师)直接联系，如果他有任何具体问题的话。

5. 有关上次会议记录的第 6 事项，Bay 机械电力公司报告说，自动喷水灭火装置的施工图以修改的水幕的计算结果做了增补。他们正在等待建筑师的审查和认可。

6. 有关上次现场会议记录的第 7 事项，当总包商拆除天花板并完成自动喷水灭火装置工程的时候，建筑师将在 1 月 4 号到此，在重新装配以前审视天花板。

标志包将由雇主进行导向性的标识。不需要建筑目录。

7. 上次现场会议记录的第 8 事项是关于协调图纸的问题，在协调图纸之内的将被议定的最后事项是有关用电管道的顶高调节。Bay 机械电力公司进行了管道系统的现场测量。

8. 上次会议记录的第 9 事项是关于 57 号检修孔，反映在 No.17.1 条提议要求中，该提议包含在第 2 号变更指令中，有微小修改的修订为提议要求 No.17.1a 条提交出来。总包商被授权继续进行该工程，且如果存在较小数额的资金修改，他将立即发送给建筑师。James(总包商)建议，一旦管道系统弯头做好就在检修孔的底部安装一个挡泥板。

总包商将在检修孔的底部就排水完成一些修改工程，这一点在本次会议中做了评审。该项工程包括角落渗水处的一个挡水坝，另外还增加一个小型污水池。这将做出时间安排并于明天提交。

9. 有关上次现场会议记录的第 10 事项，关于配电室上的 8" 混凝土板浇筑，该区域将进行全荷载检测，检测费用由总包商来承担。总包商指出剩余部分的楼梯混凝土浇筑等需要保养至少 30 天以后才能进行全荷载检测。目前已经可以在任何时间进行检测。Bay 机械电力公司一完成该区域的施工，即可进行全荷载检测。

10. 有关上次现场会议记录的第 11 事项，Kyle(投资商)表达了对于百叶窗的细节设计问题的担忧。该问题是墙洞里很潮湿。细节设计需要在安装期间仔细地观察，以确保不仅窗台而且侧板和顶部也要选准位置。

11. 上次现场会议记录的第 12 事项是关于井道盖的，总包商报告说他们已经移走了在混凝土盖上面的现有防水层，混凝土盖上只有较小区域留下一些沥青。总包商将让供应商检查井盖状况，并在浇筑混凝土之前得到认可。John & Son 公司推荐安装金属网片进行混凝土准备。委托人授权可以这样做，但是建议请求的答复需要由总包商尽快做出反应。

12. 有关上次会议记录的第 15 事项，总包商指出，他们仍然在等待二月份 12mm 玻璃的交货。

13. 有关上次会议记录的第 16 事项，总包商报告不合格的内粉刷样板已经做了更换。他们在等待建筑师的施工指令。

14. 有关上次会议记录的第 17 事项，将需要对紧靠主入口的弧形柱的装饰进行修正处理。目前这不是一个平整的安装。

同样，有许多现浇混凝土墙的区域，都有可能需要在粉刷后涂腻子面层来处理装饰问题。

建筑师 Paul 与雇主和总包商一起检查了各种现浇混凝土的状况。在混凝土面按原始合同文件被磨光之后，将要求总包商提供对混凝土面的粉刷饰面建议。这将针对所有公共区域。另外一个来自总包商的作为可接受样本的区域已被建筑师认可，总包商为建筑师准备了该样本。

15. 有关上次会议记录的第 18 事项，总包商建议的在中庭的混凝土砌块的外墙面上使用镘刀收光的建议。这个建议确实很好，建筑师要求总包商通过 Lance(工料测量师)正式报价以供参考。

16. 有关上次会议记录的第 19 事项，总包商有一个关于涂釉基座的颜色的问题。建筑师 Paul 与总包商和雇主一起检查了该区域。建议请求将通过 ATI 建筑师事务所从总包商发送给 John & Son 公司。同时，建筑师 Paul 检查了南墙砖的情况。对现有砖墙开口应当按建筑师的指示与外墙砌平。同样，在该区域下面的现浇筑混凝土应当通过预制混凝土来进行处理。建筑师 Paul 将对此发布一个建议请求。

17. 有关上次会议记录的第 20 事项，总包商将发布一个暂定于 2010 年 1 月 10 日的对水设施的封闭试验要求。

18. 有关上次会议记录的第 21 事项，委托人要求移走现在的前厅门并更换成门 50C。委托人正要求更换门、框和五金器具。建筑师将发布建议请求给 Joinery Works 公司。

19. 有关上次会议记录的第 22 事项，委托人将购买、接收和安装该合同之外的所有室内设备。关于家具合同、嵌入式家具和必需的内置家具模块化将以建议请求发给 Joinery 工程公司。家具合同的剩余部分仍然在 Joinery 工程公司和委托人之间进行合作。

20. 有关上次会议记录的第 24 事项，Sigma 建筑有限公司指出，封闭项目北面停车场里的部分停车棚似乎并不必要。停车场的交付日期暂定于 2010 年 2 月 22 日。

21. 有关上次会议记录的第 26 事项，雇主指出，目前 Lewis 公司仅接受 Bay 机械电力公司列出的预制自动喷水灭火装置的喷头保护装置。Lexicon 公司设施管理部门将与 Lewis 公司讨论这一点。

22. 关于上次会议记录的第 27 事项，建筑师要求总包商提交有关中庭地面的混凝土找平层的信息。

23. 对主入口处的现有铝制门槛状况进行了讨论。雇主正要求移走这些门框且用新的来替换。建筑师将发布建议请求给 John & Son 公司。

24. 总包商指出，有一个出现在 Bay 机械电力公司账单上要负责的公平的用水量。Ed Rushing(分包商)要求提供明细账单。

25. 断电日程暂时安排从 2010 年 3 月 11 日至 3 月 20 日。总包商对此类型的工作要求是被告知的，且应支持尽快通电。

C. 进展状况检查

1. 整体项目大约完成了 55%。
2. 挖掘 99%完工。
3. 排水/下水道 99%完工。
4. 结构混凝土 99%完工。
5. 砌砖工作 65%完工。
6. 景观美化 55%完工。
7. 工地改善 50%完工。
8. 钢结构 90%完工，包括装配。
9. 木工结构 95%完工。
10. 初粉刷 50%完工。
11. 电气初安装 70%完工。

12. 屋顶 75%完工。
13. 管道工程 45%完工。
14. 窗户安装 70%完工。
15. 消防设施 99%完工。
16. 煤气设施 99%完工。
17. 机械 50%完工。
18. 泥灰工作 35%完工。
19. 木作装配 25%完工。
20. 由于恶劣天气,过去两周里工地的生产仅仅只有 50%。

D. 项目付款

1. 委托人申明,项目预算已经审查过。且表明项目付款跟随类似于前几个月的情况,并且所有期中付款根据按工料测量师的付款证书支付。

2. Sigma 建筑有限公司确认,他们已经收到针对他们上一次付款申请的付款。

3. Bay 机械电力公司和 Joinery 工程公司抱怨他们上一次的付款被延迟,工料测量师 Lance 将在下星期之内发出付款证书,Bay 机械电力公司应该在下次申请中补充他们的未付款项证明材料。

E. 时间延长

1. 恶劣天气

对于 26 天的全部工期索赔到目前已经收到且被认可。在误期条款中只批准 15 天。7月份的 11 天误期正在审查中。

2. 其他索赔

对由于为准备钢结构施工图的工期索赔(16 天)已收悉。根据原来拒绝的情况,Sigma 建筑有限公司已经提交额外资料替换索赔。索赔的主要原因是建筑图纸上缺乏大样以及对钢结构的一些变更。这一点正在考虑之中。

F. 会议信息

下一次现场会议将在两星期后的星期二,2010 年 1 月 3 日下午 3:00 于现场办公室举行。

G. 会议资料分发

所有参加了本次会议的各方。

上述内容被认为是完整的并正确论述了所讨论的事项、给出指令和得出结论,除非本办公室得到了相反的通知。

Unit 12
Construction Risk Management

1. Introduction

The management of risks is extremely critical for project success. Risk management has been widely applied in various fields such as economics, insurance, industries, and so on. While the word "risk" means that uncertainty can be expressed through probability, risk management is a structured process for the management of uncertainty through risk assessment. All risks must be evaluated in terms of two distinct elements: the likelihood that the event is going to occur as well as the consequences, or effect, of its occurrence. Risk and opportunity are mirror opposites of each other. Opportunity emerges from favorable project circumstances and risk emerges from unfavorable events.

The inherent uncertainties are generally not only from the unique nature of the construction project, but also from the diversity of resources and activities. Moreover, risks are not always independent and static in construction projects. The effect of two events is not necessarily the sum of their individual effects. For example, one-day delay due to snow storm and the same day delay due to a design change are two independent events, but in combination they have the same consequence – no work can be done that day. Accordingly, risks are usually dynamic, that is, their characteristic, probability and impact can change during the project process.

Risk management refers to the art of identifying, analyzing, responding to and controlling project risk factors in a manner which best achieves the objectives of all participants. Additionally, effective risk management typically generates positive results on a project by improving project performance, increasing cost effectiveness and creating a good working relationship between contracting parties.

2. Risks in Construction

Construction project success is usually measured by its schedule, budget and quality which conflict is inherent. Broadly, various risks can affect these three basic factors against the success of a project. In general, the project scale and complexity have close relation to the schedule of the project; and at the same time those two aspects have relations with the impact or severity of risk, that is, in many circumstances, the larger and more complex the project is, the longer the time is required to complete the project, and more severely it will be affected by project uncertainties and risks. Thus, in large and complex projects, the potential risks in construction projects are many and varied; budget overruns and schedule slippages have been common and scope changes are inevitable as well. The main risks in construction projects can be classified into physical, technical(construction, design), political, financial, legal-contractual and environmental risks.

2.1 Contractor's Risk in International Market

The contractor faces a multitude of risks in international market. From tendering stage, the contractor needs to be able to identify the risks in the contract in order to prepare the tender. Among them are inflation, bad weather, strikes and other labour problems, shortage of materials, unforeseen conditions at the construction site, accidents (whether by fire, flood or carelessness); and innovative design that does not work or proves impossible to construct, and the interaction between liability for defective workmanship and for faults in design, because lack of coordination between design and construction is a common source of dispute. Many of the risks posed by archaeological finds, environmental or other citizen opposition are shared by the contractor. Work stoppage can affect contractors' allocation of men and materials, or prevent contractor from bidding other work. Ultimately, the contractor faces the possibility of losing a great deal of money or of being forced out of the business.

2.2 Risk of Changed Conditions

Historically, unforeseen site conditions have caused many construction claims and have driven more than some contractors into default. This important provision, sometimes referred to as a "differing site conditions" clause, is now part of the international standard documents, as well as the AlA and FIDIC documents. Some changed conditions or unforeseen site conditions might affect the cost of work. For example, Those unforeseen ground conditions can necessitate the driving of longer piles or the use of more support steel than was first planned foundation work. Both operations might disrupt and delay work, throw schedule out of kilter, and cost significantly more than a contractor could reasonably expected. Although the contractor denotes acceptance of the risk, when he is signing the contract documents, however, some contractors are still gamblers at heart and prefer to take the risks, and along with that risk potential for a windfall profit. In the presence of a changed condition, the employer should provide an equitable means of paying the contractor for overcoming conditions that neither he nor the employer could have expected from the information available at the time the contract was prepared, but it always is not the case. Changed conditions or unforeseen site conditions are not a rare case in international construction market.

Factors such as these can result in contractors experiencing significant increases in the cost of the works, as well as delay. The key questions for the contractor are accordingly:

> ➢ whether the additional costs can be recovered from the employer; and
> ➢ whether an extension of time to completion and relief from delay damages can be obtained.

3. International Project Risks

International project risks are sometimes overlooked or assessed haphazardly by some contractors; such cases have incurred colossal financial damages. For international construction, the purpose of risk management is to mitigate risks by planning for factors that can be detrimental to project objectives and deliverables. Although risk management is a relatively known and practiced process, few contractors have conquered its successful implementation. Much of what is practiced is based on intuition, personal judgment. Such risks include war, civil war, terrorism, and expropriation, inability to transfer currency across borders, and trade credit defaults by foreign customers.

Although risks such as civil unrest and economic unstability are typically outside the scope of normal business, understanding and dealing with these risks are critical for companies working internationally. Study discovered that only few of companies had in place systematic and consistent methodologies to assess political risks. Working in an international setting often requires a much wider view of the project's context than with domestic projects.

4. Risk Management

Risk management requires a systematic and practical method of dealing with both the predictable and unpredictable risks inherent in the construction market. Contractors must acquaint themselves with the risks, and they should manage and develop specific risk minimization strategies. Project risk management must be comprised of the feedback used to regulate the risk management performance. Risk management typically involves the following four distinct functions:

4.1 Risk Identification

The initial step is to identify of the risks associated with a proposed construction project or contract at the early stages of the project's life. The identification process will form the basis whereby risks, uncertainties, constraints, policies and strategies for the control and allocation of risk are established. The formulation of construction risk management is to allocate risk among the employer, the contractor, and the architect.

Risk identification is the process of determining the specific risk factors that can reasonably be expected to affect the project. Risk identification is the essential step for a successful project. Prior to negotiation, contractor should assign at least one experienced person to identify contractual and extra-contractual risks. Identification of risk factors is fundamental requirement. Risk identification can be done by approaches such as standard checklists, expert interviews, Delphi technique, comparing to other projects and facilitated brainstorming sessions.

4.2 Impact Analysis

Analysis of probability and consequences – the potential impact of these risk factors, is determined by how likely they are to occur and the effect they would have on the project if they did occur. Since risks influence all aspects of a project, each party should quantify the impact a risk will have on the project cost, schedule, quality and/or profit. Contractor must evaluate risk factors or characteristics of a risk such as the risk event, its probability of occurrence, and the amount of potential loss or gain, and analyze every possible issue or event causing or that may cause harm to the project. So the impact of possible risks can be controlled to the extent where the risks are effectively identified and managed.

4.3 Response System

There are some actions which needed to be taken responding to residual risk coming in the risk response. Sometimes reevaluation is needed. The uncertainty of a risk event as well as the probability of occurrence or potential impact should decrease by selecting the appropriate risk mitigation strategy or avoiding of the risk factors. Uncertainty is reduced by using more data and information. Risk mitigation strategies are steps taken to minimize the potential impact of those risk factors deemed sufficiently threatening to the project. Those mitigation strategies are the most common risk management and handling techniques. Four itigation strategy categories commonly used are:

➢ Avoidance – when a risk is not accepted and other lower risk choices are available from several alternatives. In case of intolerable risk and no way for mitigation of damages, the project is aborted;

➢ Retention/Acceptance – when a conscious decision is made to accept the consequences should be the event occur;

➢ Control/Reduction – when a process of continually monitoring and correcting the condition on the project is used. This process involves the development of a risk reduction plan and then tracking the plan.

➢ Deflecting/Transferring

Deflecting or transferring risks by contract is a common response ranging from total allocation of risk to another party or risk-sharing between two or more parties. Forms of sharing the risk with others include contractual shifting, performance incentives, insurance, warranties, bonds etc. The risk elements are transferred by contracting out the affected work. Project managers should be educated regarding how risks can be managed by negotiating and drafting carefully considered and project specific contract provisions. Some basic risk management concepts are:

● Public work—transfer risk to others.
● Private work—some employers are uninterested, uninformed or naive.
● Reciprocal contract provisions—minimize exposure to the risks assumed.
● Mitigate risks by requiring and enforcing compliance with insurance provisions.
● Effective risk management requires project management's attention not only during the negotiating/contracting phase but throughout the entire project.

4.4 Risk Register

In the past decades or so the use of the risk register as a key control document has gained acceptance with most clients. The risk register lists all the identified risks and the results of their analysis, evaluation and information on the status of the risk. The risk register should be continuously updated and reviewed throughout the course of the project.

The risk register should contain the following information: risk number (unique within register); risk type; author (who raised it); date identified; date last updated; description; likelihood; interdependencies with other sources of risk; expected impact; bearer of risk; countermeasures; and risk status and risk action status. All the risks, including potential variations, were subject to continuous review and modification.

The risk register is important for the following five reasons:
- monitoring and, if necessary, correcting progress on risk mitigation measures;
- identifying new risks;
- closing down expired risks;
- amending risk assessment for existing risks;
- approving the drawdown of project contingencies by the client when required.

5. Contractual Risk Management

5.1 Risk allocation in Construction Contract

- Control and documentation – creating a knowledge base for future projects based on lessons learned. The parties' risk management strategies and goals should be reflected in the language of the contract. Contractors should adopt the philosophy in the area of risk transfer negotiation that "if they don't ask, they don't get." Contractual risk transfer in the construction industry is seen most frequently in contract provisions regarding indemnity, consequential damages, differing site conditions and delay.

- Risk allocation in international construction market is established by the construction contract. The importance of the contract cannot be overemphasized. Ideally, the parties, in their contract, will assign the risks and liabilities to the party best equipped to manage and minimize them. The contracting process provides the vehicle for each party to negotiate, define and limit its rights in accordance with its goals. The risks and responsibilities associated with a specific project must be clearly allocated within the contract. In the end, the contract serves as a framework of the law between the parties and will establish which party has assumed or negated a particular risk in connection with the project. During that time the risk allocation agreed at the time of contracting can change substantially. This is especially so with regard to the availability of materials and its costs.

- Although the contract serves as the principal risk management vehicle, parties must begin managing and minimizing risks long before the contract is signed. To avoid inequities, contractors should come to the negotiating table with some idea of their risk management goals. How these risks are allocated under the contract and (if not by the contract itself) under the applicable law is accordingly important. Different contracts and different governing laws approach this in quite different ways.

Unfortunately, most contractors pay insufficient attention to the risk management process.

5.2 Contractual Indemnity

Indemnification, also known as an agreement to hold harmless, may be defined as the obligation of one party (the indemnitor) to reimburse another party (the indemnitee) for the losses the indemnitee incurs or the damages for which it may be held liable. Contracting parties normally utilize indemnification clauses to shift the risk of a variety of liabilities. For instance, the main contractor may assume the employer's risks and subcontractors may assume the main contractor's risks.

5.3 Contractual Risk Transfer

Contractual risk transfer is a form of risk management which has been employed for many years in international construction market. It involves the allocation or distribution of the risks inherent to a construction project between or among contracting parties. If done effectively, risk transfer does not grossly or inequitably allocate all risk to one party, but instead places risk upon parties according to their ability to control and insure against risk. The underlying concept for this risk transfer is to pass risk to another party who may be in a better position to monitor and protect against the risk or in a better financial position to accept and insure against the risk.

The identified four common routes for the transfer of risk as follows:
- employer to contractor;
- contractor to subcontractor;
- employer, contractor, subcontractor or architect to insurer;
- contractor or subcontractor to surety.

However it should be noted that implementing transfer of the risks to others may result in development of different contract terms, payment of higher fees or additional premiums. If risks can be transferred, their consequences can be shared or totally carried out by someone other than the employer. The employer will be expected to pay a premium for this, so responsibility for initiating this form of risk response lies with the employer.

5.4 Insurance

The insurance against the probable occurrence of risk factor is needed. Most physical risks can be insured against. For example, on engineering and construction works contracts a contractor can have many risks covered by effecting insurances such as contract works insurance, public liability insurances, and general insurance covered for plant owned or hired by them, and professional indemnity insurance.

However, insurance is not a substitute for effective risk management. Insurance is only intended to deal with measurable or known risks and serves to spread the impact of loss. It cannot deal with uncertainty itself and cannot prevent loss. Most standard forms of engineering and construction contracts require the contractor to effect a range of insurances and to extend such cover to subcontractors. Some require that, in addition, contractors effect specific insurances.

Reading

Construction Project Quality Management

1. Introduction

The construction industry is well known for its time/cost overruns and poor performance, and this can be traced back to the errors/mistakes made during the delivery of goods and services. Construction project quality management includes the processes required to ensure that the project will satisfy the needs for which it was undertaken and designed. It includes all activities of the overall management function that determine the quality policy, objectives, and responsibilities and implements them by means such as quality planning, quality control, quality assurance, and quality improvement, within the quality system.

2. Features of Construction Quality Management

Specifications of work quality are an important feature of facility designs. Specifications of required quality and components represent part of the necessary documentation to describe a facility. Typically, this documentation includes any special provisions of the facility design as well as references to generally accepted specifications to be used during construction. Quality management represents increasingly important concerns for construction project management. Defects or failures in constructed facilities can result in very large costs. Even with minor defects, re-construction may be required and facility operations impaired. Increased costs and delays are the result. Good management principle is that the work is done right at the first time.

From the point of project life circle for cost control, the most important decisions regarding the quality of a completed facility are made during the design and planning stages rather than during construction. It is during these preliminary stages that component configurations, material specifications and functional performance are decided.

Quality management during construction consists largely of insuring conformance to these original designs and planning decisions. While conformance to existing design decisions is the primary focus of quality control, there are exceptions to this rule.

First, unforeseen circumstances, incorrect design decisions or changes desired by an employer in the facility function may require re-evaluation of design decisions during the course of construction. While these changes may be motivated by the concern for quality, they represent occasions for re-design with all the attendant objectives and constraints. With the attention to conformance as the measure of quality during the construction process, the specification of quality requirements in the design and contract documentation becomes extremely important. Quality requirements should be clear and verifiable, so that all parties in the project can understand the requirements for conformance.

Second, some designs rely upon informed and appropriate decision-making during the construction process itself. For example, some deep foundation methods make decisions about types of shoring required at different locations based upon observation of soil conditions during the excavation process. Since such decisions are based on better information concerning actual site conditions, the facility design may be more cost-effective as a result.

3. Quality Management Mechanism

Development of construction quality management has been for construction organizations to move away from the traditional "fire fighting" approach to more formal quality management systems which are to plan, monitor and control their production process. The best known formal certification for quality improvement is the International Standardization Organization's ISO 9000 standard; it is also required in FIDIC conditions. ISO 9000 emphasizes good documentation, quality goals and a series of cycles of planning, implementation and review. In line with the latest ISO 9000 standard, it emphasizes customer satisfaction and continual improvement. However, current construction project practice of quality management, which focuses on fulfilling predefined procedures (set by the organization itself).

3.1 Quality Planning

Quality planning involves identifying which quality standards are relevant to the project and determining how to satisfy them.

3.2 Quality Assurance

Quality assurance is all the planned and systematic activities implemented within the quality system to provide confidence that the project will satisfy the relevant quality standards. It should be performed throughout the project.

3.3 Quality Control

Quality control involves monitoring specific project results to determine if they comply with relevant quality standards and identifying ways to eliminate causes of unsatisfactory results. Project results include both product results such as deliverables and management results such as cost and schedule performance.

The project management team should have a working knowledge of statistical quality control, especially sampling and probability, to help them evaluate quality control outputs.

Project quality management must address both the management of the project and the product of the project. Failure to meet quality requirements in either dimension can have serious negative consequences for any or all of the project stakeholders.

For example:

➢ Meeting customer requirements by overworking the project team may produce negative consequences in the form of increased employee turnover.

➢ Meeting project schedule objectives by rushing planned quality inspections may produce negative consequences when errors go.

3.4 Total Quality Management

In contrast to this traditional approach of quality management is the goal of total quality management, no defective items in TQM system are allowed anywhere in the construction process. While the zero defects goal can never be permanently obtained, it provides a goal so that an organization is never satisfied with its quality management program even if defects are reduced by substantial amounts year after year. This concept and approach to quality management was first developed in manufacturing firms in Japan and Europe, but has since spread to many construction companies. Total quality management is a commitment to quality expressed in all parts of an organization and typically involves many elements. Worker involvement in improved quality management is often formalized in quality circles in which groups of workers meet regularly to make suggestions for quality improvement. Material suppliers are also required to insure zero defects in delivered goods. However, the unique nature of each facility, the variability in the workforce, the multitude of subcontractors and the cost of making necessary investments in education and procedures make programs of total quality management in construction difficult.

4. Quality Management in Construction

The traditional quality management practices is the notion of an acceptable quality level which is an allowable fraction of defective items. Materials obtained from suppliers or work performed by an organization is inspected and passed as acceptable if the estimated defective percentage is within the acceptable quality level. Problems with materials or goods are corrected after delivery of the product.

4.1 Material Quanlity Management

In view of the procurement of construction materials required for the project, it is necessary to have a number of comparisons and selection of suppliers for supply qualification and quality assurance system to ensure quality of materials. It is essential to establish a materials management system for managing material procurement, processing, transportation, storage, and develop a materials tracking system to track the materials quantities and acceptance status. All materials will be compliance with the manufacturer's recommendations and project specifications and stored accordingly. For the purpose of insuring compliance, random samples and statistical methods are commonly used as the basis for accepting or rejecting work completed and batches of materials. Rejection of a batch is based on non-conformance or violation of the relevant design specifications.

4.2 Construction Process Quality Management

Process is known as "operation". Construction product manufacturing process is a basic part of the construction procedures, but also the basic unit of production process organization. Process quality management is to control and limit the volatility of the process quality within the boundaries of the required quality criteria, and the ultimate goal of quality control procedures is to ensure the stability of construction products quality. Construction process like formwork, steel works, concrete works, masonry works, plastering works etc. are the focuses of project quality management and quality control process.

5. Information Technology Applications in Construction Quality Management

With the fast development of information technology, the process of quality management and the relationships among quality management activities, such as inspection/test planning, inspection/test, conformance verification, feedback and nonconformance reporting, were clearly defined and computerized. And through integrating the project-specific quality management data of various project participants, IT has significant potential for assisting with the tasks of representing quality requirements, diagnosing and analyzing quality data, managing quality activities, and improving quality information flow, along with knowledge management as it pertains to construction quality management. Each hierarchy consisting of quality components will link to a database. Combined with CPM, a quality system can be developed to do timely quality inspection/test and reporting. Thus, project management team will be able to control the construction execution quality very efficiently by means of IT application.

New Words and Expressions

construction risk management 建设风险管理
probability 概率，机率；可能性，或然性
inherent 固有的，内在的；与生俱来的
diversity 多样性，差异；多样化
design change 设计变更
combination 组合，联合；结合，化合
improving project performance 提高工程项目性能
contracting parties 缔约方
severity 严重；严格；猛烈
potential risks 潜在的风险
budget overruns 预算超支
slippage 滑动，滑移；下降
legal-contractual 法律合同的
tendering stage 投标阶段
strike 罢工；抓，穿透；到达，打动
unforeseen conditions 不可预见的条件，未知的状况
at the construction site 在施工现场
innovative 创新的，革新的
archaeological 考古的
archaeological finds 考古发现
work stoppage 停工

Unit 12 Construction Risk Management

bidding other work 投标其他项目
keep out of the business 置身局外
site conditions 现场条件，现场状况
construction claims 施工索赔
default 拖欠，不到场；缺席，缺乏
necessitate 使成为必需，需要；迫使
kilter 顺利，良好状态；平衡
significantly 明显地；值得注目地；意味深长地
denote 表示，指示
signing of the contract documents 签署合同文件
gambler 赌徒，投机商人
take the risks 冒风险
windfall profit 暴利
equitable 公平的，公正的；平衡法的
colossal financial damages 巨大的经济损失
detrimental 不利的，有害的；有害的人
deliverables 可以传送的；可交付使用的
expropriation 没收；征收，征用
across borders 跨境，跨越国界
trade credit defaults 贸易赤字
civil unrest 社会动荡
economic stability 经济稳定
international setting 国际环境
acquaint 使熟悉，使认识
develop specific risk minimization strategies 制定风险最小化的具体策略
formulation 构想，规划；公式化；简洁陈述
prior to negotiation 谈判前
extra-contractual risks 合同之外的风险
standard checklists 标准清单
expert interviews 专家访谈法
Delphi technique 德尔菲法技术
brainstorming sessions 头脑风暴会议
quantify 量化，定量
residual 残渣，剩余；剩余的，残留的
appropriate risk mitigation strategy 合适的风险缓解政策
intolerable 无法忍受的，不堪的
aborted 失败的；夭折的，流产的
conscious decision 有意识的决定
contractual shifting 合同的变更

performance incentives 绩效奖励
warranties 担保
bonds 债券
mitigation 减轻；缓和，平静
deflection 偏向，偏差；挠曲
contingency planning 应急预案制定
review team 评审小组
project specific contract provisions 项目合同具体条款
reciprocal 互惠的，相互的；互相起作用的事物；倒数的
compliance with 符合，遵守
insurance provisions 保险条款
risk register 风险登记
description 著录；描述，描写，说明书，类型
likelihood 似然；可能性，可能
interdependent 相互依赖的；互助的
countermeasures 对策，策略；措施
modification 改变；修正，修改
expired 过期的，失效的；期满
drawdown 减少；水位降低
contingencies 临时的；意外事件；不可预见费
philosophy 哲学，哲理；智慧
construction industry 建筑行业
indemnity 补偿，赔偿；保障，赔偿物
in accordance with 按照，根据
principal risk management vehicle 主要风险管理工具
negotiating table 谈判桌
applicable law 法律适用范围内
contractual indemnity 合同赔偿
indemnification 赔偿，补偿
reimburse 赔偿，偿还
indemnification clauses 赔偿条款
insure against risk 投保的风险
contract terms 合同条款
additional premiums 额外的保险费
pay a premium 支付保险费
construction works contracts 建筑工程承包合同
contract works insurance 合同工程保险
public liability insurance 公共责任保险
general insurance 一般保险

professional indemnity insurance 专业弥补保险
specific insurances 特定保险

Exercises

I. Choose the best answer according to the text.

1. The inherent uncertainties are generally not only from the unique nature of the construction project, but also from _____.
    A. the diversity of resources and activities
    B. the sum of their individual effects
    C. A and B
    D. none of the above

2. According to the text, risk management refers to _____.
    A. has been widely applied in various fields such as economics, insurance, industries, and so on
    B. are not always independent and static in construction projects
    C. the art of identifying, analyzing, responding to and controlling project risk factors in a manner which best achieves the objectives of all participants
    D. none of the above

3. The main risks in construction projects can be classified into _____.
    A. physical, construction, design
    B. political, financial, legal-contractual
    C. environmental risks
    D. above all

4. According to the text, a "differing site conditions" clause, is now part of _____.
    A. the international standard documents
    B. differing site conditions
    C. the AlA and FIDIC documents
    D. A or C

5. For international construction, the purpose of risk management is to _____.
    A. understand and deal with these risks are critical for companies working internationally
    B. mitigate risks by planning for factors that can be detrimental to project objectives and deliverables
    C. transfer currency across borders, and trade credit defaults by foreign customers
    D. have in place systematic and consistent methodologies to assess political risks

6. We learn from the passage that Risk management typically involves the following distinct functions _____.
    A. risk identification and impact analysis
    B. response system and risk register

C. A and B

D. contractual risk management and insurance

7. The identified four common routes for the transfer of risk as follows _____.

   A. employer to contractor and contractor to subcontractor

   B. contractor or subcontractor to surety

   C. employer, contractor, subcontractor or architect to insurer

   D. above all

II. Decide the following statements are true or false.

1. The effect of two events is not unnecessarily the sum of their individual effects.

2. Ultimately, the contractor faces the possibility of losing a great deal of money or of being forced out of the business.

3. A changed conditions or unforeseen site conditions is a rare case in international construction market.

4. Although risk management is a relatively known and practiced process, contractors have conquered its successful implementation.

5. Study discovered that only few of companies had in place systematic and consistent methodologies to assess political risks.

6. So the impact of possible risks can be controlled the risks are effectively identified and managed.

7. The importance of the contract cannot be overemphasized.

8. Fortunately, most contractors pay sufficient attention to the risk management process.

III. Change the following words to another form and write down the Chinese meanings.

1. in terms of _____
2. elements _____
3. combination _____
4. accordingly _____
5. performance _____
6. severity _____
7. slippages _____
8. multitude _____
9. default _____
10. significantly _____
11. denotes _____
12. terms _____

IV. Give out the following words' synonym or other word in the closest meaning.

1. risk	a. unfair
2. assessment	b. cope with

3. dispute
4. ground conditions
5. equitable
6. overlooked
7. dealing with
8. impact
9. retention
10. control
11. transfer
12. compliance with
13. liabilities
14. distribution
15. Substitute

c. consequences
d. deflect
e. comply with
f. uncertainty
g. site conditions
h. allocation
i. evaluation
j. neglectived
k. argue
l. reduction
m. replace
n. responsibilities
o. acceptance

V. Put the following English into Chinese.

1. All risks must be evaluated in terms of two distinct elements: the likelihood that the event is going to occur as well as the consequences, or effect, of its occurrence.

2. Whether by fire, flood or carelessness, innovative design that does not work or proves impossible to construct, and the interaction between liability for defective workmanship and for faults in design, because lack of coordination between design and construction is a common source of dispute.

3. A changed conditions or unforeseen site conditions might affect the cost of work. For example, such unforeseen ground conditions can necessitate the driving of longer piles or the use of more support steel than was first planned foundation work.

4. In the presence of a changed condition, the employer should provide an equitable means of paying the contractor for overcoming conditions that neither he nor the employer could have expected from the information available at the time the contract was prepared, but it always is not the case.

5. There are some actions which needed to be taken responding to residual risk comes in the risk response.

6. In the end, the contract serves as a framework of the law between the parties and will establish which party has assumed or negated a particular risk in connection with the project. During that time the risk allocation agreed at the time of contracting can change substantially.

7. The underlying concept for this risk transfer is to pass risk to another party who may be in a better position to monitor and protect against the risk or in a better financial position to accept and insure against the risk.

8. Most standard forms of engineering and construction contracts require the contractor to effect a range of insurances and to extend such cover to subcontractors. Some require that, in addition, contractors effect specific insurances.

VI. Put the following Chinese into English.

1. 提高工程项目建设的性能
2. 签署法律合同文件
3. 制定风险最小化的具体策略
4. 专家访谈法，德尔菲法与头脑风暴会议法
5. 建设项目合同具体条款
6. 建筑工程承包合同
7. 合同工程保险、公共责任保险与财产保险

参 考 译 文

第 12 单元　施工风险管理

1. 引言

　　风险管理对于项目的成功与否极其关键。风险管理被广泛应用于若干领域，诸如经济、保险、工业等。尽管"风险"一词意味着不确定性可以通过可能性来表述，但是风险管理是针对通过风险评估的不确定性管理的一种结构流程。所有风险必须依据两个显著的要素来进行评价，即：事件将要发生的可能性，其发生的后果或结果。风险和机会是相互对立的两面。机会产生于有利的项目状况，但风险来源于不利的项目事件。

　　建筑工程项目固有的不确定性通常不仅来自项目独有性质，而且来自项目资源和活动的多样性。此外，在建筑工程项目中风险不总是独立和静止的。两个事件的结果并不必然是它们个别事件的总合。例如，暴风雪引起的一天延误和由于设计更改引起的天数延误是两个独立的事件，但是结合起来看，它们具有相同的后果——在那一天没有工程被完成。相应地，风险是动态的，换句话说，它们的特征、可能性和影响在项目进程中是可以改变的。

　　风险管理指在一定方式上识别、分析、响应和控制项目风险因素的艺术，它最好地实现所有参与方的目标。同时，通过改善项目实施、递增成本效力和创造良好的缔约各方之间的工作关系，有效的风险管理往往能产生项目上的积极结果。

2. 施工中的风险

　　施工项目的成功通常由进度、预算和质量等内在的冲突来衡量。大体上讲，各种风险可以影响到这三个对项目成功不利的基本因素。总的说来，项目的规模和复杂性与项目的时间表有着密切的关系；同时，这两个方面与风险的冲突或者严重性有关系，即，在许多情况下，项目越大越复杂，完成项目需要的时间就越长，且项目的不确定性和风险的影响将越严重。如此一来，在大型和复杂项目中，施工项目中的潜在风险是形形色色的；预算超限和日程延误就是普遍的，且范围变更不可避免。施工项目中的风险可以分成自然、技术(施工、设计)、政治、金融、法律和环境风险等类别。

2.1 国际市场上承包商的风险

　　在国际市场上，承包商面临着大量的风险。从投标阶段开始，为了筹备投标，承包商

需要能够识别合同中的风险。这些风险有通货膨胀、恶劣天气、罢工和其他劳工问题、材料短缺、施工现场不可预见的情况、意外事故(由火灾、洪水或粗心大意引起的),以及不能实施或证明不可能施工的革新设计,以及有缺陷工艺责任和设计缺陷之间的相互影响等,因为设计和施工之间缺乏协调是争执的普遍源头。工人停工斗争可能影响到承包商对人员和材料的配置,或者阻止承包商对其他工程的投标。最终,承包商面临着重大亏损或者被迫出局的可能性。

2.2 情况改变的风险

从历史的角度看,意料之外的现场状况引起了许多施工索赔并且不只是促使一些承包商违约。这个重要的规定,有时作为"持异议的现场状况"条款而被提及,现在是国际标准文件的一部分,也是 AIA 和 FIDIC 文件的一部分。改变了的状况或意料之外的状况可能影响工程的成本。例如,意料之外的地面状况可能必须处理更长时间的堆料,或者须使用比最初针对地基工程计划更多的承载钢材。两项操作都可能扰乱和延误工程,打破日程表的良好状态,付出比承包商能够合理预期的大得多的代价。虽然承包商表示能的接受风险,然而,签署合同文件的时候,许多承包商内心里仍然像是赌徒并宁愿冒险,与这个潜在风险相伴的是意外利润。在改变了的状况面前,雇主应当提供一种为克服这些状况而付款给承包商的公正的方式,他和雇主都不能在合同准备期间从可得到的信息中预期这些状况,但事情往往不是这样。在国际市场上,改变了的状况或者意料之外的状况并不少见。

诸如这样的一些因素可能导致承包商遭受重大的项目成本增加以及工程延误。相应地,承包商面临的重要问题是:

➢ 追加成本是否能从雇主那里收回;
➢ 能否获得竣工时间的延长和误工损失的补助。

3. 国际项目风险

国际项目风险有时也被一些承包商随意地忽略和评估;其结果就是遭受了巨大的财务损失。对于国际施工,风险管理的目的是通过对可能对项目目标和项目可交付性的不利因素做计划去降低风险。虽然风险管理相对来说是一个早就有的和长期存在的过程,但是很少有承包商能完全避免它。

虽然像社会动荡和经济不稳定这样的风险一向是超出正常业务范围的,但是理解和应对这些风险对于国际化经营的公司却非常关键。研究显示,只有很少的公司恰当地具有系统的和一贯的评估政治风险的整套方法。在国际环境中的公司运作常常需要比国内项目宽广得多的项目背景视野。

4. 风险管理

风险管理需要系统地和实用地处理建筑市场上固有的可预测和不可预测的风险的方法。承包商自己必须了解风险,并且应当设法开发具体的风险最小化策略。项目风险管理必须包括用于调整风险管理行为的反馈信息。风险管理一般牵涉以下四项截然不同的功能。

4.1 风险识别

最开始是在项目生命的早期对与所计划的施工项目或合同有联系的风险进行识别。识别过程将形成一个基础，借此，风险、不确定性、制约、政策和针对风险控制和分配的策略将建立起来。项目风险管理的公式化就是在雇主、承包商和建筑师之间分配风险。

  风险识别是决定具体的可能合理预期并影响项目的风险因素的过程。风险识别对于项目的成功必不可少。在谈判之前，承包商应当指派至少一个有经验的人去识别合同风险和额外合同风险。风险因素的识别是根本要求。风险识别可以通过诸如标准检查列表、专家访问、德尔菲技术、与其他项目做比较以及召开头脑风暴会议讨论来进行。

4.2 影响分析

  可能性和后果分析——这些风险因素的潜在影响由它们怎样发生以及如果发生了会对项目产生怎样的结果来决定。由于风险影响项目的所有方面，各方应当量化风险将在项目成本、日程、质量和/或利润上产生的影响。承包商必须评估风险因素或风险特征，如风险事件、其发生的可能性以及损失或收益的总量，且必须分析每个正在产生或可能对项目产生危害的问题或事件。因此可能风险的影响对风险被有效识别和管理的范围来说是可以得到控制的。

4.3 回应系统

  为了应对进入项目之中的余留风险，还需要采取一些风险应对行动。有时，需要做重新评估风险情况。风险事件的不确定性还有发生的可能性或潜在影响可以通过选择恰当的风险缓解策略或者避开风险因素来得到减少。使用更多数据和信息可以减少风险的不确定性。风险缓解策略的步骤是减少对项目有实质危险的潜在风险因素，这些风险缓解策略是通用的风险管理和处理技术，普遍使用的缓解策略有4类：

  ➢ 回避——当风险不能接受，且其他低风的险选择可以从几个替代方案中得到的时候。万一无法承受的风险和对于缓解损失没有办法的时候，项目将非正常放弃。

  ➢ 保留/接受——万一风险事件发生时，作出明智的决定去接受风险发生的后果。

  ➢ 控制/减少——用于持续监控和纠正项目实施进程的风险的情况。该进程涉及风险降低计划的进展状况控制，然后进行跟踪计划。

  转移/转向——当风险与其他人分担的时候。与其他人分担风险的形式包括合同转移、行动激励、保险、保证、担保等。风险要素通过分包出受影响的工程而得以转移。

  ➢ 风险转移

  通过合同来转向或转移风险是通用的风险对策，该对策可以将风险全部分配到另外的项目参与方，或者在两个或更多参与方之间分担风险。与项目参与方分担风险的形式包括合同风险转移，履约激励措施，保险，担保和保函等等。将影响项目的风险因素通过合同形式转移出去。项目经理应当是训练有素的，能够通过谈判和精心考虑的合同和具体合同条款起草来管理风险。一些基本的风险管理概念有：

- 公共工程——把风险转移给其他人；
- 私人工程——一些雇主不感兴趣、不明了情况或无经验；
- 互惠合同条款——使假定的风险暴露最小化；
- 通过要求和实施对保险条款的遵从而缓解风险；
- 有效的风险管理要求项目管理的注意力不仅在谈判/合同签署阶段，而是贯穿整个项目。

4.4 风险登记表

大约在过去几十年中，很多业主开始使用作为关键风险控制文件的风险登记表。风险登记表会列出所有已识别的风险、对这些风险的分析和评估结果以及风险状况方面的信息。风险登记表应当在贯穿整个项目的过程中不断被更新和评审。

风险登记表应当包含如下信息：风险号码(在登记表中是唯一的)；风险类型；识别者(谁识别的风险)；识别日期；最后更新日期；说明；可能性；与其他风险来源的相互关联；预期影响；风险承担者；对策；风险状况和风险行为状况。所有风险，包括潜在变更在内，须不断评审和修正。

由于下列五个原因，风险登记表是很重要的：
➢ 监控并在必要时在风险缓解措施方面纠正进展；
➢ 识别新风险；
➢ 结束到期的风险；
➢ 针对现有风险对风险评估进行修正；
➢ 当需要时通过业主来审定项目应急费的启用。

5. 合同风险管理

5.1 建筑合同的风险分配

控制和文件资料——基于所学到的教训，创建一个针对未来项目的知识库。各方的风险管理策略及目标应当在合同语言中反映出来。承包商应当采纳风险转移谈判领域中的哲学，即"如果他们不问，那么他们就没注意到"。在建筑业中合同风险转移在有关赔偿、相应的损失、有差异的工地状况和延误等方面的合同条款中司空见惯。

国际建筑市场上的风险分配由建筑合同来确定。合同的重要性不能被过分强调。理想情况下，各方在合同中将把风险和债务分配给最能胜任的一方，使其得到处理和最小化。签约过程为每一方提供了根据其目标而进行谈判、界定和限制其权利的手段。与具体项目有关的风险和责任必须在合同范围内被明确地分配。最后，合同起到各方之间法律构架的作用，且将确定哪一方承担或者取消与项目有关的特别风险。在此期间，约定好的风险分配在签约的时候可以被充分更改。这一点特别与材料的可用性和材料的成本有关。

虽然合同是主要的风险管理工具，各方必须在合同签署很早之前就开始处理和最小化风险。为避免不公正，承包商应当带着他们风险管理目标的理念出现在谈判桌上。这些风险将如何依据合同和(如果没有按合同本身)依据适用的法律进行分配变得很重要。不同的合同和不同地区的现行法律以相当不同的方式来处理这一点。

遗憾的是，大部分承包商对风险管理过程所给予的关注不够。

5.2 合同赔偿

赔偿，即保持无伤害的协议，可以定义为赔偿一方的义务，该赔偿方要针对受偿者遭受的损失或者它可能承担责任的损害而对另一方(受偿者)进行赔偿。签约各方通常利用赔偿条款转移多种债务风险。例如，总承包商可能承担雇主的风险，分包商可能承担总承包商的风险。

5.3 合同风险转移

合同风险转移是风险管理的一种形式，该形式在国际建筑市场上已经沿用多年。它涉及对于签约方之间或之中的固有风险的配置和分摊。如果能够有效地处理，风险转移就不会过于或不公地把所有风险分配到一个当事方身上，而是根据他们的控制能力把风险置于各方身上且确保免受风险危害。这种风险转移的根本概念是，把风险传给另一方，该方也许处于一个更好的监控位置并防止免受风险的危害，或者处于更好的财务地位去接受风险且确保免受风险危害。

以下是风险转移的四条已识别的常见路线：
- ➢ 雇主到承包商；
- ➢ 承包商到分包商；
- ➢ 雇主、承包商、分包商或建筑师到承保人；
- ➢ 承包商或分包商到担保人。

应当指出的是，把风险转移给别人可能导致不同合同条款的发展、更高费用的支付或者附加保险费用。如果风险可以被转移，那么它们的后果就可以被分担或者完全由某人而不是由雇主来执行。雇主将被指望为此而支付保险费用，因此开始风险回应的这种形式的责任在于雇主。

5.4 保险

防止风险因素可能发生的保险是必需的。大部分自然风险可以被防止。例如，在工程学和施工工程合同方面，承包商可能会碰到许多风险，这些风险可以通过有效的保险来承保，比如合约工程保险、公众责任保险、承保他们自有或租用的重型设备的一般保险，以及专业责任保险等。

然而，保险不是有效风险管理的替代品。保险仅仅旨在应对可测量的或者已知的风险服务扩展到损失的影响。它并不能处理不确定性本身且不能阻止损失。大部分标准工程学和施工合同形式要求承包商实现一系列的保险并把这种担保扩展到分包商。另外，有些形式还要求承包商完成特定保险。

阅读

施工项目质量管理

1. 引言

建筑行业以其时间/成本超支和拙劣运营状况而著称，且这一点可以追溯到商品和劳务递送期间所犯的过失/错误。施工项目质量管理包括必需的、确保项目满足为其而承担和设计的需要的进程。它包含综合管理职能的所有活动，这种管理职能决定质量政策、目标以及责任，并且通过质量体系内的诸如质量规划、质量控制、质量保证和质量改善来实施它们。

2. 施工质量管理的特征

工程质量规范是设施设计的一个重要特征。所需的质量和组成部分的规范代表着描述设施的必要文件资料的一部分。一般来讲，这种文件资料包含设施设计的特定条款以及通常被接受的、将在施工期间使用的有关规范的参考资料。质量管理代表着对施工项目管理的日益重要的关注。所施工设施中的缺陷或失败可能导致巨大损失。甚至由于一个较小的缺陷，就必须重新施工且设施的运营将受到损害。其结果就是成本的增加和工程的延期。良好管理原则就是工作首次就做对了。

从项目生命周期对成本控制的观点，关于已竣工设施的质量的最重要决策是在设计和规划阶段而并非在施工期间做出的。正是在这些项目初始阶段，项目组成部分的组合、材料清单和项目功能状况就被定了下来。

施工期间的质量管理多半由确保与这些原始设计一致和规划决策组成。虽然对现有设计决策保持一致是质量控制的首要焦点，但是对于这个规则仍然存在例外。

首先，意料之外的情况、不正确的设计决策或者在设施功能方面雇主想要的更改，可能需要在施工过程中对设计决策进行重新评估。虽然这些更改可能由对质量的关注而激发，但是却表明了对于重新设计所有与目标和限制有关的情况。在施工期间，由于对质量尺度的对一致性很关注，设计和施工文件资料中的质量要求规范就变得极其重要。质量要求应该是清楚的且能实施的，以至于项目中所有参与方都能了解质量要求。

其次，一些设计依赖于施工过程的认知了解和恰当的决策。例如，对一些深地基做出的关于在不同位置所需不同的支撑类型的决策，是基于以挖掘过程中对土壤状况的观察为基础的。由于这样的决策以与实际工地条件有关的更好信息为基础，设施的设计因此更加划算。

3. 质量管理机制

施工质量管理的发展对于施工组织来说已经从传统的"消防"途径转变到正式的质量管理体系，该体系一定要计划、监测和控制它们的生产流程。最著名的质量改善正规认证是国际标准化组织的 ISO 9000 标准；它在 FIDIC 合同条件中也是必需的。ISO 9000 强调适当的文件资料、质量目标和一系列规划、执行和检查周期。与最新的 ISO 9000 标准一致，它强调顾客满意度和持续改善。然而，当前的施工项目质量管理实际却注重完成预定程序(由国家标准化组织自己设置)。

3.1 质量规划

质量规划牵涉识别哪些质量标准与项目有关并决定怎样达到这些标准。

3.2 质量保证

质量保证是所有计划好的、系统的在质量体系内实施的活动，这些活动提供该项目将达到相关质量标准的信息。它将贯穿于整个项目中来执行。

3.3 质量控制

质量控制牵涉到监控具体的项目结果，从而决定这些结果是否遵从相关质量标准，并识别消除不合要求结果的原因的方式。项目结果既包括产品结果(如交付结果)，也包括管理结果(如成本和进度状况)。

项目管理团队应当具有统计学的质量控制应用知识，尤其是抽样和概率知识，从而帮助他们评估质量控制成果。

项目质量管理必须既应对项目管理又应对项目产品。在两者中的任何一方面不能达到质量要求，对任何或所有的项目利益相关者都可能造成严重的消极后果。

例如：

> 通过使项目团队过度工作来满足顾客要求，可能会在增加了的员工劳动产量的形式中产生消极后果。

> 通过仓促完成计划好的质量检查来达到项目日程目标，可能在失误未被识破的时候产生消极后果。

3.4 全面质量管理

与传统质量管理方式相比，全面质量管理(TQM)系统中不允许有缺陷事项出现在施工流程中的任何地方。尽管零缺陷目标可能从来都不能永久地获得，但是它却提供一个目标，作何组织都从来没有对它的质量管理计划满意过，即便缺陷年复一年减少到了可观的数量。这种质量管理的观念和方式首先在日本和欧洲的制造企业中得到发展，但从那时到现在已经蔓延到许多建筑公司。全面质量管理对于一个组织里所有部门所表达的质量来说是一个保证，且一向涉及许多要素。参与改善质量管理的工人常常在质量循环程序中非常固定，工人小组定期碰面对质量改善提出建议。材料供应商也需要确保所运送的货物零缺陷。然而，每个设施的独特性质、劳动力的流动性、大量的分包商，以及在培训和程序中进行必要投资的成本，使全面质量管理计划在施工中变得很困难。

4. 施工中的质量管理

传统的质量管理做法是可接受的质量水平的观念，这个质量水平是一个允许部分工作缺陷事项的。如果估价的缺陷百分比处于可接受的质量水平，从供应商获得的材料或由组织执行的工程将作为可接受物而被检查通过。对于材料或货物的问题在产品交付之后进行修正。

4.1 材料质量管理

在项目所需的建筑材料的采购方面，应针对资格和质量保障体系进行对照且挑选供应商来确保材料的质量。建立材料的采购、加工、运输、存储管理系统，以及材料跟踪系统，以跟踪材料质量和认可状况，这是最根本的。所有材料将按照制造商的技术说明和工程规范来采购，并进行储存。为确保这种遵从起见，随机抽样和统计方法通常作为接受或拒绝完成工程和材料批的基础。材料批的拒绝以不遵从或者对相关设计规范的违背为基础。

4.2 施工过程质量管理

施工过程也被认为是"操作"。建筑产品生产过程是施工过程的一个基本部分，而且是生产过程组织的基本单位。过程质量管理必须将过程质量活动的波动性控制和限制在质量标准和允许范围，并且过程质量控制的最终目标是确保稳定的施工产品质量。施工过程包括模板成形、钢结构工程、混凝土工程、砖石工程、粉刷工程等都是项目质量管理和过程质量控制的焦点。

5. 施工质量管理中的信息技术应用

随着信息技术的快速发展，质量管理过程和质量管理活动之中的关系，比如检查/检验计划、检查/检验、符合性验证、信息反馈、不合格报告，被清晰地做了定义和计算机处理。凭借整合各种项目参与方的具体项目质量管理数据，信息技术具备了重大潜力，这种潜力是针对帮助描述质量要求、判断和分析质量数据、管理质量活动、改善质量信息流等方面的，以及施工质量管理的信息知识管理。每个质量组成单元的工程质量层面均与数据库相联系。与关键路径法(CPM)相结合，质量体系可以开发用于进行及时的质量检查/检验和报告。因此，项目管理团队应用IT技术能够有效地进行施工质量控制。

Unit 13

Construction Negotiation Strategies and Skills

1. Introduction

With high competitiveness of construction environment, construction projects have become increasingly complex, where the parties involved often have conflicting objectives. Therefore, negotiation can be complicated but often present important opportunities and risks for the various parties involved. First, negotiation is a very important mechanism for arranging construction contracts. Second, as a general rule, exogenous factors such as the history of a contractor and the general economic climate in the construction industry will determine the results of negotiations. However, the skill of a negotiator can affect the possibility of reaching an agreement, the profitability of the project, the scope of any eventual disputes, and the possibility for additional work among the participants. Even after a contract is awarded on the basis of competitive bidding, there are many occasions in which subsequent negotiations are required as conditions change over time. Thus, negotiations are an extremely important task for many project managers.

2. Negotiation in Construction Management

➤ The successful delivery of a project requires the full collaboration of all concerned parties, so that the time, costs, resources, and objectives of a project can be coordinated. Therefore, negotiation has been a daily routine for construction project managers. Construction project managers seem to learn negotiating skills only through experience and observation. Therefore, practical negotiation methodologies may be useful for the construction industry in enabling project managers to handle negotiations more productively. For example, negotiation on work contracts can involve issues such as completion date, arbitration procedures, special work item compensation, contingency allowances as well as the overall price.

➤ Construction material procurement is a key business where negotiation is commonly required to reach final contractual agreement. The cost and time involved in negotiation mean that contractors must limit the number of prospective suppliers they negotiate with, and also the number of options included in negotiations. A cheap and efficient negotiation method would allow the exploration of more prospective suppliers and options.

➤ Among many alternative dispute resolution tactics, such as negotiation and mediation, negotiation has gained popularity as a method to remedy the shortcomings of litigation. Not only are the costs and times of court claims avoided, but also the involved parties have more control over the negotiation outcomes in a less hostile environment.

3. Negotiation Strategies

Negotiations involve each party using the strategy of predicting the bottom line of the other and presenting an offer that maximizes their own benefit. Negotiation consists of discussions between two or more parties around specific issues for the purpose of reaching a mutually satisfactory agreement. Traditionally, negotiation has been seen as adversarial or confrontational, e.g., talk tough and see how much you can get. This negative attitude to negotiation is deeply embedded in many cultures. Most books and courses on negotiation focus on the adversarial relationship modeled after project's commencement and hostile competitions of awarding.

The best strategy for negotiation is obtaining a win-win outcome. Successful negotiators do not try to "win at all costs". Win-win negotiating is an approach to negotiating that stresses common interests and goals. By working together, parties can seek creative solutions and reach decisions in which all parties can win. Because each negotiator has different preferences regarding each negotiable issue and option, the strategy is to make tradeoffs accordingly and achieve a higher satisfaction level. Most smart negotiators, such as excellent leaders and decision makers, believe that the key to negotiation success is quite straightforward: obtain the trust and confidence of partners and collaborators. However, we must keep in mind that sometimes negotiations are actually commercial battles or wars, opponents usually play win or lose games. The general rules should be complied with as follows:

3.1 Confidence

Negotiation is interactive and involves relationships, confidence is the value showed to be the axis for a long term business relationship. It is important when we need the consent of others to achieve our ends, when we can meet our ends better by involving others, our confidence will be our credits. Do a body check to make sure your words match your nonverbal gestures. Otherwise, you won't be taken seriously.

3.2 Gratitude

The action of appreciating others' help, suggestions and contributions showed to be important for the willingness of collaborators to want to keep contributing in future projects. It is critical to consider the impact of the spiritual values and reference practices for long term business relationships and their consequence in the economic performance of the organizations. An atmosphere of trust reduces the time required to create win-win outcomes. Cooperativeness attitude eliminates ill feelings and creates good will and outcome.

3.3 Fairness

The win-win attitude among those working in the same project demonstrated to have a positive impact even when projects were not successful in the end. On the other hand, the attitude of trying to take the credit for the work of others had a very negative impact to the outcome of the negotiation.

3.4 Transparency

To act transparently in a negotiation process regarding the positions of the parties had a positive impact on building confidence. A negotiator of well prepared and knowledgeable in the relevant field of negotiation in question will be much helpful to advance progress. The possibility of negotiating failures highlights the importance of strategy with respect to revealing information. Strategic information is something you should only give away parsimoniously and then when you get some information back.

3.5 Integrity

The act of trying to circumvent had a very negative impact in the negotiation process and it was not accepted by the decision makers. Attitudes like being friendly and empathic will be demonstrated through high integrity and socially intelligent, although we indeed need to do it sometime when opponent change his credit. However, being kept up to date via copies of e-mails, or actualized about the process of the negotiation by partners or collaborators, had a very positive impact in inspiring trust.

4. Negotiation Skills

4.1 Understanding Yourself

Probably the most important skill for an effective negotiator is a clear understanding of oneself. With a particular conflict in mind, answer the following questions about yourself as honestly as you can and prepare a brief paragraph describing yourself in a negotiation. Select a partner and tell him.

- ➢ What are my strengths? Limitations?
- ➢ Am I a good listener?
- ➢ Where am I psychologically vulnerable? Emotionally vulnerable?
- ➢ What are my prejudices and biases?
- ➢ What kind of climate do I create in negotiations?
- ➢ What are my needs during negotiation?

4.2 Defining Outcomes

➢ A second key skill for effective negotiating is to define your own "bottom line", i.e., least acceptable outcome for you. Using your sample conflict (or another example, if appropriate), determine your best outcome and your least acceptable outcome. You may wish to speculate on the same questions from the other party's point of view. In conducting negotiations between two parties, each side will have a series of objectives and constraints. The overall objective of each party is to obtain the most favorable, acceptable agreement.

➢ In light of these tactical problems, it is often beneficial to all parties to adopt objective standards in determining appropriate contract provisions. These standards would prescribe a particular agreement or a method to arrive at appropriate values in a negotiation. Objective standards can be derived from numerous sources, including market values, precedent, professional standards, what a court would decide, etc. By using objective criteria of this sort, personalities and disruptive negotiating tactics do not become impediments to reaching mutually beneficial agreements.

➢ As for two parties, one issue negotiation illustrates this fundamental point. With different constraints, it might be impossible to reach an agreement. Of course, the two parties typically do not know at the beginning of negotiations if agreements will be possible. But it is quite important for each party to the negotiation to have a sense of their own reservation price, such as the owner's minimum selling price or the buyer's maximum purchase price within both parties' acceptable range. This reservation price is equal to the value of the best alternative to a negotiated agreement.

4.3 Understanding Positions and Interests

A key technique in negotiation is to understand the difference between positions and interests, thus going beyond position to determine the underlying interests. A position is an option that one party is committed to as a solution to the conflict. An interest is the concerns, needs, and/or desires underlying the conflict, i.e., why the conflict is being raised. It is especially important to understand your best alternative to a negotiated agreement.

4.4 Silence is Golden

When the other person is a talker and you want to learn as much as you can without making any type of commitment, saying nothing and letting the other person do the talking may be the best tactic. This is also a good choice when someone says something angry, attacking or outrageous. If you say nothing, there isn't anything for the other person to counter. Silence can work wonders in a negotiation session. It effectively keeps you from talking too much, and may offer the other party the opportunity to express feelings on a particular problems or issue.

4.5 Higher Authority

The tactic of higher authority works for either person in a negotiation. Sometimes you cannot get a situation resolved by working with a particular person. Perhaps that person has decided not to comply with your request or they may not have the authority to do so. So, you go to a higher authority to obtain a satisfactory outcome. On the other hand, lacking a final say in a situation can create a very powerful position for the other person, since it provides him an opportunity to take your request to someone at a higher level in the organization.

5. Perspective on Negotiation Outcome

With additional issues, negotiations become more complex both in procedure and in result.

With respect to procedure, the sequence in which issues are defined or considered can be very important. For example, negotiations may proceed on an issue-by-issue basis, and the outcome may depend upon the exact sequence of issues considered. Alternatively, the parties may proceed by proposing complete agreement packages and then proceed to compare packages. With respect to outcomes, the possibility of the parties having different valuations or weights on particular issues arises. In this circumstance, it is possible to trade-off the outcomes on different issues to the benefit of both parties. By yielding on an issue of low value to himself but high value to the other party, concessions on other issues may be obtained. Poor negotiating strategies adopted by one or the other party may also preclude an agreement even with the existence of a feasible agreement range.

Reading

Cross Culture Communication

1. Introduction

Communication can be defined as a process through which meaning is created and exchanged. It involves sending and receiving both verbal and nonverbal messages. Communication occurs all the time, no matter what you do, you send messages, and people assign meaning to the things you do and say. Wherever you engaged in an international project, you find yourself encompassed in a diversified working environment. However, recognizing the source or nature of international diversity, can make our work relationships smoother and more productive, because we want to be able to work in an environment where we are all respected and people can work to their maximum potential. That's what keeps us going. Creating a workplace that all project participants perceive as fair and equitable, no matter what their differences are, is very important. Since communication is continuous, sometimes when people indicate that more communication is needed in progress, what they really mean is that better communication is needed.

2. Coordination in An Environment of Diversity

➢ Construction business is extremely information intensive, so the coordination is required through the integration of project information, and communication among different disciplines by architect/engineer/construction firms, subcontractors and the employer in the construction site, as views of the project may be quite different among different disciplines. And the collaboration is needed to share visions among different parties and maximize team efforts on a particular project. When it comes to working together effectively on project tasks, cultures differ with respect to the importance placed on establishing relationships early on the collaboration. Under the multicultural environment, we believe that cross culture communication through diversity is the key to the success of any project execution.

➢ International diversity in the global construction market is a common fact. Your coworkers probably come from different countries and ethnic backgrounds, practice different religions and hold different views on politics, work and problem solving. Culture is a complex concept, with many different definitions. But, simply put "culture" refers to a group or community with which we share common experiences that shape the way we understand the world. Our culture influences how we approach problems, and how we participate in groups and in communities. People's different communication styles reflect deeper philosophies and world views which are the foundation of their culture. Understanding these deeper philosophies gives us a broader picture of what the world has to offer us. Learning about people's cultures has the potential to give us a mirror image of our own. We have the opportunity to challenge our assumptions about the "right" way of doing things, and consider a variety of approaches.

➢ When we participate in a project we are often surprised at how differently people approach their work together. Some cultures view conflict as a positive thing, while others view it as something to be avoided. In the process of construction, conflict is not usually desirable; but people often are supposed to deal directly with conflicts that do arise. In fact, face-to-face meetings customarily are recommended as the way to work through whatever problems exist. But in some eastern countries, open conflict is experienced as embarrassing or demeaning; as a rule, differences are best worked out quietly. A written exchange might be the favored means to address the conflict. Asian and Hispanic cultures tend to attach more value to developing relationships at the beginning of a shared project and more emphasis on task completion toward the end as compared with westerns. Westerns tend to focus immediately on the task at hand, and let relationships develop as they work on the project. This does not mean that people from any one of these cultural backgrounds are more or less committed to accomplishing the project or value relationships more or less; it means they may pursue them differently. However, their actual participation in the project will be restricted by their organizational objectives.

3. Challenges of Diversity in International Project Execution

In addition to differences in culture and nationality, it is common to encounter other types of diversity in international project executing, although diversity is sometime viewed as an advantage in construction, it can usually adversely affect communication among members of a project. To some extent, we take these differences for granted. As we all have biases, even prejudices, toward specific groups. Sometimes we are uncomfortable around people whose habits, beliefs, or customs are different from our own. Our discomfort usually arises because we don't understand the differences, or weren't prepared to encounter them. In some cases, our discomfort or our inability to communicate with co-workers arises because of a stereotype. A stereotype is an oversimplified belief about a group of people. For example, the notion that engineers are men who wear dark-rimmed glasses and have short hair is a stereotype that is often inaccurate. Stereotypes lead us to judge people as members of a group rather than as individuals. These learned stereotypes hinder understanding. Although people within a group may have certain characteristics, each person is unique in personality, experience, ability and current life situation.

4. Cross Culture Communication Skills

➢ Communication skills are especially important when you communicate with people of diverse backgrounds. In addition to just writing or speaking effectively, you need to add elements of sensitivity, understanding and tolerance in your communication. It is important to remember not to patronize or talk down to people who do not speak business language fluently. Instead, to think of new ways to communicate will help you and your listener understanding and comfortable with each other. We should bear in mind that everyone is an individual, after all.

➢ Although all people communicate all the time, most have difficulty communicating effectively in conflict situations. Often misinterpretation is the source of the problem. Practicing communication skills can have a very beneficial effect on conflict management and resolution processes. The key to effective cross-cultural communication is knowledge. First, it is essential that people understand the potential problems of cross-cultural communication, and make a conscious effort to overcome these problems. Second, it is important to assume that one's efforts will not always be successful, and adjust one's behavior appropriately.

● The first rule is active listening. The goal of active listening is to understand your partner or opponent as well as you understand yourself. Pay close attention to what the other side is saying. Ask the partner or opponent to clarify or repeat anything that is unclear or seems unreasonable (maybe it isn't, but you are interpreting it wrong). Attempt to repeat their case, as they have presented it, back to them. This shows that you are listening and that you understand what they have said. It does not indicate that you agree with what they said— nor do you have to. You just need to indicate that you do understand them. When things seem to be going badly, stop or slow down and think.

● Second rule is to speak directly to your partner or opponent. This is not considered appropriate in some cultures, but when permitted, it helps to increase understanding. Avoid being distracted by outside parties or other things going on around you. Focus on what you have to say, and on saying it in a way that your partner or opponent can understand.

● The third rule is to speak about yourself, describe your own feelings and perceptions, rather than focusing on your partner or opponent's motives, misdeeds, or failing. By saying, "I felt let down", rather than "you broke your promise", you will convey the same information. But you will do so in a way that does not provoke a defensive or hostile reaction from your partner or opponent. (This is often referred to as using "I-statements" or "I-messages", rather than "you-messages". "You-messages" suggests blame, and encourage the recipient to deny wrong-doing or blame back. "I-messages" simply states a problem, without blaming someone for it. This makes it easier for the other side to help solve the problem, without having to admit they were wrong.)

● The fourth rule is "speak for a purpose". Too much communication can be counter-productive, they warn. Before you make a significant statement, pause and consider what you want to communicate, why you want to communicate that, and how you can do it in the clearest possible way. One method is to avoid inflammatory language as much as possible when dealing with people on the other side. Inflammatory language just increases hostility and defensiveness – it seldom convinces people the speaker is right. Although inflammatory remarks can arouse people's interest in a conflict and generate support for one's own side, that often comes with the cost of general conflict escalation. To the extent that one can make one's point effectively without inflammatory statements, the better.

Likewise, all partners or opponents should be treated with respect. It doesn't help a conflict situation to treat people disrespectfully – it just makes them angry and less likely to do what you want. No matter what one thinks of another person, if he is treated with respect and dignity – even if you think he does not deserve it – communication will be much more successful, and the conflict will be more easily managed or resolved. This means that personal attacks and insults should be avoided, as should verbal or nonverbal clues that one is disdainful of the other side.

5. Nonverbal Symbols in Cross Culture Communication

Another major aspect of communication style is the degree of importance given to non-verbal communication. The words you use are important in effective communication, but the nonverbal cues you send can be even more important. Not only is it important to pay attention to how you use language to communicate, but also it is necessary to be aware of the messages that your actions send as well. Non-verbal communication includes not only facial expressions and gestures; but it also involves seating arrangements, personal distance, and sense of time. To understand the full impact of nonverbal communication, it can be important to remind yourself that actions do speak louder than words and that communication is often unintentional. When you communicate with other people, everything you do has an impact on the meaning people assign to your messages. When your tone contradicts the words you use, people tend to weight the tone more heavily than the language when assigning meaning to what you are saying. A sarcastic tone of voice that contradicts the words used will usually lead the message's receiver to assign a negative meaning to your words.

Though used the same way in most cultures, nonverbal symbols differ among cultures. In some cultures, for example, arriving late for a social or business engagement is polite; in others, it is considered rude. In addition, different norms regarding the appropriate degree of assertiveness in communicating can add to cultural misunderstandings. For instance, English people typically consider raised voices to be a sign that a fight has begun, while some black, Jewish and Italian Americans often feel that an increase in volume is a sign of an exciting conversation among friends. Thus, English may react with greater alarm to a loud discussion than would members of some Italian American ethnic groups be.

Another common difference involves personal space. The intimate or personal space of North Americans is larger than the intimate or personal space of others. In other cultures, appropriate eye contact varies from ours. American receivers need to have eye contact about 75 percent of the time. With the French, eye contact should be maintained 100 percent of the time. With Chinese, Japanese, or other Asians, it should be maintained only about 10 percent of the time. Too much eye contact with members of Asian cultures is very offensive. Whether or not you think it is appropriate for people to form impressions of other people based on appearance, it is a fact that image and appearance play important roles in business success. If you want to be viewed as a professional, it's important to have a professional image.

New Words and Expressions

exogenous 外成的，外因的
collaboration 合作，协作；通敌，勾结
coordinate 使协调，使调和
methodology (从事某一活动的)一套方法；方法学；方法论
contingency 意外事故，偶发事件；可能性，偶然性
remedy 治疗法；补救办法；纠正办法；改正，纠正，改进；补救；治疗
adversarial 敌手的，对手的，对抗(性)的
confrontational 挑衅的；对抗的
embedded 植入的，深入的，内含的
win-win 双赢
tradeoffs (公平)交易，折衷，权衡
axis 轴，轴线
gratitude 感激，感谢；感激的样子
parsimoniously 极度俭省地，吝啬地
vulnerable (地方)易受攻击的；易受伤的；易受批评的
bottom line 概要，账本底线
tactical 战术的；策略上的；巧妙设计的；有谋略的
outrageous 粗暴的；无法容忍的；反常的；令人惊讶的

Exercises

I. Choose the best answer according to the text.

1. What can determined the result of a negotiation? _____.

    A. History of a contract

    B. General economic climate

    C. Skill of negotiator

    D. None of the above

2. The skill of a negotiator can play an important role as to _____.

    A. reaching an agreement

    B. the scope of any eventual disputes

    C. the profitability of the project

    D. the possibility for additional work among the participants

    E. subsequent negotiation results

Unit 13　Construction Negotiation Strategies and Skills

3. Dispute resolution methods may include _____.
   A. litigation
   B. mediation
   C. debate
   D. negotiation
4. Often at the beginning of a negotiation, we can define our bottom line through _____.
   A. each party to the negotiation to have a sense of their own reservation price
   B. to make an overall object for both parties
   C. insistence on personalities and disruptive negotiating tactics without using objective criteria
   D. to adopt objective standards in determining appropriate contract provisions

II. Decide the following statements are true or false.

1. The parties involved in construction projects often share the same objects and have coherent speech and thoughts throughout the whole project.
2. Negotiations are an extremely important task for many project managers.
3. Either adversarial or confrontational negotiation shall be encouraged in order to reach a mutually satisfactory agreement.
4. Collaboration and mutual trust shall be founded as the key to negotiation success.

III. Change the following words to another form and write down the Chinese meanings.

1. proceed _____
2. preclude _____
3. comply _____
4. commit _____
5. prescribe _____
6. derive _____
7. conduct _____
8. actualize _____
9. highlight _____
10. eliminate _____

IV. Give out the following words' synonym or other word in the closest meaning.

1. negotiate   a. strategy
2. objective   b. germane
3. collaboration   c. choice
4. options   d. impartial
5. outcome   e. result
6. perspective   f. bargain
7. gratitude   g. viewpoint

8. impact 　　　　　　　　　h. cooperation
9. relevant 　　　　　　　　i. thankfulness
10. prejudice 　　　　　　　j. influence
11. tactic 　　　　　　　　　k. discrimination

V. Put the following English into Chinese.

1. Negotiation is interactive and involves relationships, confidence is the value showed to be the axis for a long term business relationship.

2. A second key skill for effective negotiating is to define your own "bottom line", i.e., least acceptable outcome for you.

3. Most books and courses on negotiation focus on the adversarial relationship modeled after project's commencement and hostile competitions of awarding.

4. The best strategy negotiation is obtaining a win-win outcome. Successful negotiators do not try to "win at all costs".

参 考 译 文

第 13 单元　施工谈判策略和技巧

1. 引言

由于建筑环境竞争激烈,建筑工程变得日益复杂,其中所涉及的各方目标常常互相冲突。因此,谈判一般都很复杂,对所牵涉的各方显露出重要的机会和风险。首先,谈判对于筹备施工合同来说是非常重要的机制。其次,一般来讲,承包商的经历和建筑业中的总体经济气候之类的外因将决定谈判的结果。然而,谈判代表的技巧可能影响到达成协议的可能性、项目收益率、最终争执的范围以及各参与方之中额外工程的可能性。甚至在以竞标为基础的合同授予之后,由于情况会随着时间的推移而改变,还有许多时机,在这些时机中需要进行后续谈判。这样一来,对项目经理来说,谈判是一个及其重要的任务。

2. 项目管理中的谈判

➢ 项目的成功交付需要所有相关参与方通力协作,这样项目的时间、成本、资源以及项目目标就可以进行协调。对施工项目经理来说,谈判就成为每天的例行公事。施工项目经理似乎仅仅通过经历和观察学会谈判技巧。因此,实用的谈判方法论对于建筑业中的项目经理更有成效地处理谈判来说是很有用的。例如,工程合同方面的谈判可能涉及诸如竣工日期、仲裁程序、特殊工程事项补偿、意外事故以及总体价格等问题。

➢ 建筑材料采购是一个关键业务,其中谈判一般要达成最终合约。在谈判中涉及的成本和时间意味着承包商必须限制他们谈判的供应商的数量,还有包含在谈判中的可选办法数量。便宜和高效谈判方法将允许寻求更多的预期供应商和选择办法。

➢ 在许多可选争执解决手段中,例如谈判和斡旋,谈判作为一种补救诉讼缺点的方法受到普遍欢迎。谈判不仅涉及法院(判决的)索赔的金钱和时间被牵涉,而且所涉及各方在一个更少敌意的环境中对谈判结果有更多的支配。

Unit 13 Construction Negotiation Strategies and Skills

3. 谈判策略

谈判涉及预测对方底线和呈现使他们自己利益最大化的报价的每一方。谈判由围绕针对达成相互满意的协议目标的具体问题的双方或多方之间的商讨组成。从传统上说，谈判是对抗的、挑衅的，例如，强硬的谈论和看看你可以获得多少。这种对谈判的消极态度被深深地置入许多文化之中。大部分有关谈判的书籍和课程关注在项目开始和恶意竞争授标之后所形成的对抗关系。

最好的谈判策略是获得双赢结果。成功的谈判不用试图"不惜一切代价去赢"。双赢谈判是一个对于强调共同利益和目标的协商途径。通过协同工作，各方可以寻求创造性解决方案，并达成所有参与方在其中都可以赢的决策。因为每个谈判代表都有关于每个可协商问题和可选方式的不同选择机会，所以谈判策略就是要相应地进行折衷处理，从而实现更高的满意水平。大部分聪明的谈判者，比如卓越领导人和决策者，认为谈判成功的关键十分简单明了，即获得合作伙伴和合作者的信任和信心。然而，我们必须记住，有时谈判实际上是商业战斗或斗争，且对手通常会玩赢或输的游戏。一般应遵循的原则如下：

3.1 信心

谈判是互动的并涉及相互间的关系，且信心是长期业务关系的中心。当需要别人的赞成去获得我们想要的结局的时候，信心就很重要了。且当我们能够通过牵涉其他人而更好地达到目的的时候，我们的信心将是我们的信誉。做一个体态自测，以核实你的言辞与你的非言语姿势相匹配。否则，你将不能被认真地接纳。

3.2 感谢

感谢他人的帮助、建议和贡献的行为对有意在未来的项目中继续合作很重要。对精神价值的影响和针对长期业务关系的实际参照，及其对组织的经济运行的成果的考虑相当关键。信任的氛围会减少创造双赢结果所需的时间，合作态度会消除反感并创造良好意图和成果。

3.3 公平

在同一项目中工作的那些人的双赢态度表明，即使项目最后不成功也要具有积极的冲突。另一方面，对谈判的成果来说，试图把其他人的工作归功于自己的态度具有非常消极的影响。

3.4 透明

就各方立场而言，在谈判进程中采取透明行动，在建立信心方面具有积极影响。在谈判进行的有关领域中，准备恰当和知识渊博的谈判代表，对于促使谈判进展非常有用。谈判失败的可能性突出了关于透露信息的策略的重要性。策略信息是你仅仅应当吝啬地给予，同时你能换回一些信息。

3.5 正直

拐弯抹角的行为在谈判进程中具有非常消极的影响，并且它不被决策者接受。友好和有同情心的态度可以通过高度的正直和社交才智显示，当对手改变他的信用的时候，尽管我们有时确实需要拐弯抹角。然而，通过电子邮件的副本保持最新，或者通过搭档或者合作者实施谈判进程，在激发信任上具有非常积极的影响。

4. 谈判技巧

4.1 理解你自己

对于一个高效的谈判者来说，最重要的技巧就是对自己的清晰了解。假设你心里有一个特别的冲突，用你所能做到的诚实来回答下列关于你自己的问题，并且准备一段在谈判中描述你自己的简要内容。选择一个搭档并告诉他。

- 我有什么长处？有什么局限？
- 我是一个好听众吗？
- 我对什么心理脆弱？对什么情绪上较敏感？
- 我的偏见和偏心是什么？
- 谈判中我将创造一种什么氛围？
- 谈判期间我需要什么？

4.2 确定结果

- 有效谈判的第二个关键技巧是界定自己的"底线"，即对你来说最小的可接受结果。用你自己的冲突示例(或另一个范例，如果合适的话)，决定你想要的最好的结果和你至少可以接受的结果。你也许希望去推测来自另一方观点的相同问题。在双方之间的谈判中，每一方都有许多目标和限制。每一方的总体目标都是获得最有利的和可接受的协议。

- 根据这些战术问题，在决定恰当的合同条款时采纳目标标准通常有益于各参与方。这些标准将会规定一个特别协定或一种办法，以在谈判中获得恰当价值。目标标准可能源自许多资源，包括市场价值、范例、专业标准、法院将做出的判决等。通过使用客观的标准，个性化和非连续性谈判手段不会成为达成互利协议的障碍。

- 对于双方来说，关于某问题的谈判表明了这个根本观点。由于限制不同，想达成一个协议也许是不可能的。当然，双方在谈判的开始一向不知协议是否可能达成。但对谈判的每一方来说，具有他们自己的保留价格的判断则十分重要，比如在双方可接受范围内物主的最低售价或者买主的最高买价。这个保留价格等同于要被谈判协议的最好的可选价格。

4.3 理解立场和利益

谈判中的一个关键技术是去理解(双方)立场和利益之间的差异，以此方式超越立场去确定潜在的利益。立场是一方致力于解决冲突的一种选择。利益是冲突之下的关切、需要和/或欲望，即冲突为什么会被引起。理解你对要谈判的协议的最好备选方案尤其重要。

4.4 沉默是金

当其他人很健谈，且你想要在没做任何类型的承诺的情况下尽你所能了解信息，不说话且让其他人谈论也许是最好的战术。当有人说到愤怒的、攻击的或者蛮横的事情的时候，这也是一个很好的选择。如果你不说什么，对其他人来说也就没有任何要反驳的东西。在谈判会议上，沉默可以发挥奇效。它能有效地阻止你说话太多，且可以让对方表达对特殊问题或观点的看法。

4.5 更高权威性(领导/上级)

更高权威战术会为谈判双方中任何一方发挥作用。有时你不能通过与一个特定的人一起工作来使一种情况得到解决。或许那个人已经决定不遵从于你的要求，或者他们没有权威来这么做。所以，你寻找一个更高权威去获得一个满意的结果。另一方面，在一种情形中缺乏最终发言权可能会为对方创造一个非常强势的立场，由于他将有机会把你的要求反映到他组织(公司)中某更高的级别的上级去处理。

5. 谈判成果方面

由于额外的问题，谈判在程序和结果两者中都变得更加复杂。关于程序，问题在其中被定义或被仔细考虑的处理顺序非常重要。例如，谈判可能在一个问题接一个问题的基础上继续下去，且结果可能取决于被考虑问题的确切顺序。同样的，双方可能通过提议完整的一揽子交易协议然后继续衡量一揽子交易。至于结果，双方具有在特定问题上的不同估价或者衡量的可能性常常会出现。在这种情况下，可能会针对双方的利益在不同的问题上对结果进行折衷。通过让步于对自己是低价(不重要)的，而对对方是高价(相对重要)的问题，其他问题上(对方)的妥协就可以如愿以偿。由一方或对方采用的拙劣谈判策略，会阻止在双方可以接受的范围达成协议。

阅读

跨文化交流

1. 引言

交流即创造、交流意义的过程。它牵涉言语的和非言语的两种信息的发送和接收。交流始终在发生，无论你做什么，你都要发送信息，且人们把意义指定到你所做的和所说的事情上。无论你在哪里从事一个国际项目，你都会发现自己被包围在一个多样化工作环境中。然而，承认国际多样化的来源和性质，可以使我们的工作关系更顺畅和更有成效，因为我们想在一个我们被完全尊重的且人们能够以他们的最大潜力来行事的环境中工作。这是促使我们前进的动因。无论他们的分歧是什么，创造一个所有项目参与方都感觉公平合理的职场是非常重要的。由于交流是持续不断的，有时候，当人们暗示在进展中需要更多交流的时候，他们真正的意思是需要更好的交流。

2. 多样化环境中的协调

➢ 建筑业中心信息极其密集，且通过整合项目信息在建筑师/工程师/施工企业，以及在施工现场的分包商和雇主等不同人群中交流，协调是必需的。不同行业对项目的考虑十分不一样。为了分享不同参与方的观点在某些项目上使团队努力最大化，合作是必需的。当提到在项目任务之下一起有效地工作时，关于着眼于在合作中建立早期关系的重要性，文化显得十分不一样。在多元文化环境之下，我们认为，通过多样性、跨文化交流对于任何项目的成功执行是一个关键。

➢ 在全球建筑市场中，国际多样性是一个普遍事实。我们的同事可能来自不同的国家和民族背景，信奉不同的宗教，并持有对政治、工作和问题解决的不同看法。文化是一个复杂的概念，有着许多不同的定义。但是，简单来说，"文化"指一群体或社团，我们与其分享共同的理解这个世界的方式。我们的文化影响我们怎样处理问题，以及怎样参与到群体和社会中。不同的交流风格反映了作为他们文化基础的更深层的人生观和世界观。理解这些更深层人生观会给我们提供一幅更广阔的画面，该画面描绘了世界必须提供给我们什么东西。了解人们的文化具有对我们给出自己的镜像的潜在可能性。我们有机会去挑战我们关于做事情的"正确"方式的假设，并考虑到多种方法。

> 当我们参与一个项目的时候，我们常常惊奇于人们一起处理工作问题是多么的不同。一些文化把冲突看作是积极的事情，而另外的文化则把它视为要避免的事情。在施工过程中，冲突通常是不合意的；但人们常常被期望直接处理确实发生的冲突。事实上，面对面会见惯常被推荐为解决存在的任何问题障碍的方式。但是在有些东方国家，公开的冲突是令人为难的、屈辱的；一般说来，最好平静地解决分歧。书面交流也许是有利的对付冲突的方式。亚洲和西班牙语系文化倾向于更加重视在合作项目的开始就发展关系，并且与西方人比较起来更强调结局的任务的完成。西方人倾向于立即集中在手边的任务上，并让关系在项目的进行中得到发展。这并不意味着来自任何一种这些文化背景的人们致力于完成项目的责任不同，或者不同程度地重视彼此的关系的差别；它意味着他们可能不一样地追求达到它们的目标的方式。然而，他们在项目中的实际参与将被他们的公司目标所限制。

3. 国际项目实施中的多样性挑战

除了文化和国籍的差异外，在国际项目实施中遭遇其他多样性类型是很常见的。虽然多样性有时被视为施工中的优势，但它通常逆向地影响项目成员之中的交流。在某种程度上，我们会对这些差异不以为然。对某一群体，我们总会有不同的偏见，甚至成见。有时，我们在那些不同的习惯、信仰或者习俗的人们周围会感到不自在。我们的不自在通常因为我们不理解差异或者没有准备好遭遇它们。在某些情况下，我们与同事沟通的不自在或无能为力因保守观念(偏见)而发生。陈规老套是一种过分简单化的关于一个群体的信念。例如，那种工程师就是带深边眼镜且留有短发的人的观念是不确切的。俗套(偏见)使我们以群体成员而不是以个人为基础去对人们做出判断。虽然一个群体内的人们可能具有某种特征，但是每个人在个性、经验、能力以及当前生活状况方面是独一无二的。

4. 跨文化交流技能

> 当你与多种文化背景的人们沟通的时候，跨文化交流技能变得尤其重要。除了仅仅有效地写和说之外，你需要在你们的交流中加入敏感要素、理解和宽容。记住不要以高人一等的态度和口气对待那些不能流利讲业务语言的人们非常重要。取而代之的是，考虑新的沟通方式将帮助你和你的听众彼此感到理解和惬意。我们应当记住，毕竟每个人都是一个个体。

> 虽然所有人都一直在交流，但是大部分人在冲突情况下却会遇到有效沟通的困难。多数情况下，曲解是问题的根源。实施沟通技能在冲突管理和解决进程上具有非常有益的影响。有效跨文化交流的关键是知识。首先，人们理解跨文化交流的潜在问题并做出自觉的努力去战胜这些问题是必不可少的。其次，假设某个人的努力不会总是成功的以及适当地调整某个人的行为是很重要的。

- 第一条规则是积极的倾听。积极倾听的目标是像理解你自己一样理解你的搭档或者对手。密切注意对方在说些什么。要求你的搭档或对手澄清和重复不清楚或似乎不合理的(也许不是这样,而是你理解错了)任何事情。试图向他们重复他们提出的情况。这能表明,你在倾听且理解了他们所说的话。但不表明你同意他们所说的话,也不表明你必须同意他们所说的话。你只需要表示你确实理解他们。当事情似乎正变得糟糕的时候,应停下或放慢速度并去思考。

- 第二条规则是直接对你的搭档或对手讲。这一点在有些文化中被认为是不恰当的,但是在允许的时候,它将有助于增进理解。要避免被局外人士或你身边的其他事情分心。把心思集中在你不得不说的事情上,且以你的合作伙伴或对手能够理解的方式说出来。

- 第三条规则是讲你自己,描述你自己的感觉和认识,而不是注意你的搭档或对手的动机、劣行或缺点。通过说"我感到很失望"而不是"你失信了",你可以表达同样的意思。但是你将以不会激起你的搭档或对手的防御或敌意反应的方式来这么做。(这常常被称为"我陈述"或"我告知"的运用,而非"你告知"。"你告知"暗示着责怪,且助长接受者否认坏事或者反责怪。"我陈述"只是简单地陈述问题,没有针对问题责怪某人。这使另一方帮助解决问题更容易,而没有必要承认他们错了。)

- 第四条规则是"为目的而说"。太多的交流可能是起反作用的,他们警告说。在你进行一个有意义的陈述之前,暂停并考虑一下你想要交流什么、为什么你想要交流这个内容,你怎样才能以最清晰的可能方式来进行交流。一个方法就是当对待另一方的人员时尽可能避免使用刺激性语言。刺激性语言只会增加敌意和防范——它很少使人相信说话者是对的。虽然刺激性言语可能在冲突中激发人们的兴趣并产生某人自己一方的支持,但是那样做常常伴随着总体冲突升级。从这个意义上说,一方可以有效地表达自己的观点而没有使用刺激性语言,这是更好的结果。

同样,应当尊重对待所有参与方或对手。无礼对待人们对冲突状况毫无助益——它只会使人们愤怒且更不可能去做你想要做的。无论某人对另一人有什么看法,如果他们被以尊重和尊严来对待了——即使你认为他不值得这样对待——交流也会成功得多,且冲突会更容易对付和解决。这就意味着,个人攻击和侮辱应当避免,正如言辞的和非言辞的攻击和侮辱应当提示一方对另一方是轻蔑的那样。

5. 跨文化交流中的非言语标志

交流风格的另一个主要方面是给出非言语交流的重要性。你使用的语言在有效交流中很重要,但是你发出的非言语暗示可能更重要。不仅应重视怎样使用语言去交流,而且还应知道你的行为所发出的信息。非言语交流不仅包括面部表情和手势,而且它也涉及座位安排、个人距离以及时间观念。要了解非言语交流的完全影响,应提醒自己行为确实比言辞更有分量,并且这种交流常常是不经意的。当与别人进行交流时,你所做的一切均对你传达的信息具有影响,别人会根据你的言和行进行判断。当你的语气与你所用的言辞不一致时,别人会更注意你话里的语调含义,而不是你的用词。与你所使用的言辞不一致的挖苦语调,通常让信息接受者对你所说的话产生负面的理解。

虽然在大部分文化中以相同的方式来使用,非言语标志在各种文化中也不相同。例如在有些文化中,在社交或商务约会中迟到是有礼貌的;在其他一些国家,这被看作很不礼貌。另外，交流中坚持不同标准可能增加文化误解。例如，英国人一向认为提高的嗓音是战斗已经开始的征兆，而一些黑人、犹太人和意大利裔美国人却觉得音量的增加是朋友之间兴奋交谈的象征。于是，英国人可能比一些意大利裔美国人少数民族成员对大声讨论以更强烈警告做出反应。

另一个普遍差异牵涉私人空间。北美的亲密或私人空间比其他地方的亲密或私人空间更大。在其他文化中，目光接触的应用与我们不同。美国接受者需要目光接触大约75%的时间。对于法国人，目光接触应当保持100%的时间。对于中国人、日本人或者其他亚洲人，目光接触应当只保持10%的时间。与亚洲文化成员的太多目光接触非常令人不快。无论你认为对于人们来说基于外貌形成对他人的印象恰当与否，这都是一个事实，即形象和外貌在商业成功中扮演着重要角色。如果你想要被看作是一名专业人士，就应具有专业形象。

Unit 14

Construction Claims (1)

1. Introduction

In international construction market, construction disputes and resulting claims have become a normal and expected part of the construction process in many public, commercial and industrial projects. Contractors, in order to ensure long-term profitability, must proactively address potential claims and be prepared when claims arise. Disputes often arise between subcontractors, contractors and employers regarding performance of the project. The potential number of players in a construction dispute is limited only by the number of parties involved with a particular project. Expectations of employers, contractors, subcontractors, architects, engineers, or suppliers may be disappointed and disputes may arise at any time between the first bid and the last bill. Employers take a dim view of nonperformance by contractors, subcontractors, and others, who take an equally dim view when their performance is not rewarded by timely payment by the employer. Moreover, disputes frequently occur over the scope, timing and quality of work actually performed and materials actually delivered.

2. Causes of Construction Claims

2.1 Types of Claims

Construction disputes generate a variety of different claims that can result in different types of economic damages. An overview of why claims happen, what kinds are the most costly, and what contractor can do on the actions and events that may be compensable. Contractor must be alert when these increased costs can be established with relative certainty, liability can be determined, and liability and increased costs may be linked and result in claims. The primary causes of construction claims can be classified into the following general categories:

- ➢ Unclear or poorly drafted contracts
- ➢ Poorly coordinated contract drawings
- ➢ Formal and construction change order claims
- ➢ Disruption claims
- ➢ Acceleration claims
- ➢ Delay and extension claims
- ➢ Breach or termination contract claims

2.2 Other Types of Claims

Complications arise when the claimant has not directly contracted with the party against whom claimant wishes to file its claim. For example, claims may arise between an employer and a subcontractor or materials suppliers. Under these circumstances, the subcontractor has no cognizable claim against the employer for breach of contract because no privity exists between the parties. Other claims may arise with even more remote third parties, either against the project employer or in some cases against one another, such as financing entities, final users and other members of the construction process for whom there are no contractual remedies. These claims are often brought as tort claims (for example negligence, fraud and strict products liability), or statutory claims.

3. Claims in Construction Execution

3.1 Variation and Construction Change Claims

Variation is either an addition to, or reduction to, or any change to, the scope of work under the contract by the order of employer or employer's representative. It can also be a change to the scope in terms of substituting some of the work for something else. For example, two internal staircases could be removed and substituted for one long external staircase. A variation also arises if there is a departure from any plans, drawings, or specifications contained in the contract.

The variations involved in the pricing of direct costs and/or disruptions, delays related to formal change orders are similar to the claims for construction changes. The only major difference is that in a formal change order the employer has, in essence, admitted that something is owed for the changed work. Many times the contract provides the pricing scheme for the change. On other occasions, the employer waits for the contractor's pricing quote.

Generally, variation and construction change claims may be identified as falling into one of the following main groups:

➢ Changed conditions: Contractor must act when conditions different from that represented by the contract documents, or known at the time of bidding on the work, such as different soil conditions, or unknown obstructions, etc.

➢ Additional/Extra work: Disputes over the pricing and timing of additional work required, or even whether a piece of identified work is in the contract or not. Contractor must beware particularly of omissions in the design documents, requiring changes to make a system work, especially if they appear in a subtle way through the shop-drawing review and approval process. This is always very embarrassing for the designers, who would like to see them incorporated for compromise, so contractor may take chance.

3.2 Compensable Delays Claims

Compensable delays occur when another contract party's actions or inactions delay a contractor. The contractor may receive a time extension and damages reimbursement.

When excusable delays occur, however, the contractor may receive only a time extension. An excusable delay results from unforeseeable events beyond the employer or contractor's control, fault, or negligence, such as in force majeure circumstance of bad weather, changes in law, strikes and industrial unrest, and political agenda changes or regime change. Unusually severe weather (as compared with reasonably expected weather for the project location during the expected time period) is an example of excusable delay. If a contractor did not receive an appropriate time extension for an excusable delay, the contractor may have incurred damages through acceleration attempts to maintain timetables.

Delays that often call for both a time extension and compensation to the contractor include:
- Failure to provide the contractor site access as scheduled
- Delayed or changed design drawings
- Late delivery of employer-supplies equipment or materials
- Untimely field inspections

3.3 Acceleration Claims

Acceleration is the group of activities undertaken to make up time (production) in order to meet the originally planned completion date or to complete a project earlier than planned. Acceleration can take many forms, such as working longer shifts (overtime labor), adding second or third shifts, increasing levels of manpower and equipment, or performing various tasks concurrently and revising work sequences. Acceleration costs include:
- Premium portion of overtime and the inefficiencies associated with extended overtime;
- Higher wage rates of added shifts;
- Vendors' premiums for expedited delivery of materials;
- Equipment increases required to support added crews;
- Disruptive effects on the work force causing lower productivity;
- Extra hours associated with revised work.
- Higher wage rates of added shifts;
- Vendors' premiums for expedited delivery of materials;
- Equipment increases required to support added crews;
- Disruptive effects on the work force causing lower productivity;
- Extra hours associated with revised work.

3.4 Disruption Claims

Disruption of the contractor's work force by the employer or employer's representative resulting in reduced productivity is often compensable to the contractor. Disruptions affect the contractor's work force in many ways:
- Uneven labor force levels, including overtime;
- Inefficient work force level;
- Inefficient sequence scheduling, stacking of crafts (e.g. forcing electricians and pipefitters to work simultaneously in the same location);
- Excessive drawing changes;
- Early, late, or out-of-sequence material and equipment deliveries;

> Performance beyond contract specifications or tolerances.

3.5 Breach or Termination Contract Claims

> The claims are arising from alleged breaches of the construction contract, such claims compose the overwhelming majority of construction disputes. The contractor should be compensated for its work to prevent "unjust enrichment" of the party receiving the benefit of the work. The claim attempts to quantify the increased, unreimbursed value of the project accruing from the contractor's additional efforts that are caused by the employer. A difference between the breach contract claim and a claim related to the "changes" or "extra work" clauses in the contract lies in the rationale for recovery. Where a traditional "changes" claim is based upon the rights conferred by the contract to recover the costs of changes imposed by the employer, the breaches of the construction contract claim is based on an implied right to be reimbursed for work performed in accordance with the contract.

> The objective of the wrongful termination claims should be to put the contractor in the same position he would have been in if he had been permitted to complete the contracted work. Many contracts, however, place limitations on the types of damage recoverable if a contractor is terminated. Therefore, the appropriate damage amount should reflect the profit that would have been earned by completing the project, any costs associated with the employer's appropriation of equipment, tools or operating materials, as well as any lost profits from revenues or contracts lost due to the termination.

3.6 Variation and Acceleration Instruction/Order

Any conduct by a employer's contracting representative (architect/engineer or other representative of the employer authorized to order changes), or any event which is not a formal change order, but which requires performance of work different than anticipated or prescribed by the original contract, may constitute a variation order/instruction. There are a great many actions and events that can result in construction changes to contract work.

The contractor's acceleration claim must obtain formal instruction, namely, the applicable correspondence, meeting notes, witness statements, or other notes and records that prove that the employer or employer-representative decided to accelerate. Depending upon the applicable contractual relationships, the employer's representatives for this purpose may include the contracting officer, architect, engineer, or contractor (assuming a subcontractor accelerates).

Reading

Construction Safety Management

1. Introduction

Construction is a relatively hazardous undertaking. There are significantly more accidents due to injuries or illnesses in construction than in virtually any other industry. These work-related injuries and illnesses are exceedingly costly. Accidents during the construction process can result in personal injuries and large costs. Included in this total are direct costs (medical costs, premiums for workers' compensation benefits, liability and property losses) as well as indirect costs (reduced worker productivity, delays in projects, administrative time, and damage to equipment and the facility). Indirect costs of insurance, inspection and regulation are increasing rapidly due to these increased direct costs.

Construction safety management deals with actions that managers at all levels can take to create an organizational setting in which workers will be trained and motivated to perform safe and productive construction work. The system should outline procedures for eliminating hazards and identifying potential hazards before they become the contributing factors to unfortunate accidents. However, construction has a number of characteristics making it inherently hazardous. Large forces are involved in many operations. The project site is continually changing as construction proceeds. Workers do not have fixed project sites and must move around a structure under construction. The tenure of a worker on a site is short, so the worker's familiarity and the employer-employee relationship are less settled than in manufacturing settings. Despite these peculiarities and as a result of exactly these special problems, improving project site safety is a very important project management concern.

2. Hazard Analyses and Identify

Contractors must be made aware of all of the pre-existing workplace hazards that may affect their workers. Often this seems like common sense, but lack of documentation of the process of identifying workplace hazards can create problems. Workplace hazard identification must be completed prior to putting a project starting. Manager of Projects, Project Coordinator or Supervisor will ensure the hazard identification is performed. For example, workers are easily exposed to hazardous substances such as paints, thinners, glues, varnishes, asbestos, and also to toxic agents mainly from underground work. Sites can easily accumulate debris which can be a fire hazard or a health hazard. Drilling and excavation work can cause accidental fires or even explosion. Working at height can result in debris falling on workers or even workers falling from heights. Fire, noise and dust are common constituents in construction sites, and can be an inconvenience or danger to the neighborhood, especially in built-up areas.

3. Safety Management Organization

A well designed safety organisation for contractors, sub-contractors and interface with department is very essential. Prior to the commencement of the project, the project safety management team under the leadership of the project manager shall be organized, whose various responsibilities shall be assigned to ensure the safety, shall be controlled strictly and practiced in line with safety regulations and system. The project management team consists of the project manager, site engineers and foremen shall inspect all of the construction safety conditions on the regular basis of half a month. From the beginning of the construction, the project management team shall instill safety rules and regulations through site meetings to the operating team, so as to guarantee that all the safety rules will be strictly abided by all the workers. A safety superintendent will be appointed, whose responsibility is to supervise and check the construction safety conditions, to deter operations that violate safety rules and safety disciplines, and take necessary measures to prevent potential safety problems. The relevant safety regulations, standards and stipulations of the local government shall be respected in the project safety management.

4. Construction Safety Plan

The safety plan helps identify and eliminate a project's potential hazards. Planning is a critical area in the control and enforcement of a safety programme. It is a process that prepares, creates, implements and monitors the safety programme, thereby addreszing the workplace health and safety through an organized, step-by-step strategy. Planning starts with the company's written health and safety policy. It ensures that health and safety efforts of all project site personnel really work by designing programme that translates policy into practice. Planning entails identifying the objectives and targets which are attainable and relevant, setting performance standards for management, considering and controlling risks to all employees and to other people who may be affected by the organization's activities, and ensuring documentation of all performance standards. The safety and health programme covers a range of general safety procedures and practices. Some of them are safety training, safety meeting, safety inspection, accident investigation and reporting, job hazard analysis and control, safety promotion, and personal protective equipment, etc.

5. Construction Safety Control

During construction and commissioning activities, the safety goal is to achieve an efficient incident-free workplace and no major accidents occur on the project. The causes of injuries in construction are numerous. The largest single category for both injuries and fatalities is individual falls. Handling goods and transportation is also a significant cause of injuries. Scrupulous implementation and adherence to the construction safety procedure and requirements is needed to be observed at all levels as an on-going program. Sign boards highlighting of site disciplines and rules shall be hung the proper locations of the construction site. Prudent project managers and employers would like to reduce accidents, injuries and illnesses as much as possible. Some of these systems to identify areas of improvement and achieve enhanced construction safety status are enumerated below:

➢ Contractors safety surveillance and correction programme ;
➢ Entry passes to the work site only after induction safety training, etc.;
➢ Periodical safety audits.

One administrative control is safety professionals' functionally in implementing safety during work. Hence, contractor must develop procedures, work plans and programs that are implemented with a common understanding of safety utility. In many countries, the regulatory requirements are equally important which need to be understood and implemented in clear and unmistakable terms by all concerned including the contractor organization.

6. Safety Training

Educating workers and managers in proper procedures can have a direct impact on construction site safety. The realization of the large costs involved in construction injuries and illnesses provides a considerable motivation for awareness and education. The importance of training cannot be undermined. In order to enhance effectiveness of training, it is necessary to develop training modules and methodology. The use of modern pedagogical teaching aids such as audio-visuals, mobile training will improve the performance of training. The workers who demonstrate good safety behavior and practices should be motivated by way of rewards. Enhanced field visit by the line managers and interacting with the workers with the philosophy of "each one teach one" will go a long way in strengthening the objective of achieving safety and desired safety culture.

7. Safety Meetings

Regular safety inspections and safety meetings should become standard practices on most job sites. The dynamicity, complexity and parallel activities in construction are unavoidable at times. These activities, though planned, are carried out by the work force which is skilled in the execution of work but lack of awareness of safety requirements. Overconfidence, complacency, at times, leads to breach in safety requirements. Hence, a regular monitoring and surveillance program along with coaching and mentoring of employees during execution becomes necessary to correct the aberrations in safety implementation. In order to ensure proper coordination and communication on safety aspects on a periodical basis, it is necessary to have regular safety meeting to review the safety status and exchange of views and experience.

8. Environmental Management Systems in Construction

The construction stage site-specific health and safety plan sets out the arrangements for securing the health and safety of everyone carrying out the work and all others who may be affected by it.

The development of the ISO 9000 standards and the certification schemes has strengthened contractors to approach quality compliance. Environmental management seems to be following the same path. The attention of world-wide is centred in the publication of the new ISO 14000 standard, which provides a mechanism that links the concept of sustainable development with the construction procurement process. The system will help win more business and reduce cost in production and operation, through improving environment performance and recognizing that construction is an important industry in any economy, and it has an obligation and the potential to make a significant contribution to sustainable development through implementing ISO 14001. It is suggested that in the future environment management will become a core requirement in international construction market.

In many developed countries, the Occupational Safety and Health Administration routinely conducts site visits of work places in conjunction with approved state inspection agencies. The inspectors are required by law to issue citations for all standard violations observed. Safety standards prescribe a variety of mechanical safeguards and procedures. All Project activities will be conducted in a safe working environment, which is conducive to the efficiency and well-being of project personnel. The construction plant will be designed to ensure a good working environment for the operating staff. This will be achieved by application of sound ergonomic design principles, control of in-plant noise and use of working environment reviews during the design phase. In case of extreme non-compliance with standards, OSHA inspectors can stop work on a project. As a result, safety is largely the responsibility of the managers on site rather than that of public inspectors.

New Words and Expressions

dim 暗淡的，昏暗的；不光明的；看不清的；
subcontractor 分包商
acceleration 加速
breach 破坏；破裂；缺口；违背攻破；破坏，违反
cognizable 可辨识的，可以审理的
negligence 疏忽；[法]过失；粗心大意
fraud 欺诈；骗子
staircase 楼梯；楼梯间
substitute 代替，替换，代用
omission 省略，删节；遗漏；疏忽；[法]不履行法律责任
unrest 动荡，不安定；骚乱
expedite 加快进展；迅速完成
pipefitter [化]管工
allege 断言，宣称，辩解；提出……作为理由
reimburse 偿还，付还，归还
rationale 理论的说明；基本原理，基础理论；根据

Exercises

I. Choose the best answer according to the text.

1. Disputes often arise between _____.

    A. subcontractors

    B. employers

    C. financing entities

    D. suppliers

2. Negligence, fraud and strict products liability may cause _____.

   A. negotiation

   B. statutory claims

   C. amicable settlement

   D. tort claims

3. Which of the following items can be regarded as variation in contract conditions? _____

   A. Change of the time of bidding

   B. Unknown obstructions

   C. Omissions in the design documents

   D. Untimely field inspections

4. Which of the following items fall into the category when the contractor can receive a time extension? _____.

   A. Changes in law

   B. Strikes and industrial unrest

   C. Delayed or changed design drawings

   D. Bad weather

5. Acceleration can take many forms as _____.

   A. increasing levels of manpower and equipment

   B. revising work sequences

   C. adding second or third shifts

   D. working longer shifts

II. Decide the following statements are true or false.

1. Liability and increased costs may not be necessarily linked.

2. If only the work has not kept in pace with what has been stated in the drafted contracts, be it acceleration or delay or termination, construction claim may be aroused.

3. Normally late delivery of employer-supplies equipment or materials only gives the contractor chance to claim for time extension.

4. Acceleration may cause equipment increases required to support added crews.

5. Contracting officer, architect, engineer, or contractor normally may not be able to give acceleration instruction.

III. Change the following words to another form and write down the Chinese meanings.

1. compensate _____

2. process _____

3. reward _____

4. classify _____

5. accelerate _____

6. reimburse _____

7. schedule _____
8. beware _____
9. embarrass _____
10. allege _____

IV. Give out the following words' synonym or other word in the closest meaning.

1. breach   a. suitable
2. termination   b. delegation
3. representative   c. conclusion
4. anticipation   d. direction
5. instruction   e. expectation
6. appropriate   f. speeding up
7. claim   g. turbulent
8. excessive   h. violate
9. disruptive   i. declare
10. acceleration   j. immoderate

V. Put the following English into Chinese.

1. An overview of why claims happen, what kinds are the most costly, and what contractor can do on the actions and events that may be compensable and result in claims.

2. Other claims may arise with even more remote third parties, either against the project employer or in some cases against one another, such as financing entities, final users and other members of the construction process for whom there are no contractual remedies.

3. The claim attempts to quantify the increased, unreimbursed value of the project accruing from the contractor's additional efforts that are caused by the employer.

参考译文

第14单元 施工索赔(1)

1. 引言

国际建筑市场中，施工争议及所引发的索赔已经成为许多公共、商业和工业项目施工流程中正常的并且是意料之中的部分。为了保证长期盈利，承包商必须主动地对付潜在索赔并在索赔发生时做好准备。争议常常发生在有关项目执行的分包商、承包商和雇主之间。施工争议中的潜在参与者的数量仅仅由与特定项目有密切关系的各方数量来限制。雇主、承包商、分包商、建筑师、工程师或者供应商的期望可能是失望的，且争议可能在第一次报价和最后一次付款之间的任何时候发生。雇主对承包商、分包商以及其他当事方的不履行合同不满意，而当各参与方没有得到雇主的及时付款时，他们也会同等地不满意。此外，争议在实际完成的工程范围、时间和质量以及实际交付的材料等方面较频繁地发生。

2. 施工索赔的原因

2.1 索赔类型

施工争议产生各种不同的索赔,这些索赔可能导致不同类型的经济损失。纵观为什么索赔会发生,什么类型的索赔代价最高,以及承包商可以在可补偿的行为和事件上做什么。当这些增加了的成本可以用相对的确定性来证实时,承包商必须是警觉的,责任可以确定,且责任和增加的成本可以联系起来且导致索赔。施工索赔的首要原因可以分为以下几类:

- 含糊或拙劣起草的合同
- 有矛盾的合同图纸
- 正式和施工变更通知索赔
- (工作程序)中断(干扰)索赔
- 加速索赔
- 工期延误和延长索赔
- 违约或终止合同索赔

2.2 其他索赔类型

索赔人没有直接与想要把索赔针对其提交的当事人签订合同时,通常会遇到难题。例如,索赔可能发生在雇主和分包商或者材料供应商之间。在这些情况下,分包商没有由于违约而针对雇主的可审理索赔,因为当事人之间没有合同关系。其他索赔甚至可能对于更间接的第三方而发生,也对于项目雇主或在有些情况下对于相互之间而发生,比如金融实体、最终用户和其他施工项目成员,对所有这些当事人而言,都没有合同补救办法。这些索赔常常作为侵权索赔(如玩忽职守、欺诈和严格产品赔偿责任)或者法定索赔。

3. 施工执行中的索赔

3.1 变更和施工更改索赔

变更是根据合同条款通过雇主或雇主代表的指令对工程范围的进行增加、减少或改变。就对于别的东西的工程的某些替代而言,变更也是范围的改变。例如,内部的两个室内楼梯可以移除并用室外的一个长楼梯间取代。如果有与包含在合同中的任何计划、图纸或者规范不同,变更也会发生。

牵涉直接成本和/或关系到正式变更指令的中断、延误的定价的变更与针对施工改变的索赔相似。唯一的主要差异是,在正式的变更指令中,雇主其实已经承认,对所变更的工程来说某些东西是(对承包商)亏欠的。很多时候,合同为变更提供价格表。在其他时候,雇主等待承包商(对变更)报价。

普遍来说,变更和施工变更索赔可以被认定为主要分类成如下:

- 改变了的情况:当情况不同于合同文件所表明的那样,或者不同于有关工程的投标时所知道的那样,比如不同的土壤状况或者未知的障碍等,承包商必须采取行动。
- 附加的/额外的工程:指在所需附加工程的定价和时间方面的争议,乃至一项所认定的工程是否包含在合同里。承包商必须特别留意设计文件中的遗漏,需要变更去使系统运转的情况,尤其是如果它们通过施工图检查和批准流程在一种微妙的程度上出现的话。

对于设计师来说这总是令人尴尬的，他们愿意看到这些遗漏以折中方法而被纳入(合同)，因此承包商就可以抓住机会。

3.2 可补偿延误索赔

当另一个合同当事方的作为或不作为耽搁了承包商的时候，可补偿延误就会发生。承包商可以得到一个时间延期和损失赔偿。

然而，当可容许的延误发生时，承包商仅仅可以得到时间延期。可允许延误产生于超越雇主或承包商的控制、过失或者疏忽的不可预料事件，比如恶劣天气的不可抗力情况、法律变更、罢工和产业动乱以及政党议事日程的改变或者政体的改变。不寻常的恶劣天气(在期望的期限内与针对项目位置的合理期望的天气比较)是一个可允许延误的例子。如果承包商不能得到一个对于可允许延误的恰当的时间延期，承包商可能会因与时间表保持一致的加速企图而遭受损失。

对承包商来说，既需要时间延期又需要经济补偿的延误常常包括：
- 不能像时间表所排定的那样提供给承包商工地通道；
- 延误的或变更的设计图纸；
- 由雇主所供应的设备或材料的推迟交付；
- 不合时宜的现场检查；

3.3 加快施工索赔

加快施工是一系列的以弥补时间(生产)的施工活动，目的是去满足原计划的竣工日期或者比计划更早地完成项目。加速可以采用许多形式，比如工作时间更长的轮班(超时劳动)、增加第二或者第三班、增加劳动力强度和设备、同时完成各种任务并修订作业顺序。加速成本包括：
- 与工程延期相联系的加班工作的额外费用以及加班工作的低效率；
- 附加轮班的高工资；
- 卖方加速提交材料的额外费用；
- 增加设备所需增加的人员；
- 在引起更低生产率的劳动力方面的破坏性结果；
- 与改进的工程相联系的额外上班时间。

3.4 中断索赔

对于承包商来说，由于雇主或者雇主代表导致生产率降低的承包商劳动力的(工作程序)中断(干扰)常常是可以补偿的。中断会在许多方面影响承包商的劳动力：
- 不稳定的劳动力水平，包括加班工作时间；
- 无效率劳动力水平；
- 无效率工序进度安排、技术工人的窝工(如迫使电气专家和管道安装工在同一位置同时工作)；
- 过多的图纸变更；
- 过早、延迟或混乱的材料和设备运送；
- 超出合同规范或允许范围的操作。

Unit 14　Construction Claims (1)

3.5 违反或终止合同索赔

➢ 起因于所声称的违反施工合同的索赔占施工争议的多数情况。由于其工作会阻止得到工程好处的当事方的"不当得利",因此承包商应当被补偿。该索赔试图量化增加了的、不应赔偿的项目工程量,该工程量是从由雇主引起的承包商的额外努力而累积起来的。合同违约索赔和关系到合同中的"变更"或"额外工作"条款的索赔之间的差异在于赔偿的基本原则。传统的"变更"索赔是基于以合同授予由雇主要求的变更成本的权力为基础的赔偿,而施工合同的违约索赔是基于默认权力根据合同对已完成工程的索赔。

➢ 错误终止合同的索赔目标应当是把承包商置于他如果被许可去完成合同工程的相同位置上(他应当得到的利润)。然而,如果承包商被终止合同,许多合同把限制放到可赔偿的损失类型上。因此,合理的损失费用总额应当反映假如承包商完成合同获得的利润,该利润包括任何与雇主占用的设备、工具或者运营材料的费用,以及因终止的合同而造成的收益损失或者合同损失。

3.6 变更和加速指示/指令

任何由雇主的签约人(建筑师/工程师或雇主授权去指示变更的其他代表)签署的合同,或者任何并非正式变更指令,而是要求有别于由原始合同所预期和描述的作业情况,可能构成一个变更指令/指示。对合同工程来说可能导致施工变更的行为和事件很多。

对承包商的加速索赔必须获得正规指示,即适当的函件、会议笔记、目击者声明、或者其他笔记和记录,这些东西会证明雇主或者雇主代表决定加速。依赖于合适的契约关系,针对该目的的雇主代表可能包括签约官(甲方工程代表)、建筑师、工程师或者承包商(假定分包商加速)。

阅读

施工安全管理

1. 引言

施工是一项相对危险的工作。在施工中显著存在事实上比在任何其他行业中都多的由于受伤或疾病的事故。这些与工作有关的受伤和疾病代价极其高昂。施工进程中的事故可能导致人员受伤和财产的巨大损失。这个损失总数中有直接成本(医药费、对于工人补偿金的额外费用、责任和财产损失),还有间接成本(减少的工人生产率、项目的延误、管理时间以及设备和设施的损坏)。保险、检查和规章的间接成本由于这些增加了的直接成本而迅速增加。

施工安全管理处理那些所有级别的经理都可以采取并创建一个组织环境的行动,在该环境中,工人将被培训和激发,从而执行安全和实效的施工作业。该系统应当针对在其成为不幸事故的促成因素之前消除危险和识别潜在危险而列出程序提纲。然而,施工天生具有危险性。项目中需要巨大的力量运营。项目现场随着施工开展而不断改变。工人没有固定的项目工地,并且必须围绕着施工中的建筑物而搬迁。工人在一个工地上的聘期很短,所以与制造业的情况相比,工人的熟悉度和雇主-雇员关系更不稳定。除了这些独特性之外,也确实由于这些特殊问题,改善项目现场安全是一个非常重要的项目管理关注事项。

253

2. 分析和识别危险

承包商必须意识到所有可能影响其工人的已有的工作场所危险。这一点似乎是常识，但是由于缺乏识别工作场所危险进程的文件，因此就可能引起问题。工作场所危险识别必须在项目开工之前完成。项目经理、项目协调师或者监理师确保已执行过危险识别。例如，工人容易暴露在有害物质中，诸如涂料、稀释剂、粘胶剂、清漆、石棉，并且也会接触到地下工程的毒剂。工地堆积有易引发火灾或健康危害的碎片。钻孔和挖掘工程可能引起意外火灾乃至爆炸。高空作业可能导致碎片坠落在工人身上乃至工人从高处跌落。火灾、噪声和粉尘是施工现场的一般组成部分，且可能引起临近地区的不便和危险，尤其在高楼林立的区域。

3. 安全管理组织

针对承包商、分包商和与部门之间设计合理的组织是绝对必要的。在项目开工之前，在项目经理领导下的项目安全管理小组将被组织起来，他们的各种职责将被指定以确保安全，将被严格地控制并且与安全规程和系统一致地落实。项目安全管理小组由项目经理和现场工程师组成，且工头将以半个月定期为基础对所有施工安全状况进行检查。从施工一开始，项目安全管理小组将通过现场会议向操作小组成员介绍规章制度，以保证所有工人严格遵守所有安全规程。同时还要指定一位安全负责人，其职责是监督和检查施工安全状况，阻止那些违约安全规程和安全纪律的操作，并采取必要措施去预防潜在安全问题。当地政府的相关安全规章、标准和条令在项目安全管理中将受到尊重。

4. 施工安全计划

安全计划帮助识别和消除项目的潜在危险。规划是安全方案控制和实施中的一个决定性方面。它是一个准备、创建、执行和监控安全方案的过程，由此通过有组织的、按部就班的策略来处理工作场所的健康和安全问题。规划以公司的书面健康和安全政策开始。通过设计把政策转化为实践的方案，它确保所有施工现场人员的健康和安全努力卓有成效。规划需要识别可达到的和紧密相关的目标和对象，设定针对管理的实施标准，考虑和控制对于所有雇员和可能受组织活动影响的其他人的风险，以及保证获得所有实施标准的文件。安全和健康方案涵盖一系列普通的安全程序和惯例。其中一些是安全培训、安全会议、安全检查、事故调查和报告、工作危害分析和控制、安全推广以及个人防护设备等。

5. 施工安全控制

在施工和调试活动期间，安全目标是获得一个无事故的工作场所以及在项目上没有重大事故发生。施工中的受伤原因很多。对于受伤和致命事故两者来说，最大的单个类别是个人的跌落。处理货物和运输也是受伤的一个重要原因。对施工安全规程和要求一丝不苟地执行和遵守，作为一个正在进行的方案，在各个层面都是需要遵守的。强调工地纪律和守则的安全指示牌应当悬挂在施工现场的适当位置。有先见之明的项目经理和雇主愿意尽可能多地减少事故、受伤和疾病。这些识别改善方面和获得增强的施工安全状况系统的某些事项列举如下：

> 承包商安全监视和纠正方案；

➢ 进入工程现场的入场权的获得只有在入门安全培训之后等；
➢ 定期安全审查。

管理控制是安全专业人士在作业期间执行的安全规则。由此，承包商必须对有关安全设施的安全规程、作业计划和方案做出解释。在许多国家，受法定规章限制的要求同等重要，包括承包商在内的所有涉及各方需要理解和执行这些清楚的和不会误解的条款。

6. 安全培训

以适当的程序培训工人和经理可能在施工现场安全方面有直接的影响。对涉及施工受伤和疾病的巨大代价的领会为觉悟和培训提供了相当大的动机。培训的重要性不能被削弱。为了增强培训的效果，应开发培训模块和方法。现代教学法的教具诸如视听、电话培训的使用将改善培训的成果，表现出良好安全行为和实践的工人应当通过奖赏方式受到激发。由业务经理所巡视的加强管理的场所和以"一个教一个"的基本原理在工人之间的互相影响将在巩固实现安全和想要的安全文化目标方面大有帮助。

7. 安全会议

定期举行安全检查和安全会议应当成为大多数施工现场的标准惯例。施工中的动态性、复杂性和平行活动有时是不可避免的。这些活动，尽管是计划中的，仍由对工程的执行非常熟练但缺乏安全要求意识的劳动力来完成。有时，自负、自满导致了对安全要求的违反。由此，在执行期间的定期监控和监视方案与员工训练和指导一起对纠正安全执行中的偏差就变得很必要。为了确保以定期为基础的安全方面的正确协调和沟通，举行定期的安全会议去检查安全状况及观点和经验的交流是非常必要的。

8. 施工中的环境管理系统

施工阶段仅限工地的健康和安全计划开始为每个正在实施作业的人和所有其他可能受其影响的人得到健康和安全而做出安排。

ISO 9000 标准的发展和认证办法拉近了承包商与质量符合性的距离。环境管理的路径与此类似。全世界关注于新 ISO 14000 标准的公布，因为它将以施工采购流程来提供一个与可持续发展的概念相联系的机制。通过改善环境状况和承认建筑业在任何经济中都是一个重要的行业，该系统将帮助企业在生产和经营中赢得更多的生意，降低其生产成本。并且通过执行 ISO 14001，具有了一种对可持续发展做出贡献的义务和潜力。在未来，环境管理将成为国际建筑市场的一个核心要求。

在许多发达国家，职业安全和健康管理局将按常规与核准的国家检查机构协力指导工作场所的现场巡视。检查人员依法要求发布针对所有观察到的违反标准行为的引述。安全标准规定多种机械防护措施和规程。所有项目活动将在一个安全工作环境中被指导，这有助于提高项目工作人员的工作效率和福利。施工场地的设计将能确保针对工作人员的良好工作环境。这种设计将在设计阶段通过应用工效学设计原理、控制场地内部噪声以及使用工作环境检查等方法来实现。万一发现严重不遵守安全标准的操作，职业安全与健康管理局检查人员可以中断一个项目的作业。因此，安全主要是现场经理而非公共检查人员的职责。

Unit 15

Construction Claims (2)

1. Construction Claims Calculation

➢ One of the most contentious areas in construction claims is the calculation or estimation of lost productivity. Therefore, all direct costs of labor, equipment, materials and other costs should be captured and associated with the work according to the contract. There are two typical methods of claim calculation on whether the claim is being priced on a pre-performance basis or on an after-the-fact basis. Other direct costs associated with the claim such as field overhead, bond costs, insurance, interest and profit should also be noted on the forms.

➢ Direct costs as defined in this section include only the costs of labor, equipment and materials needed to perform the actual work within the scope of the change. It does not include the consequential effect of changes such as costs for the disruption and inefficiency created by change orders; costs of acceleration of work; and costs as a result of project extensions.

1.1 Direct Labor Costs

Direct labor costs should be based on actual or anticipated increased costs of the various craftsmen, operating engineers, laborers, etc. Rates of pay may be dictated by contract terms (such as day work schedules), or if not in the contract may be supported by various union wage scales or other supportable bases. Costs of supervision should also be calculated and noted. Regular time and overtime work should be noted, and if overtime rates are requested they should be justified on the basis that the work could not be completed on regular time, that no time extension was granted, or other appropriate basis. Documents to support labor charges include payroll records, invoices, estimates, bid takeoffs, job diaries, and other daily project reports.

Labor issues, including contract negotiations, walkouts, slowdowns, and strikes, may delay completion of a project. Depending on the nature and duration of the labor issue, the contractor may need to work overtime or double shifts to make up for time lost during a labor dispute. This significantly increases the contractor's labor cost. An extension of the contract time results in increased overhead costs and may reduce a contractor's ability to begin or continue work on other projects.

1.2 Direct Equipment and Material Costs

Equipment costs may be increased due to additional equipment needed to perform the work. Charges for equipment usage may be based on contract terms, or if not specified in the contract may be based on rental invoices or hourly rates. The appropriate price to charge is the substantiated, increased time-related costs associated with owning or providing equipment on the site to perform the work within the change. Payroll reports for operating engineers may provide evidence of when equipment was used. For contractor owned equipment, internal rates may have been developed based on the total costs of owning the equipment spread out over the useful life of the equipment. Costs such as depreciation, insurance, taxes, storage and administrative costs should be included in the rate. The rate is usually expressed in hourly, daily or weekly costs of operation. However, only excess costs incurred as a result of the change should be included.

1.3 Project Site Overhead

Site overhead is frequently referred to as preliminary and general in contract conditions or BOQ. These costs include costs of on-site project management and administration, plants rentals, storage charges, utilities, etc. Contracts usually provide for percentage mark-ups on labor and other direct costs to account for site overhead. If need be, the contractor can support its claim by reference to bid documents and estimates, or international practice. Further support can be shown by actual costs for additional time and effort spent on meetings and discussions regarding estimating and engineering with respect to the change. Unanticipated additional manpower needed to perform work may also result in additional expenditures for small tools, supplies, consumables or other miscellaneous items that were carried as general conditions.

1.4 Interest Claims

The financing of unreimbursed project costs as a result of changes can have a significant impact. Interest charges may be appropriate to recoup financing costs or the lost opportunity to utilize internal funds in a manner other than as planned. The key factors to quantifying a claim for interest is to determine
- ➢ The period over which the interest is computed; and
- ➢ The rate or cost of money.

These factors may be set forth in the contract documents or by applicable local or legal regulations.

1.5 Profit

In addition to being entitled to recover excess costs attributable to a party's breach of contract, FIDIC allows an injured contractor to recover the profit anticipated under the contract if the evidence is sufficiently certain and definite to afford a basis on which to estimate its extent. There are at least some exceptions.

2. Construction Claims Documentation

Once a potential claim or dispute has been identified, the value of developing and preserving supporting documentation cannot be overstated. It is very crucial that the contractor prepare an effective document present accurate estimated damage amounts at the complaint stage. Disputes are often won or lost on the strength of a contractor's documentation. Even before a claim is identified, it is important that the contractor keep good records of its activity on the project.

2.1 Components of Claim

A construction claim consists of two major parts:
➢ The entitlement section, which usually includes a detailed description of the actions or inactions of the party from whom relief is sought, entitling the claimant to compensation; and
➢ The damages section, which sets forth the calculations and support for the compensation claimed.

2.2 Claim Analysis

Construction claims analysis, rather than coming at the end of the claim process, should proceed concurrently with the entitlement analysis. When filing a construction claim, performing damage analyses early can result in finding alternative explanations for increased costs by presenting the contractor's own convincing records.

2.3 Delay Analysis

Construction delays are very costly. Delay analysis involves a thorough examination of the various activities of the project, pinpointing deviations from planned performance, and then quantifying the delay. Delay impact analysis requires first that the contractor review project drawings, specifications and other contract documents as well as schedules, progress logs, and similar records. Next, planned and actual performance are compared in the form of CPM network schedules to identify critical deviations. Extended costs for delays are a common and hotly contested element in pricing. Quantification of delay damages requires:
➢ an analysis to determine the type of delay;
➢ time analysis of the delay period;
➢ an analysis of the cause and liability for the delay; and
➢ an analysis to determine the costs related to the delay.

a) Schedule Analysis

A scheduling analysis representing the project is generally prepared using a computer program that plots the sequence and interdependencies of the project's significant activities. This analysis will reveal the activities' most logical sequence. Many contracts, particularly for large projects, require identification of a critical path.

b) Activity Analysis

An analysis is required of three basic types of CPM schedules. The contractor reviews the following schedules:

"As-planned" schedule. This schedule represents the planned sequence and timing of original contract work. It is important that this schedule be reviewed for reasonableness, and determined to be a realistic, achievable plan.

"As-built" schedule. This schedule sets forth the various project activities as they were actually performed, reflecting the actual sequence and duration of each activities, and the actual interrelationships among activities.

As the "as-planned" and "as-built" schedules are compared, deviations are identified. These deviations represent changes in the planned performance. As each impact is identified, the "as-planned" schedule is revised to reflect the impact, yielding an "as-adjusted" schedule, which will then be compared to the "as-built" to identify further impacts and determine the overall magnitude of the project delay and to identify major discrepancies.

After specific activities and time periods have been pinpointed through the network analysis, project records and interviews can be utilized to determine why these delays occurred and who bears the responsibility of the time extension.

c) Costs of Delay

The object of pricing an extension claim is to quantify the increased costs that were incurred only as a result of actions by the responsible party that caused a longer than planned period of performance. There typically are four types of damages associated with delay:

- extended project costs;
- escalation;
- inefficiency; and
- unabsorbed overhead

Delays in product fabrication or delivery create challenges to project completion. If products cannot be fabricated because of the unavailability of a certain material, an alternate product may need to be considered. Product substitutions increase the risk that an inferior product may be furnished in lieu of the product originally specified or selected, and increases the potential for installation conflicts when other contractor proceeds with related work based on the originally selected product. When delivery dates are not met, expedited shipping may be required to keep the project on schedule. In addition to increased shipping costs, delivery delays may adversely impact the performance of related work. Proper sequencing of the work may again be affected.

2.4 Claims Documents Backup and Records

Certain records, such as daily project logs, can constitute critical evidence in establishing entitlement to a claim. A detailed project log can document levels of manpower, the progress of the work on a particular date, and any problems that the contractor may encounter. Obviously, a project log prepared contemporaneously with the work performed will have greater weight as evidence than the verbal testimony of a project manager or foreman months or even years after the events in question. Moreover, if the claim is being presented to a fact finder from the construction industry, it is likely that the contractor's credibility will be enhanced if it maintains detailed and accurate records, particularly if the opposing party's documentation is weak. Of course, the above factors apply to all documentation that might be used to support a claim, such as cost accounting records, project correspondence, site meeting minutes, notes of conversations, internal memos and project schedules.

Large construction projects generate thousands of pages of documents. Some of those documents create the legal relationships between the parties who were actively involved in the construction process. Others vividly demonstrate how the parties dealt with issues as they came up during the course of construction.

Consider the spectrum of project documents:
- contract documents (including general conditions, particular conditions, specifications, drawings, soils reports and bonds);
- drawings (including tender set, issued-for-construction set, as-built set, shop drawings, erection drawings and coordination drawings);
- bar chart and electronic schedules(engineer approved);
- contemplated change notices, site instructions, price quotations and change orders;
- applications for payment and payment certificates;
- inspection reports and testing reports;
- minutes of site meetings;
- correspondence, inter-office memos and e-mails;
- handwritten notes of meetings and telephone conversations;
- site superintendent reports (for example, daily reports, diaries and logs).

These documents, for better or worse, complete or deficient, accurate or self-serving, comprise the complete written history of the project. One thing is very clear — the importance of these documents should never be underrated. Most of the documents are automatic and self-explanatory. However, the following items are often overlooked and are therefore worth elaborating.

a) Original Records

As noted earlier, for the prudent contractor anxious to stay solvent, records are required for estimating future work, and for protecting his contractual rights. Both of these require some form of post-contract review. However, there can be little argument that reliable data cannot be extracted from records created after the fact. Even the best of memories are fallible, and the written record serves to provide the solid reminder. Data may be extracted, analyzed and presented in a different light, but satisfactory records cannot be created later.

b) Instant memos

For example, all verbal directives should be committed to writing immediately and exchanged with the other party. This serves to keep the other party properly informed, clarify understanding if the instructions were not clear, and, of course, to preserve contractual rights.

c) Personal diaries

Diaries can provide a wealth of information. Unfortunately, they tend to be overlooked, either because the pace is so hectic that there is not time to keep one current, or alternatively, there seems to be so little of importance going on that it hardly seems worth writing. In any case, what should be recorded are solid facts, such as the make-up of various crews, sub-contractors and equipment on site, work reallocation and for what reasons, delivery problems, weather conditions, visitors to the site, discussions, and seemingly innocuous comments about the work. Needless to say, what should be avoided, are personal opinions and derogatory remarks.

d) Photographs

For record purposes, these must show what is actually going on at the time with the location and view point identified, as well as the date and photographer's name. A camera which prints the date on the negative/memory is a great start and well worth the expense. Also the photographer should realize that it is the content, and not the artistic effect, that is the most important.

e) Computer Application

As we have seen, the road to contract documentation is long and arduous. The worst part is trying to find that vital piece of information amongst the morass of paper, which is now so urgently required. Computer is so powerful that it seems impossible to do without them. However, the secret is to get data organized as early in the project as possible, then commit to consistent maintenance, regular backup and off-site storage. If this is done meticulously, the subsequent saving in time through search and find, or through spread sheet and database design and use, can be invaluable.

f) Managing the Records

As well as managing the files, the records themselves also need managing. Some simple rules can help as follows:

➢ Determine what records are to be kept, and how. Establish logs of the records, so that they can be found, referred to and/or followed up as required. Well organized contractors establish standard reference lists and code for all their contracts. This greatly facilitates managing, analyzing and comparing contracts.

➢ Once the records have been identified, ensure that they are in fact set up, maintained and used for managing the job.

➢ Review the record keeping system from time to time, because records have a habit of growing in unexpected ways - like half the correspondence showing up under Miscellaneous, and the other half under General.

In addition, some records may become obsolete or redundant, and should be discontinued. Unnecessary record keeping can waste a lot of time and money.

➢ Records also take up space and equipment. Determine the useful life of the different components, and take a systematic approach to record disposal.

➢ Take steps to ensure accuracy, reliability and hence credibility. Unreliable records can be quite useless, as well as a waste of money, and possibly even detrimental.

3. Advice for Contractor's Misapprehensions on Variation/Change

Finally, some advice, contractors should be aware of certain pitfalls of claims. Contractors generally suffer from the following misapprehensions pertaining to variation claims:

➢ That the employer is bound to pay for any change or additional work whatsoever undertaken by the contractor whether expressly directed or not;

➢ Where the scope of work is unclear or if there should be a discrepancy in the contract documents, the contractor is automatically entitled to extras;

➢ In the event work is omitted, the contractor is automatically entitled as of right to loss of profit;

➢ Prior to ordering extras, the employer must obtain the contractor's agreement to the rates for valuing the varied work;

➢ The contractor has a right to refuse to undertake varied work if he so desires in particular if there is disagreement as to the rates and time extension sought;

➢ In the situation where varied work has been undertaken, measured and valued by the quantity surveyor but payment is not effected, the contractor is automatically entitled to interest on the amount due;

➢ The employer has no right to order and the contractor is not obliged to carry out varied work in the defect liability period;

➢ The contractor has a right to call for a review of measured and valued work involving variations even after the final account has been prepared and the final certificate issued;

➢ The contractor has, in addition to the monetary claim for the varied work, a parallel right to claim for extension of time and direct loss and expense.

Reading

Construction and Engineering Consultancy

1. Introduction

Construction and consultancy services play a crucial role in infrastructural development, transfer of technology and achieving socio-economic development objectives. They together constitute one of the largest services sectors of the economy and account for a significant proportion of employment and foreign exchange earnings. In most developed and many developing countries the share of construction in the total GDP (Gross Domestic Product) ranges between 5–7 percent. Trade in construction and consultancy services is primarily through the movement of natural persons (skilled labour and professionals) and commercial presence in the form of FDI (Foreign Direct Investment), joint ventures, etc. With developments in Internet technology and advanced communications systems, there has been an increase in cross-border trade in some of these services.

2. Coverage of Construction and Engineering Consultancy

➢ Construction services encompass a wide range of services including construction work for all types of residential and non-residential buildings; civil engineering, such as construction of highways, railways, power station, bridges and tunnels, waterways and harbours; installation and assembly work of petrochemical plants; and all other activities relating to construction.

➢ Consultancy services related to construction include the preliminary study of a problem, through the development of design concepts, the preparation of a design solution for the preferred option, and the calling and evaluation of tenders, to completion and subsequent maintenance and operation of the above works. The architectural firms provide blueprints and designs for buildings, while engineering firms provide planning, design, construction and management services for building structures, installations, civil engineering works and industrial processes, etc.

➢ Construction, architectural and engineering (consultancy) services are primarily traded through commercial presence, that is, the establishment of foreign affiliates and subsidiaries of foreign companies. International construction services involve movement of unskilled, semi-skilled and skilled workers and professionals to perform a wide range of work, including designing, management and physical construction work. Increasingly, with developments in communication and Internet, cross-border supply is becoming an important component of trade in some of these services.

➢ These include the electronic transmission of designs and blueprints and on-line consulting services. However, given the capital-intensive nature of the services, the requirement of specific skills and technical know how, which may not be available locally and the strong client-oriented focus of these services, the bulk of trade would continue to take place through commercial presence and the movement of natural persons.

3. Situation of Global Consultancy

➢ Global trade in engineering consultancy services is highly skill-intensive and depends on a nation's technological capabilities. In the export of consultancy services, many industrialized countries, such as the USA, UK, France, Germany, Denmark, the Netherlands and Japan, have prevalence competition advantages over developing countries. Developed countries are the major exporters of construction, architectural and engineering services, such as overseas expansion of major engineering consulting firms in the United States and Europe, while developing countries provide the major markets. Most consultancy service products and processes are innovated in the developed countries and are licensed by the enterprises based there. The developed countries themselves also specialize in a particular sector; for example, the US firms lead in offshore drilling technologies and power, French firms in nuclear power plant construction, while Japanese firms in high-speed railroad. Construction services supplied internationally are typically related to large-scale projects, such as airports, harbours and petrochemical plants and are often undertaken by specialized contractors with local sub-contracting.

➢ Globally, there is an increasing trend towards integrated engineering and project management services. Construction of manufacturing turnkey projects whereby a single company or a consortium provides a range of services including design engineering, construction, maintenance, management and financing. The ability to provide a total service package is becoming an important advantage in the international market. This trend has been particularly prominent for highly capital-intensive industries such as oil drilling and refinery, electric power station, high-speed railroad and cement factory etc. where contracts are frequently awarded to engineering contractors on an EPC basis. Most major international companies have the technical, management and financial base to support large turnkey projects. Sometime, Project Management Consultancy engages a contract with client to provide service package for the complex and large project, generally on a "cost plus fee" arrangement.

➤ With liberalization, there has been an increase in privatization and foreign direct investments in infrastructure construction projects. Most of these foreign investments and joint ventures are in the form of BOO (Build-Operate-Own), BOT (Build-Operate-Transfer), PPP/PFI (Public Private Partnership/ Private Finance Initiative) projects. Construction and engineering services are primarily traded through commercial presence mainly supplied through FDI in construction projects, joint ventures and foreign presence in the form of BOO, BOT and PPP/PFI operations.

➤ Moreover, global commercial presence depends to a large extent on the ability of the companies to develop financial strength and raise their professional and technological standards to compete with foreign companies from countries. In international market, large construction and infrastructure projects are generally awarded by government and public sector undertakings. Hence, inter-governmental and bilateral relations play an important role in determining the award of the contract.

Developed countries have well-established international banking industry, such as the USA, UK, EU, Australia, Japan and Korea. Black & amp, Veatch Corp, MWH, PB (Parsons and Brinckerhoff) and Jacobs are all the leading global engineering, construction and consulting company providing services include scientific and specialty consulting, as well as all aspects of engineering construction, operations and maintenance.

4. International Consultancy Constraints

➤ Construction, engineering and architectural services are characterized by significant barriers to entry of new firms, especially in the international markets. The selection criteria for consultants and contractors tend to give considerable weight to non-price factors, such as past international experience, size of firms, reputation and affiliations of firms. The selection of consultancy service is usually based on the expertise, experience and business relation rather than low price. Many clients have a long-established and satisfactory relationship with their consultants, so they choose those appropriately skilled and experienced consultants to undertake the work. There are many types of project where previous experience can be relied on to establish a fair percentage fee for the required engineering services. Cost estimation may range from use of global historical records and experience. More importantly, most of the decisions which will determine a project's life cycle costs, savings and success are made at the conceptual and design stages. It is therefore important for most clients to select the consultant who will contribute most to the overall success of the project.

➤ Developing countries' firms seemed trapped in a vicious circle—many international clients reject them for lack of experience; on the other hand, they cannot gain experience if they are not able to secure international contracts. Firms from developed countries are organized on a transnational basis and possess requisite managerial expertise, information systems, and linkages and scale for operating overseas affiliates and joint ventures. Only few enterprises from developing countries are equipped and qualified to do so.

➢ China has been a big international player in the global trade of construction, but architectural and engineering services currently occupies a limited portion of international market share. Chinese companies have also explored the possibilities of joint ventures with foreign construction and engineering consultancy companies whereby Chinese consultants can provide the detailed engineering and development of requisite expertise while the foreign company can provide the conceptual design and process know-how. Chinese construction and engineering companies specialize in specific industries and very few of the companies are currently in a position to undertake all types of engineering and related work, namely, engineering consultancy and turnkey projects.

5. Engineering Design Offshore Services

With respect to the movement of international professional consultancy, many developed countries are seeking outsources to keep competitive advantages. The outsourcing comprises a wide range of services including design and architecture. Other services that lend themselves to outsourcing continue to be those that are of repetitive and data processing nature, such as Computer Aided Drafting (CAD), mapping and Geographical Information System (GIS).

Engineering design offshore services transfer ideas and designs into functional components that can be manufactured and marketed in a short time period. The common composition of team for engineering design offshore services include design leaders, design engineers, program managers, detailers, technicians, specialist in tooling and die design & manufacturing. The potential manufacturing sectors wherein the offshore consultancy opportunities exist include electronic design automation, automotive and infrastructure.

New Words and Expressions

contentious 引起争论的，有争论的；爱争论的；爱议论的
consequential 作为结果的，间接的；重要的
payroll 工资名单；工资总支出，工薪总额
takeoff (飞机的)起飞；[喻](经济的)起飞；开始；起跳
overhead 管理费用，经常费用
preliminary 初步的，初级的；预备的；开端的；序言的
BQ 工程量清单
reimburse 偿还，付还，归还
recoup 补偿，收回；偿还；[法]扣除，扣留
attributable 可归因于……的；由……引起的

overstate 夸大(某事)；把……讲得过分；夸张
pinpoint 确定，准确地指出；精准定位
spectrum 范围；系列，范围，幅度
contemplate 注视，凝视；盘算，计议；周密考虑
superintendent 监督人，管理人；主管
prudent 小心的，慎重的；精明的，节俭的
hectic 繁忙的，忙乱的；兴奋的，狂热的
derogatory 不敬的
arduous 努力的；艰巨的；难克服的；陡峭的
morass 缠作一团；困境
obsolete 废弃的；老式的，已过时的
redundant 多余的，累赘的
detrimental 有害的；不利的
pertain 关于，有关；适合；附属，从属
parallel 平行的；相同的，类似的

Exercises

I. Choose the best answer according to the text.

1. Direct costs as defined in this section include _____.
    A. costs of acceleration of work
    B. costs of equipment
    C. costs of labor
    D. costs of materials

2. Direct equipment costs include _____.
    A. administrative fees
    B. taxes
    C. excess costs incurred as a result of the change
    D. depreciation

3. Project site overheads can be found _____.
    A. in BQ
    B. in Particular conditions
    C. by reference to international practice
    D. preliminary

4. Construction claims documentation consists of _____.
    A. claims analysis
    B. entitlement analysis
    C. damage analyses

D. delay analysis

5. Project documents often include _____.

   A. specifications

   B. site instructions

   C. payment certificates

   D. minutes of site meetings

II. Decide the following statements are true or false.

1. Field overhead, bond costs, insurance, interest and profit should not be regarded as direct costs.

2. The substantiated, increased time-related costs associated with owning or providing equipment on the site to perform the work can be used to price the equipment used in the project.

3. Project site overhead is usually stated as a defined number in the contract.

4. Construction claims analysis, rather than coming at the end of the claim process, should proceed concurrently with the entitlement analysis.

5. As-adjusted schedule is yielded when comparing as-panned schedule and as-built schedule, and according deviations are reflected.

III. Change the following words to another form and write down the Chinese meanings.

1. estimate _____
2. reimburse _____
3. utilize _____
4. recoup _____
5. overstate _____
6. reimburse _____
7. deviate _____
8. contest _____
9. pinpoint _____
10. facilitate _____

IV. Give out the following words' synonym or other word in the closest meaning.

1. extension	a. divergence
2. variation	b. disparity
3. disagreement	c. old-fashioned
4. misapprehension	d. deleterious
5. detrimental	e. mixed
6. obsolete	f. expenses
7. discrepancy	g. license
8. miscellaneous	h. escalation
9. entitlement	i. error
10. overhead	j. diversion

V. Put the following English into Chinese.

1. A project log prepared contemporaneously with the work performed will have greater weight as evidence than the verbal testimony of a project manager or foreman months or even years after the events in question.

2. Needless to say, what should be avoided, are personal opinions and derogatory remarks.

3. If this is done meticulously, the subsequent saving in time through search and find, or through spread sheet and database design and use, can be invaluable.

4. Where the scope of work is unclear or should there be a discrepancy in the contract documents, the contractor is automatically entitled to extras.

参 考 译 文

第 15 单元　施工索赔(2)

1. 施工索赔计算

➢ 施工索赔中最有争议一个方面之一，是对损失的生产力的计算或评估。因此，与工程相关联的所有劳动、设备、材料的直接成本和其他成本应当根据合同进入计算。两种基本的索赔计算方式为索赔是在以工程实施之前的定价基础上还是在工程实施后的基础上。其他与诸如工地管理费用、保函成本、保险、利息和利润有关的直接成本也应当在索赔表格中注明。

➢ 正如在本章所指出的那样，直接成本仅仅包括需要在变更范围以内去完成实际工作的人工、设备和材料成本。它不包括变更的后续结果，比如由变更指令产生的对于中断和低效的成本；工程加速成本；项目延期结果的成本。

1.1 直接劳工成本

直接劳工成本应当以实际的或预期的各种技术工、操作工程师、普工等的增加成本为基础。工资费用可能由合同条款(如计日工价格表)来决定，或如果没有在合同里则可能由各种工会工资等级标准或者其他可引用的标准来决定。监理成本也应当被计算和注明。应该注明正常工作和加班工作，且如果加班费用被要求(支付)的话，那么需证明这些工程不能按正常时间完成，工程延期不被准许，或者其他恰当的根据之上，即这些费用是合理的。支持人工费用的文件包括工资单记录、发票、估价单、投标估算、工作日志以及其他日常项目报告。

劳工问题，包括合同谈判、退出组织、怠工以及罢工等，可能延误项目的竣工。根据劳工问题的性质和持续时间，承包商可能需要加班或者双班轮换来弥补劳工争议期间失去的时间。这显著增加了承包商的人工成本。合同的延期会导致间接成本的增加，并可能减少承包商在其他项目上开始或继续工作的机会。

1.2 直接设备和材料成本

由于完成工程需要额外设备，因此设备成本可能会增加。设备使用费用可能以合同条款为基础，或者如果没有在合同中规定，则可能以租金发票或者计时工资为基础。要收取的钱是证明了的、增加的与时间有关的成本，该成本与属于自己的或者工地上所提供的在变更范围以内去完成工程的设备有关。薪资总额报表对操作工程师来说可能提供什么时候使用过设备的证据。对于承包商所拥有的设备来说，内部费用可能基于拥有设备的、分散在设备的有效寿命期间的总成本而产生。像折旧、保险、税收、贮存和管理成本等成本应当包括在费用中。该费用通常以小时的、每天的或者每周的运营成本来表示。然而，只有由于变更而引起的过量成本应该包含在内。

1.3 项目现场管理费

现场管理费在合同条件或工程量表里经常被称为通用费(开办费)。这些成本包括现场项目管理和执行成本、机械租赁费、贮存费用、工程设施等。合同通常规定通过对人工一定百分比和其他直接成本的加价来计算现场管理费。如果需要的话，承包商可以通过参考投标文件和估价单或者国际惯例来支持其索赔。进一步的证据表示可以根据就变更工程的估价和工程设计而进行会议和讨论所增加的额外时间和精力的实际成本来支持。未曾料到的完成工程导致的人工也可以通过针对小工具、日用品、消耗品或者其他混杂事项的额外支出计入通用费内。

1.4 利息索赔

由变更引起的未偿付项目费用的融资可能具有显著影响。对于收回融资成本或在一定程度上利用内部基金而不是按计划预算，利息计费可以是合理的。对于利息的量化索赔的关键因素是决定
- ➢ 利息在其间被估算的期限；
- ➢ 资金费用或成本。

这些因素可能在合同文件中规定或者由适用的当地法律条例来详细解释。

1.5 利润

除了有资格去收回(索赔)由于一方违反合同造成的成本增加之外，如果证据足够肯定和确切并提供评估其利润根据的话，FIDIC 允许受损害承包商根据合同去收回(索赔)预期利润。至少还有一些免责条款。

2. 施工索赔证明资料

一旦识别出潜在的索赔或争议，展开和保存支持其证明资料的价值就不能被夸大。在投诉阶段，承包商准备表明精确估计的损失总量的有效文件是非常关键的。争议常常基于承包商的证明文件而获胜或失败。甚至在一项索赔被识别之前，承包商在项目上保持其良好活动记录也是很重要的。

2.1 索赔的组成部分

施工索赔由两个主要部分构成：
- ➢ 授权部分，该部分通常包括某方的作为或者无作为，来自该方，则寻求责任被减轻，同时使索赔人对赔偿有资格；
- ➢ 损失部分，该部分详尽地解释对于索赔补偿的计算和支持。

2.2 索赔分析

施工索赔分析应当与(可索赔)资格分析一起进行,而不是索赔过程结束的时候才开始。当提出施工索赔时,通过向承包商方展示有说服力的记录,尽早做出损失分析可以促使找到对增加成本的可替代解释。

2.3 误期分析

施工误期的代价很高。误期分析涉及对各种项目活动的彻底检查、对来自计划施工的执行偏差进行准确定位,然后对误期进行量化。误期影响分析首先要求承包商对图纸、规范和其他合同文件、进度计划、进度日志以及类似记录进行评审。接下来,要对计划完成和实际完成的情况与关键路径法(CPM)网络图进行对比,以识别关键性偏差。由误期产生的成本增加在定价中是普遍存在的中,且常引起强烈的争论。误期损失的量化要求如下:

- ➢ 决定误期类型的分析;
- ➢ 延误期间的时间分析;
- ➢ 对误期原因和所负责任的分析;
- ➢ 决定关系到误期成本的分析。

a) 进度计划分析

代表项目的进度计划分析一般使用计算机程序来做出重要工作项目活动的顺序和相关衔接。这种分析将揭示项目活动最符合逻辑的顺序。许多合同,尤其是针对大型项目的合同,要求具有关键途径的识别。

b) 工作分析

对这三个基本的关键路径法(CPM)日程类型来说,分析是必需的。承包商会检查下列进度计划:

计划工作进度。该进度代表原合同工程的计划顺序和时间安排。该进度计划应当针对合理性进行检查,且确定为可实施的和可实现的计划,这一点很重要。

实际完成工作进度。该进度展示各种项目活动实际的实施情况,反映每项活动的实际顺序和持续时间,以及这些活动里的实际相互关系。

对计划工作和实际完成工作进度进行对照,偏差也就得到了识别。这些偏差表示已经计划的实施的变更。由于每个影响得到了识别,所以"计划"进度做了修订去反映影响,从而产生一个"调整"进度,该进度于是将与"实际完成"进度进行对照,从而识别(对工程)进一步的影响,并确定项目误期的总体影响性,识别主要的进度偏差。

在具体活动及时间经由网络图分析准确定位之后,项目记录和面谈情况可以用来确定这些误期为什么会发生以及谁将承担工期延误的责任。

c) 误期成本

对延期索赔的定价目标是,通过引起比计划的实施期限更长的责任方,去量化仅仅作为行动结果而发生的增加成本。通常与误期有关的损失有四种类型:

- ➢ 项目成本增加;
- ➢ 物价上涨(费用增加);
- ➢ 无效率;
- ➢ 无法消化的管理费增加。

在产品组装或者交付中的误期会形成对项目竣工的挑战。如果由于某种原材料无法弄到而不能组装产品的话,就需要考虑一种替代的产品。产品替换会增加次等产品被供应来代替原来规定或挑选的产品的风险,并且,当其他承包商继续进行相关的基于起初挑选的产品的工程时,会增加安装冲突的可能性。当交货日期没有得到满足时,加速运输对于保持项目按时间表运作是必需的。除了增加的运输成本之外,交货误期可能相反地影响到有关工程的实施。工程的恰当排序可能再次受到影响。

2.4 索赔文件证据和记录

某些记录,比如每日项目日志,可能构成索赔资格确立的决定性证据。一份详细的项目日志可以证明人力水平、在特殊日期的工进展以及承包商可能遭遇的任何问题。显然,在所讨论的事件发生几个月或者几年之后,与施工同期准备的项目日志将具有比项目经理或工头的口头证词作为证据的分量更大。此外,如果索赔正被展现给来自建筑行业的调查者,在项目日志保持详细和精确记录的情况下,特别是在对方的文件材料有欠缺的情况下,承包商的信誉将得到加强,这一点是很有可能的。当然,上述的因素适用于用来支持索赔的所有证明材料,比如成本会计记录、项目信函、现场会议记录、谈话笔记、内部备忘录以及项目进度表等。

大型建筑项目会产生数千页的文件。那些文件中的一些文件会创建被积极牵涉施工过程中的各方之间的法律关系。其他文件则表明,随着施工过程中争端的出现,各方是怎样处理这些争端的。

对项目文件的范围可以做如下考虑:
- 合同文件(包括通用条件、特殊条件、规范、图纸、土壤报告和保函);
- 图纸(包括投标图纸、施工图纸、竣工图、施工安装图、装配图、协调图等);
- 横道图表和电子进度表(经工程师批准的);
- 预期变更通知、现场指令、报价表和变更指令;
- 期中付款申请和付款证书;
- 检查报告和检测报告;
- 现场会议记录;
- 来往信函、办公室交互备忘录和电子邮件;
- 会议手写记录和电话交谈记录;
- 现场管理负责人报告(如每日报告、日记和日志)。

这些文件,不论好坏,是完整的还是残缺的,是精确还是自用的,都是组成完整的项目书面历史。有一点非常明确——这些文件的重要性从来都不应当被低估。大部分文件是自然而然的且是不言自明的。然而,下列事项常常被忽视,因此值得精心准备。

a) 原始记录

正如最初指出的那样,对于急切地想要保持偿付能力的谨慎的承包商来说,记录对估算工程和保护其合同权利而言是必需的。这两项需要合同(项目)后评审的一些形式。然而,可能存在一些小争论,即可靠数据不能从在事实之后产生的记录里抽取。甚至最好的记忆力也难免有错误,且书面记录有助于提供可靠的提示。数据可能以不同的角度被提取、分析以及显示,但是令人满意的记录不可能在后来产生。

b) 即刻备忘录

例如,所有口头权威指令应当立即以书面形式保留下来,且与另一方进行交流。这有助于使另一方得到及时的通报，如果指令不清楚还可对指令进行澄清，并且，会自然地保护自己的合同权利。

  c) 个人日记

  日记可以提供丰富的信息。不幸的是，日记却常被忽视，要么因为计划进度太忙乱以致没有时间记日记，要么正发生的事情似乎不重要不值得记录。无论如何，应当记录下来的是可靠事实，比如若干工作人员的补充、现场分包商和设备、工程再分配及其原因、交货问题、天气状况、工地参观者、讨论，以及关于工程的看来似乎无关紧要的评论。不用说，应当避免的是个人观点和诋毁性的评论。

  d) 照片

  为了记录目的，还必须标明在某个时候某个地点发生什么事以及所识别的角度，还有日期和摄影师姓名。把日期印在底片上/存储器上的照相机是一个良好的记录开端且物有所值。摄影师还应该意识到，最重要的不是艺术效果，而是内容。

  e) 计算机应用

  正如我们所看到的那样，通向合同文件的道路是漫长而艰巨的。最糟糕的是，因为现在急需这份资料，就设法在乱作一团的文件中找到致命的一份资料。计算机具有强大的功能以至于似乎没有它们不可能进行的工作了。然而，秘诀是要在项目中尽可能早地使数据变得有条理，然后保持维护、定期备份和离开现场存储等习惯。如果这一点做得一丝不苟的话，那么通过搜索和发现或者通过表格以及数据库设计和使用而获得的后续时间节约，则非常宝贵。

  f) 记录管理

  除了管理卷宗，记录本身也需要管理。对一些简单的有帮助的规则列举如下：

  ➢ 确定什么记录是要保存的，以及怎样保存。建立记录的日志，以便根据需要能够找到、参考和/或跟踪它们。管理得当的承包商会建立标准的参考清单，并对把所有合同进行编码。这极大地便于对合同进行管理、分析和比较。

  ➢ 一旦记录被识别，就要确保它们事实上为了管理这件工作而被建立、维护和使用的。

  ➢ 时不时检查记录，以保持系统正常，因为记录具有以意外的方式增长的属性——像信函的一半以混杂的状态显示出来，而另一半则正常地显示一样。

  另外，一些记录可能变得过时或者多余，且应当被终止。不必要的记录保存会浪费许多时间和资金。

  ➢ 记录也会占据空间和设备。确定不同部件的使用寿命，然后采用系统的方式去处置记录资料。

  ➢ 采取步骤确保精确性、可靠性以及因此而来的可信性。不可靠的记录可能是十分无用的，也是对资金的浪费，并且甚至是不利的。

  3. 针对承包商对变更/改变的误解的忠告

  最后给出一些忠告：承包商应当知晓某些索赔陷阱。承包商一般会遭受下列关于变更索赔的误解：

  ➢ 雇主一定会为任何改变或由承包商承担的额外工作付出代价，不管是否明确地受到指导；

> 在工程范围不清楚的情况下，或者在合同文件中存在不符合之处的情况下，承包商自动地被赋予对额外收费事项的权利；
> 如果工程被遗漏了，承包商自动地被赋予对利润损失的权利；
> 在对额外收费事项做出指令之前，雇主必须得到承包商对于估价改变的工程费用的同意；
> 如果对方非常想了解是否存在关于所寻求的费用和时间延长的分歧，承包商则有权拒绝承担变化的工程；
> 在变更工程被工料测量师(估料师)测量和估价，但是付款没有生效的情况下，承包商自动拥有获得到期利息的权利；
> 在缺陷责任期间，雇主没有权利对承包商下达指令，且承包商没有义务去完成变更工程；
> 承包商有权要求评审涉及变更的已测量和已估价的工程，甚至在决算已经准备好且竣工交付证书已发布之后；
> 除对变更工程的费用进行索赔之外，承包商具有对工程延期和直接损失和费用进行索赔的平行权利。

阅读

建筑和工程咨询

1. 引言

建筑和工程咨询服务在基础设施发展、技术转让和实现社会经济发展目标方面扮演着关键性角色。它们共同构成经济的最大服务行业之一，并且占有就业和外汇收入的重大比例。在大部分发达国家和许多发展中国家，建筑份额在全部 GDP(国内生产总值)中的 5%～7%变化。建筑和咨询服务中的贸易主要通过自然人(技术工人和专业人士)的活动以及用国外直接投资(FDI)、合资企业等形式的商业参与来实现。随着因特网技术和先进通信系统的发展，在这些服务的某些方面跨境贸易有所增长。

2. 建筑和工程咨询的覆盖范围

> 建筑服务围绕广泛的服务内容，包括针对所有类型的住宅和非住宅建筑工程；土木工程，如公路、铁路、电站、桥梁和隧道、航道和港口建设；石油化学工厂的安装和装配工程；以及所有其他与建筑有关的活动。
> 关系到建筑的咨询服务，包括问题的初步研究，凭借概念设计的发展，对于首选办法的设计方案准备、招标和评标、竣工和后续维护以及上述工作的具体操作来完成。建筑公司为建筑物提供蓝图和设计，而工程咨询公司则为建筑结构、安装、土木工程项目以及工业流程等提供规划、设计、施工和管理服务。
> 施工、建筑和工程(咨询)服务主要通过商业参与来交易，即建立外资公司的外国子公司和附属机构(分公司)。国际建筑服务牵涉完成一系列工程的不熟练、半熟练和熟练工人以及专业人士的调动，包括设计、管理和具体的施工工程。逐渐地，随着通信和因特网的发展，跨境供给正成为这些服务的某些方面的重要贸易组成部分。

> 包括设计和蓝图的电子传送以及在线咨询服务。然而，考虑到服务的资本密集型特性、特定的技能和在当地也许不能得到的专有技术的要求，以及这些强力以委托人为导向焦点的服务，贸易的主要部分将通过商业参与和自然人的调动继续发生。

3. 全球咨询业形势

> 工程咨询服务的全球贸易是高度技术密集型的行业，且取决于一个国家的技术能力。在咨询服务的出口中，许多工业化国家，比如美国、英国、法国、德国、丹麦和日本，具有高于发展中国家的普遍竞争优势。发达国家是主要的施工、建筑和工程服务输出国，比如美国和欧洲的主要工程咨询公司的海外扩展，而发展中国家则提供主要的市场。大部分咨询服务产品和流程在发达国家得到了革新且得到了基于那些地方的企业的许可。发达国家自身也专攻一个特殊领域；例如，美国公司领先于海底钻探技术，以及能源项目；法国公司领先于核电站施工，而日本公司领先于高速铁路。国际上供给的建筑服务一向与大型项目有关，例如机场、港口和石油化学工厂，且它们常常由专业化的承包商通过当地分包来承担。

> 从全球看，存在一个朝着整合的工程和项目管理服务渐增的趋势。由单一的公司或者联营企业会提供一系列服务，包括设计工程、施工、维护、管理和融资的总承包交钥匙项目的施工。提供总体服务包的能力正成为国际市场上的重要优势。这个趋势对于高度资本密集型产业比如石油钻探和提炼、电站、高速铁路和水泥厂等来说尤为突出，在这些产业中合同常常以 EPC 为基础授予工程咨询承包商。大多数国际公司具有技术、管理和金融基础去支持大型交钥匙项目。有时，项目管理咨询公司对复杂和大型项目与业主签订提供一揽子服务的合同，一般以"成本加酬金"合同方式进行。

> 由于放宽限制，在基础设施工程领域有了私有化和外国直接投资的增加。这些外国投资和合资的大多数采用 BOO(建造—运营—拥有)、BOT(建造—运营—转让)以及 PPP/PFI(公私合伙/私人主动融资)形式。建筑和工程服务主要通过商业参与来进行交易，这些商业参与主要由 FDI 以 BOO、BOT 和 PPP/PFI 运营的形式在建筑工程、合资和外国参与中来提供。

> 此外，全球商业参与很大程度上取决于公司开发财力并提升其专业和技术标准从而与来自各国的外国公司进行竞争的能力。在国际市场上，大规模建筑和基础设施项目一般由政府和公共事业部门授予。因此，政府间和双边关系在决定合同的授予中扮演着重要角色。

发达国家具有根深蒂固的国际银行业，比如美国、英国、欧盟、澳大利亚、日本和韩国。Black & amp, Veatch Corp、MWH、PB(Parsons 和 Brinckerhoff)和 Jacobs 是所有主要的全球工程、施工和咨询公司，提供科学和专业的咨询服务，以及工程建设、运营和维护各方面的服务。

4. 国际咨询限制

> 施工、工程和建筑服务的特征在于新公司进入的显著壁垒，尤其在国际市场上。对咨询师和承包商的挑选标准倾向于对非价格因素给予相当大的重视，比如过去的国际经验、公司规模、公司名声和公司联系。咨询服务的挑选原则通常基于专业知识或技能、经

验和业务关系而非低价格。许多委托人具有跟他们的咨询师长久建立的满意关系,所以他们选择那些技能合适的和有经验的咨询师来承担业务。有许多项目类型,在这些项目中,针对所需的工程咨询服务,以前的经验可以期望用来建立公平的费用比例。成本估价可以根据全球历史记载在经验的范围内变化。更重要的是,大部分决定项目生命周期成本、节约和成功的决策是在概念和设计阶段做出的。因此对于多数委托人来说,挑选最有助于项目的总体成功的咨询师是很重要的。

> 发展中国家的公司似乎陷于一个恶性循环中——因缺乏经验许多国际委托人拒绝与他们合作;另一方面,如果他们不能弄到国际合同的话,他们就不能获得经验。发达国家的公司组织在一个跨国的基础上,并且针对运作海外附属公司和合资公司占有必不可少的管理专业知识、信息系统以及联系和规模。只有少数来自发展中国家的企业具备资格。

> 中国已经成为全球建筑贸易中的一个重要国际角色,但是目前建筑和工程咨询服务只占有国际市场份额的有限部分。中国公司也探索了与外国建筑和工程咨询公司共同经营的合资企业的可能性,借此,中国咨询师可以提供详细的工程咨询和必要的专业技术,而外国公司能够提供概念设计和流程专有技术。中国建筑和工程咨询公司在特定行业(并且极少数)公司目前能够承揽所有类型的工程和相关项目,即工程咨询和交钥匙项目。

5. 工程设计离岸服务

谈到国际职业咨询师的调动,许多发达国家正在寻求外包从而保持竞争优势。外包由一系列服务构成,包括设计和建筑艺术。其他适合于外包的服务仍旧是那些重复的和数据处理特性的服务,诸如计算机辅助设计(CAD)、地图绘制和地理信息系统(GIS)。

工程设计海外服务把理念和设计转换成在短期内可以制造和投入市场的功能成分。工程设计海外服务团队的一般构成包括设计总监、设计工程师、规划经理、大样设计师、技术人员、加工和模具设计和制造方面的专家。海外咨询机构存在于潜在的制造部门包括电子设计自动化、汽车业和基础设施。

Unit 16
Contract Dispute Resolution

1. Introduction

The international construction project is one that comprises a diversity of interests, professions and procedures which interact to create a completed project. A construction project occurs on-site and the construction activities represent a collective effort from specialists who belong to various disciplines. Although participants may share a common goal of completing a particular project, their actual participation is restricted by their organisational objectives. Thus, it will result in incompatibility errors which are considered risks that discovered during the course of construction phase and generate change orders, construction disputes, cost overruns, time delays, compromise to quality, frustration, and stakeholder dissatisfaction. This potential is heightened when parties that work together have different philosophies regarding the implementation of the project.

Disputes may arise over quality of work, over responsibility for delays, over appropriate payments due to changed conditions, or a multitude of other considerations. The mechanism for contract dispute resolution can be specified in the original contract. Contractual disputes are time consuming, expensive and unpleasant. If unresolved in time, construction disputes can become very expensive, considering the finances, personnel, time lost, and the opportunity costs. Quantifiable costs include hiring of attorneys, expert witnesses and the dispute resolution process itself. The less visible costs (e.g., company resources assigned to the dispute, lost business opportunities) and the intangible costs (such as damage to business relationships, potential value lost due to inefficient dispute resolution) are also considerable, although quite difficult or impossible to quantify.

In the highly competitive multiparty environment of construction, disputes can arise for many reasons, such as the complexity and magnitude of the work, the lack of coordination among the contracting parties, poorly prepared contract documents, inadequate planning, financial issues, and disagreements about the methods of resolving on-the-spot or site-related problems. Any one of these factors can derail a project and lead to complicated litigation or arbitration, increased costs, and a breakdown in the communication and relationships among parties.

It is important to keep lines of communication between the contracting parties open at all times when dealing with claims and to avoid adopting entrenched positions. The procedures applicable to dispute resolution in the contract should be adhered to but this does not preclude "without prejudice" discussions taking place between the contracting parties throughout the process, with a view to arriving at a settlement of the dispute. From the onset of a dispute, it is important to manage the disagreement actively and positively at the appropriate senior level, in order to encourage early and effective settlement. Unnecessary delays and inefficiencies can lead to rapid escalation of costs.

In international construction contracts, the two parties to the contract are the contracting authority (the employer) and the contractor. The employer may delegate some functions to the employer's representative to assist in the execution of the contract. The common dispute resolution procedures available to the two parties are negotiation, mediation, arbitration and, finally, limited recourse to the judicial system.

2. Negotiation

Negotiation as a dispute resolution process commences after the dispute has arisen and the parties necessitating a need to negotiate. Negotiation is where two or more parties attempt together to reach an agreement on a disputed matter. It involves unaided discussions between the disputing parties without legal representation. Negotiation in dispute resolution takes many forms. It ranges from an informal chat or telephone conversation to highly structured process taking place over long period of time.

Negotiation is by far the most common form of dispute resolution. The objective of sensible dispute management should be to negotiate an acceptable settlement as soon as possible so as to minimize costs. Negotiation is, usually, the most effective form of dispute resolution in terms of management of time and costs. It should be the preferred approach to most disputes. It should be remembered that, even if a dispute progresses to mediation and subsequently arbitration, it will still be possible, or indeed may be necessary, to continue to negotiate with the employer in parallel with these procedures on a "without prejudice" basis to seek a settlement that will minimize the level of costs incurred.

3. Mediation

Mediation is a flexible process designed to assist the parties to resolve a dispute by agreement. The essential feature of mediation is achieving an agreement between the parties. The mediator acts as a facilitator who assists the two parties to negotiate and acts as a catalyst. The mediator must convince the parties that it is in their interest to work together to settle disputes. The mediator must be impartial, sympathetic and must establish credibility and trust with the parties.

Mediation is a non-binding procedure for dispute resolution whereby an independent mediator is engaged by the parties to the contract to broker a settlement between them on the matters in dispute. It has advantages in bringing a third party's views to bear on the issues in dispute and is faster and less costly than arbitration. It has the advantage that the mediator will try to assist the parties to resolve the dispute in any way acceptable to both parties. If settlement is reached, the mediator will bring the parties back together to formalize the terms of the agreement. After an agreement is made, it is generally enforceable.

Without question, mediation is a low risk process that can save time and money. The process also tends to be non-adversarial and thereby helps to preserve important business relationships. Further, if successful, mediation brings finality, as there are no awards to convert to judgments, potential appeals or the need to chase payments. Notwithstanding the above, if either party lacks a commitment to discuss settlement in good faith, the process may represent a waste of time and expense. Consequently, if the positions of the parties are too polarized or the facts make settlement unlikely, mediation may not be appropriate.

4. Arbitration

Arbitration is an alternate to litigation. Disputes may be routed directly into arbitration thus by-passing the requirements of Clause 20.4 of FIDIC, in the event that there is no DAB (Dispute Adjudication Board) in place. It originated as a method of resolving disputes, quickly and without legal formality. This is the most commonly found dispute resolution method stipulated in building contracts. No party is compelled to submit a dispute to arbitration unless both parties agree to do so within the terms of the contract. Once agreed to the method of arbitration the dispute cannot be litigated. Arbitration is the process by which a dispute between two or more parties is referred for determination by another person or persons other than the court after hearing both sides in a judicial/legal manner. The proceedings enable a determination by a knowledgeable person usually from the discipline appropriate to the matter in dispute and received in a manner which reflects the contractual and commercial aspects of the project. Arbitration is a private process and facilitates the parties to keep the details of their dispute private.

Arbitration is a binding procedure governed by statute whereby the parties to a contract refer a dispute to an arbitrator and agree to be bound by his decision. If the parties fail to agree on an appropriate arbitrator, either party may refer to the body named in the contract to nominate an arbitrator. The arbitrator is required to apply the burden of proof according to the law and has the power to decide all procedural and evidential matters.

The arbitrator may decide to hold hearings where direct evidence, both witness and expert, may be given on behalf of each of the parties, followed by cross-examination by the other party. At the conclusion of the hearings, the arbitrator is required to deliver, normally within a reasonable period, an award which is final and binding on the parties and legally enforceable. An award may also be a consent award in the event of a settlement being reached by the parties in the course of the proceedings as a means of recording the settlement, including the allocation of costs. Within 30 days of receiving an Arbitrator's award either party may request the arbitrator to interpret the award and to correct any arithmetical errors or make an additional award on claims presented to him but omitted from the award.

While arbitration can have many advantages over litigation in terms of cost and time, this is not always the case. In fact, there has been increasing criticism in some cases concerning the cost and quality of arbitration proceedings. Nonetheless, arbitration continues to be a widely-used process to resolve construction claims and clearly has certain benefits over litigation under many circumstances.

5. Adjudication

This is a process of making an award by a procedure similar to arbitration. The main difference between adjudication and mediation is that the adjudicator does not look for a consensual compromise but judges the issues between the parties and are bound to give a decision, whether it is acceptable or not by the parties concerned. The philosophy of adjudication is that people who appreciate the strength and weaknesses of their positions and the risk of legally binding processes, and can amicability resolve their disputes outside a formally structured process through independent third party. The reasons for emergence of adjudication are due to accelerating pace of business necessitating the disputes to be resolved without any delay

Disputes result in a substantial dilution of effort, delays and diversion of capital. The FIDIC conditions of contract include provisions for the submission, consideration and resolution of claims and disputes under a number of different clauses. The primary clause of interest here, clause 20, deals specifically with claims, disputes and arbitration. It envisages the establishment of a Dispute Adjudication Board, known as the DAB.

A DAB is a panel of experienced, respected, impartial and independent reviewers. The DAB members are provided with the contract documents, plans and specifications and become familiar with the project procedures and the participants, and are kept abreast of project progress and developments. The DAB procedure was conceived as a method of primary dispute resolution. Thus the procedures should facilitate prompt reference of disputes to the board as soon as project level negotiations have reached an impasse, or the referral to the board only after multiple levels of employer and contractor reviews is inconsistent with the process and counter-productive in terms of time and expense.

FIDIC conditions of contract state that that the DAB's decision shall be binding on both parties, who shall promptly give effect to it unless and until it shall be revised in an amicable settlement or an arbitration award. It is therefore essential that the membership of the DAB is mutually agreed upon by the parties and not imposes at other party. FIDIC Clause 20.7 states that in the event that neither party has served a notice of dissatisfaction and the decision has become final and binding then any failure to comply with the decision may be referred to arbitration.

6. Litigation

The process of resolving a dispute by judicial settlement is known as litigation. Historically, litigation in court was the most common way to resolve intractable disputes arising in the construction context. Unfortunately, litigation can be time-consuming, expensive and unpredictable. However, reservations exist in the international construction market over concerning litigious disputes, particularly in relation to time and cost and the slow pace of justice. Litigation nevertheless has a place in the construction as much as any other methods of resolving disputes and parties must be able to have recourse to it, in cases of

- ➢ Where the arbitrator has mis-conducted himself or the proceedings;
- ➢ Where an award has been improperly procured;

➢ Where one party requests certain matters be set aside or remitted to the reconsideration of the arbitrator on the basis of an error of law on the face of the award.

The court may set aside an award where it feels any of these grounds have been substantiated or may decide to remit the matters referred or any of them for reconsideration by the arbitrator or may make an alternate award.

The court has generally been reluctant to intervene unless the arbitrator has made an award which shows on its face an error of law so fundamental, or clearly wrong, that the courts cannot stand aside and allow it to remain unchallenged. The court's entitlement to interfere with an award by an arbitrator is significantly circumscribed and the courts will not interfere without very good reason. The policy of the law is to uphold the certainty of arbitration awards, once they have been made.

In considering the best way to resolve a construction dispute, however, many factors need to be evaluated. Although time and cost are important, other issues may have greater importance. The contractor will need to consider the need to conduct analysis of claim discovery, the benefits or disadvantages of trying the case before someone with or without experience in the construction industry, and procedural problems, if the case involves a multi-party dispute, and differences in judicial review.

Reading

Engineering Innovation—Building Information Modeling

1. Introduction

Building Information Modeling (BIM)—an innovative new approach to building design, construction, and management introduced by Autodesk in 2002—has changed the way industry professionals worldwide think about how technology can be applied to building design, construction, and management. Building information modeling supports the continuous and immediate availability of project design scope, schedule, and cost information that is high quality, reliable, integrated, and fully coordinated. Among the many competitive advantages it confers are:

➢ Increased speed of delivery (time saved);
➢ Better coordination (fewer errors);
➢ Decreased costs (money saved);
➢ Greater productivity;
➢ Higher-quality work;
➢ New revenue and business opportunities.

For each of the three major phases in the building lifecycle—design, construction, and management—building information modeling offers access to the following critical information:

➢ In the design phase—design, schedule, and budget information;
➢ In the construction phase—quality, schedule, safety and cost information;

➢ In the management phase—performance, utilization, and financial information.

The ability to keep this information up to date and accessible in an integrated digital environment gives architects, engineers, contractors, and employers a clear overall vision of their projects, as well as the ability to make better decisions faster—raising the quality and increasing the profitability of projects.

Although building information modeling is an approach and not a technology, it does require suitable technology to be implemented effectively. Examples of some of these technologies, in increasing order of effectiveness, include:
➢ CAD;
➢ Object CAD;
➢ Parametric Building Modeling.

The concept of building information modeling is to build a building virtually, prior to building it physically, in order to work out problems, and simulate and analyze potential impacts. The heart of building information modeling is an authoritative building information model.

2. Building Information Modeling benefits

Building Information Modeling(BIM) is used to refer to two different things: the process of building information modeling and the resulting model (the building information model). BIM is the development and use of a computer software model to simulate the construction and operation of a facility. The resulting model, a Building Information Model, is a data-rich, object-oriented, intelligent and parametric digital representation of the facility, from which views and data appropriate to various users' needs can be extracted and analyzed to generate information, which can be used to make decisions and improve the process of delivering the facility. Building information modeling is an approach to building design, construction, and management. Building information modeling is, essentially, the intersection of two critical ideas:

➢ Keeping critical design information in digital form makes it easier to update and share and more valuable to the firms creating and using it;

➢ Creating real-time, consistent relationships between digital design data—with innovative parametric building modeling technology—can save significant amounts of time and money and increase project productivity and quality.

BIM uses include visualization; scope clarification; partial trades coordination; collision detection/avoidance; design validation; construction sequencing planning/phasing; plans/logistics; marketing presentations; options analysis; walk-throughs and fly-throughs; virtual mock-ups; and sight-line studies.

BIM can help construction professionals create such a model for different interests, including architects, engineers, contractors, subcontractors, fabricators, suppliers and others offering myriad virtual details in the design, construction, and management phases of the building lifecycle, and sort out and work with the problems before hand. For example, imagine walking into a building, walking through the lobby, removing the ceiling tiles and looking at the utilities in the ceiling space—before the building is even built, however, you will foresee what you need to tackle in advance.

3. BIM 4D Models

BIM 4D Models link components in 3D models with activities from the design, procurement, and construction schedules. The resulting 4D production model of a project allows project stakeholders to view the planned construction of a facility over time on the screen and to review a 3D model for any day, week, or month of the project.

4D models enable a diverse team of project participants to understand and comment on the project scope in a proactive and timely manner. They enable the exploration and improvement of the project executing strategy, improvements in constructability with corresponding gains in on-site productivity, and the rapid identification and resolution of time-space conflicts. 4D models have proven particularly helpful in projects that involve many stakeholders, in projects undergoing renovation during operation, and in projects with tight, urban site conditions. Tight site conditions, a must-met completion deadline, and many non-construction stakeholders have made the project idea for the application of 4D project management. The 4D model enabled the project team to produce a better set of specifications and design drawings for the construction of the project, resulting in fewer unplanned change orders, a smaller construction team, and a comfortable completion of the project ahead of schedule.

4. BIM in Design

BIM is a very powerful architectural design and coordination tool for project-wide design and documentation. The project design team members typically rely on a number of purpose-built models including:

- 3D conceptual design model
- Detailed geometric design model
- Structural finite element analysis model
- Structural steel fabrication model
- Design coordination model
- Construction planning and sequencing model
- Equipment inventory model
- Energy analysis model
- Fire/life safety and egress model
- Cost analysis model

It is very rare that a single technology is being used on any one building project between different companies and/or across all phases of the project lifecycle. BIM has had a tremendous, positive impact on design, visualizing and communicating the essence of a complex facility to a broad audience. It helps designer solve a number of problems involving challenging geometry on plans, elevations and section drawings, and it can generate as "views" from a single design model, are always consistent. Structural engineers can have great success in sharing their concrete and steel 3D object models with architect to integrate into architectural model and data sharing.

5. BIM in Construction

In the construction phase of the building lifecycle, Building Information Modeling (BIM) makes available concurrent information on building quality, safety, schedule, and cost. The contractor can accelerate the quantification of the building for estimating and value-engineering purposes and for the production of updated estimates and construction planning. The consequences of proposed or procured products can be studied and understood easily, and the contractor can quickly prepare plans showing site use or renovation phasing for the employer, thereby communicating and minimizing the impact of construction operations on the employer's operations and personnel. Building Information Modeling also means that less time and money are spent on process and administration issues in construction because document quality is higher and construction planning better. The final result is that more of the employer's construction investment goes into the building than into administrative and overhead costs.

5.1 Cost Estimating

Both the main contractor and the subcontractor will benefit greatly from accurate take-off quantities and a good construction-sequencing view to determine how crowded the site will be when they arrive. Such as an accurately detailed BIM 3D model will give wall and ceiling subcontractor not only the location and interrelation of each wall-and-ceiling item, but also the materials of what exactly comprises each component for an accurate take-off quantity, through visualizing the project contractors make sure all the constructing pieces are included.

Armed with this information, the experienced estimator will, and does, work up an accurate quote without having to look around corners and imagining the architect as to what he or she really intended. Given this a clear view of the construction sequencing, the BIM 3D model will then afford the estimator a firm basis for a good bid.

5.2 Construction Quality and Safety

Public organizations and private companies in several countries have successfully led many BIM-based projects with considerable interest and effort. In fact, several public organizations have recommended delivering BIM data, which is checked with quality control according to BIM modeling standards. The high quality control of BIM can be applied to both physical and logical conditions. From designing, a preliminary review of the quality of the functional, aesthetic, engineering and environmental aspects of the facilities can be carried out by using software tools prior to the final evaluation. Since the BIM quality check is based on BIM guidelines and standards, a quantitative review is possible, and in most cases, automatic verification can be done through the software itself. Such a system can help in the prevention of the initial selection of poor designs.

Construction safety professionals can use BIM to improve construction safety. Once a 3-D model is created, it can be used for many purposes, including worker safety training and education, safety planning and employee involvement. Safety professionals need not be experts in model creation or its technical aspects; they simply need a basic understanding of BIM, which is essentially a 3-D computer-aided design drawing. Craft men will be able to identify the sequence of activities, and material and tool requirements before work started. Pre-task planning offers the most opportunities to use BIM for construction safety. By virtually looking at the elements to be built, employees were able to better identify the hazards and control measures so the task could be completed faster and more safely. Such as duct works, which involve in identifying access as a significant concern and are able to bring in aerial lifts. The crew will identify falls as a hazard and devise control measures (e.g. fall protection devices). The piping will be installed in a tunnel and required much welding.

6. BIM in the Management

In the management phase of the building lifecycle, Building Information Modeling makes available concurrent information on the use or performance of the building; its occupants and contents; the life of the building over time; and the financial aspects of the building. Building Information Modeling provides a digital record of renovations and improves move planning and management. It accelerates the adaptation of standard building prototypes to site conditions for businesses, such as retail, that require the construction of similar buildings in many different locations. Physical information about the building, such as finishes, tenant or department assignments, furniture and equipment inventory, and financially important data about leasable areas and rental income or departmental cost allocations are all more easily managed and available. Consistent access to these types of information improves both revenue and cost management in the operation of the building.

In general, BIM is growingly changing the way employers, designers, engineers, contractors, subcontractors and fabricators approach building design, construction and operation.

7. Constructability Review

➢ As projects get more and more complex, the issue of constructability becomes important. Constructability infiltrates all parts of a project, especially those related to the engineering and architectural professions. With projects becoming more and more complex and time frames shorter and shorter, implied warranty and severe professional liability issues may arise.

Constructability is a project management technique for reviewing construction processes from start to finish during the pre-construction phrase. It will identify obstacles before a project is actually built to reduce or prevent error, delays and cost overruns. It is referred to as:

● the extent to which the design of the building facilitates ease of construction, subject to the overall requirements for the completed building;

● a system for achieving optimum integration of construction knowledge and experience in planning, engineering, procurement and field operations in the building process, and balancing the various project and environmental constraints to achieve overall objectives;

● a system for achieving optimum integration of construction knowledge in the building process and balancing the various project and environmental constraints to maximize achievement of project goals and minimize building performance barriers to improving constructability.

Constructability issues not only involve issues of buildability, but also the sequence of construction and integration of systems in a logical sequence using standard substructures.

➢ Building design has a significant impact on construction productivity and quality. Design professionals need to be aware of the potential issues and claims implied by a design's constructability or buildability profile. When a project has inherent constructability issues, resulting litigation can involve delay claims, change order issues and disputes, and owner's dissatisfaction with delivery.

In extreme situations, direct claims may be made against the design principal for poor plans, specifications or estimates, or schedules that have made the project difficult to build, or more costly or time consuming than anticipated.

Litigation usually involves the claims which clearly include issues relating to constructability. The constructability claims arise because almost all of these factors relate to inadequate communication, lack of coordination, and inexperienced project teams.

8. Constructability Review Objectives

The main objective of a constructability review should be to minimise or eliminate potential change orders and schedule delays during construction by ensuring that the construction documents are fully co-ordinated, complete and buildable. A constructability review should also seek to eliminate redundancy in quality control reviews performed by different entities involved in the project, such as architects, peer reviewers and permitting agencies. The review objectives are as follow:

➢ Enhance early planning
➢ Minimize scope changes
➢ Reduce design-related change orders
➢ Improve contractors productivity
➢ Develop construction-friendly specifications
➢ Enhance quality
➢ Reduce delays/Meet schedules
➢ Improve public image
➢ Promote construction safety
➢ Reduce conflicts/disputes
➢ Decrease construction/maintenance costs

New Words and Expressions

diversity 多样化
multitude 大量，许多；大众，人群
entrench 用壕沟围绕或保护……；牢固地确立……；挖掘壕沟
mediation 调停，调解，斡旋
in parallel with 与……平行，与……同时，与……并联
catalyst [化]触媒，催化剂；[喻]触发因素；促进因素
polarize 使极化；使偏振；使两极分化
litigation [律]打官司；诉讼
arithmetical 算术的，算术上的
dilution 稀释
envisage 想象，设想；正视，面对
abreast 并列，并肩地；并排；不落后于；并排的；并肩的
impasse 绝境；僵局；死路；死胡同
circumscribe 在……周围画线；划定……范围；限制；限定
intractable 难对付的，难管教的，倔强的

Exercises

I. Choose the best answer according to the text.

1. Contractual disputes costs may include _____.
   A. damage to business relationships
   B. hiring of attorney
   C. expert witnesses
   D. lost business opportunities

2. In the highly competitive multiparty environment of construction, disputes can arise for _____.
   A. quality of work
   B. different organizational objectives
   C. different philosophies regarding the implementation of the project
   D. lack of coordination among the contracting parties

3. The common dispute resolution procedures available to the two parties are _____.
   A. amicable settlement
   B. arbitration
   C. negotiation
   D. litigation

Unit 16 Contract Dispute Resolution

4. Meditator's role can also be interpreted as _____.
   A. arbitrator
   B. catalyst in negotiation
   C. facilitator
   D. autarchy

5. The main difference between adjudication and mediation is that _____.
   A. the former can necessitating the disputes to be resolved without any delay
   B. the former is more formal
   C. adjudicators are bound to give a decision, whether it is acceptable or not by the parties concerned
   D. adjudicator does not look for a consensual compromise

II. Decide the following statements are true or false.

1. It is possible for both parties to work on disputes when they happen.

2. Negotiation involves unaided discussions between the disputing parties with legal representatives.

3. Among the dispute forms, litigation is the most widely used one and the most effective form of dispute resolution in terms of management of time and costs.

4. Adjudication is the most commonly found dispute resolution method stipulated in building contract.

5. Once agreed to the method of arbitration the dispute cannot be litigated.

III. Change the following words to another form and write down the Chinese meanings.

1. envisage _____
2. arbitrator _____
3. adjudicator _____
4. litigation _____
5. resolver _____
6. circumscribe _____
7. preclude _____
8. quantify _____
9. compatibility _____
10. compromise _____

IV. Give out the following words' synonym or other word in the closest meaning.

1. impartial   a. obedience
2. amicable   b. unsubstantial
3. submission   c. interchange
4. resolution   d. unprejudiced
5. intangible   e. significant

6. alternate   f. friendly
7. considerable   g. compassionate
8. credibility   h. rational
9. sympathetic   i. determination
10. sensible   j probability

V. Put the following English into Chinese.

1. Any one of these factors can derail a project and lead to complicated litigation or arbitration, increased costs, and a breakdown in the communication and relationships among parties.

2. It should be remembered that, even if a dispute progresses to Mediation and subsequently arbitration, it will still be possible, or indeed may be necessary, to continue to negotiate with the employer in parallel with these procedures on a "without prejudice" basis to seek a settlement that will minimize the level of costs incurred.

3. Notwithstanding the above, if either party lacks a commitment to discuss settlement in good faith the process may represent a waste of time and expense. Consequently, if the positions of the parties are too polarized or the facts make settlement unlikely, mediation may not be appropriate.

参 考 译 文

第 16 单元 合同争端的解决

1. 引言

国际建筑工程融合了多方利益、众多行业及一系列实施步骤，这些因素相互作用并创建一个竣工项目。建筑项目出现于现场且施工活动代表隶属不同学科专家的共同努力。虽然各参与方可能分担完成一个特定项目的共同目标，但是他们的实际参与受其组织目标的限制。于是，这种情况会导致互不相容的差错，这些差错被认为是施工过程中所发现的风险，并会引起变更指令、施工纠纷、成本超支、时间延误、质量损害以及权益方的不满。当一起工作的各方就项目的执行持有不同理念时，这种可能性会显著升高。

纠纷可能会在工程质量、误期责任、因条件变化导致的恰当赔付或者大量的其他需考虑因素等方面发生。对于合同纠纷解决的机制可以是在原始合同中做出明确规定。合同纠纷旷日持久、代价高昂且令人生厌。若不及时解决，就财务、人事、时间损耗和机会成本而言，施工纠纷可能会使代价变得很大。可计量成本包括律师雇用、专家证人及纠纷解决过程本身的费用。不太明显的成本(如分配到纠纷上的公司资源、失去的业务机会)和无形成本(如业务关系的损害、因效率低下的纠纷解决导致的潜在价值损失)也是相当可观的，量化这些成本十分困难或者是不可能的。

在高度竞争的多方参与的施工环境中，纠纷可能由诸多原因引起，诸如工程的复杂性和艰巨性、缔约各方之间缺乏协调、准备欠妥的合同文件、不充分的规划、财务问题以及关于解决当场的或者与工地有关问题的办法的分歧。这些因素中的任何一个都可能使项目脱离既定进程,并导致复杂的法律诉讼或仲裁、成本增加以及各方之间沟通和关系的破裂。

在处理索赔问题且避免采取坚定立场时,随时保持签约各方之间沟通渠道的畅通非常重要。为了达成纠纷的和解,合同中适用于解决纠纷的规程应当得到遵循,但这并不排除贯穿整个过程中发生于签约各方之间的"无偏见"磋商。从纠纷一开始,为了促使及早和有效和解,在适当的公司高层积极和坚定地处理分歧是非常重要的。不必要的误期和低效可能导致成本迅速增长。

在国际施工合同中,合同当事双方是订约权威(雇主)和承包商。雇主可能托付一些职责给其代表去协助合同的执行。当事双方都可得到的解决的共同纠纷的规程是谈判、调解、仲裁,以及最后对于司法系统的有限追索权。

2. 谈判

谈判作为解决纠纷的过程,开始于纠纷发生且各方都觉得有必要进行谈判之后。谈判就是两方或多方试图一起在所争议的问题上达成协议。谈判涉及无法律代理情况下纠纷各方之间的无外援商讨。纠纷解决谈判采取许多形式。谈判形式从一次非正式聊天或电话交谈到较长时期内发生的高度复杂过程不等。

谈判显然是解决纠纷的最普遍方式。明智的纠纷管理目标应当是尽快议定一种可接受的和解以便使成本最小化。就时间和成本管理的角度而言,谈判通常是解决纠纷最有效的方式,它对于大部分纠纷来说是首选途径。应当牢记的是,纵然纠纷进入了调解及随后的仲裁阶段,在"无偏见"基础上去寻求将使成本水平最小化的和解,继续就这些规程同步地和雇主进行谈判,仍然是可能的,或者确实可能是必要的。

3. 调解

调解是一个可变通过程,意在协助各方通过协议来解决纠纷。调解的本质特征是在各方之间达成协议。调解人起到服务商的作用,其协助双方进行协商并发挥催化剂的作用。调解人必须说服各方一起努力解决纠纷是出于他们共同的利益。调解人必须公正、有同情心且必须建立与各方的信誉和信赖。

调解是针对纠纷解决的无约束协调程序,借此,独立调解人会被当事各方所青睐,并就争议问题以中间人的身份促成各方之间达成和解。引入第三方意见对纠纷问题产生影响有诸多好处,并且比仲裁更快捷且成本更低。它还有的好处是,调解人设法以各方能接受的任何方式协助各方解决纠纷。如果达成和解,调解人会把各方带回谈判桌并使协议条款书面化。签署之后的协议通常是可强制服从的。

毫无疑问,调解是低风险的能节约时间和资金过程。该过程也倾向于无对抗性,也因此有助于维护重要的业务关系。此外,如果调解成功,它会带来一个定局,也就是不存在转化为判定、潜在上诉或者追讨欠款的必要的裁决。尽管有上述情形,如果任何一方缺乏承诺去真诚地商讨和解的话,调解过程就代表着时间和开支的浪费。因此,如果各方的立场过于极端或者事实上已经不可能和解,调解就是不恰当的。

4. 仲裁

仲裁对于诉讼来说是一个替代方案。若所属地方没有争端裁定委员会(DAB),则纠纷可能直接进入仲裁程序，这样就越过施工合同条件(FIDIC)第 20.4 款。仲裁作为快速且在没有法律手续的情况下来解决纠纷的一种方法而出现。仲裁是建筑合同中规定的最普遍认可的纠纷解决办法。没有任何一方被强迫让纠纷接受仲裁，除非双方在合同条件之内同意这么做。一旦同意仲裁，就不能对纠纷提起诉讼了。仲裁是一个过程，通过该过程，双方或多方之间的纠纷在以司法/法律方式听取双方的证词之后，由另一人或多人而绝不是法院为了获得裁定而进行提交。经过通常来自合乎纠纷事件的学科的博学多识人士，以及以反映出项目的合同和商业状况的方式，这些仲裁程序使一项裁定成为可能。仲裁是一个私人过程并且便于各方保持其纠纷细节的私密性。

仲裁是受法规支配的具有约束力的程序，合同各方借此把纠纷交由仲裁人处理并同意受其裁定的约束。若当事各方未能与仲裁员有相同看法，任何一方可求助于合同指定的机构，由其推荐一名仲裁人。法律要求仲裁人应用举证责任并有权决定所有程序及举证事宜。

仲裁人可以决定举行听证会，在听证会上，由另一方的反诘问所跟随，直接证据，既有证人也有专家，可能代表当事人的每一方而被给出。在听证会完结阶段，仲裁人被要求在一个合理的期限内给出最终的、约束各方的且合法强制服从的裁决。在作为记录和解的方式，包括成本的分配的仲裁进程中，和解由各方达成的情况下，裁决可能是一致同意的裁决。在收到仲裁人裁定的 30 天以内，任何一方都可以要求仲裁人解释裁决并纠正任何计算错误，或者就呈现给其但却从裁决中遗漏掉的索赔做出额外裁定。

虽然就成本和时间而言仲裁具有超过诉讼的诸多优势，但事情并不总是如此。事实上，在有些情况下存在越来越多的关于仲裁程序的成本和质量的指责。虽然如此，仲裁继续是广泛使用的解决施工索赔的过程，并且无疑地在很多情况下具有超过诉讼的某种好处。

5. 裁定

裁定是通过与仲裁类似的程序做出裁决的过程。裁定和调解之间的主要差异是，裁定人不去寻找一致同意的妥协而是去判定各方之间的问题且一定要做出决定，而不管其决定当事人接受与否。裁定的理念是人们意识到他们立场的优点和缺点以及合法约束过程的风险，并且能够经由独立的第三方友善地在正式安排的过程之外来解决他们的纠纷。裁定出现的原因是业务步伐的加快以及没有延误地促使纠纷得到解决。

纠纷会导致大量精力的削弱、误期以及资金的分散。根据许多不同的条款，施工合同条件(FIDIC)包括索赔和纠纷的提交、补偿和解决办法。此处基本的利益条款是第 20 条，特别用来处理索赔、纠纷和仲裁方面的问题。此条款对纠纷裁定委员会，即大家熟知的 DAB 的建立做了设想。

DAB 是一个有经验的、受尊重的、公正的和独立的评论家组成的专门小组。DBA 成员要被提供合同文件、施工图纸及规范，并熟悉项目程序和项目参与方，且能与项目进展和事态保持同步。DAB 程序被设想为首要的纠纷解决方式。因此，项目等级谈判一进入僵局，或者该程序便于委员会迅速提出争端解决参考，或者在业主和承包商在各层面的审议与程序和对费用及时间产生负面效应的情况下，提交到争端仲裁委员。

FIDIC 合同条件规定，争端裁定委员会(DAB)的裁定对当事双方都附有义务，双方应当立即使该裁定生效，直到该裁定以友好和解或者仲裁裁决来做出修正。因此，DAB 的全体会员被合同双方互相赞同且不强迫另一方是绝对必要的。FIDIC 第 20.7 条规定，如果当事人没有接到不满意的正式通知，且裁定是决定性的并有约束力的，那么对遵从裁定义务的任何不执行都会交由仲裁处理。

6. 诉讼

通过司法决定解决争端的过程被称为诉讼。从历史的角度来看，法庭诉讼是解决发生在施工环境中的棘手争端的最普遍方式。遗憾的是，诉讼耗费时间，代价高昂且不可预测。然而，在国际建筑市场上，关于诉讼的争端，尤其是关于时间、成本以及司法解决的缓慢进程方面，人们还是持有保留意见。尽管如此，诉讼在建筑业中占有与其他争端解决办法同样多的一席之地，且当事各方在以下情中一定能够获得来自诉讼的援助：

- 仲裁人对自己和仲裁程序玩忽职守；
- 不正当获得的裁决；
- 在从裁决表面看来的法律错误基础上，当事人一方要求解决被搁置一边或者被推迟到仲裁人再审议中的某些问题。

在法院觉得这些理由的任何一些已经被证实，或者可能决定推迟处理所提交的问题，或者为了仲裁人再审议而推迟处理这些问题中的一些问题，或者可能做出一个替代裁决的情况下，法院可能会把一个裁决搁置一边。

法院一般不愿干涉，除非仲裁人做出了在表面上就显示出在法律层面上基本的或者明显错误的裁决，以至法院不能袖手旁观并允许该裁决仍然不受争议。法庭干涉由仲裁人做出的仲裁裁决的权利是有很大限制的，没有非常充分的理由，法院是不能干涉的。一旦做出裁决，法律政策将维持仲裁裁决的确定性。

然而，就解决建筑争端的最好方式而言，许多因素需要进行评估。虽然时间和成本是重要的，但是其他问题也具有更大的重要性。若诉讼案件牵涉多方争端以及司法审查中的分歧，那么承包商需要考虑对索赔强制性透露、在建筑行业中有经验或没有经验的某人之前对案件进行尝试的好处或不利以及对程序问题进行必要的分析。

阅读

工程创新——建筑信息模型

1. 介绍

建筑信息模型——2002年由Autodesk引入的建筑设计、施工和管理的一种创新型方法——已经改变了全球业内行家看待技术如何应用于建筑设计、施工和管理的方式。建筑信息模型支持连续和即刻地获得项目设计范围、进度和成本信息，这些信息具有高质量、可靠、集成化和充分协调的特点。在许多竞争性优势中，该模型所具有的优势如下：

- 增加项目交付速度(节约时间)；
- 更好的协调性(较少失误)；
- 减少成本(节约资金)；
- 更高生产率；
- 工程质量更高；
- 新的收益和商业机会。

对于建筑生命周期的三个主要阶段——设计、施工和管理——的每一个阶段来说，建筑信息模型都可以为其提供如下关键信息：
> 设计阶段——设计、设计进度和预算信息；
> 施工阶段——质量、施工进度、安全和成本信息；
> 管理阶段——工作状况、利用和财务信息。

在一个集成的数字环境中，保持该信息及时更新并且便于获取的能力给予建筑师、工程师、承包商和雇主一个清晰的项目总体构想，还有使更好的决策变得更快的能力——提高质量并增加项目的盈利性。

虽然建筑信息模型只是一种方法而非技术，但它确实需要合适的、有效实施的技术。在渐增的效能状况中，这些技术的例子包括：
> 计算机辅助设计；
> 目标计算机辅助设计；
> 参数建筑模型。

建筑信息模型的概念就是，为了解决问题并模拟和分析其潜在影响，在从物理上建造之前，去虚拟地建造一个建筑物。建筑信息模型的实质是一个可靠的建筑信息模式。

2. 建筑信息模型的益处

建筑信息模型(BIM)用于两件事情：建筑信息模型的过程和作为结果的模式(建筑信息模式)。BIM是运用计算机软件来模拟设施的施工和运营的发展结果。作为结果的模式，建筑信息模式，是一个数据丰富的、以目标为导向的、智能的和参数的设施数字表示，从该数字表示，适合于不同用户需要的视图和数据可以被提取和分析并生成信息，该信息可以用于决策并改善项目设施交付的流程。建筑信息模型是一种建筑设计、施工和管理的方法。该模型在本质上是两个关键概念的交叉：
> 保持关键设计信息的数字形式，使它更容易更新和共享，并使公司对它的创建和使用更有价值；
> 在数字设计数据之间创建实时的一致关系——以创新型参数建筑模型技术——可以节约大量的时间和资金，并提高项目的生产率和质量。

BIM的作用包括：可视化；明确项目范围；各工种的协调；各工种间的协调；冲突检测/规避；设计确认；施工工序规划/分段；材料计划/物流；营销展示；优化分析；步行漫游和飞行漫游；虚拟模型和基准线研究。

BIM可以帮助施工专业人士为了不同的兴趣而创建这样一个模型，这些专业人士包括在建筑生命周期的设计、施工和管理阶段提供无数虚拟详细资料的建筑师、工程师、承包商、分包商、装配商、供应商及其他人员，并且预先分类和解决问题。例如，在建筑物还未建造之前，想象走进一幢建筑，穿过大厅，移开吊顶板材，查看棚顶空间的效用，这样就可以预见你需要预先解决的问题。

3. BIM 四维模型

BIM四维模型以来自项目设计、采购和施工进度的活动来连接三维模型的组成部分。作为结果的项目四维模型允许项目利益方随时间的推移在电脑屏幕上就能查看已计划实施的施工,并针对项目的日、周、月进度对三维模型进行检查。

四维模型使项目参与方的不同团队能够以一种前摄的和适时的方式去理解和评判项目范围。他们能够探索和改善项目执行策略,以现场生产率的相应收益去改善可施工性,并快速确认和解决时间-空间冲突。四维模型被证实在有些项目中尤其有帮助,这些项目涉及许多利益方,例如在那些在运营期间进行革新的项目和带有狭小的城市工地条件的项目。狭小的工地条件、必须满足的竣工最后期限,以及许多非施工项目利益方已经做了对四维项目管理模型应用理念的实施。四维模型能够使项目团队针对项目的施工产生一套更好的规范和设计图,从而导致更少的非计划变更指令、更小的施工队伍及轻松而提前的项目竣工。

4. 设计中的 BIM

对于整个项目的设计和文件资料来讲,BIM 是非常强大的建筑构架设计和协调工具。项目设计团队成员依赖许多为特定目的建造的模式,包括:

- ➤ 三维概念设计模式
- ➤ 详细的几何设计模式
- ➤ 结构限定元素分析模式
- ➤ 钢结构装配模式
- ➤ 设计协调模式
- ➤ 施工规划和进度模式
- ➤ 设备库存模式
- ➤ 能量分析模式
- ➤ 火灾/生命安全和出口模式
- ➤ 成本分析模式

单一技术用于不同公司间的和/或横跨项目生命周期所有阶段的一个建筑项目中,非常罕见。在设计、形象化并把复杂设施的要素与广大受众进行交流方面,BIM 具有巨大的积极的影响。它帮助设计师解决许多牵涉在平面图、正视图和剖面图方面需要遇到几何的问题,并且它能够产生来自单一设计模式的"视野",这些"视野"总是相一致的。在把混凝土和钢筋的三维目标模型与建筑师分享从而整合建筑学模型和数据分享方面,结构工程师可以获得极大成功。

5. 施工中的 BIM

在建筑生命周期的施工阶段,建筑信息模型(BIM)产生关于建筑质量、安全、进度和成本方面的可得到的同步信息。承包商可以加快对项目的预算量化和价值工程分析,并产生对建筑造价和施工计划的不断更新。承包商可以很容易地研究和理解设计所提议的或者业主所采购的产品的建造结果,承包商可以迅速准备工地的施工图纸或为雇主做阶段整修安排,由此可减少在运营期间雇主和人力方面对项目运营的影响。BIM 也意味着承包商在项目施工中的流程和管理问题上用更少的时间和资金花费,因为有了更高的项目文件质量和更好的项目施工规划。最终结果是,雇主的项目投资更多地进入建筑而不是花费在管理和项目管理费中。

5.1 成本估算

总包商和分包商都将从精确的启动工程量和良好的施工顺序考虑中获得极大的益处,

从而在它们都付诸实施的时候确定工地会处于怎样的状态。例如，通过使项目承包商的想法形象化，从而确保所有的施工部分都包括在内，一个精确而复杂的 BIM 三维模型不仅能够对墙体和顶棚分包商提供墙体—顶棚的位置和相互关系，而且可以提供对于精确的启动工程量的确切构成每个部分的材料。

以这样的信息装备起来，不必调查现场各个角落以及推测建筑师到底打算做什么，有经验的评估师确实可以准确算出报价。考虑到施工顺序的，BIM 三维模型将帮助评估师达到优秀投标。

5.2 施工质量与安全

在一些国家，凭借极大的兴趣和努力，公共组织和私营企业已经成功地带动了许多基于 BIM 的项目。事实上，一些公共组织建议发起 BIM 数据，根据 BIM 模型标准，这些数据与质量控制标准相符。BIM 的高品质控制在物理和逻辑两种条件下都可以应用。从设计开始，通过运用软件工具，设施的功能性、美观性、工程学及环境诸方面的质量初步检查在最终评估之前就可以实现。由于 BIM 质量核查建立在 BIM 指导原则和标准的基础之上，定量的检查就成为可能，且在大多数情况下，自动核查可以通过软件来完成。为预防出现拙劣的设计，这样一个系统是大有助益的。

建筑安全行家也可以运用 BIM 来改善施工安全。一旦三维模型创建起来，就可以用于很多目的，包括工人安全培训和教育，安全规划与员工参与。安全行家不必在模型创建或者模型技术方面是专家；他们仅仅需要对 BIM 有基本的了解，即本质上是了解三维计算机辅助设计作图法。在工程开始之前，行业人士能够确定活动顺序、材料及所需工具。任务前规划针对施工安全提供了大部分运用 BIM 的机会。通过虚拟查看需要建造的基本部分，员工能够更好地识别危险和控制措施，因此可以更快更安全地完成任务。比如管道铺设，这就涉及识别作为重要事项的施工通道以及带来空中升降机。全体工作人员能辨别掉落是一种危险并想出控制措施(如防掉落装置)。管道会被安装在隧道中并焊接牢固。

6. 管理中的 BIM

在建筑生命周期的管理阶段，BIM 可以产生以下可得到且并存的信息：建筑的使用或性能；建筑使用者和内容；随着时间变化的建筑的使用寿命；建筑的财务状况。BIM 提供修整好的数字化记录，并改善行动计划和管理。为了满足商业需要，如零售活动在不同的位置需要类似的建筑施工，BIM 会加快针对工地条件的标准建筑样板的调整。关于建筑的物理信息，如润饰、占用者和部门分配、家具和设备清单、可出租方面财务上的重要数据以及出租收入或部门成本分摊，全部都容易管理，可利用。对这些类型信息的前后一致的获取通道会使收益和建筑运营中的成本管理得到改善。

总体来说，BIM 正逐渐改变着雇主、设计师、工程师、承包商、分包商和装配商处理建筑设计、施工及运营的方式。

7. 可施工性检查

> 由于项目越来越复杂，可施工性问题就变得非常重要。可施工性渗透到项目的各个部分，尤其是与工程设计和建筑设计专业相关的部分。由于项目越来越复杂且项目交付期限又越来越短，内在担保及严重的职业责任问题就会应运而生。

可施工性是在施工前阶段,帮助自始至终检查施工流程的一种项目管理技术。它会在项目实际建造之前识别施工障碍,以减少或预防过失、误期及成本超支。它涉及如下方面:
- 根据竣工建筑的总体要求,建筑设计在多大程度上有助于施工;
- 为了实现建造过程中在规划、工程设计、采购和野外运作方面的施工知识和经验的最佳整合,平衡各种项目和环境限制以实现总体目标的一个系统;
- 为了实现建造过程中施工知识的最佳整合,平衡各种项目和环境限制,以使项目目标实现最大化且使对于改善可施工性的建筑性能障碍最小化的一个系统。

可施工性问题不仅涉及项目可建性,而且涉及在使用标准支撑结构的逻辑顺序中的施工顺序及系统整合。

➢ 建筑设计在施工生产率和质量方面具有重大影响。设计专家需要意识到由设计的可施工性和可建性概况所暗示的潜在问题及索赔。当项目具有内在的可施工性问题时,所导致的诉讼可能包括误期索赔、施工变更指令问题和争端、业主对项目交付的不满等。

在极端情况下,拙劣的施工图纸、规范或估价,或者使项目建造困难的日程安排,或者比预期更高昂的成本或时间消耗,导致的直接索赔对设计负责人不利。诉讼通常涉及索赔,这些索赔显然包含与可施工性有关的问题。因为所有这些因素几乎都与项目团队的沟通不充分、缺乏协调和经验不足有关,可施工性索赔也就随之出现了。

8. 可施工性检查

可施工性检查的主要目标应当是通过确保施工文件的充分协调性、完整性及可建性,使施工期间潜在的变更指令和进度误期最小化或者被完全消除。可施工性检查也应该设法消除由牵涉项目的不同实体——诸如建筑师、同级检查人员和获准代理机构——所实施的质量控制检查中的过剩现象。检查目标如下:
➢ 加强早期规划
➢ 范围变更最小化
➢ 减少与设计有关的变更指令
➢ 提高承包商的生产率
➢ 开发施工友好型规范
➢ 提高质量
➢ 减少误期/符合进度
➢ 改善公共形象
➢ 增进施工安全
➢ 减少冲突/争端
➢ 降低施工/维护成本

参 考 文 献

[1] Standard Prequalification Document Prequalification of Bidders User's Guide[M]. Asian Development Bank, September 2010.

[2] Standard Bidding Documents Procurement of Works & User's Guide[M]. The World Bank Washington, D.C. May 2006, revised March and April 2007.

[3] B.W. Totterdill. FIDIC users' guide: A practical guide to the 1999 Red and Yellow Books[M]. Published by Thomas Telford Publishing, 2001.

[4] B. W. Totterdill. FIDIC users' guide: A practical guide to the 1999 Red Book[M]. Published by Thomas Telford Publishing, 2001.

[5] Ashworth, A. Contractual Procedures in the Construction Industry[M]. Fifth Edition, Prentice Hall, 2005.

[6] Hackett, M. & Robinson, I.. Pre-contract Practice and Contract Administration for the Building Team[M]. Oxford: Blackwell Publishing, 2003.

[7] A Guide to the Project Management Body of Knowledge (PMBOK® Guide)[M]. Fourth Edition, Project management Institute, 2008.

[8] Managing Successful Projects with PRINCE2[M]. Trade paperback, Stationery Office Books (TSO), 2009.

[9] Lewis, James. Project Planning, Scheduling & Control: A Hands-On Guide to Bringing Projects in on Time and on Budget[M]. Fourth Edition, McGraw-Hill Professional, 2005.

[10] Keith Potts. Construction Cost Management[M]. Taylor & Francis Publishing, 2008.

[11] Halpin, D.. Construction Management[M]. 3rd Edition, John Wiley & Sons, Inc. 2006.

[12] Chris Hendrickson, Tung Au. Project Management for Construction[M]. Prentice Hall College Division,1989.

[13] Sears, S. K., Sears, G., and Clough, R.H. Construction Project Management[M]. 5th Edition, John Wiley & Sons, NJ, 2008.

[14] Geoffrey Schmitt. Contracting in the Global Market Place: Shaping the Change XXIII FIG Congress[A]. Munich, Germany, October 2006.

[15] Low, S.P. and Jiang, H. (2003) Internationalization of Chinese construction enterprises[J]. ASCE Journal of Construction Engineering and Management, Vol.129, No.6.

[16] John Kunz & Martin Fischer. Virtual Design and Construction: Themes, Case Studies and Implementation Suggestions[A]. CIFE Working Paper #097,Version 10: October 2009, Stanford University.

[17] Russell V. Keune. Architectural Services in Global Trade in Professional Services[A]. Sixth Services Experts Meeting Domestic Regulation and Trade in Professional Services Paris, 15-16 February 2007.

[18] Gary Gereffy, Mario Castillo, Karina Fernandez-Stark. The Offshore Services Industry: A New Opportunity for Latin America[A]. Inter-American Development Bank, 2009.

[19] Sathy Rajendran, Brian Clarke. Building Information Modeling: Safety Benefits & Opportunities[J]. Professional Safety, October 2011.

北京大学出版社土木建筑系列教材(已出版)

序号	书名	主编	定价	序号	书名	主编	定价
1	建筑设备(第2版)	刘源全 张国军	46.00	50	土木工程施工	石海均 马哲	40.00
2	土木工程测量(第2版)	陈久强 刘文生	40.00	51	土木工程制图	张会平	34.00
3	土木工程材料(第2版)	柯国军	45.00	52	土木工程制图习题集	张会平	22.00
4	土木工程计算机绘图	袁果 张渝生	28.00	53	土木工程材料(第2版)	王春阳	50.00
5	工程地质(第2版)	何培玲 张婷	26.00	54	结构抗震设计	祝英杰	30.00
6	建设工程监理概论(第3版)	巩天真 张泽平	40.00	55	土木工程专业英语	霍俊芳 姜丽云	35.00
7	工程经济学(第2版)	冯为民 付晓灵	42.00	56	混凝土结构设计原理(第2版)	邵永健	52.00
8	工程项目管理(第2版)	仲景冰 王红兵	45.00	57	土木工程计量与计价	王翠琴 李春燕	35.00
9	工程造价管理	车春鹏 杜春艳	24.00	58	房地产开发与管理	刘薇	38.00
10	工程招标投标管理(第2版)	刘昌明	30.00	59	土力学	高向阳	32.00
11	工程合同管理	方俊 胡向真	23.00	60	建筑表现技法	冯柯	42.00
12	建筑工程施工组织与管理(第2版)	余群舟 宋会莲	31.00	61	工程招投标与合同管理	吴芳 冯宁	39.00
13	建设法规(第2版)	肖铭 潘安平	32.00	62	工程施工组织	周国恩	28.00
14	建设项目评估	王华	35.00	63	建筑力学	邹建奇	34.00
15	工程量清单的编制与投标报价	刘富勤 陈德方	25.00	64	土力学学习指导与考题精解	高向阳	26.00
16	土木工程概预算与投标报价(第2版)	刘薇 叶良	37.00	65	建筑概论	钱坤	28.00
17	室内装饰工程预算	陈祖建	30.00	66	岩石力学	高玮	35.00
18	力学与结构	徐吉恩 唐小弟	42.00	67	交通工程学	李杰 王富	39.00
19	理论力学(第2版)	张俊彦 赵荣国	40.00	68	房地产策划	王直民	42.00
20	材料力学	金康宁 谢群丹	27.00	69	中国传统建筑构造	李合群	35.00
21	结构力学简明教程	张系斌	20.00	70	房地产开发	石海均 王宏	34.00
22	流体力学	刘建军 章宝华	20.00	71	室内设计原理	冯柯	28.00
23	弹性力学	薛强	22.00	72	建筑结构优化及应用	朱杰江	30.00
24	工程力学	罗迎社 喻小明	30.00	73	高层与大跨建筑结构施工	王绍君	45.00
25	土力学	肖仁成 俞晓	18.00	74	工程造价管理	周国恩	42.00
26	基础工程	王协群 章宝华	32.00	75	土建工程制图	张黎骅	29.00
27	有限单元法(第2版)	丁科 殷水平	30.00	76	土建工程制图习题集	张黎骅	26.00
28	土木工程施工	邓寿昌 李晓目	42.00	77	材料力学	章宝华	36.00
29	房屋建筑学(第2版)	聂洪达 郄恩田	48.00	78	土力学教程	孟祥波	30.00
30	混凝土结构设计原理	许成祥 何培玲	28.00	79	土力学	曹卫平	34.00
31	混凝土结构设计	彭刚 蔡江勇	28.00	80	土木工程项目管理	郑文新	41.00
32	钢结构设计原理	石建军 姜袁	32.00	81	工程力学	王明斌 庞永平	37.00
33	结构抗震设计	马成松 苏原	25.00	82	建筑工程造价	郑文新	39.00
34	高层建筑施工	张厚先 陈德方	32.00	83	土力学(中英双语)	郎煜华	38.00
35	高层建筑结构设计	张仲先 王海波	23.00	84	土木建筑CAD实用教程	王文达	30.00
36	工程事故分析与工程安全(第2版)	谢征勋 罗章	38.00	85	工程管理概论	郑文新 李献涛	26.00
37	砌体结构(第2版)	何培玲 尹维新	26.00	86	景观设计	陈玲玲	49.00
38	荷载与结构设计方法(第2版)	许成祥 何培玲	30.00	87	色彩景观基础教程	阮正仪	42.00
39	工程结构检测	周详 刘益虹	20.00	88	工程力学	杨云芳	42.00
40	土木工程课程设计指南	许明 孟茁超	25.00	89	工程设计软件应用	孙香红	39.00
41	桥梁工程(第2版)	周先雁 王解军	37.00	90	城市轨道交通工程建设风险与保险	吴宏建 刘宽亮	75.00
42	房屋建筑学(上:民用建筑)	钱坤 王若竹	32.00	91	混凝土结构设计原理	熊丹安	32.00
43	房屋建筑学(下:工业建筑)	钱坤 吴歌	26.00	92	城市详细规划原理与设计方法	姜云	36.00
44	工程管理专业英语	王竹芳	24.00	93	工程经济学	都沁军	42.00
45	建筑结构CAD教程	崔钦淑	36.00	94	结构力学	边亚东	42.00
46	建设工程招投标与合同管理实务	崔东红	38.00	95	房地产估价	沈良峰	45.00
47	工程地质(第2版)	倪宏革 周建波	30.00	96	土木工程结构试验	叶成杰	39.00
48	工程经济学	张厚钧	36.00	97	土木工程概论	邓友生	34.00
49	工程财务管理	张学英	38.00	98	工程项目管理	邓铁军 杨亚频	48.00

序号	书名	主编	定价	序号	书名	主编	定价
99	误差理论与测量平差基础	胡圣武 肖本林	37.00	114	建筑工程安全管理与技术	高向阳	40.00
100	房地产估价理论与实务	李 龙	36.00	115	土木工程施工与管理	李华锋 徐 芸	65.00
101	混凝土结构设计	熊丹安	37.00	116	土木工程试验	王吉民	34.00
102	钢结构设计原理	胡习兵	30.00	117	土质学与土力学	刘红军	36.00
103	土木工程材料	赵志曼	39.00	118	建筑工程施工组织与概预算	钟吉湘	52.00
104	工程项目投资控制	曲 娜 陈顺良	32.00	119	房地产测量	魏德宏	28.00
105	建设项目评估	黄明知 尚华艳	38.00	120	土力学	贾彩虹	38.00
106	结构力学实用教程	常伏德	47.00	121	交通工程基础	王富	24.00
107	道路勘测设计	刘文生	43.00	122	房屋建筑学	宿晓萍 隋艳娥	43.00
108	大跨桥梁	王解军 周先雁	30.00	123	建筑工程计量与计价	张叶田	50.00
109	工程爆破	段宝福	42.00	124	工程力学	杨民献	50.00
110	地基处理	刘起霞	45.00	125	建筑工程管理专业英语	杨云会	36.00
111	水分析化学	宋吉娜	42.00	126	土木工程地质	陈文昭	32.00
112	基础工程	曹 云	43.00	127	暖通空调节能运行	余晓平	30.00
113	建筑结构抗震分析与设计	裴星洙	35.00				

相关教学资源如电子课件、电子教材、习题答案等可以登录 www.pup6.com 下载或在线阅读。

扑六知识网(www.pup6.com)有海量的相关教学资源和电子教材供阅读及下载(包括北京大学出版社第六事业部的相关资源)，同时欢迎您将教学课件、视频、教案、素材、习题、试卷、辅导材料、课改成果、设计作品、论文等教学资源上传到 pup6.com，与全国高校师生分享您的教学成就与经验，并可自由设定价格，知识也能创造财富。具体情况请登录网站查询。

如您需要免费纸质样书用于教学，欢迎登陆第六事业部门户网(www.pup6.com)填表申请，并欢迎在线登记选题以到北京大学出版社来出版您的大作，也可下载相关表格填写后发到我们的邮箱，我们将及时与您取得联系并做好全方位的服务。

扑六知识网将打造成全国最大的教育资源共享平台，欢迎您的加入——让知识有价值，让教学无界限，让学习更轻松。

联系方式：010-62750667，donglu2004@163.com，linzhangbo@126.com，欢迎来电来信咨询。